PART 3   *Ruptured Bodies, Ruptured Tales:*
         Masculine Injury and Transcendence in
         Turn-of-the-Century U.S. Literature

    5   What a Beating Feels Like: Authorship, Dissolution,
        and Masculinity in Upton Sinclair's *The Jungle*   *159*

    6   Behind the Lines: Homoerotic Anxiety
        and the Heroic in Stephen Crane's
        The Red Badge of Courage   *171*

Conclusion: Beyond Influence, Beyond Homoeroticism,
              and Beyond the Pleasure Principle in
              F. Scott Fitzgerald's *The Great Gatsby*   *191*

        Notes   *211*
        Index   *249*

ILLUSTRATIONS

1. Henry James, *American Journal 1*, Cambridge, December 26, 1881   *151*
2. Henry James, *American Journal 1*, Cambridge, December 26, 1881   *152*
3. Henry James, *The Pocket Diaries*, Thursday, July 21, 1910 through Saturday, July 23, 1910   *154*

Finally, I am grateful to my son, Ross, for both patience and independence in advance of his several years, and to my wife, Helena Michie, for her always valuable editorial advice; for the child care that often made needed additional work time possible; and for her steadfast and affectionate belief that I could and would complete this book, in the face of occasional evidence to the contrary.

Monumental Anxieties

Authoring the Self

GENDER, IDENTITY, AND AUTHORIAL SELF-CONSTRUCTION IN NINETEENTH-CENTURY U.S. CULTURE

*I*n this book, I trace the consequences of an interlaced set of conditions in a set of traditionally valued masculine texts for which those conditions are crucial. These texts include Nathaniel Hawthorne's *The Scarlet Letter;* Edgar Allan Poe's trio of detective stories, "The Murders in the Rue Morgue," "The Murder of Marie Roget," and "The Purloined Letter"; Henry James's *Roderick Hudson, The American, The Ambassadors,* and *The Wings of the Dove,* which I read as an interrelated sequence; Upton Sinclair's *The Jungle;* Stephen Crane's *The Red Badge of Courage;* and by way of concluding, F. Scott Fitzgerald's *The Great Gatsby.*

In the chapters that follow, I suggest these texts are corporately marked by the crisis-driven strength of their authors' desire for the cultural authority of achieved authorship, and that this desire has a consequent priority over the overt content of the narrative the author produces. This priority creates a generally—but not always—unconscious narrative of authorial self-making that underwrites and shapes the manifest content of the narrative in which it evolves, a narrative that has particularly crucial consequences for the representation of sexuality and gender. If these dynamics seem, on one hand, self-reflexively literary in the now familiar sense that literature always in part describes the possibilities and perils of its own operations, they also are key to the representative power of each of these texts in the context of middle-class U.S. culture in the nineteenth and early twentieth centuries. The narrative of authorial self-making that dominates each of these texts, I argue, enacts a literary version of the general cultural narrative of masculine development, which assumed a stable and important shape in the first half of the nineteenth century. According to this narrative, a male subject had to move from a mother-centered household to a masculine place in the world, a difficult transition in which the new middle-class problem of vocational choice occupied a crucial position. If masculinity in this narrative served as a target of individual aspiration and desire for men, femininity functioned as the difficult-to-erase trace of the shaping labor of the mother, much broader than the culturally celebrated moral virtues proper mothers supposedly breathed into the psyches of their sons.

In the case of the authors I treat here, a number of factors exacerbated the narrative construction of masculine identity. First, the much noticed productive presence of women in nineteenth-century literary culture called the masculinity of literature into question and made visible the important cultural labor of women concealed beneath the idealizations of maternity. Male writers had to deal explicitly with the cultural problem of feminine influence, complicated by the undeniable presence of women competitors in the literary marketplace. Second, literature as a profession was one in which the anodyne of professional success was (and is) difficult to achieve, and all the texts I analyze are marked by the struggles of their authors to secure their literary reputations. Third, partly as a consequence, male writers found themselves famously alienated from what might be called the masculinity of commerce, and they had to negotiate a treacherous relation to masculine authority that could not be attained by simple appeal to the cultural position of literature. Finally, in the midst of masculine strivings, the texts I discuss are troubled by same-sex desires that disrupt rather than nurture masculine self-construction, desires that arguably inhabit the broader cultural narrative of male development as well but have gone largely unrecorded. I attempt to trace in this book, then, a broad and important cultural narrative as it assumes a complex, specifically literary textual form.

I hold in this book to my paradigm and the specific texts that, through the process of interpretation, generate new and different versions of it. I explicitly do not intend to generate a model useful for the interpretation of all texts, or even all those by men. Other authors may be less driven by the vocational anxieties of authorship than the writers I discuss here; other authors may have a less vexed relation to a maternity imagined as originary and constitutive of male cultural attainment; other authors may be less plainly troubled by desires for other men. Some crucial authors for a study of nineteenth-century masculinity, such as Walt Whitman, write chiefly in genres such as poetry that require the articulation of complex and different authorial dynamics. Women authors, in general, write against different developmental narratives that deserve a careful articulation in their own terms. Authors from nondominant cultural traditions must be understood not only in relation to patterns of cultural dominance, but in terms of their complex inheritances from those traditions. My assumption has simply been that to try to do more would be inevitably to do less in terms of marking out the tradition on which I have chosen to focus. I by no means, however, intend to deny the importance of other versions of U.S. literature, or even to deny the value of efforts to construe the texts I write about in a different set of terms.[1]

In this introduction, I develop the historically informed paradigm of male authoring that governs this book. I indicate how the broad narrative of male development in the nineteenth century functions in terms of the pursuit of literary masculinity and comes to inhabit narrative dynamics specific to the novel. These dynamics, in turn, control the representation of sexuality and gender in the novels I analyze.

Having generated this paradigm for masculine writing in the United States, I use it to construct a series of readings of important nineteenth- and twentieth-century texts in the body of *Monumental Anxieties*. In the first of three sections, "Purloined Letters: The Fiction of Nathaniel Hawthorne and Edgar Allan Poe," I begin with a consideration of *The Scarlet Letter*, arguably the most contested text in nineteenth-century literary and cultural studies of the United States. I employ biographical and cultural information to situate Hawthorne's story of authorial self-making and to examine his complicated rendering of the relation of femininity and homoeroticism to writing. In a linked and shorter discussion centering on Poe's "The Purloined Letter," the cultural anxiety of authorship gets figured in terms of the contested psychodynamics of his detective fiction, which, I argue, both reveals and obscures the cultural appropriation of women's labor.

In part two, "Circuits of Desire: Authority in the Early and Late Fiction of Henry James," my analysis focuses specifically on an intertextual analysis of the crucial opposition in James between threatening and difficult-to-narrate queer desires, on one hand, and heterosexually constructed and heavily aestheticized authority, on the other. I suggest James sequentially distributes this opposition between two early texts, *Roderick Hudson* and *The American*, and between two late texts, *The Ambassadors* and *The Wings of the Dove*, and that the authority of the late texts consists in their formalization of this opposition, but not in its resolution.

In part three, "Ruptured Bodies, Ruptured Tales: Masculine Injury and Transcendence in Turn-of-the-Century U.S. Literature," I again focus on the cultural and the biographical to situate crises of gender and sexuality that are exacerbated by the terms of authority in naturalist texts. I argue that *The Jungle,* despite its documentary efforts, is a powerfully projective text that stages an uncanny crisis of authorial self-making in relation to a disruptive and deforming femininity. I suggest that *The Red Badge of Courage,* in contrast, explores a disruptive homoeroticism lodged in Henry Fleming's charged encounters with corpses. These encounters are defined and contained by their position out of the narrative line of battle, a line that produces a deeply ironized authority for Crane and a deeply ironized manhood for Fleming, thus gothically concluding and unveiling the nineteenth century's necrophiliac linking of homoeroticism and death.

Finally, in my conclusion, I suggest that the formal perfection of Fitzgerald's *The Great Gatsby* lies in its magisterial manipulation and formalization of the anxieties identified in previous sections of this book.

Each reading I construct in this book, while informed by historical and cultural issues described in the introduction, works within slightly different idioms, determined by its utility for interrogating particular authors and texts. My interest in each case has been to pay attention to the distinctive detail of each text, even while arguing for their structural similarity. I will refer here, in passing, to two issues that may be relevant for a reading of this book: the question of biography and the question of genre.

My use of biographical information will vary from chapter to chapter and author to author and reflects some ambivalence on my part about this mode of argument. In general, where useful biographical information exists indicating the relation of a particular author to matters of gender or sexuality, I make reference to it. Clearly, for example, the strong biographical evidence of James's homosexuality that has been amassed in recent decades helps authorize a reading of the complex homoeroticism in his fiction. On the other hand, my arguments finally are textual and do not rest on or require a foundation of biographical evidence. Indeed, evidence of feminine influence and same-sex desire may be remarkably sparse in biographies of male writers, for the obvious reason that such formations have been difficult to acknowledge fully and exist as a kind of cultural unconscious. The absence of evidence of active homosexual relations with other men in the life of a particular writer, for example, by no means precludes homoeroticism as a question in his fiction. Neither does the absence of direct feminine contributions to a male writer's work (though evidence of such contributions is, again, of interest where it exists) suggest that feminine influence is not a relevant category for analysis, since, as I will later suggest, such influence is a structural product of nineteenth-century gender relations. Though I give an historical account of the dynamics I discuss in this book in this introduction, in general I operate on the assumption that evidence of a phenomenon at work within a literary text constitutes real evidence and should be regarded as such.

Monumental Anxieties also covers a wide range of work across conventional genre boundaries. Upton Sinclair's socialist naturalism, Henry James's high modernism, Edgar Allen Poe's detective fiction, and Hawthornian romance clearly occupy in many regards different regions of the nineteenth-century literary universe, although it is a difficult if not impossible enterprise to specify theoretically essential distinctions between genres that can resist deconstructive critique. This book will suggest that certain culturally produced dynamics of male authoring are in fact remarkably consistent across such ostensible differences between authors and texts and, with some differences, consistent from the nineteenth to the twentieth centuries. One of these consistencies involves, in fact, the practice of invoking the category of the "real" as a consistent strategy for claiming intellectual and social authority for particular male characters within fiction, and by extension for the work of fiction itself. Clearly, for example, naturalist fiction authorizes itself as a genre by claiming truth-value for its (usually) masculine imaginings of the world. Though I see no reason why distinctions cannot be made between fictions on the basis of claims to representational accuracy so long as one carefully specifies the target of representation, it is nonetheless the case that claims to realist accuracy are generally broad and unfocused and, as a consequence, unmask themselves as power-appropriating strategies of warrantless self-authorization. Within the fiction I analyze in *Monumental Anxieties,* the claim to realist authority involves a resistance to the emotional and ethical demands of women, and a related claim to an unencumbered existence in social space imagined as public and masculine by virtue of its demand for certain kinds of knowledge and expertise. Genre, consequently, might be thought of more productively in terms of its functioning within the gender dynamics of particular texts rather than as a way of absolutely distinguishing one text from another. In almost all cases, such claims exist to be deconstructed and serve as an avenue to an ironic reading of the development of a text's central characters.

*A*uthorship as a profession emerged with the explosive impact on U.S. culture of the growth of the publishing industry from roughly 1830 to the Civil War. In this period, publishing was transformed from a small, relatively local industry that primarily published books written by European authors to a national industry capable of developing individual texts by U.S. authors into best-sellers and delivering wealth to individual authors, who became cultural celebrities as a result.[2] If authoring, as embodied by such persons as Fanny Fern, Harriet Beecher Stowe, James Fenimore Cooper, and Catharine Maria Sedgwick, suddenly emerged as a potentially lucrative profession, it was nonetheless one of considerable struggle for many male writers who have been posthumously rewarded by twentieth-century readers. Many of the male authors of the now traditional canon shared the need to support a family, for example, a need that typically affected women either through the death of a male provider or, as in Elizabeth Stuart Phelps's *The Story of Avis,* the male provider's physical and/or mental collapse. These writers, with the notable exceptions of Whitman and to some extent Thoreau, did not seek the voluntary poverty of a bohemian lifestyle; they had little if any interest in Chatterton's garret. Even the disreputable Poe had his young wife to support for eleven years until her death, and one of the engines that drove his career was a ceaseless and desperate need for income. Hawthorne had a wife and three children, and his movement into novel writing in the 1850s was provoked as much by the failure of his short fiction to produce adequate profits as by purely aesthetic considerations. Melville struggled to support a family for years on a series of novels still famous both as aesthetic successes and as commercial failures.

To the burdens of supporting a family in a middle-class lifestyle one might add the pressures of the remarkable flux of Jacksonian culture. While the debate continues regarding the actual prominence of the nascent middle class in the period before the Civil War, the dynamic changes of pre–Civil War culture are not generally debatable.[3] If the truth is that most wealthy members of U.S. culture remained wealthy, financial rises and falls were common enough to produce substantial anxieties regarding the stability of class position.

For women the activity of writing often existed in a crisis-ridden relation to the true vocation of maternity, despite the attractions of writing as a career relatively open to women. For many male writers, a commitment to literature also involved a crisis of vocation of varying severity, produced in their case by the possibility of pursuing professions that presented better odds of success. A number of literary notables came to writing as part of a vocational crisis. John Greenleaf Whittier, for example, speaks to this crisis in an early short story entitled "The Nervous Man." According to Whittier's artist hero, "Time has dealt hardly with my boyhood's muse. Poetry has been to me a beautiful delusion. . . . I can, indeed, make rhymes now, as mechanically as a mason piles one brick above another; but the glow of feeling, the hope, the ardor, have passed away forever. I have long thought, or rather the world has *made* me think, that poetry is too trifling, too insignificant a pursuit for the matured intellect of sober manhood. I have half acquiesced in the opinion of Plato."[4] Perry Miller argues that abolition allowed Whittier both to satisfy his severe conscience and to gratify his powerful ambitions. Here is how Whittier describes his change of direction in a letter: "Disappointment in a thousand ways has gone over my heart and left it in the dust. Yet I still look forward with high anticipations. I have placed the goal of my ambitions high—but with the blessings of God it shall be reached. The world has at least breathed into my bosom a portion of its own bitterness, and I now feel as if I would wrestle manfully in the strife of men. If my life is spared, the world shall know me in a loftier capacity than as a *writer of rhymes*."[5] Finally, the young Whittier sounds the note of feminization, which I will come back to as an important component of the anxiety of authorship for nineteenth-century men. Looking around him, he sees that other men "bear no evidence of manly and vigorous exertion. They have no character of thought. . . . We are becoming effeminate in everything—in our habits as well as our literature."[6] Whittier would join poetry to the masculinizing enterprise of abolition before eventually achieving his greatest success with the nostalgic and saccharine domesticity of *Snowbound*.

The young Hawthorne echoed Whittier's uncertainty in a letter he wrote as a young man to his mother: "Shall you want me to be a Minister, Doctor or Lawyer? A Minister I will not be." In still another letter he asks, "[W]hat do you think of my becoming an Author, and relying for my support upon my pen. . . . But Authors are always poor Devils, and therefore Satan may take them."[7]

In later years, Hawthorne explained that, despite the effort he had invested in his writing, his career had been a kind of accident of indecision: "I sat myself down to consider what pursuit in life I was best fit for. . . . And year after year I kept on considering what I was fit for, and time and my destiny decided that I was to be the writer that I am."[8] W. D. Howells, born in 1837, remembered both having as a youth a strong sense of literary vocation and recognizing the difficulty of ever supporting himself by writing alone, based on the difficulties of other established authors: "If I thought of taking up some other calling it was as a means only; literature was always the end I had in view, immediately or finally. I did not see how it was to yield me a living, for I knew that almost all the literary men in the country had other professions; . . . there was then not one who earned his bread solely by his pen in fiction, or drama, or history, or poetry, or criticism, in a day when people wanted very much less butter on their bread than they do now. But I kept blindly at my studies."[9]

In *Notes of a Son and Brother*, Henry James reflected at length on the vocational struggles of both himself and the artistically inclined William, neither of whom was encouraged by the family to cultivate art as a profession.[10] According to James, "What we were to do instead was just to *be* something, something unconnected with specific doing, something free and uncommitted. . . . The 'career of art' has again and again been deprecated and denounced, on the lips of anxiety or authority, as a departure from the career of business, of industry and respectability, . . . but it was perhaps never elsewhere to know dissuasion on the very ground of its failing to uplift the spirit in the ways it most pretends to" (47–48). The elder Henry James's critique of the "career of art," in other words, was more or less from the bohemian side of respectability, so that Henry, Jr., remembered his "own repeated appeal to our parent for some presentable account of him that would prove us respectable. Business alone was respectable—if one meant by it, that is, the calling of a lawyer, a doctor or a minister" (64–65).[11] Meanwhile, his parents worried about the consequences of his habit of inveterate novel reading.

The anguish of Hawthorne, Whittier, Howells, and James was characteristic of a host of writers who more often than not came to writing as a career after a vocational crisis of variable severity. Emerson came to literature after abandoning the ministry; Irving abandoned the law; Longfellow refused to study law; Melville tried and abandoned innumerable careers; Thoreau tried and abandoned teaching school; Poe was expelled from West Point; James Russell Lowell studied law and gave it up; and even a generation later the young Henry James, almost unthinkably given the aging Master's love of ruminative gaping pauses and intricately crafted dependent clauses, attempted the study of law at Harvard.

The experiences of vocational crisis were by no means confined to male *writers*. Again these were forms of crises that were to some extent broadly typical of middle-class young men in the nineteenth century. The ongoing transformation of the nineteenth-century economy, fueled by forces such as geographical mobility, urbanization, and explosive population growth, meant that sons would often find work in positions that barely existed as possibilities for older generations.[12] The entire category of the "white-collar" job, for example, was a nineteenth-century contrivance involving a separation of workplace from home and a segregation within the workplace of nonmanual and manual labor. The growth of "white-collar" positions, in turn, marked the growth of the middle class, for whom the possibility of rising serves as an ideological bedrock.[13] At the same time, these common crises seem more intense in the case of male writers because of the nature of writing in nineteenth-century culture. In no period will the decision to support oneself primarily by writing, and especially primarily by writing fiction, offer the relatively secure route to success promised by the traditional professions, such as law and medicine, or by a solid start in business.

G. Stanley Hall's massive *Adolescence,* published in 1905, is suggestive in this regard, as he codifies and expands the nineteenth century's developmental crises.[14] Hall persistently urges that adolescence as a biologically grounded phase be protected from the "complex business organization" that is absorbing "ever more and earlier the best talent and muscle of youth and now dominates health, time, society, politics, and lawgiving." To Hall, "the complete apprenticeship . . . needs repose, leisure, art, legends, romance, idealization, and in a word humanism," traits he sees being exterminated "in our very kindergartens." If Hall here argues for the increased protection of what he regards as a sacred period of development, he overlooks the extent to which the object of his study has been produced, not by the relentless extension of work into childhood, but by its deferral. His attempt to make vocational concerns recede even further from the late childhood of the middle class is evident in his appropriation of the term "apprenticeship," here completely stripped of its function in an earlier artisan culture. If the crisis of this deferral is general rather than specific, Hall also indicates why such a crisis might have an unusual magnitude for the literary young. Even in the act of obviously celebrating "art, legends, and romance," he assumes their status as permanently adolescent and prevocational and not consistent with achieved adult identity (1:xvi–xvii).

A confirming account of the relation of adolescent bookishness to real masculine identity occurs in Alfred J. Beveridge's *The Young Man and the World,* also published in 1905. Beveridge urges his young readers to "make good with the American father," a man who "has 'been through the mill,' until the softness is pretty well ground out and little remains but the granite-like muscle of manhood. He is a pretty stern proposition; and if there is anything he won't stand it is pretense, make-believe. . . . They have lived so much longer than you have that the accretion of daily experience has given them a variety of information beside which your book knowledge is a sort of wooden learning, lifeless and artificial. . . . No, decidedly, don't 'get too smart for father.'"[15]

If the hope of class mobility became the central pillar of social ideology in the nineteenth century, concealing and justifying an increasing concentration of wealth, the efforts of the upwardly mobile might also be fueled by the specter of calamitous failure. As Carroll Smith-Rosenberg puts it,

> The newly emerging bourgeoisie had few resources with which to resist disintegration. The beneficiary of the commercial and industrial revolutions, it consisted of an inharmonious grouping of quite disparate economic and social components: an older mercantile elite; new wholesale merchants only just risen from peddler to prince; smaller shopkeepers; the new industrial entrepreneurs; the equally new professionals. So ill-assorted an amalgam could scarcely be considered a solidified class. Certainly its membership demonstrated extreme instability. Specie shortage, bank wars, acts of nature such as fires and shipwrecks, the uncertainty of new markets, all could destroy budding careers, throw families into want and despair.[16]

Some kind of family catastrophe is the originating event of much nineteenth-century domestic fiction, a catastrophe that forces the heroine to confront the world without a covering male presence.[17] Such catastrophes mark male lives as well, and their possibility produces a broad preference in the nineteenth century for the sturdy and persistent in male character over mercurial brilliance: A properly formed male should be tough to knock off his feet and should fight through his reverses. As Beveridge pitilessly puts it, "A man who cannot get up when he is knocked down is of no use in the world" (80). In general, there would be little sense of social safety to cushion the vocational decisions of the young or the old. The converse of a hoped-for brilliant success, failure and ruin, would be in sufficient evidence to seem a significant possibility.

Henry Ward Beecher speaks to this emphasis on the stalwart in his *Addresses to Young Men,* given in the winter of 1843 to 1844 and circulated throughout the nineteenth century.[18] He observes: "Every few years, Commerce has its earthquakes. . . . The hearts of men fail them for fear; and the suddenly rich, made more suddenly poor, fill the land with their loud laments. But nothing strange has happened. When the whole story of commercial disasters is told, it is only found out that they, who have slowly amassed the gains of useful Industry, built upon a rock" (22). Patient industry is the quality that eludes the "geniuses" who "abound in academies, colleges, and Thespian societies; in village debating clubs; in coteries of young artists, and among young professional aspirants." These are "known by a reserved air, excessive sensitiveness, and utter indolence; by very long hair, and very open shirt collars" (26–27). This genius is "usually impatient of application, irritable, scornful of men's dullness, squeamish at petty disgusts" (28). Yet even in literature, masterpieces come from "an almost incredible continuance of labor upon them" (29). Misfortune may happen, but its lesson is to work harder: "To be pressed down by adversity has nothing in it of disgrace; but it is disgraceful to lie down under it like a supple dog. Indeed, to stand composedly in the storm, amidst its rage and wildest devastations; to let it beat over you, and roar around you, and pass by you, and leave you undismayed,— this is to be a MAN" (43).

These bedrock qualities, however, are undermined by the desire-producing images of capitalist culture, which teaches a scorn for honest, manual labor. As opposed to politics, for example, "[h]ow disgusting in contrast is the mechanic's life; a tinkering shop,—dark and smutty,—is the only theater of his exploits; and labor, which covers him with sweat and fills him with weariness, brings neither notice nor praise. The ambitious apprentice, sighing over his soiled hands, hates his ignoble work;—neglecting it, he aspires to better things,—plots in a caucus; declaims in a bar-room; fights in a grog shop; and dies in a ditch" (40–41). Beecher's lectures develop a kind of dense semiotic field in which literature, as a vocation, would have to know itself. On the one hand, a desire to produce great art might represent a high and difficult-to-achieve aspiration and so conform to nineteenth-century ideas of striving upward. On the other, art involved a suspicious turning away from conventional masculine commerce toward "long hair" and "open shirt collars" and might seem less like labor than erratic indolence. It did not represent a reliable path to the dependable solidity of bourgeois masculinity.

As a consequence of the crisis of vocation in middle-class life, the achievement of a vocational identity came to represent a key stage in the developmental narratives of individual men. The achievement of a stable position in the world of work symbolized one's final emergence from the mother-dominated world of childhood into the adult masculine world, but gaining such a position was not an escape from family relations so much as a reproduction of them. The man with a solid and stable beginning might legitimately aspire to a family of his own. Both the drive toward a vocation, then, and the consequence of attaining one were family matters, and the problems of authority and authorship must be understood in these terms.

Nineteenth-century culture gave to women important responsibility for the care of young children and for the early cultivation of "character," regardless of the differing practical degrees to which men chose to involve themselves in such matters. This cultivation occurred in an increasingly self-enclosed domestic space that nonetheless served the needs and necessities of a nascent industrial capitalism. As Gillian Brown has argued, "domestic individualism" provided a balm to the increasing uncertainty of the economic relations and, by providing a basis for secure self-definition apart from "the market," enabled such uncertainty to exist.[19]

At the same time, according to Mary Ryan, middle-class families strove to prepare their male children for a fluid economy shifting in ways that were difficult to foresee. The increasing emphasis on education and "character" arguably equipped sons to confront a variety of situations in a variety of locations. Internalized ideals were transportable. Rather than relying on Calvinist force as a method of compelling obedience from children, starting about 1830 domestic culture self-consciously explored maternal strategies for building character through the manipulation of affection and guilt.[20] The results of this early training were supposed to endure as testimony to a mother's influence.

The primacy of the mother in early care shifted the father's primary responsibility to later periods in the development of the child. Fathers would continue to serve as symbolic heads of the family and as sources of discipline and to supervise formal education, but the father's role, especially early in the child's life, had diminished by the beginning of the nineteenth century. A major locus of paternal responsibility involved the later task of guiding the male child's difficult entry into the wider masculine world.[21] Ryan reports, for example, numerous examples in Oneida County of an active interest displayed by fathers in their sons' careers.[22] By the 1840s, custody law in the United States reflected this division of labor, the father's time of primary influence beginning when the son was about the age of ten.[23] That earlier childhood was the province of the mother seemed embodied even by clothing styles. Until the age of six—the dawn of active boyhood—the male child would wear loose-fitting feminine gowns.[24]

The division of labor in child rearing then, despite the inevitable complexities and differences that pertained to individual situations, produced a standard narrative of male development in which the male child moved from a female-centered, domestic world of childhood to a stable position in and identification with a nondomestic outside world of masculine economic, political, and recreational activity. This change in a number of ways involved rupture, symbolized by a change of dress and by the social separation of masculine and feminine spaces and activities.[25]

The negotiation of this narrative was anything but simple for young men. If achieved masculine identity required a resolution to the problem of vocation, this resolution might not occur until well into the subject's twenties, setting up a long and difficult period of liminality.[26] In an increasing number of cases before the Civil War, as young men struggled to find their economic feet, the family offered continuing support. Ryan suggests that by 1860, for example, 40 percent of young clerks were living with kin, as opposed to 20 percent a decade earlier. In the 1850s, 40 percent of native-born males between the ages of fifteen and thirty were living with their parents, a figure that rose to 60 percent by 1860. Only 35.3 percent of white-collar workers between the ages of twenty-five and twenty-nine were married.[27] Hawthorne's decision to live in his mother's household in the years following his graduation from Bowdoin, often taken as a sign of reclusiveness and pathology, was, then, not an unusual one for a young man in a vocational quandary.

Even success in negotiating the problem of male vocation did not produce a clear break from the feminine influences of childhood. A maternal feminine presence in the masculine psyche seems to have been, if anything, deliberately cultivated in the middle classes of the United States. This cultivation is apparent, not only from literature, but from the numerous health manuals, sermons, and advice books, which despite their limitations constitute some of the best sources for understanding middle-class masculinity in the nineteenth century. As reformer O. S. Fowler, an early writer on men's health, urged in 1867, "Behold thy mother! Make love to her, and her your first sweetheart. . . . Nestle yourself right into her heart, and hers into yours."[28] According to Albert J. Beveridge, "She has her own way, too, of getting this nourishment of the verities into your character. It is done not so much by preaching to you . . . as it is by her very presence. . . . Don't be afraid that that will make you effeminate and soft. . . . I have seen one of this kind of fellow hold in awe a mob of cowboys and plainsmen when passions were aroused and blows had already been struck" (61–62). Paradigms of the masculine in the nineteenth century, perhaps more than in the homophobically haunted twentieth century, have a place for the feminine within them, however incoherent the terms of its definition.

This place, however, was characterized less by liberal tolerance for broad feminine influences than by a psychic and cultural defense against them, just as the doctrine of "separate spheres" operated against a social reality of expanding opportunities for women.[29] If the mother has primary responsibilities for child care until the child reaches an age near adolescence, then even many of the child's practical skills must be traced to feminine training. The mother, or in the bourgeois family perhaps a female surrogate, will teach the male child speech, recite or read to the child his first stories, sing him his first songs, subject him to his first discipline and punishment, introduce him to toilet training, provide him with his first experience of play, teach him to use eating implements, help him clothe himself, treat his cuts and bruises, encourage him to walk, and teach him to count. If the child-centered ideologies that emerged about 1820 signify the intensive care needed to equip a child to function in the complicated world of capitalist democracy, the figure entrusted with providing this care was largely the mother.

The reduction of a mother's influence to emotional, moral, and religious training is, then, a containing sentimental fiction that seems to extend women's power while in fact drastically circumscribing it.[30] Such circumscription, however, is a foundational—and perhaps the foundational—task of nineteenth-century masculinity. The massive contributions of women to the male child's development in the early stages of life must somehow be rendered compatible with adult masculine identity. In nineteenth-century literature the mechanisms for the denial of women's contributions to culture break down for two reasons. First, the presence of women in literary endeavors made the denial of aspects of feminine influence an especially difficult task. Second, male authors in the United States may have felt equally alienated from dominant cultural ideas of masculinity, in part because art was persistently figured in feminine terms.[31]

As I have argued, the mother will make a broad and crucial contribution to male development in a culture that makes child care a feminine job. In the case of literature, this contribution is difficult to suppress because of the significant presence of women in culture as both writers and readers of literature.[32] Indeed, as many critics have pointed out, the biggest sellers of the 1850s, the decade of *The Scarlet Letter, Moby Dick, Walden,* and *Leaves of Grass,* were all written by women: Susan Warner's *Wide, Wide World,* Harriet Beecher Stowe's *Uncle Tom's Cabin,* Maria Cummins's *The Lamplighter,* and E.D.E.N. Southworth's *The Hidden Hand.* The prominence of women in literary endeavor had enormous consequences for male writers and for the vocational crisis of writing. The active participation of women in nineteenth-century literary culture suggests that women were active bearers, not just of language or fantasy or originary contacts with cultural formations emptied of any specific content, but of literary *culture* in a robust and complicated sense. A number of male writers in the United States have had important if undervalued relations to women: Hawthorne's vital but largely unspecifiable relation to his remarkable sister, Ebe, or Emerson's relation to his brilliant and eccentric aunt, Mary Moody Emerson, or Richard Harding Davis's relation to his mother, Rebecca Harding Davis, come especially to mind. These important interpersonal ties represent moments in which the contributions of women to culture surface with some clarity, but they serve as metonymic signs for other contributions lost or nearly lost, contributions that may surface only in single lines of memoirs or biographies. According to Octavius Brooks Frothingham in 1882, for example, George Ripley had a "dearly beloved sister, Marianne, a woman of superior mental gifts, as well as of the highest personal qualities, closely acquainted with many prominent men and women of her time." James Whitcombe Riley had not only a father but a mother who wrote poems and contributed them to local papers. E. P. Roe had a mother of whom he reportedly said, "Such literary tendencies as I have are derived from her, but I do not possess a tithe of her powers." W. H. Prescott upon his mother's death reportedly spoke both of his mother's love of reading and writing and of her importance as a "guiding influence."[33]

These kinds of hints do not represent reliable biographical data in any particular case. On one hand, literary history and Western history in general have systematically discounted and suppressed women's contributions to culture. On the other, such comments as the ones quoted above may often represent a sentimental urge to acknowledge women in a language that has little real content aside from a desire to praise. Empty encomiums to maternity represent an important device through which the contributions of women are contained by a narrowly defined maternal bond between mother and son, and through which an excavation of the positive and negative content of real relations is avoided.

Such praise can also represent a desire to have a particular kind of culturally desirable mother, even if such a figure seems missing from a writer's actual history. Biographers have long puzzled, for example, over Henry James's famous praise in his journals of Mary James, a woman about whom no one else, so far as I can tell, has found much positive to say: "She was our life, she was the house, she was the keystone of the arch. She held us all together, and without her we are scattered reeds. She was patience, she was wisdom, she was exquisite maternity. Her sweetness, her mildness, her great natural beneficence were unspeakable."[34]

It may be that James simply uses conventional praise here to repress aspects of his relationship to his mother that were difficult and painful to express. James's formulaic description also conventionalizes him in terms of masculine culture. Her "perfect" maternity, we find out a page later, consists, in part, of her estimable willingness to "lay herself down in her ebbing strength and yield up her pure soul to the celestial power that had given her this divine commission" after her children "had reached a full maturity and were absorbed in the world and in their own interests" (230).

It is possible that if we understood the lost history of James's relations to his mother we would better understand his matricidal celebration of her virtues. To argue that the death of a mother always justifies such grief is to replicate an idealization of maternity that empties out the labor of real women in such roles. In James's novels, particularly *The Wings of the Dove* and *The Ambassadors,* the obligation of men such as Densher and Strether to women such as Kate Croy and Maria Gostrey is explicitly *not* related to biological maternity but to the acquisition of knowledge women acquire by virtue of their own cultural position. James's celebration of Mary James's "exquisite maternity" serves as a metonymic way of owning up to and yet containing a cultural debt broader than that owed to the standardized sacrifices of maternity. Such a broader debt is denied forcefully in *The Bostonians,* the novel written in this period of James's career. James may or may not sympathize with Ransom's contentious and even violently masculine views about cultural politics.[35] Whether he does or not, such views position Ransom as a man who owes absolutely none of his ideas to women, even as Verena Tarrant apparently has no substantive ideas of her own to give. Olive Chancellor apparently does have ideas, but an implication of her love for women is that she will not "love" or mother men, which in James chiefly stands for a flow of cultural information and cognitive skills. The fringe male characters who do have obligations to women's culture, the intensely mothered Henry Burrage and the culturally mothered Mathias Pardon, are both reduced by it. *The Bostonians* massively defends itself against patterns of feminine influence that the older James would explore.

A cultural debt to women does not have to be funneled through familial or personal relations with specific women. Any inveterate reader in the nineteenth century, such as James, would, as a matter of course, read books written by women, who might be either popular cultural presences, such as Southworth or Warner, or women of substantial reputation, such as Harriet Beecher Stowe, Jane Austen, George Sand, or George Eliot. The influences of such women upon male work might be directly acknowledged, as James acknowledges Eliot in the preface to *The Portrait of a Lady.*[36] Such influence might also surface in the form of aversion, as in Melville's domestic *Pierre* or James's own *The Bostonians,* and this aversion helps shape entire literary movements in the cultural history of the United States, though the emergence of anything so complex as a literary movement is an overdetermined phenomenon that involves much more than gender. Alfred Habegger has argued that for writers such as James the adventure of style serves to masculinize literature and demarcate it from a feminine mass culture.[37] Style produces what Richard Poirier refers to as "a world elsewhere."[38] In this world, masculine expertise can be clearly differentiated from, in Hawthorne's famous phrase, "a damned mob of scribbling women."

Samuel Goodrich, a pre–Civil War New England publisher, bookseller, and author of the Peter Parley books for children, suggests in his 1857 memoirs the importance of women as contributors to male literary development, the difficulty of seeing through the containing tropes of sentimentality in order to judge the precise nature of this contribution, and the power of style in masculinizing adult male writing.[39] Goodrich remembers his maternal grandmother and his mother as sources of his "literary" character. The author claims that his upper-class grandmother "sang me plaintive songs—told me stories of the Revolution; . . . she described Gen. Washington, whom she had seen; and the French officers, Lafayette, Rochambeau, and others, who had been inmates of her house. She told me tales of even more ancient date, and recited poetry, generally consisting of ballads, which were suited to my taste. And all this lore was commended to me by a voice of inimitable tenderness, and a manner at once lofty and condescending" (89).

If his grandmother was a source of literature and history, equally important were the poetic tendencies of his mother: "I have no doubt that I inherited from my mother a love of the night side of nature—not a love that begets melancholy, but an appetite that found pleasure in the shadows as well as the lights of life and imagination. Eminently practical as she was—laborious, skillful, and successful in the duties which Providence had assigned her . . . she was still of a poetic temperament. Her lively fancy was vividly set forth by a pair of the finest eyes I have ever seen—dark and serious, yet tender and sentimental" (156–157). In his adolescence, as he roamed the country like a young Wordsworth, it is his mother's "scraps of solemn poetry from Milton, Young, and Watts" that, he claims, acted as "lightning-rods to conduct to my lips some of the burning emotions of my breast" (155–156). Though he "could not then write a reliable line of sense or grammar," he "planned poems, and even dreamed of literary fame" (156).

Goodrich immediately follows this recollection with a portrait of his Bible-reading father as, in fact, the source of his style: "You will gather from what I have said that my father not only prayed in his family; . . . he always read a chapter in the sacred volume. In our family Bible it is recorded that he thus read that holy book through, in course, thirteen times. . . . He was an excellent reader, having a remarkably clear, frank, hearty voice. . . . The direct, simple style of the Bible entered into my heart, and became for a long time my standard of taste in literary composition" (157). Goodrich is able safely to contain the relation of his literary interests to women by suggesting a masculine authority over style. His grandmother chiefly serves as a source of historical tales of great men. His mother's potentially threatening tendency to Byronic passion, on the other hand, is safely ensconced within his father's clarity and good sense.

This is nostalgia, however, for the simple world of the late eighteenth century: Goodrich was born in 1793. In the decades before the Civil War, such simplicity, real and imagined, would increasingly yield to the complexities of mass culture. Such culture, full of scribbling women, fundamentally resisted the ordering gaze of everyday male authority. The imposition of order on this world required greatness of a transcendent kind.

If many novels in the eighteenth century were published anonymously, as Cathy Davidson has suggested, in the years before the Civil War literature was understood and discussed in terms of authors, who might earn a measure of fame as a consequence.[40] The highest category in terms of which authorship was discussed, and one generally not available to women writers such as Fern, was that of "genius," which according to Nina Baym was "the hoped-for end of every novelistic venture" (259).[41] Though the term comes with built-in ambiguities, regarding, for example, whether the quality of genius pertains to the work or its producer, it clearly implied the possibility of transcendent cultural authority that appealed to a number of traditionally celebrated male authors of antebellum literature.[42] By lifting an author above the masses, the idea of genius carried a built-in defense against the anxiety of commercial failure at the same time that it exalted the idea of literature. In all cases of its use, the trope of genius, as the highest pinnacle of writing, expresses a distinction in favor of serious culture and against the popular and conventional, and hence it helps to make elite transcendence the goal of serious literature. It also, needless to say, produces a large fund of resentment against more successful popular writers.

Such writers, commonly referred to en masse, are typically described in terms of abjection—of illegibility, of unthinkable proliferation, of waste, of body fragments, of monstrous reproductive maternity—which serve as the polar opposite of the authority of genius, and yet which serve as a slough of despond into which unrealized genius might fall. Even if popular literature, much of it written by women, contains stable and even comforting representations of the domestic, its overwhelming presence in the literary marketplace threatens the intelligibility of culture to the author. If Hawthorne famously referred to contemporary women writers as a "damned mob of scribbling women," he expressed an even deeper animus in a note written to his publisher, James T. Fields, regarding the books of Camilla Crosland. Complains Hawthorne, "I really don't know that I have said any more than truth, in a good-humored mood, will warrant; but, nevertheless, I can very well conceive of a person's tossing the books aside as tedious twaddle. My favorable opinion of the book has evaporated, in the process of writing it down. *All* women, as authors, are feeble and tiresome. I wish they were forbidden to write, on pain of having their faces deeply scarified with an oyster-shell."[43] If one presumes Hawthorne's punishment fits the crime, an implicit message to Fields is that women have already "deeply scarified" themselves in the act of writing novels. At the same time, Hawthorne's initial opinion seems to have been at least moderately favorable and to have had some relation to historical reality. The real locus of conflict has been in his own ambivalence-ridden psyche. This ambivalence has made *him* produce an apparently deficient piece of writing (which has not been recovered), and this authority-diminishing complicity has produced his gesture of angry distancing from "tedious twaddle." He himself, in other words, has been "deeply scarified."[44] The implication of trash or waste in characterizing such books as "twaddle" to be "thrown aside" is reinforced by Hawthorne's choice of the "oyster shell" as his implement of imagined violence. An oyster shell is a waste object from which the oyster has perhaps been consumed and in any case is missing, and which certainly has no pearl. The wound it makes is a product of its worthless, rough character.

Waste explicitly characterizes contemporary literature to Samuel Goodrich. To Goodrich, the antebellum period marks a decline from the properly hierarchical scene of reading he remembers from his own youth:

> Books and newspapers . . . were read respectfully, and as if they were grave matters, demanding thought and attention. They were not toys and pastimes, taken up every day, and by everybody, in the short intervals of labor, and then hastily dismissed, like waste paper. The aged sat down when they read, and drew forth their spectacles, and put them deliberately and reverently upon the nose. These instruments were not as now, little tortoise-shell hooks, attached to a ribbon, . . . but they were of silver or steel, substantially made, and calculated to hold on with a firm and steady grasp. . . . Even the young approached a book with reverence, and a newspaper with awe. How the world has changed![45]

Goodrich's sense of contemporary culture as actively disruptive to properly reflective honest-to-goodness reading also extends to his own activity as a writer. As he confesses in regard to his own publications, "I feel far more of humiliation than of triumph. . . . I have written too much, and have done nothing really well."[46]

The sense of democratic culture as a realm of illegible and feminized waste also informs James Russell Lowell's comments on the situation of literature in an essay on Poe in 1845, the same Poe who himself consists, to Lowell, of "two-fifths sheer fudge":

> Our capital city, unlike London or Paris, is not a great central heart . . . but resembles more an isolated umbilicus, stuck down as near as may be to the center of the land. . . . Boston, New York, Philadelphia, each has its literature almost more distinct than those of the different dialects of Germany; and the Young Queen of the West has also one of her own, of which some articulate rumor barely has reached us dwellers by the Atlantic. Meanwhile, a great babble is kept up concerning a national literature, and the country, having delivered itself of the ugly likeness of a paint-bedaubed, filthy savage, smiling dandles the rag baby upon her maternal knee.[47]

Lowell's metaphors bespeak a desire for central and autonomous authority, a "great heart," which would rescue literature from the "umbilicus," a grotesque metaphor that suggests an incomplete separation from the feminine and an absence of discrete, comprehensible identity. The national literature—with the possible exception of the "Young Queen of the West"—is a grotesque "rag baby" sitting upon a "maternal knee" rendered grotesque by association.

As Lora Romero suggests, throughout the nineteenth century, male authors in fact regularly conflate mass production and female generativity, and see such generativity as a potentially dangerous extension of female domestic power, which inhabits a Foucauldian profusion of microscopic sources, and which lacks a central, identifiable source.[48] The possibilities and perils of such circulation of the feminine are, in fact, a source of uncertainty and ambivalence for male authors about the capacity of capitalist culture to serve the construction of masculine authority. On one hand, a struggle with the formidable figure of the domestic mother might well be usefully shifted to the exterior, impersonal world of commerce. On the other hand, this latter realm could itself be embraced only ambivalently because of the oft-noted alienation of vocationally troubled (now celebrated) male authors from the perceived intellectual anarchy of commerce as well. One might find in commerce, finally, a terrifying potential to feminize, involving the expansion of feminine power Romero charts and a corresponding diminishment of masculine intellectual authority, lodged in a capacity to confer order on reality.

The movement to escape the domestic power of the mother in the exterior masculine world, a movement, again, part of conventional male developmental patterns in nineteenth-century culture in the United States, would thus be threatened by the complexity of imagining an intellectual place for oneself in the amorphous, dangerously feminizing world of commerce. This world would have to be transcended, since its incipient modernism routinely swamps the ordering efforts of the nineteenth century's most capacious minds, by a desire for a transcendently male form of authority.

The variety of anxieties and indeterminancies I have been discussing are usefully displayed by Walt Whitman's 1871 *Democractic Vistas*. In what follows, Whitman's fascination with the reproductive power of capitalism, embodied by the "proud, crashing, ten-cylinder presses," coexists uneasily with the degrading, persistently feminine mass culture it produces:

> Not but that doubtless our current so-called literature, (like an endless supply of small coin,) performs a certain service, and may-be, too, the service needed for the time, (the preparation-service, as children learn to spell). Everybody reads, and truly nearly everybody writes, either books, or for the magazines and journals. The matter has magnitude, too, after a sort. . . . There is something impressive about the huge editions of the dailies and weeklies, the mountain-stacks of white paper . . . and the proud, crashing, ten-cylinder presses, which I can stand and watch any time by the half hour. Then, (though the States in the field of imagination present not a single first-class work, not a single great literatus,) the main objects to amuse, to titillate, to pass away time . . . are yet attain'd. . . . To-day, in books, in the rivalry of writers, especially novelists, success, (so-call'd) is for him or her who strikes the mean flat average, the sensational appetite for stimulus, incident, persiflage, &c. and depicts, to the common calibre, sensual, exterior life. To such, or the luckiest of them, as we see, the audiences are limitless and profitable. . . . While this day, or any day, to workmen portraying interior or spiritual life, the audiences were limited, and often laggard—but they last forever. . . . Behold the prolific brood of the contemporary novel, magazine-tale, theatre-play, &c. . . . What is the reason . . . that we see no fresh local courage, sanity, of our own—the Mississippi,

> stalwart Western men, real mental and physical facts, Southerners . . .
> in the body of our literature? . . . But always, instead, a parcel of dan-
> dies and ennuyees, dapper little gentlemen from abroad, who flood
> us with their thin sentiment of parlors, parasols, piano-songs . . .
> whimpering and crying about something, chasing one aborted con-
> ceit after another.[49]

The reference to the "prolific brood" of the novel once again associates general culture with an engulfing maternity, an implication affirmed in the suggestion of "aborted" birth in the final quoted phrase. Whitman sets up a first
line of defense for serious art against the sprawl of mass culture by declar-
ing its zone the "interior or spiritual." Even the interior, however, has been
corrupted by effeminate men and their "parlors" and "parasols," which generates a longing for the distant worlds of the "Mississippi," "Southerners,"
"stalwart Western men" and the stability of "real mental and physical facts."

It is no wonder that for Whitman such conflict can only generate a fantasy of sublime transcendence into "the daring launching forth of concep-
tions in literature, inspired by them, soaring in highest regions, serving art
in its highest, (which is only the other name for serving God, and serving
humanity)" (245). This transcendence is in stark juxtaposition to the only
listed use of common literature, which is the feminine one of teaching children to spell. This last metaphor suggests that common literature may indeed
have a positive effect as the beginning of a teleological process with stalwart
manhood and\or the masculine sublime as its desirable end.

For any writer, desirable ends can only be accomplished through the
process of writing. For the writers and texts I discuss in this book, the multiple pressures on middle-class men in the United States produce the act of
writing as a crisis of self-definition, particularly for writers who have previously achieved no identity-confirming successes.[50] If it is the nature of writing
that one's successes themselves require reconfirmations, these reconfirmations
may still lack the intensity of first efforts to demonstrate the capacity to serve
as the author of a book or to achieve greatness for the first time. Such pressures may also be increased dramatically by a variety of other biographical
factors.

It is only by completing a manuscript that the writer earns the title *author* and the cultural authority this title implies. The multilayered stakes in
claiming such a status in the U.S. culture of the nineteenth century have, I
hope, been made clear by previous sections of this introduction. Vocational
identity is at stake; masculine identity is at stake; money is at stake; cultural

authority is at stake; and, with authority, the cultural possibility of coherent, autonomous subjectivity. This subjectivity must be capable of resisting or transcending the abjectifying "feminizing" forces of mass democratic culture.[51]

The idea of achieving the status of author may, in fact, serve as one of the chief motives of the writing process. This motive may take priority over even the idea for one's book in the genesis of writing.[52] As opposed to beginning with an idea about which to write, in other words, one might well begin with a determination to become an author and only the vaguest sense of the eventual content of one's narrative. In such a case, the would-be author searches for a subject that will lend itself to the construction of a satisfactory book based on his or her sense of what a book must or should be. For established writers the search for a subject consonant with the production of authorship may be equally insistent as earlier ideas are exhausted by the process of writing. The subject of a narrative, then, may be generated as a vehicle for a desire to achieve the imagined good of authorship and thus serve as the narrativization of this desire. The urge to complete the project at hand for the sake of the story itself will correspond as well to the vocational urge to realize oneself as an author successfully. These two different strands or emphases of the composing process will often be inextricably intertwined in a submerged narrative of composition that varies in detail and accessibility from author to author and from text to text.

This narrative of composition is typically one of crisis. If a successfully written text ends by solidifying a writer's claim to authorship, this claim is at risk until the text is completed. Henry James, always instructive about questions of writing, describes his own midcompositional perils in the course of writing *Roderick Hudson,* his first novel of ambitious scope:

> Yet it must even then have begun for me too, the ache of fear, that was to become so familiar, of being unduly tempted and led on by "developments"; which is but the desperate discipline of the question involved in them. . . . Really, universally, relations stop nowhere, and the exquisite problem of the artist is eternally but to draw, by a geometry of his own, the circle within which they shall happily *appear* to do so. . . . All of which will perhaps pass for a supersubtle way of pointing the plain moral that a young embroiderer of the canvas of life soon began to work in terror, fairly, of the vast expanse of that surface. . . . It is one of the silver threads of the recoverable texture of that embarrassed phase, however, that the book was not finished when it had to begin appearing in monthly fragments. . . . To

have "liked" so much writing it, to have worked out with such conviction the pale embroidery, and yet not, at the end of so many
months, to have come through, was clearly still to have fallen short
of any facility and any confidence.[53]

James's account speaks eloquently of the pressures on his younger self to bring
the narrative to completion and of the necessary constriction such formal requirements impose on the possible multiplication of events and circumstances
in the middle of the novel. As he says, apart from such requirements, "[r]eally,
universally, relations stop nowhere." This sense of infinite possibilities and
choices, of infinite difficulties, suggests that the (many) moments of
midcomposition threaten defacement of the aspiring author, uncompensated
by the genesis of any real narrative authority.[54] If this is a crisis of the story,
it at the same time is a crisis of "facility and . . . confidence" because the
writer has nothing but the confidence of previous experience to guarantee a
favorable outcome: The story may, indeed, turn out badly, and the related attempt to confirm oneself as an author may fail. In this space, the writer may
be literally devoid of identity, since other kinds of vocational identity may
have been surrendered in order to write and the identity available through
writing has not yet been gained. This crisis can be resolved only by forestalling
the potentially infinite complications of incident and meaning in midnarrative
and by completing the text.

At the same time, James's account suggests that he "liked" even the
difficulties of composition despite the existence of his text only in the form
of serialized "fragments." James's texts in general display a persistent unease
with settled endings, especially with the bête noire ending of the marriage
plot, and work to conclude in ways that preserve the contingency and openness of midcomposition. To rephrase one of the claims James makes above,
he works indefatigably to make relations seem to stop nowhere, despite the
necessity, in writing, that composition stop them.

James is quite conscious of an opposition in art between the ragged,
the tawdry, the incomplete, the unknown or half-perceived, and the unruffled
and consistent surface of finished composition. He is aware that compositional "finish," like the gilt surfaces of the upper-class world he treats, tends
to expunge and conceal these things, yet such finish is a valued component
of literary achievement. As he puts it in the preface to *The Spoils of Poynton,*
the artist begins with

the stray suggestion, the wandering word, the vague echo, at touch
of which the novelist's imagination winces as at the prick of some

sharp point: its virtue is all in its needle-like quality, . . . [t]he fine-
ness . . . that communicates the virus of suggestion. . . . Strange and
attaching, certainly, the consistency with which the first thing to be
done for the communicated and seized idea is to reduce almost to
nought the form, the air as of a mere disjoined and lacerated lump
of life, in which we may have happened to meet it. . . . The reason
is of course that life has no direct sense whatever for the subject and
is capable, luckily for us, of nothing but splendid waste. Hence the
opportunity for the sublime economy of art, which rescues, which
saves, and hoards and "banks," investing and reinvesting these fruits
of toil in wondrous useful works.[55]

It is impossible to know exactly how ironic James might be about the commercial ugliness of his metaphors for the finished text. It is clear that even
the name of his central heroine in *Spoils,* the exquisitely ugly "Fleda Vetch,"
privileges the half-known and flayed underside of gilt surfaces. This text, in
fact, ends with all its rawness intact. The apocalyptic but somewhat random
burning of Poynton operates as a spectacular distraction from its absence of
any suitable ending at all.

　　The opposition I have been discussing in James corresponds in some
ways to Roland Barthes's opposition between "pleasure" and "bliss" in literature:

Text of pleasure: the text that contents, fills, grants, euphoria; the
text that comes from culture and does not break with it, is linked to
a *comfortable* practice of reading. Text of bliss: the text that imposes
a state of loss, the text that discomforts (perhaps to the point of a
certain boredom), unsettles the reader's historical, cultural, psychological assumptions, the consistency of his tastes, values, memories,
brings to a crisis his relation with language. Now the subject who
keeps the two texts in his field . . . enjoys the consistency of his
selfhood (that is his pleasure) and seeks its loss (that is his bliss).[56]

Such a pleasure is constituted by the shattering of the repressive force of systems of cultural and literary meaning, in the service of what those systems
necessarily exclude, though the nature of the excluded may not itself be known
or knowable. In the space thus created, signs and relations shuffle themselves,
and something new or lost or unexpressed may threaten to enter the realm of
the symbolic. The writer might well cultivate the crisis of midcomposition
as a way of enacting his or her aggression against a series of other possible

identities, utterly impossible and life-denying, that miss some mark that writing strives to define. Such resistance may occur on the behalf of desires incompatible with or annihilated by the endings of linear narrative at a particular historical moment.[57]

*A*mong the wayward yearnings and marginalized states of being that might potentially surface in midwriting, two often but not necessarily related sorts are of particular significance for this book: feminine identifications and homoerotic desires.

The midperiod of composition furnishes a possible space for an exploration of feminine identifications, a space in which the culturally unacknowledged might be explored, and a space of potentially narrative-threatening disorder. Earlier in this introduction, I suggested that even common acknowledgments of feminine influence in U.S. culture function to suppress and confine the much broader contributions of women to nineteenth-century culture and to the specific development of individual men. These contributions, then, function themselves as what we might think of as a cultural unconscious, as buried experience not easily expressed in the conventional narratives culture provides to male and female subjects.

There are two related aspects to the exploration of the feminine in a masculine text. The first is that such an exploration may be an involuntary product of the crisis of composition precisely because the position of not having reached the end of one's story, not having solidified one's claim to authorship, equals a feminizing failure of vocation. Feminization, in these terms, is an involuntary condition from which the male subject must strive to emerge. The second, however, is that the feminization of midcomposition may be consciously or unconsciously cultivated, just as—and I argue this later—the homoerotic may be consciously or unconsciously explored. If narrative must move toward a closure that produces masculine authority through an erasure of the feminine, it is not clear that such closure, however necessary, adequately represents the trajectory of desire.

I have argued that to position the maternal as simply pleasure and oblivion, however, is itself a repression of the wider contributions of women to male development and Western culture. These masculine debts have a complicated relation to the problem of getting to the end of one's story. The difficulty male artists in the United States have in identifying with culturally dominant paradigms of masculinity is both cause and effect of the association of art as an activity with femininity or feminization. How may culture be reimagined in a way that grants a stable masculine position to the writer?

How may the fiction writer realize through his work the goal of conventional masculine development?[58]

This imagined position might get represented in terms of the symbolic positions of the family, but ideally it will imagine a place for the male artist in the masculine realm of exterior, nondomestic social and economic power. It may express the final interdependence of these realms, as happens at the end of *The Scarlet Letter,* when Dimmesdale realizes his paternal relation to Pearl and his public, social position simultaneously. The construction of such a position, indistinguishable from finding an ending for one's book, recapitulates the nineteenth century's standard narrative of male development, in which an important relation to the maternal yields to a clearly masculine place in the world. At the same time, taken synchronically, narrative simply makes clear the terms of the problem: A powerful and constituting relation to femininity must somehow coexist with a clear and supported claim to masculine identity, and the latter *requires* that the former be curtailed.

The crucial and complicating dynamics of homoerotic desire, to which I have thus far given less attention, also commonly inhabit narrative middles of much nineteenth-century U.S. fiction. Although I use the term *homoerotic* repeatedly in this book to discuss desires between men not yet made visible by the twentieth century's reifying discourse of homosexuality, the content of this term must remain somewhat open. An analytic relation to the body must be at best imperfect, a fact that consistently disrupts a nineteenth-century masculinity invested in its own rationality. It is easiest to describe sexual desires in the common terms of power relations, but such terms leave out the particular bodily relations between two persons that comprise a crucial element of erotic experience. What is at stake, to ask a simple but extremely difficult question, when two persons touch? What is the desire to touch? I will not attempt to chart such an intellectual abyss here. My use of *homoerotic* is meant to insist, however, upon my sense that texts written in the United States in the nineteenth century register physical desires between men that cannot be easily articulated or accounted for rationally. Particularly in the years before "homosexuality" existed as an articulated social position, it would have been difficult if not impossible to imagine a fully articulated homosexual narrative, even given the cultural reality of erotic desire between men.[59] The prehistory of homosexuality in the nineteenth century consists of half-buried, half-emergent associations, whether memories, characters, or events, that do not get carried out and enacted at the level of plot.[60] The liberatory openness of midcomposition, then, repeatedly furnishes a space in which the bliss of imperfectly apprehended desires might be explored. Such explorations have often been ignored, nonetheless, in the critical histories of each of the texts I talk about.[61]

I do not mean, however, that physical desires exist in some magic space apart from power relations; I only mean that their analysis is not exhausted by them. Whatever the ultimate sources of homoerotic regard for other men in nineteenth-century literature, this regard necessarily assumes much of its manifest shape from the kind of socially dominant ideas and paradigms I have been tracing in this introduction. Given that developed ideas of homosexuality only emerge at the century's end, homoerotic desire must be heavily inflected by the nineteenth century's prominent and developed discourse of gender.

The nineteenth century's ongoing efforts to essentialize and divide men and women on the basis of gender had the consequence of creating extremely powerful bonds between members of the same sex, evident, as Leslie Fiedler observed years ago in *Love and Death in the American Novel,* in such cultural productions as the novels of the Leatherstocking saga, *The Adventures of Huckleberry Finn, Billy Budd,* or *Moby Dick.*[62] The ideal of separate spheres created an artifical and exaggerated divide between men and women and injected gender into every area of public life. If, for men, aspiration commonly involved identification with a real or imagined figure of the same gender, such identification itself could easily cross into erotic desire. As Jonathan Dollimore observes, writing about another period, a kind of eroticism inhabits "the necessary identifications of male bonding." These indentifications "produce an intensity of admiration some of which just cannot help but transform into deviant desire for, rather than just honourable imitation of, 'man's' most signficant other (i.e. man). And it occurs so easily—almost passively— requiring little more than a relinquishing of the *effort* of emulation, the erasure of *'to be like'* and the surrender to what remains: *'I desire . . . you.'"*[63] For the literary men I am discussing in this book, moreover, the (inevitable) reality of gender indeterminancy and authority-denying chaos of U.S. culture gives birth to emulative desires of transcendent intensity. This intensity is evident throughout the texts I discuss, from *The Scarlet Letter* to *The Ambassadors* to *The Great Gatsby.* Each text contains an aching desire to achieve a position of acceptable manhood, a desire both blocked and, as a consequence, rendered sublime.

A powerful desire for the stuff of masculinity, then, may often create homoerotic desire for the body of the other man as its inevitable by-product. Alternatively, desire for other men that may come from other sources, such as a primarily homosexual orientation, may have difficulty understanding and expressing itself apart from ideas of aspiration and identification. Henry James's primary orientation (whatever this means) was almost certainly homosexual. Nevertheless, as I will demonstrate, his textual inscription of the homoerotic has much in common with that of *The Scarlet Letter* by Hawthorne, an author who, based on accounts of his relations with Sophia, might be thought of as primarily heterosexual.[64]

The male novelists I discuss here (with the exception of Fitzgerald, whom I treat briefly at the end of the book) anticipate Freud's well-known oedipal separation of erotic desire and cultural identification.[65] This is apparently because standard emulative desires in the nineteenth century had no place in their structure for erotic desires that were their by-product, or that existed in addition to them. The erotic, consequently, comes to exist in a complicating, disruptive relation to desires that should properly be emulative and aim at the attainment of a properly masculine position. The author, in other words, should properly emulate the masculine authority of authorship and successfully complete his book, but this process is complicated by the presence of difficult-to-narrate, culturally prohibited desires for other men, and it is complicated as well by the complexities of feminine influence, which interfere with the construction of masculine authority in terms of the dominant heterosexual plots of the nineteenth-century novel.

The narrative consequences of these intertwined deadlocks, I will suggest, are often violence: violence against women and violence against other men as well. In the former case, violence takes the form of a forcible imposition of deadening cultural roles on top of cultural complexities that are also textually represented, an imposition that may be accompanied by literal fantasies of extermination, as in Poe's detective tales or as in James's *The Wings of the Dove*. In the latter case, violence may also take the form of fantasies of extermination aimed at making the textual embodiment of a problem narratively disappear, as in the death of Roderick in *Roderick Hudson*. Violence may also function as a liberation of and excuse for caretaking between men, given that violence furnishes the chief set of terms through which many men experience their mutual relations as matters of the body. The wounded man, in the case of Roderick, or of Crane's soldiers, may be looked at and touched.

In situations of unresolvable conflict, finally, one should also look for figurations of transcendence undercut by an ironic presence of the repressed and denied. Such transcendence is at stake in one of the nineteenth century's most useful passages for the consideration of literary masculinity, Henry James's autobiographical account, in *A Small Boy and Others,* of his childhood experiences in the Galerie d'Apollon of the Louvre.[66]

The paintings James recalls from his family's stay in Paris all have entangled implications in terms of gender, sexual, and family dynamics. For example, Delaroche's *Les Enfantes d'Edouard* might well suggest William's own difficult struggles, since it depicts the "long-drawn odd face of the elder prince" as "sad and sore and sick" and strikes the young Henry as "a reconstitution of far-off history of the subtlest and most 'last word' modern or psychologic kind," despite, as he recalls, never having "heard of psychology" (344). Young Henry's obsession with the imagined ease of other males seems reflected by Delaroche's treatment of "the noble indifference" of Charles the First "at his inscrutable ease" (344–345). Couture's *Page with a Falcon* would seem to support John Paul Eakin's argument that the young James was plagued by an inability to "show" anything of his intricate and rich inner world. In Couture's painting, Henry writes, the "splendid fair youth . . . shows off the great bird on his forefinger with a grace that shows *him* off" (342). In the Louvre itself, James singles out Gericault's *Le Radeau de la "Méduse"* as "*the* sensation, for splendour and terror of interest, of that juncture," as he feels himself "hang again, appalled but uplifted" on his male guide's arm (350). This painting, which depicts the survivors of a famous shipwreck moments before rescue, contains manifold hints of anxiety: The ship's name, *Medusa,* suggests sexual anxiety and fetishism, and though the painting does not specifically depict it, the survivors of the wreck of the *Medusa* notoriously engaged in cannibalism, which suggests James's obsessive concern in his autobiographical writing with questions of imaginative appropriation, or "taking in," to use the metaphor he associates with his younger self.

James associates with the Géricault a group of paintings that seem individually less evocative but collectively still located on the dangerous but invigorating ground of crossed and blurred sexual boundaries: "Guérin's Burial of Atala, Prudhon's Cupid and Psyche, David's helmeted Romanisms, [and] Madam Vigée-Lebrun's 'ravishing' portrait of herself and her little girl" (350). James himself acknowledges the provocative implications of such paintings when he comments that they served as a "foretaste . . . of all the fun, confusedly speaking, that one was going to have, and the kind of life, always of the queer so-called inward sort, tremendously 'sporting' in its way . . . that one was going to lead" (350).

If art provides James with a forum for exploring a world of complex identifications and disjunctions, it also suggests to him the possibility of grounding masculinity in its transcendence. The Louvre as a whole, and especially the Galerie d'Apollon, serves as "a prodigious tube or tunnel through which I inhaled little by little, that is again and again, a general sense of *glory.*

The glory meant ever so many things at once, not only beauty and art . . . but history and fame and power, the world in fine raised to the richest and noblest expression. The world there was . . . the local present fact . . . of the Second Empire, which was . . . new and queer and perhaps even wrong, but . . . so amply radiant and elegant that it took . . . under its protection with a splendour of its insolence, the state and ancientry of the whole scene" (346–347). This "glory" stands for a masculine power established and supported enough that it can withstand even the indeterminacy of its own contents and origins. It exists, as a consequence, as an almost pure abstraction, as money, or power, or fame, but something that transcends even these, akin to the splendor of God.

If glory suggests transcendence, this transcendence must still be earned through the labor of writing, and it works practically to justify whatever costly compromises the narrative must make in order to guarantee its creation. If the author stands finally detached from his creation, the writer strives within it, pushing and shoving the story to completion. The former identifies only with the formal perfection of the work. The latter most identifies with whatever or whoever advances the plot, a relation that often turns the struggles of the chief character into a representative of the struggles of the writer himself. In Hawthorne's *The Scarlet Letter,* the subject of the next chapter, I will argue that Arthur Dimmesdale serves as such a representative for Nathaniel Hawthorne.

PART 1

Purloined Letters

THE FICTION OF
NATHANIEL HAWTHORNE
AND EDGAR ALLAN POE

*T*he value of Nathaniel Hawthorne's *The Scarlet Letter* and Edgar Allan Poe's trio of detective stories, "The Murders in the Rue Morgue," "The Mystery of Marie Roget," and "The Purloined Letter," in the context in which I read them here, consists in their agonistic baring of the cultural processes through which masculine identity is constructed. In fiction, the mechanism of this construction is the process of writing, which works to produce the writer in the position of author. As I suggested in my introduction, however, authorial anxieties are themselves useful versions of the broader masculine anxieties of U.S. culture—hence the complicated but real representative value of texts that are also self-reflexively literary. The exposure of the mechanisms of masculine self-construction in these antebellum texts has particular value because masculinity, as it develops in the nineteenth and twentieth centuries, increasingly defends its integrity through the obfuscation and forgetting of debts to and suppressions of women that Hawthorne and Poe expose. Their contributions to the remodeling of masculinity before the Civil War allow a scrutiny of its emerging structure.

CHAPTER 1

Gender and the Scene of Writing

HOMOPHOBIA, THE FEMININE, AND NARRATIVE IN NATHANIEL HAWTHORNE'S *THE SCARLET LETTER*

It is sweet to be remembered and cared for by one's friends . . . sweet to think that they deem me worth upholding in my poor walk through life. And it is bitter, nevertheless, to need their support. It is something else besides pride that teaches me that ill-success in life is really and justly a matter of shame. I am ashamed of it, and I ought to be. The fault of a failure is attributable—in a great degree, at least—to the man who fails. I should apply this truth in judging of other men; and it behooves me not to shun its point or edge in taking it home to my own heart. Nobody has a right to live in this world, unless he be strong and able, and applies his ability to good purpose.
—Hawthorne, letter to George Hilliard

*T*his chapter is the consequence of a long process of thinking about Hawthorne's *The Scarlet Letter,* a text that to a large extent has served as the genesis of this project as a whole.[1] Hawthorne's introductory "The Custom-House" manifestly sets up the interrelations of masculine anxieties, feminine identifications, and authorship as subjects for consideration.[2] He links an introduction that angrily advertises its alienation from conventional masculinity to the narrative that follows by establishing Hester Prynne's threatening *A,* which he finds in the Custom-House, as the origin of his writing project. The novel that follows constructs itself as a successfully completed and masculinity-confirming project by establishing mechanisms of exchange through which the cultural goods Hester's femininity signifies can eventually be commodified, misremembered, and absorbed by masculine literary culture. Prior to the text's reconsolidation of masculine identity, however, Dimmesdale's dislocation from a conventional relation to a stabilizing and idealized femininity produces a mobility of desire in his relations to other men. If the forces of commodification—at work here through Hawthorne's labor of writing—produce a useful rupture (for men) between the reality of feminine contributions to male identity and the distorted representation of those contributions in culture, they also produce a midcompositional space in which desire itself can circulate via a substitution of one object of uncertain identity for another.

The central effort of the text, then, becomes the homophobic control of the disruptive eroticism of Dimmesdale's relation to Chillingworth, whom I will treat as the (pre)homosexual in the text. *The Scarlet Letter* manages its problem by returning to its focus on the drama of Hester and Dimmesdale, its commitment to heterosexual narrative now reinforced by its panicked staging of homoeroticism as the disintegration of identity and, by extension, a disintegration of the narratives on which identity is based. Hawthorne completes his text by discovering the utility of the separation between identification and desire. Even as Dimmesdale absorbs Hester's rebellious sensibility, the text suggests that the ultimate inspiration for his election day sermon comes from a bodiless God, a move that simultaneously suggests the masculinity of cultural production and suppresses the erotic nature of his relations to other men.

Because *The Scarlet Letter* is essentially a drama of the writing of narrative as the writing of masculine identity, my analysis will center on three scenes of writing that shadow the text's three structuring scaffold scenes: first, the idealized scene of romance writing in "The Custom-House" that Hawthorne juxtaposes to the creative sterility of masculine relations; second, the midnarrative scene of Dimmesdale's decomposition in his study; and third, Dimmesdale's triumphant writing of his election day sermon.

Waiting for Hester: The First Scene of Writing

At the time of the publication of *The Scarlet Letter*, Hawthorne was desperate for authorial success. Prior to its publication, his literary career, in his own terms, had been something less than an unqualified success. Hawthorne never regarded his tales and sketches as especially noteworthy achievements, a derogatory habit of mind evident, even if exaggerated, in an 1837 letter to Longfellow: "As to my literary efforts, I do not think much of them. . . . [I]f my writings had made any decided impression, I should probably have been stimulated to greater exertions; but there has been no warmth of approbation, so that I have always written with benumbed fingers."[3] Indeed, even after the long years of seclusion and effort, Hawthorne's income from his writings was scarcely sufficient to support his wife and children. A combination of serious financial needs and political opportunities accounts for his assumption of the post of chief surveyor of the Salem Custom-House.

Hawthorne's tenure in this position, however, serves, if anything, to intensify his conflicts. As the text states, he feels marginal and unrecognized as a writer in this commercial world: "It is a good lesson . . . for a man who had dreamed of literary fame, and of making for himself a rank among the world's dignitaries by such means, to . . . find how utterly devoid of significance, beyond that circle, is all that he achieves" (26–27). Hawthorne's problem as an author, consequently, has two crucial aspects. His own efforts at authorship, in his own eyes, are too unsubstantial to earn him the acclaim he seeks, and authorship itself, as an achieved status, seems devalued in the world of "The Custom-House."

Hawthorne responds in kind with an angry devaluing of the masculine world of commerce.[4] He finds signs of dissolution everywhere, scornfully describing the few persons who thrive in the Salem Custom-House as animals, contrivances, mainsprings, magnets, or books of record. The rest of its denizens are pictured in various stages of decline, the sense of which is reinforced by Hawthorne's general use in his introduction of a rhetoric of decay and disintegration, which, I will suggest in the next section, indicates homoerotic/homophobic dynamics at work in *The Scarlet Letter*. His ancestors, he says, "have mingled their earthly substance with the soil" until the soil itself suggests "the mortal frame" (9). The old Custom-House officers have a jollity that resembles "the phosphorescent glow of decaying wood" (16); the dining companions of the inspector are now all "food for worms" (19); and Surveyor Pue, when they dig him up, is "an imperfect skeleton, some fragments of apparel, and a wig of majestic frizzle, which, unlike the head that it once adorned, was in a very satisfactory state of preservation" (30). Those who lose their positions in the Custom-House have been metaphorically beheaded, and the superiority of Hawthorne's own party lies partly in their refusal to ghoulishly "kick the head which they have just struck off" (41).

While chief surveyor of the Custom-House, however, Hawthorne shares its milieu, and seems to share in its entropic swirl. Nearly bereft of creative energy, the bored author finds himself in a land of the dead located precisely between the worlds of literature and of public office: "Poking and burrowing into the heaped-up rubbish, . . . reading the names of vessels that had long ago foundered at sea or rotted at the wharves, . . . glancing at such matters with the saddened, weary, half-reluctant interest which we bestow on the corpse of dead activity,—and exerting my fancy, sluggish with little use" (29). Even after finding the *A* that inspires his eventually successful act of writing, while he continues in such an atmosphere of masculine decline the energy the letter imparts cannot fire Hawthorne's "intellectual forge." As a consequence, Hawthorne tells us that his characters remain, redundantly, "dead corpses," who "stared me in the face with a fixed and ghastly grin" (34). Hawthorne remains immersed in quotidian masculinity and unable to unite "petty and wearisome incidents, and ordinary characters" by finding "their indestructible value." As a consequence, he imagines that at a future date he will only recall "a few scattered fragments and broken paragraphs" of this commercial world (37).

If this fragmentation reflects the conflicts of striving to compose a complex narrative in the midst of difficult circumstances, it may also represent an unconscious shadow of lesser anxieties related to "The Custom-House" as a separate compositional problem. These anxieties would be muted precisely by the ameliorating completion of *The Scarlet Letter,* and narratively contained by the completion of the introduction, with its prophecy of fame and triumph, generations hence, for the author of "THE TOWN PUMP." Just as the writing anxiety of the introduction may belong both to itself as a project and to the novel that follows, Hawthorne's concluding lines both do and do not refer to the already completed narrative that follows. Though his "town pump" allusion seems to explicitly refer to "A Rill for the Town Pump" and hence even ironically invoke one of his most minor published pieces, this pump stands near the marketplace in Salem, analogous to the site of the scaffold in Boston where Hester Prynne suffers and Dimmesdale confesses. His allusion might suggest a bond, consequently, between his authorial trials and the trials of Hester Prynne and between his triumph and Dimmesdale's triumphant election day sermon.[5] It ambitiously if covertly gestures, in other words, toward authorial fame based on the completion of Hawthorne's most famous text and toward the continuity of introduction and romance, even as it signifies the separate integrity of "The Custom-House" as a writing project that will produce fame, if at all, in a lower key.

"The Custom-House" itself positions Hester's *A* as a key element in its twin crises of masculinity and authorship. In the midst of masculine and authorial entropy, the moping author finds Hester's creation in a pile of Custom-House rubbish, and, pressing it to his breast, immediately feels a "burning heat . . . as if the letter were not of red cloth, but red-hot iron." The "heat" this letter imparts, inextricably entangled in the feminine, serves as an imagined countervailing force to male disintegration. Hawthorne employs in reverse the relation that Mark Seltzer argues is characteristic of later naturalist prose. If in naturalism the masculine trope of force serves to counteract the potentially engulfing femininity of nature, Hawthorne here renders energizing force as feminine and suggests that the disarray of the material world is masculine.[6] This disarray is itself ambiguous in terms of gender, since it finally suggests the feminization of possessing insufficient feminine force. The Old General, for example, the male toward whom Hawthorne feels the deepest affiliation and respect in his introduction, has a secure masculine status that has a feminine passion as one of its fundamental constituents. The general still has a "heat that . . . was not yet extinct" but resembles "a deep, red glow, as of iron in a furnace" (21). As a consequence, "[t]he closer you penetrated to the substance of his mind, the sounder it appeared" (20). This informing energy, in turn, seems allied to the general's "young girl's appreciation of the floral tribe" (23).[7]

If the letter's heat suggests its ability to effect a transfer of passion to a desultory author desperately in need of it, its status as a letter also suggests its capacity to serve as a carrier of writing or authorship in a more explicit sense. It not only might inspire Hawthorne's own efforts but already comes wrapped in its own narrative, itself inspired by Hester Prynne's life, but penned by Surveyor Pue as her history and transferred to Hawthorne by him. In similar fashion, we might reflect that, after all, the entire narrative has been produced by Hawthorne himself and transferred to the reader, however inspired he might be by the prior life history of Anne Hutchinson he has received from masculine Puritan sources. Though Hawthorne eventually consigns Hester to an enclosed domesticity in *The Scarlet Letter,* the letter itself is not identical to the empowering potential of a private, domestic femininity. On the contrary, if it retains its heat or passion even in commercial settings, it comes to Hawthorne through the Custom-House mechanisms of commerce and exchange, passed from one surveyor to another. It is because Hester's letter circulates that its acquisition and use by Hawthorne are possible.

On both the levels of masculinity and authorship, then, the figure of the scarlet letter arguably reflects and even exacerbates conflicts that also make it necessary, and hence it points to the depth and complexity of those conflicts for Hawthorne. Just as the letter itself seems marked by the gender conflicts and ambiguities of its production, by symbolically donning the letter Hawthorne acquires a visible mark of his alienation from masculinity. This alienation derives both from his identification with the femininity of feeling and from his connection to the ambiguous feminization of literary production, and it seems to predate his fortuitous finding of the scarlet letter, given his often bitter invocation of Salem's malaise from his introduction's opening pages.

The Old General, whom I discussed earlier, seems to point Hawthorne toward the antidote of achieved authorship. However flower-loving and feminine, the general safely enfolds his deviance within an embracing masculinity certified by his successful military past—the hero of Fort Ticonderoga could not be anything but essentially male. This masculinizing success makes it possible to disregard the traces of any underlying self-divisions or ambiguities, so that Hawthorne can benignly refer to his "true and simple energy" (23).

The yet-to-be-successful author certifies the general as a role model by echoing his heroic "I'll try, Sir" (23) in his even more emphatic response to Surveyor Pue's injunction to write: "I will!" (34). Significantly, though effort alone provides a basis for a redeeming masculinity in the general's "I'll try," Hawthorne's "I will" requires actual execution. Otherwise, the superior assurance of Hawthorne's declaration immediately deflates into "I didn't" or "I couldn't" or "I was mistaken." The author's possession of a masculine identity, in other words, must still be earned even after this statement of determination.

Hawthorne's alienation from the desiccated, patriarchal world of the Custom-House leads him to seek an alternative scene of writing, one which "womankind, with her tools of magic, the broom and the mop," might visit on a more regular basis (7). He finds such a place, not surprisingly, in the domestic surroundings of the home. The famous scene of romance writing, however, seems as much like a scene of having-written as a place of the "seething turmoil" of composing *The Scarlet Letter* (43). Lit by "glimmering coal fire" and "moonlight," the empty apartment contains

> the chairs, with each its separate individuality; the centre-table, sustaining a work-basket, a volume or two, and an extinguished lamp; the sofa; the book-case; the picture on the wall;—all these details, so completely seen, are so spiritualized . . . that they seem to lose their actual substance, and become things of intellect. Nothing is too small or too trifling to undergo this change. . . . A child's shoe; the doll, seated in her little wicker carriage; the hobby-horse. . . . Thus, . . . the floor of our familiar room has become a neutral territory, somewhere between the real world and fairy-land, where the Actual and the Imaginary may meet. (35–36)

To Hawthorne, "at such an hour, and with this scene before him, if a man, sitting all alone, cannot dream strange things, and make them look like truth, he need never try to write romances" (36).

In this case, the romance written may be *The Scarlet Letter,* of course, but also seems to be precisely the scene itself, which Hawthorne has constructed as a meeting place of "the Actual and the Imaginary." Though fetish objects abound, located undecidably between self and other, masculine and feminine, adult and child, and energizing the author's imagination, the whole seems regulated by a salubrious and de-eroticized economy, in which the author's enormous acts of appropriation are balanced by his power to make a reparative return. Indeed, though a comforting and stable exterior reality exists here, defending the author against madness and enveloping the felt femininity of composition in a feminine domestic environment, one senses that the work producing the scene, even from objects such as (probably) his wife's "work-basket," chiefly is his, as he confers upon the objects the "dignity" of "intellect" (35). So confident, ideally, does the author-at-home seem that Hawthorne reports without comment or emotional response a visit from what seems to be his recently departed mother: "It would be too much in keeping with the scene to excite surprise, were we to look about us and discover a form, beloved, but gone hence, now sitting quietly in a streak of this magic moonshine, with an aspect that would make us doubt whether it had returned from afar, or had never once stirred from our fireside" (36).[8] That such a ghostly visitation could occur *without exciting surprise* strikes one as an astounding claim. Rather than testifying to the narcotic power of domestic life, however, it indicates Hawthorne's sense of his creative power, propitiating the spirits precisely through the act of engineering their return from the land of the dead. The maternal figure fits seamlessly into his completed composition, which guarantees through its look of normality the harmony of a psyche threatened by its own contradictions.[9]

It is possible to see threatening potentials of the feminine, however, lurking both within and outside of this scene intellectualized by the "magic" of moonshine. For example, in one of Hawthorne's 1848 letters to Sophia, written during his tenure as Custom-House surveyor, he confesses that "I really am half afraid to be there alone, and feel shy about looking across the dimly moon-lighted chamber. I expend a great deal of sentiment as often as I chance to see any garment of thine, in my rambles about the house or any of the children's playthings. And after all, there is a strange bliss in being made sensible of the happiness of my customary life."[10] In this passage, both Hawthorne's own desires and the object world seem less successfully "composed" into harmony; as a consequence, the fetish structure of the scene seems more sexual and more insistent. The energy generated by the relation between the masochistically helpless author and Sophia's clothing generates a disintegrating "strange bliss" that is only partly domesticated by the author's reference to the pleasures of his "customary life," which apparently benefits from looking not so customary after all.

Neither can the domestic be securely sequestered from the conflicts of the broader social world. Hawthorne's sentimental sense of the rightness of the maternal presence at his fireside, a rightness that would be somehow disfigured even by the presence of surprise, suggests as its counterpart the wrongness of women in a variety of other complex, real-world roles, especially of women who have entered the trade of literature.[11] An example of the anger such wrongness could generate occurs in his sketch of Anne Hutchinson, Hester Prynne's most important historical model and a woman who did not sit quietly by the fire:

> We will not look for a living resemblance of Mrs. Hutchinson, though the search might not be altogether fruitless. . . . The hastiest glance may show, how much of the texture and body of cis-atlantic literature is the work of those slender fingers, from which only a light and fanciful embroidery has heretofore been required. . . . As yet, the great body of American women are a domestic race; but . . . there are obvious circumstances which will render female pens more numerous and more prolific than those of men . . . and . . . petticoats wave triumphant over all the field. . . . [T]here is a delicacy . . . that perceives . . . a sort of impropriety in the display of woman's naked mind to the gaze of the world.[12]

Underlying this passage's dominating unease with women outside of the domestic sphere are suggestions of considerable ambivalence and conflict, evident, for example, in the mixture of allure and repulsion in the display of a "woman's naked mind to the gaze of the world." The idea that public women are naked is repeated by Hawthorne in a later comment on Fanny Fern's *Ruth Hall*. As he says to Ticknor, "I must say I enjoyed it a good deal. . . . Generally, women write like emasculated men . . . but when they throw off the restraints of decency, and come before the public stark naked, as it were—then their books are sure to possess character and value."[13]

As one reads the remainder of the sketch, one finds additional evidence of the positive side of Hawthorne's ambivalence despite the disciplinary terror of Hutchinson's end: She leaves only "an infant daughter . . . amid the terrible destruction," who "was bred in a barbarous faith, and never learned the way to the Christian's Heaven."[14] Nevertheless, before this apocalypse, Hawthorne writes, "in the midst, and in the centre of all eyes, we see the Woman. She stands loftily before her judges, with a determined brow, and unknown to herself, there is a flash of carnal pride half hidden in her eye, as she surveys the many learned and famous men whom her doctrines have put in fear. They question her, and her answers are ready and acute; . . . the deepest controversialists of that scholastic day find here a woman, whom all their trained and sharpened intellects are inadequate to foil" (23). Hawthorne's ca-pacity to admire such a woman, as he later admires Prynne, indicates the re-markable depth of Hawthorne's conflicts. The goodness of his domestic scene of writing, then, may lie not in its alterity to a world of public women that Hawthorne unconditionally and totally opposes. Rather, it rescues him from the disintegrating effects of his ambivalent perception of such a world—from identification, titillation, and resentment.

If women in public, and particularly writing women, generate such con-flict for Hawthorne, the hostility leveled at other men in "The Custom-House" finally seems only the more remarkable. A scene in which Hawthorne has under his command an unmixed "patriarchal body of veterans" (12) proves not just unsatisfactory but absolutely disabling, and rather than attempt to reconcile himself to the masculinity it represents or to reconcile such mas-culinity to him, Hawthorne repudiates it as a realm of absolute decay and disintegration with even more concentrated spleen than he brings to the prob-lem of scribbling women.

One cause of this rejection might be the face value one of an absolute difference between the values Hawthorne holds and the assumptions of the world of politics and business "The Custom-House" represents, though I be-lieve such distinctions can be exaggerated just as Hawthorne exaggerates them here. As I have argued earlier, the dilemmas of male artists are generally ho-mologous with the broad developmental and vocational dilemmas of middle-class masculinity, even as Hawthorne's love of the domestic is itself a middle-class cultural ideal.[15] Hawthorne even exaggerates his personal alien-ation from the masculine world, since he continued to dabble in politics and gained the appointment of U.S. consul at Liverpool, in part as a consequence of his campaign biography of Franklin Pierce. (According to opponent Horace Mann, "If he makes out Pierce to be a great or brave man, it will be the great-est work of fiction he ever wrote.")[16] Even given revenge as one of Haw-thorne's motives in writing his introduction, it is not clear why the terms of his rejection of the masculine world would be its want of integrating feminine passion, if the presence of women in the public world is also a cause of anxiety and alarm.

The answer, as I will suggest in the next section of this chapter, may be less the distance Hawthorne feels from such a masculine world than the dangerous terms of his attraction for it. In the absence of an anchoring relation to a private and idealized heterosexuality, Hawthorne's relations to other men are disintegrating because of their potential eroticization, and the distancing anger of "The Custom-House" is in part his homophobic response. The positive erotic potential of such relations surfaces in the text of *The Scarlet Letter* itself, to which I now turn.

Dangerous Exultations: (Homo)Sexuality, Disintegration, and the Second Scene of Writing

Hawthorne's *The Scarlet Letter* contains much that we, as contemporary readers, would recognize as the machinery of homophobia and, of course, of the homoeroticism homophobic structures both admit and work to suppress. *The Scarlet Letter* contains the kind of erotic triangle that, as Eve Kosofsky Sedgwick has argued, can function as a disguise of and a conduit for homoerotic desire.[17] Both Chillingworth and Dimmesdale have relations with Hester Prynne, the former as the cuckolded husband, the latter as her adulterous lover. Throughout the novel, however, we rarely see either male having contact with Prynne; instead, they take up residence with each other.

The categories of "homosexuality" and "homophobia" are, needless to say, problematic ones to invoke in terms of U.S. culture before the Civil War, as I indicated in my introduction. In the case of *The Scarlet Letter,* however, their figuration is uncannily and proleptically appropriate to the formalization of such categories at century's end. In general I agree with Michael Warner's recent comment, made in terms of *Walden,* that "historians may have given too much credit to the power of merely lexical changes. The genealogy of the modern vocabulary of hetero/homosexuality can be seen already in Thoreau's framing of the problem."[18] As I believe *The Scarlet Letter* helps show, in other words, both homosexuality and homophobia have clear prehistories in which their later forms are already strikingly evident. I intend this turn-of-the-century lexicon here, nevertheless, to be understood with an implicit parenthetical *pre* attached, a prefix that, however awkward, preserves the question of historical difference as an open and a difficult one.

Just as Hawthorne's access to Hester's letter depends on its circulation as a literary commodity, the conditions of possibility for Dimmesdale's intimacy with Chillingworth are the circulation and mobility of nascent capitalist culture. Chillingworth is not knowable, either in terms of his position in the world as Hester's husband or of his private character, a condition of impersonal anonymity that allows him maximum freedom to manipulate his self-presentation to ingratiate himself to the town and the minister. In fact, he spans and thus ruptures systems of cultural signification, as we see when he first enters the novel as a hodgepodge of acquired characteristics: "By the Indian's side, and evidently sustaining a companionship with him, stood a white man, clad in a strange disarray of civilized and savage costume. . . . Although, by a seemingly careless arrangement of his heterogeneous garb, he had endeavoured to conceal or abate the peculiarity, it was sufficiently evident to Hester Prynne that one of this man's shoulders rose higher than the other" (60). The incongruous worldliness of one "whose sphere was in great cities" attracts the young minister (121). Dimmesdale finds in the physician's eclectic worldliness an escape from the narrow intellectual confines of his own world: "There was a fascination for the minister in the company of the man of science, in whom he recognized an intellectual cultivation . . . with a . . . freedom of ideas, that he would have vainly looked for among the members of his own profession. In truth, he was startled, if not shocked, to find this attribute in the physician. . . . It was as if a window were thrown open, admitting a freer atmosphere into the close and stifled study" (123).

Dimmesdale's "kind of intimacy" with the exotic Chillingworth flourishes outside the minister's range of normal homosocial and heterosexual relations (125). The minister has been exiled from the latter by the peculiarities of his situation, and Chillingworth fills the resulting gap in his living situation as a substitute for a wife: "After a time, at a hint from Roger Chillingworth, the friends of Mr. Dimmesdale effected an arrangement by which the two were lodged in the same house. . . . There was much joy throughout the town, when this greatly desirable object was attained. It was held to be the best possible measure for the young clergyman's welfare; unless . . . he had selected some one of the many blooming damsels, spiritually devoted to him, to become his devoted wife" (125). This excursion from convention, however, generates for Dimmesdale a set of anxieties directly and obsessively related to Chillingworth's body and his own as interpretive problems. Despite Dimmesdale's own "strong animal nature" (130), "he looked doubtfully, fearfully,—even, at times, with horror and the bitterness of hatred,—at the deformed figure of the old physician. His gestures, his gait, his grizzled beard, his slightest and most indifferent acts, the very fashion of his garments, were odious in the clergyman's sight; a token, implicitly to be relied on, of a deeper antipathy in the breast of the latter than he was willing to acknowledge to himself. For, as it was impossible to assign a reason for such distrust and abhorrence, so Mr. Dimmesdale, conscious that the poison of one morbid spot was infecting his heart's entire substance, attributed all his presentiments to no other cause" (140). Conventionally, of course, the unnamed "morbid spot" could be taken to signify Dimmesdale's guilt at his unconfessed adultery with Hester Prynne and his paternal responsibility for Pearl; but the passage also contains ample evidence of homophobic hysteria. Such a reading is supported by an ensuing scene. In it we are told that Chillingworth penetrated his patient's innermost chambers, "laid his hand upon his bosom, and thrust aside the vestment that, hitherto, had always covered it even from the professional eye" (138). His look at the sleeping Dimmesdale produces a "wild look of wonder, joy, and horror! With what a ghastly rapture . . . bursting forth through the whole ugliness of his figure, and making itself even riotously manifest by the extravagant gestures with which he threw up his arms toward the ceiling. . . . But what distinguished the physician's ecstasy from Satan's was the trait of wonder in it!" (138). The physician's "ghastly rapture" and "ecstasy," which follow the disrobing of the minister, suggest that what has occurred is some sort of erotically charged, physical violation. It is far from clear, however, how Chillingworth's violation of the sleeping Dimmesdale should be understood, particularly since all interpretations have implications that are politically difficult and pertain, directly, to the relation of homophobia and desire.[19]

The potentially homophobic reading of this scene as rape rests in part on the biographical speculation of James R. Mellow that Hawthorne was molested as a youth by his uncle, Robert Manning.[20] This may or may not have happened, but as an argument it exists in a circular relation to passages such as this in Hawthorne's fiction. The reason to read this scene as a literal rape, in other words, is the possibility of a rape in Hawthorne's past life; the reason to posit such a rape of Hawthorne, at the same time, is that his fiction contains such passages. With a slight adjustment of vision, we might just as easily argue that Dimmesdale's unconsciousness in the scene represents a desire to have some sort of erotic contact with the older man and yet to escape any responsibility for enacting such a prohibited desire. This reading, in turn, if what Hawthorne represents is a metonymy for rape, arguably masks a sexual violation as the desire of the victim. The apparent split, meanwhile, between a reading of the scene as one of phobic depiction of violent molestation and a reading of the scene as one containing covert positive desire encourages a simplified either/or relation to the problem of homophobia in *The Scarlet Let-*

ter. Lacking Whitman's sublimated language of comradeship, in other words, and several psychic light-years from Whitman's expansive desire to tear the doors of guilt from their jambs, much of Hawthorne's access to the homo-erotic was through a culturally available language of prohibition metony-mically linked, as we shall see in the next section, to masturbation phobia. At the same time, since *The Scarlet Letter* is finally a fantasy produced by Hawthorne, the homophobia of the text works to suppress or repress some-thing *it itself is producing*. Its homophobia, in other words, must be more than simple negation.

If the reader faces an interpretive conundrum at this point in the text, it is a conundrum in which Hawthorne's narrative enthusiastically joins by positing the body as a complex interpretive problem with no solutions. What does Chillingworth see that generates "wonder" even in his own scientific psyche? If he has discovered the first traces of Dimmesdale's own emerging *A,* the letter in no way clarifies the mystery of its appearance on the minister's breast. Instead, it sends Chillingworth into an orgasmic physical joy that pre-sents his own body as an interpretive problem. How are we to understand his extravagant ecstasy, which stands in direct contrast to the "profound depth" of Dimmesdale's own "remarkable" (138) repose? Between the activity of the former and the lassitude of the latter, Hawthorne positions Dimmesdale's usual sleep habits, but only through a metaphor that coyly defamiliarizes even this normal activity as a natural mystery: "[H]e was one of those persons whose sleep, ordinarily, is as light, as fitful, and as easily scared away, as a small bird hopping on a twig" (138).

Even when he is awake, Dimmesdale's bodily actions and their motives are finally opaque both to himself and to the scrutinizing reader. Shortly be-fore Chillingworth succeeds in physically examining his breast, the minister has suddenly "rushed out of the room " (137) to escape from Chillingworth's invasive questions. Dimmesdale, we are told, "was sensible that the disorder of his nerves had hurried him into an unseemly outbreak of temper, which there had been nothing in the physician's words to excuse or palliate. He marveled, indeed, at the violence with which he had thrust back the kind old man" (137).

Chillingworth reads this "outbreak" as proof of the minister's capacity for passionate adulterous sin, but he offers no help in reading the nature of such passion, except to pose it in opposition to coherent selfhood: "But see, now, how passion takes hold upon this man and hurrieth him out of himself! As with one passion, so with another! He hath done a wild thing ere now, this pious Master Dimmesdale, in the hot passion of his heart!" (137). The mark of such passion is its capacity to problematize identity by rupturing the borders of the body. The minister "hurrieth . . . out of himself" even as Chillingworth's own ecstasy "burst forth" from his "figure" several pages later (138). At the same time the nature of this passion—and whether it should be understood in heterosexual, homosexual, or some other set of terms—remains ambiguous: "As with one passion, so with another!" (137). All erotic passion in *The Scarlet Letter* threatens the bodily integrity and rational self-control of its possessor.

If the relations of Dimmesdale and Chillingworth produce a variety of bodily signs, sensations, and passions that the text presents as beyond the constraints of normal subjectivity, and hence beyond fully intelligible explanations, this disruptive potential of homoerotic relations between men often extends to heterosexual relationships as well. The emergence of homophobia must be understood as part of a broad erotophobia that characterizes heterosexual male culture in the nineteenth century. In Cooper's *The Pathfinder,* for example, the hero is plunged into the erotic abyss of the body by his love for Mabel Dunham. Normally, Pathfinder is so perfectly at one with his body that he can raise Killdeer, aim, fire, and strike his target as an instantaneous mental/physical fact—shooting as an act of sublime transcendence. When Dunham meets his advances with only sincere friendship, however, the stalwart scout experiences a meltdown Cooper describes in terms of alien possession: "The pent-up feelings would endure no more, and the tears rolled down the cheeks of the scout, like rain. His fingers again worked convulsively at his throat, and his breast heaved, as if it possessed a tenant of which it would be rid, by any effort, however desperate. . . . 'The sarjeant was wrong—' exclaimed the guide, laughing, amid his agony, in a way to terrify his companion by the unnatural mixture of anguish and light-heartedness."[21] For Pathfinder, the presence of women serves as a disruption of the imaginary homosocial relations of his wilderness adventures, but it also protects those adventures from the disruptive force of erotic energies precisely by specifying them as the problem of women. Pathfinder and Chingachgook never have to deal with each other's throbbing bodies on the trail, as Mabel Dunham both occupies the erotic and graphically dramatizes its dangers. Why, after all, would the noble scout want to introduce such erotic hysteria into homosocial relations?

In part, the disruptive power of the erotic has to do with lack of an adequate vocabulary for bodily sensations of pleasure and pain, as Elaine Scarry has argued.[22] The resistance of this erotic or desiring body to rational control and regulation becomes the target of an immense cultural effort at rationalization throughout the nineteenth and twentieth centuries. On the one hand, such discourses come to have substantial disciplinary power in relation to social and sexual behavior; on the other, they never fully succeed in putting this body in its place or alleviating the anxiety of its otherness to the self. As Freud's own privileging of the sexual in his decentering of consciousness suggests, erotic experience can generate endless layers of rational explanation without being fully reducible to it. Any subject organized around his own rationality must be permanently self-divided.

Much anxiety about the body and its potential doings can be found beneath the surface of the nineteenth-century advice book, except that the palliative of the advice book was always the same: the regulative rationality of bourgeois life. This rational normalcy was precariously propped against a gothic sense of the costs of transgression of middle-class standards—sinners in the hands of an angry doctor. Even moderate writers on men's health regarded the body's capacity for passionate excess as a threat to rational masculinity. Dangerous activities included masturbation or excessive masturbation; nonprocreative sexuality outside the containing frame of the family; often, excessive sexuality even within marriage; and the related bodily ills imagined to be linked to behavior such as idleness, gambling, and the consumption of alcohol. The key to male health was the mind's capacity to understand and subdue the body.[23]

One of the most interesting and important nineteenth-century accounts of the unsettling relation of the body to identity occurs in health reformer Sylvester Graham's well-known *A Lecture to Young Men,* published in 1834 in Providence, Rhode Island.[24] Reason collapses as a successful arbiter of the relation between mind and body in Graham's text, and this collapse results from the rigor with which Graham considers the interrelations between the two. Roughly Hawthorne's contemporary, Graham provides a remarkably accurate nineteenth-century reading of the symptomology of Dimmesdale as a victim of sexual sickness. Graham shares Hawthorne's profound sense, in other words, of the calamitous consequences for reason of an erotic free fall into the body.[25]

To Graham, the danger of sexuality consists in the capacity of body and mind to corrupt each other. Left to itself, the prelapsarian body would be ruled by an instinct that would regulate sexuality according to reproductive need. The condition of modern culture is such, however, that such natural controls no longer function. Among all the animals, only "proud, rational man" could destroy the "government of instinct" through the cultivation of a surplus eroticism (14–15). It is by abusing his organs and depraving his instinctive appetites, through the devices of his rational powers, that the body of man has become "a living volcano of unclean propensities and passions" (14). If rationality is to some extent the villain, however, it also offers a postlapsarian solution, because humans are "endowed with rational powers to *ascertain* those constitutional laws, and moral powers to *prevent* that excess" (14).

The danger of such excess, to Graham, is less the loss of semen, the retention of which most nineteenth-century health authorities agreed was crucial for male health, than the "peculiar excitement of the nervous system" produced by the male orgasm (23). This orgasm generates such "powerful agitation" that "the brain, stomach, heart, lungs, liver, skin—and other organs—feel it sweeping over them, with the tremendous violence of a tornado" (20). The natural body, in other words, might first be corrupted by the mind, but the body could then corrupt the mind in turn by virtue of the disruptive power of sexual excitement. Sexuality cannot be understood exclusively at the level of the body nor of the mind and works indefatigably to corrupt the rationality entrusted with its control.

Masturbation for Graham poses a special threat because it engages the mind in a mutually corrupting, indeterminate relation to the body that compromises its independent, regulatory function. He argues that in masturbation "the mental action, and the power of the imagination on the genital organs . . . are exceedingly intense and injurious; and consequently the reciprocal influences between the brain and genital organs become extremely powerful, and irresistible and destructive" (40). In other words, the masturbator and sexual profligate in general would come to have a "diseased association of the cerebral and genital organs" (63). Graham in effect predicts that in the case of a sexual profligate, like Dimmesdale, we will find, in Chillingworth's phrase, a "strange sympathy between body and mind," as each feeds the passions of the other (138).

Significantly, Graham seems quite conscious of sexual relations between men as a dangerous and disruptive form of sexual activity. As Carroll Smith-Rosenberg indicates, a number of nineteenth-century health writers suggest that masturbation might lead to homosexual activity and attribute to the masturbator the effeminacy associated with the figure of the homosexual later in the century.[26] Graham is quite firm concerning the risk of male-to-male transmission of masturbatory technique, which frequently is "communicated from one boy to another; and sometimes a single boy will corrupt many others." Graham claims to "have known boys . . . at the age of twelve and thirteen almost entirely ruined . . . and many of them went to the still more loathsome and criminal extent of an unnatural commerce with each other!" (42–43).

The violator of Graham's standards of sexual propriety risks a free fall into paranoia and guilt: "Beginning with occasional dejection of spirits, he goes on in his transgressions, till . . . a deeper gloom . . . gathers in permanent darkness over his soul. . . . If he endeavors to give his thoughts to the most solemn and sacred subjects still he is haunted with images of lewdness. . . . Filled with self contempt. . . . he has no relish for the ordinary amusements and pleasures of life. . . . He is continually tormented with indefinite anxiety and fear!—and is constantly full of disquietude, anguish, and dread!" (58–61). Such an account serves as an apt description of Dimmesdale's guilt-ridden psychic state.

Graham's text indicates the extent to which homophobia in the nineteenth century must be understood as part of a broader erotophobia, which differentially applies at times to almost all forms of sexual activity. The anxiety in heterosexual masculine culture concerning same-sex desire cannot be understood against a background of untroubled heterosexuality. As T. Walter Herbert has indicated, "the ideal of self-sovereign middle-class manhood produced an autophobic sexuality, such that erotic arousal was chronically attended by dread and was experienced as disgust and guilt when it was felt to stray beyond the boundaries of self-control" (143). Indeed, in Graham's work, though heterosexual activity, masturbation, and homosexual activity exist as separate categories, the borders of these categories always seem blurred and all three seem to contribute to the same set of consequences. The differences among categories in this hierarchy of horror arguably derive from the success of the well-known male tactic of displacing the anxieties of heterosexuality onto the female body. In masturbation, on the other hand, the dangers of eroticism to a privileged rationality must be confronted by the subject as part of himself rather than as a particular kind of danger in his environment. In homosexuality, dangerous eroticism must be experienced at least as internal to masculinity, in part because no bar of morphological difference separates the heterosexual and homosexual man.[27] In addition, the anxieties even of heterosexuality have generated massive and complex defenses against the threat of sexuality to dominant paradigms of male rationality. The locus of such defenses is precisely the heterosexual and heterosexualizing narratives of Western culture, which imply, by metonymically sliding from the heterosexual to the heterosocial, or from the problem of eroticism to the problem of male-female relations, that sexuality can be narrativized into sense. I will return to the question of the interrelation between heterosexuality and narrative in *The Scarlet Letter* in the final section of this chapter.[28]

Graham serves as a valuable model for the demonic Chillingworth.

Though wearing the mask of benevolence and speaking as a confidant, Graham violates the privacy of the young men he studies, even as Chillingworth invades Dimmesdale's chamber, authorizing a broad cultural surveillance of their habits and behavior and tortuously demonizing sexual pleasure. Both Graham and Chillingworth embody the hysteria occasioned by the breakdown of abstract reason before what cannot, by its very nature, be made reasonable. What reason denies ends by pervading it in demonized, obsessive form. Chillingworth begins the study of Dimmesdale "with the severe and equal integrity of a judge, desirous only of truth, even as if the question involved no more than the air-drawn lines and figures of a geometrical problem, instead of human passions, and wrongs inflicted on himself" (129). Beginning with the assumption that his problem is somehow bodiless, the physician falls victim to a passion Hawthorne describes in powerfully physical and anal erotic terms: "He now dug into the poor clergyman's heart, like a miner searching for gold; or, rather, like a sexton delving into a grave, possibly in quest of a jewel that had been buried on the dead man's bosom, but likely to find nothing save mortality and corruption" (129).

In homoerotic terms, in ironic contrast to the most obvious import of his name, Chillingworth serves as a figure of excess passion, one whose avidity causes him to violate the privacy of Dimmesdale's person and whose appearance suggests the disintegrative force of eroticism upon masculine identity. Though Hawthorne initially suggests that Chillingworth suffers from an erotic absence caused by his excessive absorption in mental life, one page later it becomes clear that his threat is, in fact, a phallic one, associated as much with sexuality and the body as with the mind. We are told that "his look became keen and penetrative. A writhing horror twisted itself across his features, like a snake gliding swiftly over them, and making one little pause, with all its wreathed intervolutions in open sight" (61). By the end of the narrative Chillingworth's enterprise becomes completely demonized. Hawthorne tells us that "there came a glare of red light out of his eyes; as if the old man's soul were on fire, and kept on smoldering duskily within his breast, until, by some casual puff of passion, it was blown into a momentary flame" (169). Hawthorne's remarkably mobile imagery, from head to breast; from fire to dusky smoldering; and, at a "casual puff of passion," back to a flame, suggests the disintegrative force of passion upon Chillingworth's person.[29]

If we take the disarray of Chillingworth's clothing for a sign of the disruptive presence of homosexuality, if we regard Chillingworth, like Claggart in *Billy Budd,* as the (pre)homosexual figure in the text, then the "chill" in the text would seem to belong less to Chillingworth than to the phobic

Dimmesdale, flying in panic back to the masculinity-confirming environs of the nuclear family.[30] Such a flight may give an additional layer of ironic significance to Chillingworth's remark, at the final scaffold scene where Arthur affirms his nuclear family ties: "'Hadst thou sought the whole earth over,' said he, looking darkly at the clergyman, 'there was no one place so secret,— no high place nor lowly place, where thou couldst have escaped me,—save on this very scaffold'" (253).

Though, again, in a conventional reading Dimmesdale needs to confess in order to save himself from Chillingworth's sadistic manipulation of his guilt, in a homoerotic context it is difficult not to see Dimmesdale's appearance as a way of sanctioning his official heterosexuality, however painful, in a sphere from which his older friend has been excluded. Chillingworth's error has been to attempt to generate this sphere in the absence of conventional heterosexual desires. As he says to Hester, "My heart was a habitation large enough for many guests, but lonely and chill, and without a household fire. I longed to kindle one! It seemed not so wild a dream,—old as I was . . . —that the simple bliss, which is scattered far and wide . . . might yet be mine" (74). The consequence of this effort, in homophobically loaded language, is her "false and unnatural relation with [his] decay" (75). Thereafter, he surfaces in the narrative as her rival for Dimmesdale's affections.

As argued earlier, if one finds evidence of homosexuality in the nineteenth-century novel in the United States, one often finds it in odd, narratively detached places. Just as the difficulty of the body as an object of knowledge in the nineteenth century perpetually threatens a masculinity dependent on rational self-knowledge, the homoerotic surfaces in the midst of conventional narratives that constitute stable and knowable social experience and grant access to social power. These conventional narratives, often versions of the "marriage-plot," in general reflect the cultural dominance of heterosexuality.

The crisis of the homosexual and heterosexual in *The Scarlet Letter*, then, cannot be understood apart from the crucial dynamics of composition and authorship at work in the text. The heterosexual plot, involving Hester and her *A,* essentially narrativizes the construction of the self as author. The linear pressure of narrative toward closure operates in heterosexual terms involving Dimmesdale's relation to Prynne and, in fact, produces a heterosexual model of writing involving the appropriation of the feminine for masculine creativity. The homoerotic dynamics of the novel remain divorced from the text's will-to-authorship but are no less a product of the dynamics of writing. This complex interrelation is evident in Hawthorne's second scene of writing, which occurs almost precisely at the midpoint of his narrative.

Hawthorne's title of this chapter, "The Interior of a Heart," locates its discussion inside the body, and yet because of the metaphorical implications of "heart," it also collapses any easy distinction between mind and body, a collapse evident in Dimmesdale's masochistic practice of flailing himself with a "bloody scourge" and "laughing bitterly at himself the while" (144). This self-torture, in turn, produces torturing visions:

> It was his custom, too, as it has been that of many other pious Puritans, to fast. . . . He kept vigils, likewise, night after night, sometimes in utter darkness; sometimes with a glimmering lamp; and sometimes, viewing his own face in a looking-glass, by the most powerful light which he could throw upon it. . . . In these lengthened vigils, his brain often reeled, and visions seemed to flit before him. . . . Now it was a herd of diabolic shapes. . . . Now a group of shining angels. . . . [N]ow came the dead friends of his youth, and his white-bearded father, with a saint-like frown, and his mother, turning her face away as she passed by. Ghost of a mother,—thinnest fantasy of a mother,—methinks she might yet have thrown a pitying glance towards her son! And now . . . glided Hester Prynne, leading along little Pearl. . . . None of these visions ever quite deluded him. . . . [H]e could discern . . . that they were not solid . . . like yonder table of carved oak, or that big, square, leathern-bound and brazen-clasped volume of divinity. (145)

In the idealized account of romance writing in "The Custom-House," Hawthorne posited a relation to a scene of domesticity that allowed the author access to certain gendered cultural commodities, maintained their comfortable exterior status, and redeemed the transactions through the author's sense of his beneficent productivity. Here, Dimmesdale suffers a decomposition as a subject graphically marked by the physical extremity of his flagellating efforts at self-discipline. Unlike the successful writer's appropriation of his or her environment under the sheltering umbrella of imagination, Dimmesdale's psyche lacks any stabilizing relation to exteriority: calamitous projection so constitutes his world that the sufferer requires an act of will even to latch onto the stabilizing but nonproductive presence of "yonder table of carved oak." Unlike the everyday substance of this table, or unlike the "big, square, leathern-bound and brazen-clasped" Bible, Dimmesdale cannot stabilize his selfhood by imagining it in physical terms as a domestic object. Dimmesdale's tortured soul and emaciated body conspire equally in the production of his hallucinogenic visions. They engage in the kind of mutual disruption predicted by Graham in the passages cited earlier, and together they create a perceptual whirlpool that envelops and shatters the comforting illusion of an everyday world.[31]

This chapter immediately follows the scene in which Chillingworth violates the minister's person, in order, we imagine, to see traces of the emerging *A*. It immediately precedes the chapter in which Dimmesdale, for no reason identified in the narrative, abruptly leaves his study for a midnight vigil, joined eventually by Hester and Pearl in a foreshadowing of the heterosexual tableau that ends the novel.[32]

This heterosexual tableau serves as one of the romance's three scaffold scenes, which together stand in stark contrast to Dimmesdale's decomposition evident in the preceding chapter. These scenes always visually express a bourgeois reality of normal relations—between men and women; between judgers and judged; between the righteous and the sinful; between husband, wife, and child—that stabilizes and creates the underlying turmoil of Hawthorne's text. They prevent the exploration of other kinds of relations in the daylight of rational reality and press them into a nether world, and Dimmesdale keeps dropping into this nether world and swimming back to the scaffold, where Hawthorne waits with a towel.

This sequence of four chapters in the middle of the text, taken together, suggests a surfacing of the homoerotic exactly at the moment of the novel's greatest disruption of its own intelligibility. Much of the detail of Dimmesdale's breakdown, replete with angels, parents, demons, and Hester and Pearl, is essentially uninterpretable, as if language and Dimmesdale's psyche have been here stretched to a breaking point. The two preceding chapters, "The Leech" and "The Leech and His Patient," detail the nature of the domestic intimacy between Chillingworth and Dimmesdale, ending with Dimmesdale's violation. The energies liberated in Dimmesdale's masturbatory study, in turn, are immediately recontained by the novel's return to its heterosexual plot and its congruent insistence on its own containing narrative structure.

The extremity of the passage indicates not only that the text's homoerotic investments threaten the necessary movement of its narrative but that Hawthorne's creatively necessary access to feminine passion may be threatened as well. The "thinnest fantasy" of the "[g]host" of a mother "turning her face away," a triple denial of imaginative access to the maternal, indicates the disabling consequences not only of Dimmesdale's betrayal of Prynne but of the practices that immediately precede this fantasy of maternal disapproval (145). Though Prynne is a less aversive presence in the fantasy than Dimmesdale's mother, the rebellious passion that defines her value in *The*

Scarlet Letter has also been withheld from Dimmesdale to this point in the narrative. Reconnecting Dimmesdale to this passion will be the chief task of the second half of the text. In "The Interior of a Heart" the homoerotic tensions in the novel have reached a climax of disintegration; the heterosexual climax, involving Dimmesdale's theft of the letter, his triumphant sermon, and his reconciliation with Prynne and Pearl, is yet to come.

Splitting the Letter: "Rough-Looking Desperadoes" and the Final Scene of Writing

If relations between Dimmesdale and other men are complex sites of psychic, sexual, and narrative disintegration, this phobic rendering reenergizes *The Scarlet Letter*'s heterosexual plot, focusing on the evolution of the long-suppressed relations between the minister and Hester Prynne. Indeed, it is Hester's dismay at the minister's condition, visible during their mid-narrative vigil on the scaffold, that moves her to action. This plot effectively stages a theft of the feminine for writing through the commodification of Hester's letter.

Though Hester initially seems to receive the *A* from Puritan patriarchy, in important senses she is actually its origin, since she makes the letter as an embodiment of her passion, in an act that is linked to the nearly simultaneous, natural creation of Pearl: "On the breast of her gown, in fine red cloth, surrounded with an elaborate embroidery and fantastic flourishes of gold thread, appeared the letter A. It was so artistically done, and with so much fertility and gorgeous luxuriance of fancy, that it had all the effect of a last and fitting decoration to the apparel which she wore" (53). If what the Custom-House lacked was passion, Hester here overflows with it as a consequence of natural fecundity. This link reinforces a structure of feeling that associates passion and femininity and prevents passion from circulating freely from one man to another. With this passion, however, comes a tendency to intellectual and cultural criticism that represents a transgression of an ideal domestic role. Hester, "with a mind of native courage and activity . . . had habituated herself to such latitude of speculation as was altogether foreign to the clergyman" (217). Even the term "latitude" reverses the usual polarity of gender: Hester is associated with space, freedom, the outside, and Dimmesdale with claustrophobic enclosure.

This surplus, not just of conventionally feminine feeling but of capacity in a broad sense, has biographical sources in the circle of remarkable women who surrounded Hawthorne in his life. His debts to women's culture, impossible to specify with absolute precision, were clearly much more complicated than any simple capacity to feel he may have derived. In *Family Themes and Hawthorne's Fiction,* Gloria Ehrlich provides evidence of the sources of Hawthorne's anxiety about the interrelations of literature and gender, which surface in *The Scarlet Letter* with special force. According to Ehrlich, Hawthorne's recently departed mother and his moody, brilliant sister, Ebe, serve, in addition to Anne Hutchinson, as models for Hester Prynne. What Ehrlich refers to as the "inner circle" of Hawthorne's youth was composed entirely of women who seem to have contributed significantly to the development of his literary interests (100). Nina Baym reminds us that Julian Hawthorne credits Nathaniel's mother with a major role in shaping his sensibility "by encouraging him to read poetry, romance, and allegory."[33] Sister Ebe, older by two years, seems to have been an even more important influence on Hawthorne's developing sensibility. According to Hawthorne in a letter to William Ticknor, Ebe was "the most sensible woman I ever knew in my life, much superior to me in general talent, and of fine cultivation. . . . [S]he has both a physical and intellectual love of books, being a born bookworm." Despite the possibility of rhetorical inflation on Hawthorne's part, his esteem for his sister's ability is generally warranted.[34] Known for her unconventional opinions and combative outspokenness, Ebe served as a reader of her brother's early manuscripts, a collaborator on some projects for magazines, and a procurer of books from the Salem Athenaeum. Despite her talent, her literary activity, such as it was, was essentially private. Her attractive features and dark hair, her intelligence, her dangerous opinions, and her penchant for solitude all suggest the heroine of *The Scarlet Letter.*

Still another important and highly cultured woman in Hawthorne's life was his wife, Sophia, who seems to have been Ebe's antithesis. Hawthorne expresses the difference between the two and the compelling nature of Ebe's character in an 1839 letter to Sophia: "You must never expect to see my Sister E. in the day-time. . . . I never imagine her in sunshine; and I really doubt whether her faculties of life and intellect begin to be exercised till dusk. . . . Their noon is at midnight. I wish you could walk with her; but you must not, because she is indefatigable, and always wants to walk half round the world, when once she is out-of-doors."[35] It undoubtedly is too easy to cast Sophia as the one-dimensional Phoebe of *The House of the Seven Gables,* even though Phoebe was Hawthorne's pet name for his wife in his letters. Her own letter writing, for example, often is easily as lively and interesting as Hawthorne's affectionate, but simple and patronizing, letters to her. Her "Cuba Journal," written from 1833 to 1835 before her marriage to Hawthorne, was praised and circulated in Boston, though after her marriage Hawthorne seems to have discouraged any public outlet for her talents.[36] These talents were partly sacrificed, much like Hester Prynne's, to the incessant demands of motherhood. Hawthorne has no difficulty imagining even an extension of these demands in an 1847 letter: "Ownest Phoebe, . . . Well; when our children—these two, and three or four more—are grownup, and married off, thou wilt have a little leisure, and mayst paint that Grecian picture that used to haunt thy fancy. But then our grandchildren—Una's children, and Bundlebreech's,—will be coming upon the stage. In short, after a woman has become a mother, she may find rest in Heaven, but nowhere else."[37] It seems fair to conclude, consequently, that Hawthorne derived considerable profit from the service of a number of women of exceptional talent, a service that continued after his death when, freed for the public sphere, Phoebe edited his journals and correspondence.

If *The Scarlet Letter,* at the moment of Dimmesdale's scene of writing, has opened itself to such powerfully centrifugal pressures, how can the text achieve what I earlier spoke of as the necessity of closure? To a large extent, *The Scarlet Letter* moves toward its ending by erecting a contrived barrier of gender difference within the letter Hester wears. This barrier consists, in the second half of the text, of a bar between feeling and thought.[38] The scarlet letter, according to Hawthorne, was her passport to the latter, ushering her "into regions where other women dared not tread. Shame, Despair, Solitude! These had been her teachers,—stern and wild ones,—and they had made her strong, but taught her much amiss" (199–200). Though Hester could think and apparently think well, and though Hawthorne himself may have biographically profited from such feminine rebelliousness, such effort still might cost her "the ethereal essence, wherein she has her truest life. . . . A woman never overcomes these problems by any exercise of thought. They are not to be solved, or only in one way. If her heart chance to come uppermost, they vanish. Thus, Hester Prynne, whose heart had lost its regular and healthy throb, wandered without a clew in the dark labyrinth of mind" (165–166).

Hawthorne's statement on Hester's behalf, in fact, predicts the text's own devices, as it will engineer for Hester a "felt" rather than a "thought" solution and crowd her back into the corner of True Womanhood. It is significant, however, that this process completes itself only as a textual denouement. It is not as the sentimentalized and chastened maternal figure at novel's end that Hester aids Dimmesdale; on the contrary, she contributes the complex sum of her being to the pitiful minister's resurrection. The text, then, constructs an enabling defense against its appropriation of the feminine even as it proceeds to appropriate it, thus continuing in the mode of its own earlier account of the circulation of Hester's sewing in the Boston community. What the Puritan community officially condemns, it unofficially uses, circulating and absorbing Hester's art with an enabling unconsciousness of its exploitation of her prohibited passion: "Vanity, it may be, chose to mortify itself, by putting on, for ceremonials of pomp and state, the garments that had been wrought by her sinful hands. Her needle-work was seen on the ruff of the Governor; military men wore it on their scarfs, and the minister on his band; it decked the baby's little cap; it was shut up, to be mildewed and molder away, in the coffins of the dead" (82–83). Likewise, Hester's passionate rebelliousness comes to inhabit Dimmesdale's sermon in a sublimated and unrecognizable form. The imposition of a gendered understanding upon Hester's complex being in this part of the novel converts this being into a commodified form that can be absorbed without threatening the process of rebuilding Dimmesdale's masculinity. It is this crucial process of forming the feminine for use that the final sentimentalization of Hester works to forget, by placing her in a voluntarily occupied domestic realm, one that obscures the violence of patriarchal culture's power to refigure the feminine to nurture and protect masculine identity. For masculine identity to be secure, the nature of its constitution must be forgotten.

Because Hester is barred from writing, the letter as writing, as opposed to the letter as feeling, seems to be circulated by patriarchal culture through her and has a masculine origin and character, even if, in terms of acquisition, it still has a female source. Luce Irigaray describes the relation between processes of "splitting" and commodification in *This Sex Which Is Not One*: "*In order to become equivalent, a commodity changes bodies. . . . A commodity—a woman—is divided into two irreconcilable 'bodies'*: her 'natural' body and her socially valued, exchangeable body, which is a particularly mimetic expression of masculine values."[39]

I would alter Irigaray's terms in order to describe the circulation of Hester's letter. The splitting in this text is not so much between the commodified and the natural as between that which must circulate as an essentially masculine commodity and that which can circulate as the "feminine." The consequence of this splitting is the evisceration of the maternal as a category, in order that women in such a reduced role serve as a stable mirror in terms of which men can preserve the distinct integrity of masculine character. The chief threat here is constituted less by what Irigaray characterizes as "woman" as a sign of the dependence of male "economic structures" and "sexuality" on "the work of nature" than by women as full cultural participants, unless she means "nature" to imply a broad spectrum of relations masculine identity must repress, including its relation to the irrational abyss of its own body (185). Far down the list of the threats women may represent to men in Western culture is the mere fact of natural reproduction. Women and children, or, as Hawthorne puts it, the "image of Divine Maternity, which so many illustrious painters have vied with one another to represent," serves as one of Western culture's favorite images (*Scarlet Letter,* 56).

Hawthorne's repressive refiguration of Hester occurs in her forest interview with Dimmesdale, when she is subject to a castration by the text. Hawthorne conceals this castration in a way consonant with the function of "true womanhood" in U.S. culture: he tries to convince us that her loss of power is actually a gain, and that she desires her loss.

When Hester throws away her *A,* we discover, with a perceptual shock, that a separation between her body and her badge is actually possible, and that this badge might indeed be acquired and employed by another. According to Hawthorne, "[T]here lay the embroidered letter, glittering like a lost jewel, which some ill-fated wanderer might pick up, and thenceforth be haunted by strange phantoms of guilt, sinkings of the heart, and unaccountable misfortune" (202). At this moment of the text's self-blinding, we might remember that Hawthorne himself might be counted among the finders of the letter, and that he converts its imagined (but not, therefore, less real) finding into one of nineteenth-century literature's most successful authorial acts.

For Hester, of course, the loss is celebrated as liberatory. The release of her hair, "dark and rich, with at once a shadow and a light in its abundance," fetishistically compensates for the letter's loss, as suddenly we are told, "There played around her mouth, and beamed out of her eyes, a radiant and tender smile, that seemed gushing from the very heart of womanhood" (202). The textual transformation of Hester's defeminizing habit of thought earns her the right to circulate in the economy of heterosexuality.[40]

The passionate sexuality the text now finds in Hester and its clarification of what belongs to whom issues a call to the heterosexual in Dimmesdale and readjusts his relations to masculinity as well. Suddenly, the text persistently associates masculinity with violence and physical activity, which operates to open up the maximum possible space between Dimmesdale and both other men and women. Though hardly an Olympic hurdler, as Dimmesdale returns to town we find that he "leaped across the plashy places" and "thrust himself through the clinging underbrush" (216). Along the way he resists temptations to violate the souls of several parishioners, suddenly struck by impulses to "do some strange, wild, wicked thing or other . . . yet growing out of a profounder self than that which opposed the impulse" (217). He finds himself tempted to issue "blasphemous suggestions . . . respecting the communion-supper" to a "good old man" who "addressed him with . . . paternal affection and patriarchal privilege" (217–218); he finds himself tempted to utter an argument "against the immortality of the human soul" to a "most pious and exemplary old dame; poor, widowed, lonely" (218–219); and he finds himself tempted to assault the purity of a "maiden newly won" (219) to the Gospel. As his final encounter, Dimmesdale meets a drunken sailor and, in telling language, yearns "to recreate himself with a few improper jests, such as dissolute sailors abound with, and a volley of good, round, solid, satisfactory, and heaven-defying oaths" (220).

What Hawthorne figures as a liberation of Dimmesdale's primal inner self, triggering the reaction-formation of his ultraconventional and law-loving sermon, actually represents the work of repression upon both of the sources of psychic trouble for men in *The Scarlet Letter*. Dimmesdale's violence institutes a break with the feminine by performing an assault upon it, suggesting the aggressive outlawry of nineteenth-century boys' culture that helps engineer the child's transition from maternal to paternal realms. This break remains visible in the minister's callous disregard for Hester's material situation at text's end, despite his profession of care for her soul. It ruptures and denies as well his eroticized relations to other men and prepares the way for his identification with the transcendental and bodiless masculinity of the law.

The general tumult of the marketplace, marked by swordplay, rough men, and military bands, serves to discipline Hester, who seems helpless and out of place in the novel's final scenes, reduced and silenced by public space. Indeed, she fails to attract even a sympathizing glance as Dimmesdale passes, "so remote from her own sphere, and utterly beyond her reach. . . . She hardly knew him now! He, moving proudly past, enveloped, as it were, in the rich music . . . so unattainable in his worldly position, and still more so in that far vista of his unsympathizing thoughts" (239). Hester suffers the final indignity, again figured in positive terms, of being barred from the symbolic altogether as she hears Dimmesdale's sermon. She hears instead only the reflection of the figural reduction of her own contribution to it:[41] "Muffled as the sound was by its passage through the church-walls, Hester Prynne listened with such intentness, and sympathized so intimately, that the sermon had throughout a meaning for her, entirely apart from its indistinguishable words. These, perhaps, if more distinctly heard, might have been only a grosser medium, and have clogged the spiritual sense. . . . It was this profound and continual undertone that gave the clergyman his most appropriate power" (243–244).

These final marketplace scenes of Dimmesdale's ambiguous triumph deploy two versions of masculinity, each of which exists as the mirror image of the other. On the one hand, the chapter entitled "The Procession" deploys masculinity as indistinguishable from unified state power, embodied by Hawthorne in the figures of "Bradstreet, Endicott, Dudley, Bellingham, and their compeers,—who were elevated to power by the early choice of the people. . . . They had fortitude and self-reliance, and, in time of difficulty or peril, stood up for the welfare of the state like a line of cliffs" (238).[42] The other prominent male presences in the marketplace are sailors, who were, we learn, "rough-looking desperadoes, with sun-blackened faces, and an immensity of beard. . . . From beneath their . . . hats . . . gleamed eyes which, even in good nature and merriment, had a kind of animal ferocity. They transgressed without fear or scruple, the rules of behavior that were binding on all others" (232). These desperadoes suggest a fantasy of a masculinity unified by the absence of both external law and guilt-inducing relations to women. In the motherless and fatherless expanse of the sea, Hawthorne's sailors are a self-created law unto themselves and "had been guilty, as we should phrase it, of depredations on the Spanish commerce, such as would have perilled all their necks in a modern court of justice" (233). As in Dimmesdale's outbreak of rebelliousness, Hawthorne again suggests the power of fantasy violence to detach masculinity from the conditions of its constitution.

Dimmesdale chooses solidarity with the law and thus reinvents himself as a Puritan patriarch. In the final scene of writing in *The Scarlet Letter,* Dimmesdale composes his election day sermon with a new authorial power and confidence. Having flung his previous manuscript in the fire "with a sentence broken in the midst" (223), he ordered food and "wrote with such an impulsive flow of thought and emotion, that he fancied himself inspired; and only wondered that Heaven should see fit to transmit the grand and solemn music of its oracles through so foul an organ-pipe as he. . . . Thus the night fled away. . . . There he was, with the pen still between his fingers, and a vast, immeasurable tract of written space behind him!" (240). Now tracing his inspiration, not to Hester, but to a disembodied God speaking through "so foul an organ-pipe as he," Dimmesdale engineers a rewriting of writing, figuring composition as a single, integrated flow. Only the trope of transcendent inspiration, as opposed to multifaceted and bodily centered conflict, can provide the necessary authority for his text. In the process, he abandons the dangerous and disruptive ground of his intimacy with Chillingworth for a conventional identification with masculinity as authority. Chillingworth tells Dimmesdale, in fact, that the scaffold represents the only place where he "couldst have escaped me" (253). The only escape from desire, in other words, is a commitment to the straitjacket of a paternal identification that insists on its difference from the erotic possibilities Chillingworth represents.

Written through a passion that has its source in Hester, Dimmesdale's sermon achieves a religious and artistic triumph. As Amy Schrager Lang indicates, "His art, in which private, feminine experience informs masculine public statement, is not, by this means, feminized but completed" (187). He may be said symbolically to actualize an enduring dream of a writer in the United States: establishing the political centrality of art; gathering the faithful in a victory that is at once masculine and socially transforming; healing the split between private self and public role. As author, rather than brood about the progenitress of authoring, Dimmesdale creates a fantasy in which he is progenitor of his people: "[A]s he drew towards the close, a spirit as of prophecy had come upon him, constraining him to its purpose as mightily as the old prophets of Israel were constrained; only with this difference, that, whereas the Jewish seers had denounced judgments and ruin on their country, it was his mission to foretell a high and glorious destiny for the newly gathered people of the Lord" (249). Finally, then, *The Scarlet Letter* ends with the genesis of a fiction of patrilineal generation. Indeed, so caught up in the spirit of authoring is Dimmesdale, that he even admits, or almost admits, paternity of Pearl.[43]

It is when squarely placed within the masculinity-confirming environs of public, political culture that Dimmesdale can admit, paradoxically, that his relation to Hester is a powerful source of the letter he has and the letters he produces. Lest we think this identification with Hester means identity, however, Dimmesdale is simultaneously moved to assert a masculine difference. He insists that his *A* is bigger than hers: "Now, at the death hour, he stands up before you! He bids you look again at Hester's Scarlet Letter! He tells you, that, with all its mysterious horror, it is but the shadow of what he bears on his own breast" (255). The irony, of course, is that his letter is so shadowy that some of the assembled multitude later deny its existence. Dimmesdale is either thwarted or protected by the daylight of rational vision, which by definition rebuffs manifestations of the phantasmic and repressed.

The Scarlet Letter's final consolidation of masculine identity occurs in its "Conclusion," when Hester returns to live a life of sentimental service in the community that shunned her. The cultural labor men appropriate from women is never consonant with imagined contributions of the culturally celebrated true woman or mother. This figure emerges after the genesis of masculine identity and represents a forgetting that seeks to consign the complex cultural contributions of women to the grave of an idealized oblivion. Hester's "voluntary" return, then, occurs as an effect of the text's previous operations, but it also functions as an after-the-fact disavowal of the appropriation those operations performed. The letter, one feels assured, will not be re-purloined. This Hester has little or nothing to lose. Yet the text's closure is nonetheless imperfect and incomplete, as a sign, perhaps, that the work of cultural repression always leaves disruptive traces through which its nature can be read. Hawthorne's ambiguous motto comes to mind: "'Be true! Be true! Be true! Show freely to the world, if not your worst, yet some trait whereby the worst may be inferred" (260).

*I*t is appropriate, then, that *The Scarlet Letter* ends with Hawthorne's meditation on an unquiet grave. Few things, certainly, can exceed the opacity of his final paragraph:

> And, after many, many years, a new grave was delved, near an old and sunken one, in that burial ground beside which King's Chapel has since been built. It was near that old and sunken grave, yet with a space between, as if the dust of the two sleepers had no right to mingle. Yet one tombstone served for both. All around, there were monuments carved with armorial bearings; and on this simple slab of slate—as the curious investigator may still discern, and perplex himself with the purport—there appeared the semblance of an engraved escutcheon. It bore a device, a herald's wording of which might serve for a motto and brief description of our now concluded legend; so somber is it, and relieved only by one ever-glowing point of light gloomier than the shadow:—
> "ON A FIELD, SABLE, THE LETTER A, GULES." (264)

The gothically complex lyricism of Hawthorne's conclusion fixes our attention on the couple as a tragic problem unresolvable even in death—but one to be put away, perhaps, as unresolvable. It forcefully distracts us from the third party of the triangle, Chillingworth, who "shrivelled away, and almost vanished from mortal sight, like an uprooted weed" (260). Significantly, perhaps, it is his elimination as a physically present threat that produces Hawthorne's most explicit meditation on the content of his relations with Dimmesdale:

It is a curious subject of observation and inquiry, whether hatred and love be not the same thing at bottom. Each, in its utmost development, supposes a high degree of intimacy and heart-knowledge. . . . [E]ach leaves the passionate lover, or the no less passionate hater, forlorn and desolate by the withdrawal of his object. Philosophically considered, therefore, the two passions seem essentially the same. . . . In the spiritual world, the old physician and the minister— mutual victims as they have been—may, unawares, have found their earthly stock of hatred and antipathy transmuted into golden love. (260–261)

In heaven, perhaps, the physician who had "dug into the poor clergyman's heart, like a miner searching for gold; or, rather, like a sexton delving into a grave" (129), will join the tortured Dimmesdale in mutually satisfying, if non-physical, affection.[44]

CHAPTER 2

'Edgar Allan Poe and the Purloined Mother

$\mathcal{H}$awthorne's account of Hester's circulating letter and the effect of this circulation in the construction of authorial identity have a double in antebellum literature: Poe's "The Purloined Letter." Like Hawthorne, Poe as an author had complex and ambivalent relations to women, and just as for Hawthorne, these relations made the problem of working out the terms of male authority difficult and complex.

The strength of Poe's mournful desires for idealized lost women, beginning with the early loss of his actress mother, Eliza Poe, has long been a theme of Poe criticism.[1] Kenneth Silverman suggests in his recent biography that Poe's obsession with this lost figure inhabits his work not only thematically, in terms of his numerous poems and stories about the death of women, but in the allusions to the stage that honeycomb his works.[2] In his later life, Poe's desire to be comforted and cared for by women produces a series of relations to nineteenth-century women poets, whose literary efforts he supported. These include such figures as Sarah Anna Robinson Lewis, Frances Sargent Osgood, and Sarah Helen Whitman, to whom Poe had a tempestuous failed engagement.[3] If Poe's life is complexly entangled in nineteenth-century women's culture, however, it is also marked by desires for masculine respect, evident in his early struggles with John Allan, his surrogate father, and in his ambitions, which according to Silverman were palpable as well from an early age: "Those who knew him at school later remembered him as blatantly competitive, 'eager for distinction,' 'ambitious to excel,' 'inclined to be imperious'" (24).[4] If Poe's later ambitions would inhabit less conventional forms, they are still evident in the reach and scope of his literary output and the masculine claims to authority evident in his literary voice.[5] Even if Poe's work functions ironically to undercut the cultural foundations on which such authority rests, a sense of its ambition survives even the revelation of its deconstructive perversity. Successful charlatanism of a high order itself requires a mastery of mass culture and stakes a claim to a resentful authority of its own.[6]

Poe, then, is a figure whose work is marked by exacerbated forms of the unstable gender conflicts of nineteenth-century U.S. culture. Poe's trio of detective stories, "The Murders in the Rue Morgue," "The Mystery of Marie Roget," and the third story, on which I will focus here, "The Purloined Letter," ambiguously either unveils or replicates the violence of U.S. culture's suppression of women and appropriation of the feminine—as always, the complexity of Poe's relation to questions of gender makes his intentions difficult to assemble.[7] The first two tales depict the use of a sensationalized and graphic violence against silenced women to masculinize the ambiguous cultural terrain of androgyny for men. "The Purloined Letter," in contrast, offers a relatively subdued vision of the poisonous symbolic violence culture employs against women, engineering a commodified exchange of the feminine that both exposes and conceals the absorption of feminine value into a masculinizing circuit of power. As in the case of *The Scarlet Letter,* the gender indeterminacy that "The Purloined Letter" strives to resolve through commodification opens the tale to the representation of homoerotic desires as well, as the story's suppression of women also suppresses their mediating function in relations between men.

Most readings of Poe's trio of detective tales, however, have not taken up feminist issues. They tend to construct readings of the tales as uncanny psychoanalytic allegories, analyze Poe's theories of ratiocination, or specify his relation to mass culture, but generally fail to address the visible circuit of misogynist violence the stories contain. This violence directly serves the construction of masculine authority lodged in Dupin, one of Poe's most masterful characters. Taken corporately, such readings participate in the processes of cultural suppression and absorption of the feminine that the story itself records.[8] In this chapter, then, I hope to fashion a reading of Poe's tale that reflects nineteenth-century anxieties about authorship and consequent aggressions toward women.

Like *The Scarlet Letter,* Poe's stories conduct a complex and ambivalent campaign to claim an ambivalence-ridden space of androgyny as safely masculine space.[9] We learn in "The Murders in the Rue Morgue" that Dupin, the hero-detective of the tales, has, like Hawthorne's narrator in "The

Custom-House," experienced downward mobility from "a variety of untoward events," despite originally coming from "an illustrious family" (179); he also seems to have fallen into literary pursuits. "Books . . . were his sole luxuries," Poe tells us (179), and he lives with the narrator of the stories in a homo-erotically charged dusky solitude during the daytime, "reading, writing, or conversing, until warned by the clock of the advent of the true Darkness" (180).

Dupin's habits, which also unfit him for life in the masculine world of business and commerce, merely prepare the ground for his apotheosis as the master of the middle-class world of newspapers and crimes, which would be precisely the most likely scene of his rejection. Dupin's triumphs depend on scorned mental traits that have no place in a world of male "mathematical" analysis, traits like association, identification, and intuition, which for Dupin are literary in their application. Much of his crime-solving information comes from a close reading of written accounts of the crime. At moments of greatest analytic intensity, his voice, "usually a rich tenor, rose into a treble which would have sounded petulantly but for the deliberateness and entire distinctness of the enunciation" (180).

In Dupin, whose "Bi-Part Soul" might be split into "the creative and the resolvent" (180), Poe has created a character whose power depends directly on his access to feminine capabilities that have generally positive functions in the tales. They allow Dupin to function and to compete even in the world of masculine violence, and the idea that such capabilities should be treated with contempt is precisely the rhetorical target of the tales. Like Hawthorne's Old General, the hero of Fort Ticonderoga, Dupin's "femininity" actually makes him more masculine than the men he humiliates.

The entire trilogy, including both "The Murders in the Rue Morgue" and "The Mystery of Marie Roget," both acknowledges and suppresses the relation between Dupin's feminine powers and a historical, social, and psychological dependence on actual women. The stories acknowledge this influence in tacit ways, through the presence of the feminine in Dupin; through the focus on issues of creativity and art, the area of public life in the nineteenth century where the role of women is most important; and through the crucial presence of actual women characters in all three tales, which figures the question of Dupin's femininity as a matter of the relation of actual men to actual women. This relation is suppressed through the terrible violence in the tales directed against women and, after the figurative murder of the mother, a refiguring of influence as a matter between men. The narrator's relation to Dupin and his exploits and Dupin's own functioning much of the time in the role of narrator produce a commodification of the feminine as literature to be exchanged between men.

In the first two of these three tales, all women characters are horribly murdered and mutilated. Both the mother and daughter in "The Murders in the Rue Morgue" are killed in the presence of possessions and money and have disreputable associations with the public realm: "Upon the floor were found four Napoleons, an ear-ring of topaz, three large silver spoons, three smaller of *métal d'Alger,* and two bags, containing nearly four thousand francs in gold" (182). The old lady uses tobacco and snuff and is rumored to have told fortunes. There is little sense here of any possible contribution of such women to the formation of male character or to male vocational abilities. Indeed, Dupin discovers this horrible crime through newspaper reports, so that the women have already been killed into print, the question of influence discounted through the circulation of brutality and death. To solve the crime, Dupin needs no specific relation to any particular women or their bodies in terms of which he might experience obligation or guilt. He needs only access to the graphic reports of the popular press.

Much the same might be said of "The Mystery of Marie Roget," to which I have already alluded.[10] The real-life victim, Mary Rogers, on whom Poe's tale is based, worked in a New York cigar store. Roget works in a local *"parfumerie"* and consequently, like the women killed in the Rue Morgue, is associated with the public sphere and with commerce (214). Once more, Dupin reads of the murder in the popular press, and his investigation consists to a large extent of juxtaposing notices of the case from the assembled periodicals of Paris. Nothing in Poe surpasses the violence of this composite description of Roget's body, which is even more extensive than what I quote here. To Dupin, of course, this description is all fodder for analysis:

> The face was suffused with dark blood, some of which issued from the mouth. No foam was seen, as in the case of the merely drowned. There was no discoloration in the cellular tissue. About the throat were bruises and impressions of fingers. The arms were bent over on the chest, and were rigid. . . . On the left wrist were two circular excoriations, apparently the effect of ropes, or of a rope in more than one volution. A part of the right wrist, also, was much chafed. . . . A piece of lace was found tied so tightly around the neck as to be hidden from sight; it was completely buried in the flesh, and was fastened by a knot which lay just under the left ear. This alone would have sufficed to produce death. (201)

As in the case of "The Murders in the Rue Morgue," this death seems to preclude consideration in terms of maternal influence, because of the conventional separation between the maternal and fallen sexuality; because the maternal does not conventionally inhabit language that is so abstracted, so coldly clinical; and because the language circulates in the public, urban, commercial sphere in which Roget works. Poe positions Roget as a woman from whom nothing can be gotten except sexual pleasure, even before her murder and mutilation. This absence, however, does not preclude Dupin's access to the feminine; rather, it allows him to incorporate feminine characteristics all the more securely within the competitive rationality of male culture.

The third of these three stories, "The Purloined Letter," contains a female victim of crime, the Queen, whose title and political activities, at least, suggest a figure as powerful as Hawthorne's queen in exile, Hester Prynne. Indeed, one might even argue that the story enacts a kind of gender equality. But as soon as this maternal presence is admitted to the story, a concomitant intensification of anxiety about feminization seems to occur. In "The Purloined Letter," Dupin feels forced to conduct his most thoroughgoing argument *for* the masculine virtue of a power of identification and for the poetic to which it is linked. In the symbolic presence of the Queen, he makes this argument in correspondingly filial terms. Dupin's example of identification is a schoolboy, about eight, who might (and throughout the nineteenth century increasingly would) be taught by a woman teacher, and who in any case would be subject to maternal power. This lad wins marbles from his friends playing "even and odd" by the following technique: "I fashion the expression on my face, as accurately as possible, in accordance with the expression of his, and then wait to see what thoughts or sentiments arise in my mind or heart, as if to match or correspond with the expression" (231). Dupin suggests that this capacity for identification is necessary for all sound thinking and is at the heart of the villain D——'s brilliance. At the same time, this conventionally feminine capacity for empathy is refashioned as a competitive masculine technique, which both protects its masculinity and suppresses any homoerotic implications of actual feeling between men. The question of this technique is a metaphor for the larger question of literary thinking and its place in masculine culture. The plodding, unidimensionally male Prefect is categorically incapable of appreciating the criminal brilliance of D——. According to Dupin, "This functionary . . . has been thoroughly mystified; and the remote source of his defeat lies in the supposition that the Minister is a fool, because he has acquired renown as a poet. All fools are poets; this the Prefect *feels*; and he is merely guilty of a *non distributio medii* in thence inferring that all poets are fools" (232). Dupin's emphasis on the determining use of feeling in the genesis of the Prefect's attitude toward poets ridicules the role of undeveloped crude intuition in generating the latter's plodding contempt toward the creative. The Prefect, in other words, scorning the emotive, can only feel in an utterly unconscious way, whereas the Minister D——— reasons "as poet *and* mathematician," although as "mere mathematician, he could not have reasoned at all" (232). Though this comment reverses the hierarchy between the poet and mathematician, it also may contain a deeper implication that as a "mere mathematician" one does not and cannot exist. For D——— and Dupin, the power of an unavoidable recourse to feeling exponentially increases in its power by coupling it with a masculine, analytic distance.

The schoolboy's method, of course, lies at the bottom of all method in "The Purloined Letter": to ascertain the nature and place of the letter, one must assume the character of the letter's possessor. In the initial theft, the Minister "fathoms" the Queen's secret in her boudoir, an act that leads the Prefect to observe that the villain "dares all things, those unbecoming as well as those becoming a man" (227). Dupin, too, when he steals the letter back, wears dark green shades, complains of weak eyes "to be even" with the criminal (234), and proceeds from this position to find the missing document. Both the Minister and Dupin engage in an elaborate play of cross-dressing, in which the converse of a conventional masculine commitment to energy, ambition, and the outdoors necessarily suggests feminization. Dupin, in his attempt to re-purloin the letter, finds the Minister "at home, yawning, lounging, and dawdling, as usual, and pretending to be in the last extremity of *ennui*" (234). Nevertheless, Dupin tells us that "[h]e is, perhaps, the most really energetic human being now alive" (234).

This play between Dupin and D——— suggests again *The Scarlet Letter* and the relation between Dimmesdale and Chillingsworth that dominates the center of Hawthorne's book. In the case of both, scenes of pseudodomesticity are presented as masks of a violent masculine desire for power, except that violence itself finally serves to mask the problems of feminization and homoerotic desire central to both narratives. In both cases, homosocial/homoerotic competitions work to occlude the female figure involved and to stage the feminine as a problem to be solved between men.

Significantly, Dupin first mistakes the letter's location. As he says, "I paid especial attention to a large writing-table near which he sat, and upon which lay confusedly, some miscellaneous letters and other papers, with one or two musical instruments and a few books. Here however, after a long and very deliberate scrutiny, I saw nothing to excite particular suspicion" (234). Despite this apparent error, Dupin's next glance infallibly locates the letter: "At length my eyes . . . fell upon a trumpery filigree card-rack of pasteboard, that hung dangling by a dirty blue ribbon, from a little brass knob just beneath the middle of the mantel-piece. In this rack, which had three or four compartments, were five or six visiting cards and a solitary letter" (234–235).[11] In fact, the movement of Dupin's gaze from the desk to the card rack traces a connection between a general masculine creativity lodged in such activities as writing, reading, and music (the latter a pure signifier of art or beauty because of its disconnection from the practical world) and a culturally specified femininity. To Marie Bonaparte, the card rack that holds the letter in fact serves as "almost an anatomical chart" of the female body, one from "which not even the clitoris (or brass knob) is omitted."[12] With its "dirty blue ribbon," and with any number of cards and one ambiguously phallic letter inserted in its "trumpery filigree" and "pasteboard" compartments, this is, without doubt, a fallen card rack. Its degraded condition, much like the descriptions of the corpses of women in the previous stories, utilizes the conventional nineteenth-century opposition of sexual degradation and maternity to suppress the problem of feminine influence represented by the Queen.

The circulating letter itself suffers a mutilation suggestively similar to that which explicitly occurs to women's bodies in the first two tales. According to Dupin,

> It was torn nearly in two, across the middle. . . . [I]t was, to all appearance, radically different from one of which the Prefect had read us so minute a description. Here the seal was large and black, with the D—— cipher; there it was small and red, with the ducal arms of the S—— family. Here, the address, to the Minister, was diminutive and feminine; there the superscription, to a certain royal personage, was markedly bold and decided. . . . But, then, the *radicalness* of these differences, which was excessive; the dirt; the soiled and torn condition of the paper, so inconsistent with the *true* methodical habits of D—— . . . were strongly corroborative of suspicion. (235)

What this letter represents, as the thing circulated and contested, clearly becomes an interpretive key to the story. The context established by the first two tales suggests that women are the primary targets of violence; the Queen's status as the initial victim of the crime committed in "The Purloined Letter" reinforces this pattern. If we see that the letter is mutilated like a female body, should its contents in fact be seen as feminine? Or does the Minister's interest in disguise suggest that we reverse this identification? Should we see it as a masculine, phallic object by virtue of its insertion into the feminine card rack? In what sense can it ever be thought of as feminine, if, as the circumstances of the story seem to imply, it was initially composed by a man and circulated through her? Isn't the Queen caught in a circuit of masculine dominance in any case, so that even her participation, at best, can be as a relay in masculine transactions?

The presumption that the letter the Queen receives has a masculine origin is itself based on the game of gender expectations. The Queen's anxiety when D—— appears might suggest a letter from a lover, particularly since questions of honor are involved, but such an assumption normatively confines the Queen to the realm of the personal, when the very fact of the blackmail of the Queen suggests she functions at the level of the political as well. Dupin himself later seems to confirm that the letter has masculine origins when he comments on D——'s concealment of it. When he purloins it, "the address, to the Minister, was diminutive and feminine." In the description of the missing letter given by the Prefect, in contrast, "the superscription, to a certain royal personage, was markedly bold and decided" (235). Nonetheless, there is no reason to presume that only men write with a bold and decided style. D—— himself masquerades as a feminized male in the story and, consistent with his feminization, is apparently responsible for the feminine handwriting the letter displays when in his possession. Considering the tale's pattern of repetitions, the possibility of a masquerade in the opposite direction certainly suggests itself. Given the tale's commitment to homoeroticism and androgyny, in fact, there is no particular reason to presume that the lover of the Queen, if she has one, is male in any case. If the central project of "The Purloined Letter" is, as I have argued, to establish the masculinity of androgyny, its method is to commodify and loosen the relation of feminine traits to the Queen. The circuit of exchanges that suggests that the contents of the letter are masculine, then, ambiguously employs and exposes patriarchy's first line of defense. Finally, the letter has been most successfully masculinized when, after its successive exchanges, the Queen receives her property back through the mastery of Dupin.

The next line of defense, in the last of a series of stories devoted to the appropriation of the feminine, might be the conventional position that the contents of the letter are irrelevant and unknowable in any case. The lack of reference to its contents tempts us to empty out the letter and treat it as an abstract signifier, a pure commodity that can be readily exchanged precisely because of its convertibility.[13] It is not at all clear, however, that we should accept the inevitability of the letter's indeterminacy if we must surrender to an actual suppression of knowledge in order to do so. What if, in other words, the indeterminacy of the letter constitutes less its essential nature than the operation of a desire that the contents of the letter be emptied out precisely through its circulation in masculine hands? That this letter has content is beyond question, and, regardless of what the reader knows, surely D—— and Dupin have every opportunity to read the letter and do so. It is nevertheless true that between D—— and Dupin the content of the letter appears to have no direct meaning beyond certifying the abstract value of a central chess piece in a game of wits. To the Queen, the content of the letter is paramount, and this content thus also comes into play between the Queen and both contestants who have connections to her person. It is she whom the Minister is attempting to blackmail, and it is she for whom Dupin acts as a "partisan" (236). As they circulate between Dupin and D——, then, the contents of the letter, which in the context of the reading I am producing here represent what actually is being purloined, are abstracted and suppressed. The blankness of the letter evacuates the position of the Queen as one about which very little can be said of a concrete nature, while shifting emphasis to the homoerotic competition between Dupin and his double. The final gesture of the story minimizes the extent to which Dupin has acted on the Queen's behalf at all: His object apparently has been, in addition to money, revenge for "an evil turn" done him by D—— at Vienna (236).

The epigraph to "The Murders in the Rue Morgue," however, suggests that one should not yield too quickly to apparent interpretive difficulties of hidden knowledge: "What song the Syrens sang, or what name Achilles assumed when he hid himself among women, although puzzling questions are not beyond all conjecture" (175). This epigraph itself poses complicated difficulties in understanding the operation of gender in these tales.[14] It juxtaposes an allusion to the other-worldly song of the "Syrens," which irresistibly penetrates (like Marie Roget's perfume?) and destroys men, to a situation in which men manipulate feminization as a disguise and hence subject it to agency and control. In both cases, questions about the precise content of the experiences alluded to remain.[15]

Because this tale has such a pared-down, symbolic efficacy, it has lent itself to psychoanalytic allegory. It is possible to accommodate the historical situation of gender in the nineteenth century and preserve its significance in psychoanalytic and theoretical discourses through the application of a model of the fetish. Typically, the fetish engineers precisely the kind of suppression of maternal influence executed by "The Purloined Letter" itself even as it places the fact of this suppression in plain sight.[16] The classic fetish involves a male defense against castration, concealing the lack of the mother by granting to her the profoundly unnatural fetish object. According to Freud, "it remains a token of triumph over the threat of castration and a safeguard against it."[17] Even though Freud sees that fetishism both defends against castration and asserts it, his model continues in both cases the persistent association between women and "lack" and hence acts in accord with the fetish rather than rendering an adequate account of it (219).

Fetishism should be understood not in terms of an originary equation of women and lack nor in terms of a hallucinated maternal phallus, a concept that empties out the mother or the feminine as an authentically productive cultural position. By far the most important operations of gender take place in the symbolic realm where the terms of identity are set and threatened; it is in this realm that masculinity appropriates cultural value and consigns femininity to the position of "lack."[18] It may be that masculine integrity is haunted by memories of a pre-oedipal mother, shadow memories that logically imply the dissolution of identity, but it is equally possible to suggest that the threat of dissolution comes from traces of the ongoing work of patriarchy—the performative work of coalescing masculine identity through an evisceration of the feminine in the realm of material, historical experience. Because this evisceration involves an ongoing act of misrecognition, the identity on which it depends is itself threatened by the often barely perceptible reality of women's contributions to culture; by the guilt and denial that shadows conventional male relations to women; and perhaps by desire itself, if we are inhabited by a desire to find some originary mother, undamaged by the operations of patriarchal culture.[19] The artifactuality of fetish objects, then, suggests the status of gender difference as itself a function of commodification.[20] If the fetish, classically, suggests a desire to confer a lost wholeness upon the maternal body, it also defensively maintains male identity by suggesting that such wholeness could never possibly (and must not) exist. It repeats as well an originating commodification through which the feminine has been emptied out.[21] The suppression of the content of the Queen's letter in Poe's tale and its exchanges suggest such a process.

A compressed version of this process can be found in another famous Poe tale, "Ligeia." The narrator of this tale profits from Ligeia's immense wisdom. As he says, "[H]er knowledge was such as I have never known in woman—but where breathes the man who has traversed, and successfully, *all* the wide areas of moral, physical, and mathematical science?" Convinced of her utter superiority, the narrator resigns himself, "with a child-like confidence, to her guidance through the chaotic world of metaphysical investigation" (82).

Her intellectual and spiritual power comes to center for the narrator in her mysterious eyes. Although I will quote the narrator at some length, it is difficult to do full justice to the obsessiveness of his description:

> They were, I must believe, far larger than the ordinary eyes of our own race. They were even fuller than the fullest of the gazelle eyes of the tribe of the valley of Nourjahad. . . . The "strangeness," however, which I found in the eyes, was of a nature distinct from the formation, or the colour, or the brilliancy of the features, and must, after all, be referred to the *expression*. Ah, word of no meaning! behind whose vast latitude of mere sound we intrench our ignorance of so much of the spiritual. The expression of the eyes of Ligeia! . . . What *was* it? I was possessed with a passion to discover. Those eyes! those large, those shining, those divine orbs! they became to me the twin stars of Leda, and I to them devoutest of astrologers. . . . I mean to say that, subsequently to the period when Ligeia's beauty passed into my spirit, there dwelling as in a shrine, I derived, from many existences in the material world, a sentiment such as I felt always aroused, within me, by her large and luminous orbs. Yet not the more could I define that sentiment, or analyze, or even steadily view it. (80–81)

In the course of this description, Ligeia's eyes become progressively objectified and abstracted from the body and the self of which they are a part. The narrator is less and less capable of giving an account of *what* the eyes represent precisely. He claims to find himself "*upon the very verge* of remembrance, without being able, in the end, to remember" (81), but this fortunate forgetting forces a displacement of his quest into figuration and metaphor and allows him to find the inspiration of Ligeia's eyes in other cultural sources:[22] "I recognized it, let me repeat, sometimes in the survey of a rapidly growing vine—in the contemplation of a moth, a butterfly, a chrysalis, a stream of running water. . . . And there are one or two stars in heaven . . . in a telescopic scrutiny of which I have been made aware of the feeling. I have been filled with it by certain sounds from stringed instruments, and not unfrequently by passages from books" (81). As a final step in this process, the feminine quality of Ligeia's eyes finds its most apt expression in the famous, never found quotation from Joseph Glanville: "And the will therein lieth, which dieth not. Who knoweth the mysteries of the will, with its vigor?

For God is but a great will pervading all things by nature of its intentness" (81). The narrator's remarks suggest a trajectory of transformative absorption. The feminine mystery of Ligeia's eyes has been abstracted away from its source and absorbed into masculine authority, a ludicrous and unsuccessful replica of Dimmesdale's appropriation of Hester's *A* or of the commodification of the feminine at work in "The Purloined Letter."

The narrator's perception of his beloved in "Ligeia" actually resembles the narrator's perception of Dupin in Poe's detective tales.[23] In the first of the three detective stories, "The Murders in the Rue Morgue," the narrator also finds himself captivated by Dupin's remarkable and overpowering learning. The narrator is "astonished . . . at the vast extent of his reading" and feels his soul "enkindled within me by the wild fervor, and the vivid freshness of his imagination" (179). If the mysterious Ligeia inhabits "a large, old, decaying city near the Rhine" (79), Dupin and the narrator take up residence in a "time-eaten and grotesque mansion, long deserted through superstitions" (179). To the narrator of "Ligeia," her remarkable abilities are marked by an opposition between control and passion, a disturbance that surfaces at the level of the voice: "Of all the women whom I have ever known, she, the most outwardly calm, the ever placid Ligeia, was the most violently a prey to the tumultuous vultures of stern passion. And of such passion I could form no estimate, save by the miraculous expansion of those eyes which at once so delighted and appalled me—by the almost magical melody, modulation, distinctness, and placidity of her very low voice—and by the fierce energy . . . of the wild words which she habitually uttered" (81). To the narrator of "The Purloined Letter," Dupin's analytic brilliance is also marked by a mixture of icy calm and suppressed passion, a conflict that surfaces in his voice, which transgresses gender in the opposite direction. Despite his "wild fervor" (179), when Dupin thought, "[h]is manner . . . was frigid and abstract; his eyes were vacant in expression; while his voice, usually a rich tenor, rose into a treble which would have sounded petulantly but for the deliberateness and entire distinctness of the enunciation" (180). If Dupin's eyes, in contrast to the fetishized eyes of Ligeia, go "vacant" and empty when deep in the analytic activity at which he excels, "The Purloined Letter" nonetheless focuses on vision as a source of power, as the relative capacities of Dupin, D——, and the Prefect depend upon their respective abilities to see or not see an object hidden in plain sight.

The congruences between the two stories help fill in the suppressed position of the Queen in "The Purloined Letter." If Ligeia seems to pose a more obvious and potent threat to the integrity of male subjectivity, it is because she has been less successfully contained in the appropriating framework of exchanges: her power is initially posited as her own. The narrator of "Ligeia" realizes, in fact, that he has *"never known* the paternal name of her who was my friend and my betrothed" (79). This distinction suggests that the Queen survives in "The Purloined Letter" in part because the frame of the story reproduces symbolic rather than literal violence in order to negate and contain her cultural presence. "Ligeia," of course, might suggest that death itself is an inadequate containment of the feminine in any case, but her death is psychologically symbolic rather than real. Unlike many of Poe's dead women, of whom Ligeia is an example, the graphically murdered women of "The Murders in the Rue Morgue" and "The Mystery of Marie Roget" stay stone-cold dead in their graves.

These congruences also suggest the indeterminacy of sex and gender that underlies Poe's construction of masculine authority. Just as the narrator of "Ligeia" speaks of himself as that character's "betrothed" (79), the narrator of Poe's detective stories has an intensely homoerotic and perhaps homosexual relation to Dupin.[24] Each comes to serve as the primary companion of the other, in the absence of any perceptible erotic interest in women. As this passage from "The Murders in the Rue Morgue" suggests:

> It was a freak of fancy in my friend (for what else shall I call it?). To be enamored of the Night for her own sake; and into this *bizarrerie,* as into all his others, I quietly fell; giving myself up to his wild whims with a perfect *abandon.* The sable divinity would not herself dwell with us always; but we counterfeit her presence. At first dawn of the morning we closed all the massy shutters of our old building; lighted a couple of tapers which, strongly perfumed, threw out only the ghastliest and feeblest of rays. By the aid of these we then buried our souls in dreams—reading, writing, or conversing, until warned by the clock of the advent of the true Darkness. Then we sallied forth into the streets, arm and arm. (179–180)

Convinced that Dupin's society is "a treasure beyond price," the enthralled narrator is "permitted to be at the expense of renting, and furnishing" their joint domicile (179). This relation is an ongoing one, unmodified by the adventures the stories record.

The homoerotic energies of "The Purloined Letter" are foregrounded by the story's negation of the position of the Queen. In the previous two stories, the relations of Dupin to his rivals have been mediated by a focus on the bodies of women. A facade of heterosexual interest is maintained by the heterosexual nature of the crimes—men killing and mutilating women—in a culture in which violence and sexuality are routinely if horrifically entwined. In "The Purloined Letter," the need to control the Queen as a cultural producer suppresses her function as the guarantor of the heterosexuality of male homosocial relations, and Dupin is left in an erotically ambiguous face-to-face encounter with D——, who serves as both his rival and double. This doubling leaves evident what Luce Irigaray characterizes as the "homosexuality" of the sociocultural order (192). If, as Eve Kosofsky Sedgwick remarks, Irigaray's use of the term "homosexuality" doesn't seem very sexual, it nevertheless is the case that this face-to-face encounter between men with chiefly their own relation at stake, this matching of bodies, is always potentially erotic, as is any disruption of the precarious balance of sameness and difference in conventional bourgeois relations.[25] In particular, the processes of identification that serve as the chief investigative method of this story require for their application a high degree of similarity between men, and they presuppose a high degree of attention to the bodies of other men as a source of morphological signs of the mind one attempts to fathom. In Dupin's example of the boy playing "even and odd," to which I referred earlier, the use of this method actually involves a physical miming of the other person's expression, which produces, in turn, a replica of that person's internal state. Thus, when Dupin visits D—— in search of the letter, he replicates the latter's pose of feminized lassitude: "I found D—— at home, yawning, lounging, and dawdling, as usual, and pretending to be in the last extremity of *ennui*. He is, perhaps, the most really energetic human being now alive. . . . To be even with him, I complained of my weak eyes, and lamented the necessity of the spectacles, under cover of which I cautiously and thoroughly surveyed the whole apartment, while seemingly intent only upon the conversation of my host" (234).

The story displaces the potential eroticism of this domestic matching of minds and bodies, an eroticism particularly evident because of the larger context of Dupin's homoerotic relationship to the narrator, into the savage and violent competition the story records. Even the framing emphasis on detection projects outward the mystery to be solved, away from difficult questions of the erotic in terms of the detective's own body. It discovers and solves its own mystery in the body of the other, toward which it finally acknowledges no erotic connection. If the homoerotic is palpably present in "The Purloined Letter" in any case, it only serves to fuel Dupin's violent drive for mastery as a form of sublime transcendence. Dupin's interest in D—— and the case, we eventually learn, has been produced by a competitive desire for revenge for "an evil turn, which I told him, quite good-humoredly, that I should remember" (236). Relations between men are always dangerously marked by violence and danger, as the quotation Dupin writes on the substitute letter he leaves for D—— suggests:

—Un dessein si funeste
s'il n'est digne d'Atrée, est digne
de Thyeste. (236)

Thyestes has seduced Atreus's wife in Crebillon's play. In return, Atreus kills and cooks Thyestes' sons and feeds them to him at a banquet. Hence, despite or perhaps because of his domestic life with the narrator, Dupin returns heterosexuality to its buffering role and simultaneously suggests that desires between men, presented here in oral form, harbor within them grotesque and cannibalistic violence. Just as in *The Scarlet Letter,* such desires pose a fantasied threat to the integrity of the subject, an anxiety that is expressed in terms of a threat to the integrity of the masculine body.

The effects of the closing quotation replicate in sensational form the effects of the device through which Dupin re-purloins the letter. During Dupin's first visit, he purposely leaves a gold snuff box in order to provide a context for a second visit. He arranges a distraction so that the letter might be surreptitiously seized:

"The next morning I called for the snuff-box, when we resumed, quite eagerly, the conversation of the preceding day. While thus engaged, however, a loud report, as if of a pistol, was heard immediately beneath the windows of the hotel, and was succeeded by a series of fearful screams, and the shoutings of a mob. D—— rushed to a casement, threw it open, and looked out. . . . The disturbance in the street had been occasioned by the frantic behavior of a man with a musket. He had fired it among a crowd of women and children. It proved, however, to have been without ball, and the fellow was suffered to go his way. . . . The pretended lunatic was a man in my own pay." (235)

Dupin's ruse suggests that D——'s feminization is a cover for a passionate, conventionally masculine interest in violence. Since Dupin stages this violence and obviously shares such an interest, the relation of doubling arguably continues, but only in terms of the rupturing distance violence produces, evident in the sudden distinction in their respective objects of attention. Dupin's choice of ruse shifts attention to the family, since this shot has been fired in a crowd of "women and children," a narrative detail that calls attention to itself by its apparent superfluousness. *Any* shot fired on a crowded street, after all, would almost undoubtedly create the desired disturbance, since even sturdy adult men would be thrown into a panic by a lunatic with a pistol. The story has no apparent need to specify women and children as the victims of Dupin's orchestrated terror, a terror that would be little diminished, one notes, by the subsequent discovery that the apparent lunatic in question had improperly loaded his gun.

These narrative details suggest the extent to which "The Purloined Letter" has as its unconscious the terroristic violence against women that has served as the focus of the prior stories, the trace of which here reemerges. This apparently irrelevant violence masculinizes the question of method in "The Purloined Letter" and suggests the failure of the story's system of homosocial exchanges to sufficiently contain and negate the Queen. Anyone, finally, might utilize empathy to understand and predict the behavior of others; it is Dupin's ruse that most effectively genders the letter's retrieval and restoration.

The incident suggests the ingrained and troubling uses of violence between men and against women in the culture of the United States. Violence sublimates same-sex desire and reinforces paranoid distances between men. At the same time, it terrorizes and subjugates women who are necessary to establish the heterosexuality of the masculine order. In the case of this episode, it might not be too much to say that Dupin's violence in "The Purloined Letter" functions to terrorize women into mothers, since it is culture's eternally hyphenated relation between women and children that his apparently random violence cements.

PART 2

～⁂⁂⁂～

Circuits of Desire

AUTHORITY IN THE EARLY AND LATE FICTION OF HENRY JAMES

*T*he novels of Henry James are natural subjects given the central themes of this book: the narrative construction of authority and authorship and the pressure exerted by such constructions on the representation of gender and sexuality. No U.S. writer has had a stronger will to cultural authority or a more exalted sense of the authority of literature than Henry James. As Richard Brodhead says, "[A]uthorship never had the status merely of a secular profession for James, but instead of a vocation in the religious sense: a life-structuring task through which one both performs one's work in the world and discharges one's obligations to the source of one's being."[1] The demanding terms of this engagement virtually guaranteed that no public response to his work could serve as an adequate validation of his efforts, a shortfall of appreciation that would contribute heavily to the cavernous depressions that punctuated his creative career. Indeed, one obvious message of the prefaces to the New York edition, prophetic of its subsequent commercial failure, is that the only adequate reader of James in the nineteenth century was James himself.

John Carlos Rowe, in *The Theoretical Dimensions of Henry James*, has described the conflict between James's quest for authority and his concomitant identification with the disempowered positions of women.[2] This conflict is complicated in turn by the question of James's apparent homosexuality, the importance of which has become more and more clear in the decade since the publication of *The Theoretical Dimensions of Henry James*. Recent work on James's sexuality, in turn, generally has not addressed how that sexuality intersects with his problematic desire for authority of a conventionally masculine kind. It is James's sexuality, I will argue, that disrupts the construction of authority in his texts and that crucially governs his deployment of women. If women serve as a threat to male authority in literature, the use of female characters also allows its narrative construction in terms of the dominant heterosexuality of the tradition of the novel. This construction occurs through the telling of a successful story, and successful stories in an oppressively heterosexual culture must be told in heterosexual terms.

James's relation to this fact of social power produces an agonizing dialectic in his fiction, which I will establish in terms of two sets of paired texts. In the uneven but still compelling *Roderick Hudson,* his first major novel, James demonstrates the power of homoerotic investment to block the construction of narrative authority and, at great cost to the novel, seeks refuge in the heterosexual and heterosexualizing glare of Christina Light. In *The American,* chastened by his brush with narrative disaster in his previous book, James holds resolutely to the conventional lines of the heterosexual marriage plot and produces authority out of a distanced and ironic critique of manhood in the United States of the nineteenth century, a critique that nonetheless proves paradigmatic for his later fiction. In *The Ambassadors* and *The Wings of the Dove,* James borrows massively from his earlier two texts for the revisionary project of establishing formal control over the relation of heterosexual and homosexual desire in his fiction. Nonetheless, this later pair repeats the dialectical relation between homosexual and heterosexual texts in reversed order. *The Ambassadors* comically acknowledges but radically marginalizes same-sex desire in Strether's project of heterosexual self-construction. *The Wings of the Dove* focuses primarily on the exploration of perverse and deviant desire but does so under the countervailing shelter of Milly's heterosexualizing wings.

CHAPTER 3

Early Authorizations in Roderick Hudson and The American

*J*ust as Hawthorne composed *The Scarlet Letter* in the midst of enormous career pressures, James needed to demonstrate in his first two major texts that his vocational choice had been a correct one. The young author's tentative and incomplete mastery of his craft is a theme of James's treatment of both novels in the prefaces to the New York edition. His lengthy progress from early awkwardness to later mastery produces the general narrative that runs throughout the prefaces, a narrative first announced in the preface to *Roderick Hudson* as the "wondrous adventure" of the artist's "whole unfolding."[1] If James journeys toward increasing consciousness, however, he nevertheless consistently argues that large portions of the process of literary composition must remain unconscious. In considering the source of the revisionary impulse even so late as the preface to *The Golden Bowl,* James speaks to "the manifold delicate things, . . . the inscrutable, the indefinable, that minister to deep and quite confident processes of change. It is enough, in any event, to be both beguiled and mystified by evolutions so near home, without sounding strange and probably even more abysmal waters."[2] It is by glancing back at his early work, James argues in the preface to *Roderick Hudson,* that the artist profits from his notes' "own tendency to multiply, with the implication, thereby, of a memory much enriched" (1040).

Compared to this retrospectively produced consciousness, the forward-moving process of writing *Roderick Hudson* is described as a "shy and groping duration" in which he attempted to make plain the "ache" of his love for

Italy: "One fact about it indeed outlives all others; the fact that, as the loved Italy was the scene of my fiction—so much more loved than one has ever been able, even after fifty efforts, to say!—and as having had to leave it persisted as an inward ache. . . . Little enough of that medium may the novel . . . seem to supply; yet half the actual interest lurks for me in the earnest, baffled intention of making it felt" (1042). This "baffled intention" largely characterizes the young author's floundering in the midst of his first major novel. James remarks that he had "but hugged the shore" on previous occasions; now, he had "put quite out to sea" with a "'complicated' subject" (1040). That the novel began to appear in serial form before its completion only added to the pressures on James in this "embarrassed phase" (1041). As James remarks, "[T]o have 'liked' so much writing it . . . and yet not, at the end of so many months, to have come through, was clearly still to have fallen short of any facility and any confidence, though the long-drawn process now most appeals to memory, I confess, by this very quality of shy and groping duration" (1042).

Such uncertainties and difficulties for the roughly thirty-year-old James have echoes in both the anxieties of Roderick and those of his mentor, the thirtyish Rowland Mallet. If Roderick embodies the dilemmas of a young visual artist whose place in the art world has yet to be earned, Rowland more specifically embodies the novelist's problem of how to complete his narrative. James's novel begins with the question of what Rowland Mallet will do with his life and money, and it is this problem that must be answered in order for the narrative to find its proper end. As Rowland says to his cousin Cecilia, "Do you know I sometimes think that I'm a man of genius, half finished? The genius has been left out, the faculty of expression is wanting; but the need for expression remains, and I spend my days groping for the latch of a closed door."[3] His decision to serve as mentor for Roderick is framed as an "unimpeachable inspiration" to set Roderick "on the path of glory." Cecilia, meanwhile, if she is to be robbed of Roderick's company, looks forward to accounts of the sculptor's progress from "stage to stage," accounts that she requires Rowland to write (199).

In one of these epistolary midnarrative accounts, Rowland confesses his own bafflement and despair at Roderick's disintegration. As he indicates, "When I think of a little talk we had about the 'salubrity of genius,' I feel my ears tingle. If this is salubrity, give me raging disease! . . . I don't understand a jot; it's a hideous, mocking mystery; I give it up! I don't in the least give it up. . . . I sit holding my head by the hour, racking my brain, wondering what under heaven is to be done" (357). The authority most immediately threatened in this passage is Rowland's own, since it is the accuracy of his own claim of the "salubrity of genius" that has come into question. James figures his crisis of authority as an agonizing crisis of composition, since hours of holding one's head in one's hands and racking one's brain suggest the presence of a desk or table, and since these metaphors come to Rowland in the throes of writing. James, in turn, admits to an analogue of Rowland's anxiety in his preface. His problem as a young novelist resulted from the difficulty of representing Roderick's fall: "Roderick's disintegration, a gradual process, and of which the exhibitional interest is exactly that it *is* gradual and occasional, and thereby traceable and watchable, swallows two years in a mouthful . . . and thus renders the whole view the disservice of appearing to present him as a morbidly special case. . . . My mistake on Roderick's behalf . . . is that, at the rate at which he falls to pieces he seems to place himself beyond our understanding and our sympathy" (1047). "The thing escapes . . . with its life" (1047), James concludes. In so escaping, needless to say, the text helps preserve the life of the young author as well.

The difficulty of sufficiently narrativizing Roderick's collapse, in turn, also interestingly recapitulates at least part of the problem with Roderick. Even in the early stages of the novel, we are warned that Roderick lives "too fast," having seized the "key-note of the old world" in less than a month (225). This tendency to narrative foreshortening extends in an even more extreme form in his art. James's sculptor works only from inspiration of an exalted sort, hoping to reassert the capacity of the ancients to "understand beauty in the large, ideal way" (243). James understandably spends only a little time describing statues that Roderick intends as pure instantiations of idealized subjects. Roderick's problem is in part that he can never, by definition, have a procedure. When Roderick was inspired, as Rowland Mallet observes, his "day passed in a single sustained pulsation" (232). When Roderick was uninspired, his day correspondingly disintegrated: "[D]iscontented with his work, he applied himself to it by fits and starts, he declared that he didn't know what was coming over him; he was turning into a man of moods" (262). Not surprisingly, unlike a novelist or a corrupt sculptor, Roderick finds subjects hard to come by: "A sculptor is such a confoundedly special genius; there are so few subjects he can treat, so few things in life that bear upon his work, so few moods in which he himself is inclined to it" (314). Roderick paradoxically can be quite voluble about his failures and dry spells; about a Hudson success there is nothing or little to say. To offer explanations or analysis would be to indulge in the grotesque contortions Roderick's art obdurately refuses.

Hudson is opposed by the knowing Gloriani, later to reappear in *The Ambassadors*, an artist who eschews inspiration for technique and cleverness, and about whose work there is apparently everything to say even if James doesn't say it.[4] Indeed, Rowland invites Gloriani to his dinner for Roderick in part because Gloriani is "a great talker, and a very picturesque one" (237). Gloriani represents "art with a worldly motive, skill unleavened by faith, the mere base maximum of cleverness." He promises, when Roderick "finds himself sitting face to face with his lump of clay, with his empty canvas, with his sheet of blank paper, waiting in vain for the revelation to be made," to teach him "how to console" himself (247–248).

Roderick's talent and his art, then, by their nature resist narrativization. His sense of sculpture echoes that of Walter Pater's *The Renaissance*, published in 1873 and an immediate sensation. Eric Savoy, in a recent essay on the interrelations of James, Pater, and homotextual relations, provides evidence from James's letters that James sent a review of Pater's text to *The Independent* in 1873, a review that has subsequently disappeared, and finds numerous ensuing echoes of Pater's critical language in James's own. There is little doubt, then, that James had given Pater's writing serious consideration prior to writing *Roderick Hudson*.[5]

In his section on Winckelmann Pater discusses the difference between sculpture and other forms of expression:

> In poetry and painting, the situation predominates over the character; in sculpture, the character over the situation. Excluded by the proper limitation of its material from the development of exquisite situations, it has to choose from a select number of types . . . independently of any special situation into which they may be thrown. Sculpture finds the secret of its power in presenting these types. . . . This it effects not by accumulation of detail but by abstracting from it. . . . Men and women, again, in the hurry of life, often wear the sharp impress of one absorbing motive. . . . All such instances may be ranged under the *grotesque;* and the Hellenic ideal has nothing in common with the grotesque.[6]

The introduction of Pater to the question of *Roderick Hudson,* and through Pater to Winckelmann as well, suggests the crucial importance of the problem of homoeroticism to this early text of James. As Pater knew, Winckelmann's aesthetics were not separable from his interest in young men, and he serves as the forerunner of later Victorian efforts to justify same-sex desire in terms of classic forms of ideal beauty. According to Pater, "[T]hat his affinity with

Hellenism was not merely intellectual, that the subtler threads of temperament were inwoven in it, is proved by his romantic, fervent friendships with
young men. He has known, he says, many young men more beautiful than
Guido's archangel. These friendships . . . perfected his reconciliation to the
spirit of Greek sculpture" (123). Pater later quotes Winckelmann to this effect: "I have noticed that those who . . . are moved little or not at all by the
beauty of men seldom have an impartial, vital, inborn instinct for beauty in
art. To such persons the beauty of Greek art will ever seem wanting, because
its supreme beauty is rather male than female" (123). As Robert Aldrich observes, Winckelmann is an important eighteenth-century forefather of "northern" gay men who journey to Mediterranean lands in search of sexual pleasure
and social tolerance.[7] At least late in his life, according to Michael Moon's
recent essay focusing on the Venetian sections of *The Wings of the Dove,*
James himself may well have been one of these men.[8]

   James advertises with some explicitness that his talented young sculptor embodies questions of homoerotic desire.[9] At the beginning of *Roderick
Hudson,* as Rowland Mallet searches for marriageable women, his cousin
Cecilia offers him a male substitute, and in terms that highlight physical attractiveness as an issue: "If I refused last night to show you a pretty girl, I
can at least show you a pretty boy" (177). She refers, of course, to Roderick's
statue *Thirst,* but Rowland moves from collecting the statue to collecting
Roderick, as pretty as the sculpture himself with his "admirably chiselled and
finished" features and a smile that plays over them "as gracefully as a breeze
among flowers" (181). Mallet, interestingly, is of Dutch descent, which in
this novel suggests that he is an early Winckelmannesque prototype of the
northern European gone "Mediterranean" over an attractive youth. Like the
Winckelmann we get in Pater, who "was thirty years old before he enjoyed a
single favour of fortune" (119) and who "suffered too much" in his youth
and thus deserved the beauty of Rome (114), Rowland is the product of a
desolate childhood and, despite his father's wealth, "the education of a poor
man's son" (174). Rowland, too, finds himself feeling that "life owed him . . . a
compensation" (370).

   The language of Roderick's death also suggests that the novel has been
driven by Rowland's erotic desires. Certainly, Roderick's fatal Alpine plunge
has been uncannily foreshadowed by Rowland's Christlike scene of temptation earlier in the narrative, when he contemplates contributing to Roderick's
destruction, as he arguably does, in order to wrest from him the affection of
Mary Garland. The temptation to somehow destroy Roderick by helping the
"graceful and beautiful" youth plunge like "a diver . . . into a misty gulf"

generates imagery of physical violation and dishonor between Rowland and Roderick (371). In attendance are oddly disreputable monks, including a "shabby, senile, red-faced brother," who admits Rowland to a Franciscan convent with "maudlin friendliness," and a replacement monk "reading his greasy little breviary" (372). The wonder of this garden in a monastery, high on the mountain, is "how it keeps from slipping down, in full consummation of its bereaved forlornness into the nakedly romantic gorge beneath" (372).

The interweaving of the erotic with death and disaster suggests a profound fear of erotic engagement, a fear of what would happen to Rowland should he plunge into that "nakedly romantic gorge." At the same time, Rowland's ethical temptation is a narrative temptation as well. If overt homosexuality is not generally narratable as itself in the nineteenth century, in what forms might such desires be narrated? One such form, as I suggested in the introduction, is the plot of death and disaster, which authorizes a violent and genocidal penetration of the male body, and which also produces emergencies that authorize the expression of tenderness and the giving of care. The most culturally acceptable culmination of desire between men involves the annihilation or near annihilation of one of the parties, and it is to this narrative that *Roderick Hudson* succumbs. Even as it foregrounds Rowland's love for Mary Garland as the precipitating cause of his break with Roderick, even as Roderick continues to act out his fatal attraction to Christina Light, it uses the emergency of Roderick's disappearance to produce a shadowing climax of sexual desire and frustration. Beside himself with anxiety, Rowland searches for Roderick at "low, foul doors" of chalets on which he "thumped" with "nervous, savage anger" (508). He then encounters the antithesis of desire, an odd "cretin" at one of the doors who "grinned at Rowland over his goitre" (508). Finally, Rowland finds Roderick's body, which looks "admirably handsome" (510) despite the likelihood of finding some "horrible physical dishonor" (509). It was "as if Violence, having done her work, had stolen away in shame" (510). The text is mute as to the source of this violence; the cliff from which he has fallen only lifts "its blank and stony face above him, with no care now but to drink the sunshine on which his eyes were closed" (510). Roderick has turned his face to the wall.

Earlier in this discussion, I quoted James to the effect that Roderick's decline is insufficiently narrativized. This insufficiency, I would argue, is produced by and contributes to the text's anxiety over sexual desire between men. If desire between men in the nineteenth century lacks relatively accessible narrative forms, then the lonely and difficult attempt to work out the terms of such narratives exists in a state of tension with the author's attempt to write himself into the "facility" and "confidence" of authorship (1042). If James bravely makes such an attempt in *Roderick Hudson,* he nonetheless indicates in his preface that, after many months in the midst of composition, he still had an incomplete and difficult-to-manage book on his hands.

Roderick Hudson is saved as a narrative by the advent of Christina Light, a woman of such devastating beauty that all men supposedly have little choice but to desire her, and a character who suggests a cultural need for precisely such heterosexualizing mythic figures to exist.[10] She not only guarantees that *Roderick Hudson* can be read as a heterosexual novel; she presents a heterosexual narrative of Roderick's fall. As James suggests, in the absence of other fully articulated causal narratives, she functions as the "well-nigh sole agent of his catastrophe" (1047–1048), despite the failure of this explanation "to commend itself to our sense of truth and proportion" (1048). So useful does the red-herring princess nonetheless prove that James would employ her again in *The Princess Casamassima,* this time as a flashy disguise of his preoccupation with relations between Paul Muniement and Hyacinth Robinson.

The American

An understanding of the complex interrelations between sexuality and narrative in *Roderick Hudson* also helps clarify the problems of James's next major production. The pressures on James to produce a successful work, especially given the emotional complexity of continuing to rely on the financial support of his family, were intense.[11] He would respond to these pressures in *The American* by writing a novel that focuses on a protagonist, on the whole distinctly unlike himself, in a novel that contains much less in the way of deviant desire to trouble the unfolding of its heterosexual plot. It is in part by avoiding difficulties confronted in *Roderick Hudson,* then, that James produces his first major, fully realized production, one that attracted significant critical attention in the United States from its serialization in the *Atlantic Monthly,* and one that earned him a period of financial security.[12]

If *Roderick Hudson* marks a process of earnest and disturbed striving for both characters and author, *The American* would be written in a much different key, one attuned to its different protagonist, Christopher Newman, and to what I will be identifying as a formidable and characteristic "ease." This ease even dominates James's memories of the writing of the book in his preface to the New York edition. In it, James admits to "an eagerness on behalf of my recital, that must recklessly enough have overridden anxieties of every sort. . . . I seem to recall no other like connexion in which the case was met, to my measure, by so fond a complacency, in which my subject can have appeared so apt to take care of itself" (1053). Though James ruefully remarks that he might, in fact, "have taken much better care of it" (1053), he nonetheless now has "no memory of a disturbing doubt; once the man himself was imaged to me (and *that* germination is a process almost always untraceable), he must have walked into the situation as by taking a pass-key from his pocket" (1056).

Two elements are largely missing from *The American* that disrupt and complicate the narrative surface of *Roderick Hudson* and make for James's compositional ease: a direct encounter with complicated questions of homoeroticism and a related crisis of literary authority within the narrative such an encounter produces.

The American, by and large, focuses on Newman's heterosexual relations, as if the lesson of *Roderick Hudson* had been learned all too well, and leaves undeveloped and narratively isolated the erotic implications of its encounters between men. I say this despite the plausible arguments of Cheryl Tornsey and William Veeder that important homoerotic dynamics are at work in Newman's travels with Babcock in chapter 5 of the novel. Tornsey suggests Babcock is modeled on C. S. Peirce, who traveled briefly with Henry in the seventies, and reads the statue Newman gives Babcock, a monk with a capon visible through the gap in his robe, in terms of a thematics of fetishization, castration, and feminization traditionally associated with the homoerotic.[13] Veeder, in the course of making an argument about homoeroticism in *The Portrait of a Lady,* suggests that Babcock is a critical representation of William James, whom a number of critics have seen as an early and important object of Henry's homoerotic desires.[14]

Whatever desires the scene contains, the traces of homoeroticism in it are muffled and difficult to read, and they are muffled and difficult to read because they exist at a substantial remove from the story of Newman's failed courtship of Claire de Cintre: they lead to little and have no larger context in the novel. This marks a distinct difference between *The American* and *Roderick Hudson,* to which the brief chapter on Babcock, with its monks, its grotesque sculpture, its meditations on "'art for art'" and moralism, might be taken to allude.[15] Babcock might, in fact, be more at home in the earlier text but finds in Newman a maddeningly complacent subject. Even after his anguished letter, Newman will not respond in kind. After all, "[h]is good nature checked his resenting the young minister's lofty admonitions, and his tough, inelastic sense of humor forbade his taking them seriously" (582).

Newman's gift of the statue to the minister, then, suggests a vulnerability Newman does not share. Whatever desires inform their relationship, the self-conscious unease is all on Babcock's side.

A much more central male friendship in the novel occurs between Newman and Madame de Cintre's brother, Valentin, but in terms of this relationship the narrative actively refuses questions of same-sex desire instead of cordoning them off in individual relationships. This refusal is evident in Newman's visit to Valentin's rooms, located in the basement of an old house with "one of those large, sunless, humid gardens" behind it (610). In this interior, located safely within the interior of James's heterosexual plot, *The American* suggests the potentially disintegrative force of erotic relations between men. The "low, dusky, contracted" room is "crowded with curious bric-a-brac" (610):

> Here and there was one of those uncomfortable tributes to elegance
> in which the upholsterer's art, in France, is so prolific; a curtained
> recess with a sheet of looking-glass in which, among the shadows,
> you could see nothing; a divan on which, for its festoons and furbe-
> lows, you could not sit: a fire-place draped, flounced, and frilled to
> the complete exclusion of fire. The young man's possessions were
> in picturesque disorder, and his apartment was pervaded by the odor
> of cigars, mingled with perfumes more inscrutable. Newman thought
> it a damp, gloomy place to live in, and was puzzled by the obstruc-
> tive and fragmentary character of the furniture. (610)

James's description is seductively anal, yet the apparently "straight" Newman does not or will not get it. His participation in his new surroundings is fundamentally thwarted by his sense of the unnaturalness of Valentin's dusky, androgynous, and scented nest. Nothing can be used in the manner to which Newman is accustomed, and he fails to appreciate that familiar objects might be put to new uses. Far from suggesting narcissism, this world disturbs his self-image, much as Valentin's shadowy, decorative mirror refuses to return a comforting reflection. At this moment, prophetic of *The Ambassadors,* Newman could be said to personify a U.S. readership so obdurately heterosexual as to render futile the depiction of discordant desires.

The reading of this encounter as homoerotic receives reinforcement by the text's panic in the next paragraph, in which Valentin himself takes rhetorical but hollow-sounding steps to assure us of his overwhelming heterosexual interests: "[H]e had a vast deal to say about women, and he used frequently to indulge in sentimental and ironical apostrophes to these authors of his joys and woes. 'Oh, the women, the women, and the things they have made me do!'" (611). As opposed to *Roderick Hudson,* where Rowland and Roderick always have an important and unmediated bond to each other despite their simultaneous interests in Mary Garland and Christina Light, the relation between Valentin and Newman occurs in order to further Newman's courtship of Madame de Cintre. If the narrative contains a clue to the potential strength of the bond between Newman and Valentin, it lies hidden by the latter's extermination. James gets him out of the way rather than explore either the nature of his relationship to Newman, after Madame de Cintre's entombment in a Carmelite grave, or the relation Valentin would finally have, in life, to his family's disgraceful behavior. Instead, Valentin dies in a seamy defense of heterosexual manly honor.

The less-than-brilliant Newman effectively has little in common with his author, as the narrative quickly makes clear. As has been commonly noted, James suggests that an important cause of Newman's limitations, or an important associated symptom of the cause, is his failure to appreciate art and literature, or art and literature of the right type.[16] Thus, at the novel's beginning, he cannot judge the atrocious nature of Madame Noemie's copies, and in regard to women we are told that "many of the common traditions . . . were with him fresh personal impressions; he had never read a novel!" (541–542).[17] In *Roderick Hudson,* James makes the genesis of literary authority an internal and direct matter, as the aesthetically minded Hudson and Mallet struggle like James to construct positions of secure authority for themselves in the world. In *The American,* the authority of author and character are inversely proportional as a consequence of the ironic distance between the two. James's authority, in other words, will depend on the skill with which he surgically dissects his long-legged and laconic countryman. Such men, James shows, are not impenetrable.

The American settles into an effective analysis of its heterosexual hero. Though his account is essentially negative in regard to Newman, James proceeds to construct a paradigm of heterosexual manhood that serves as an important core of his later fictions, a paradigm consistently associated with the trope of "ease." This "ease," with its desiring relationship to normative masculinity, is invoked from the beginning of the novel in the opening description of Newman: "On a brilliant day in May, in the year 1868, a gentleman was reclining at his ease on the great circular divan which at that period occupied the centre of the Salon Carré, in the Museum of the Louvre" (515). The implications of this ease, however, are complex and contradictory.[18] On the one hand, Newman's ease represents his heterosexual masculine strength, blissfully convinced of its agency in the world. Newman, we are told, "appeared to possess that kind of health and strength which, when found in perfection, are the most impressive—the physical capital which the owner does nothing to 'keep up'" (516). This kind of ease is actually a kinetic energy, and at one point in the novel James tells us that "to move at his ease" Newman "needed . . . imperatively the sense of great risks and great prizes" (562). This ease is all readiness.

On the other hand, Newman's journey to Europe represents a more dangerous kind of ease as well, one associated with lassitude and retrogression. Newman has come to Europe in order to turn his back on the world of earnest masculine striving, looking for an ease of pleasure and for matrimony. As he puts it, "I don't want to work at pleasure, any more than I played at work. I want to take it easily. I feel deliciously lazy, and I should like to spend six months as I am now, sitting under a tree and listening to a band" (534).

In the tangled reality of Europe, Newman's ease is ultimately mistaken, yet penultimately has its enabling aspects as well. To put it simply, Newman actually comes close to marrying Claire de Cintre because he presumes he can; he sees none of the obvious problems. Even in regard to Madame de Cintre's fatally formidable mother, Newman blithely confesses to Mrs. Tristram that "after all it was very easy to get on with her; it always was easy to get on with out-and-out rascals" (678). If such equanimity lures one to disaster, its absence, on the other hand, may also prove disabling. M. Nioche, Madame Noemie's embattled father, lacks all ease and all agency in confronting the chances of existence: "His little ill-made coat, desperately brushed . . . told the story of a person who had 'had losses.' . . . Among other things M. Nioche had lost courage. Adversity had not only ruined him, it had frightened him, and he was evidently going through his remnant of life on tiptoe" (520–521). In contrast, Newman rhetorically asks Valentin, "What should I be afraid of? You can't hurt me unless you kill me by some violent means. . . . I can't die of illness, I am too ridiculously tough. . . . I can't lose my wife, I shall take too good care of her. I may lose my money . . . but . . . I shall make twice as much again. So what have I to be afraid of?" (713).

The perpetually uneasy James undertakes an answer to Newman's question, systematically suggesting the genesis of Newman's character in repression and denial. Newman has his merits and abilities to be sure, as a long tradition of criticism on the novel has suggested, and in his relation with Noemie Nioche, James goes so far as to tell us that his hero in fact "understood her better than he confessed" (572), but he lacks a normal Jamesian breadth of perception, hovering, in fact, not far across the border from James's fools. Some of this narrowness is no doubt due to the obliviousness of a traveler to a strange land, but Newman ignores the potential dangers of such obliviousness: he does not know and fails to sense the dangers of not knowing.[19]

Certainly, what we know of Newman's past suggests that he has had ample opportunity to learn the dangers of the world. By age fourteen, for example, "necessity had taken him . . . into the street," an allusion, one must presume, to the unmentioned loss of his parents. He had contracted "a bitter sense of the waste of precious things" in the Civil War and had later, from unspecified incidents, known "bitter failure as well as brilliant success." He had claimed "ill-luck" as "his bedfellow" and had periods in which "whatever he touched turned, not to gold, but to ashes" (532–533). He ought, in short, to have a well-honed sense of the possibility of disaster, of the necessity of caution, and of the machinations of humanity. Instead, he seems to have derived from his experience a polished talent for forgetting the wounds of the past and reconstituting a blanket of masculine self-sufficiency. Traces of these old wounds, however, surface at odd moments with the overwhelming force of the repressed.

Such a surfacing is evident in the incident that sends Newman fleeing to Europe. In the middle of a feud with a competitor, we are told, he feels "mortal disgust" as "abruptly as an old wound that begins to ache" (536). The wound in this case would seem related to Newman's disgust for the "waste" of the Civil War, but this surfacing so traumatizes Newman that he flees without even determining if his competitor gets the large sum of money at stake. In a stunning act of blindness, he famously proclaims himself a new man and heads for what he describes, with equal blindness, as a new world.

The wrecked Newman must seek to reconstitute himself through what Tristram calls the "easily learned" (534) art of leisure. This leisure represents a rebellion against a masculine world of business, linked for Newman with "waste" and onrushing death. Leisure means a swerve back to childhood, back to being a "new man inside" his "old skin" (536), and to being "as simple as a little child" (534). The fact that Newman's own childhood reached an abrupt end at fourteen, after unnamed, repressed disasters, only reinforces the sense that Newman's newness has ironic implications beyond seeking it in the old world of Europe: Newman turns to a reconstitution of his tragically lost and shattered past.

Numerous passages suggest a specific, conventionally Freudian object of desire. Newman, in searching for a wife, wants to be reborn as a "new man," and in that newness to become again a child and to recover the "old-world" relation to the breast. Even as Newman is describing to Tristram the events that brought him to Europe, for example, his eyes unconsciously betray the nature of his desire. He notes that "buxom, white-capped nurses, seated along the benches, were offering to their infant charges the amplest facilities for nutrition. There was an easy, homely gaiety in the whole scene, and Christopher Newman felt that it was most characteristically Parisian" (530). Shortly thereafter, Newman repeats the observation, a repetition that reflects James's anxiety that we perceive the point. This time he observes sentimentally that "nurses and babies . . . imparted to the scene a kind of primordial, pastoral simplicity" (532).

Newman romances Claire de Cintre into a deceivingly attractive incarnation of such regressive desires, as he slides in his fantasy between the positions of parent and child. The former inhabits his desire to take care of her; the latter is a kind of unencumbered visual nursing as he drinks in the features of his prize: "[H]is desire to interpose between her and the troubles of life had the quality of a young mother's eagerness to protect the sleep of her first-born child. Newman was simply charmed. . . . Newman at last was enjoying, purely, freely, deeply. Certain of Madame de Cintre's personal qualities—the luminous sweetness of her eyes, the delicate mobility of her face, the deep liquidity of her voice—filled all his consciousness" (675–676).

The new-found satisfaction of the European world addresses the oral aches in which Newman's American dissatisfactions were expressed. When Newman enters San Francisco James compares him to Benjamin Franklin but specifies that he lacks "the penny loaf necessary to the performance" (532–533). When he is pushed in the street at fourteen, it is "to earn that night's supper" (532). His success consists in the fact that "afterwards, whenever he had none, it was because he had gone without it to use the money for something else, a keener pleasure or a finer profit" (532–533). His hunger comes to be partially palliated by masculine satisfactions that substitute for an ease-conferring female attachment. Finally, however, the very terms of attaining that substitute nurture through competitive masculine relations fill him with "disgust"—a word that implies oral revulsion and an inability to eat (536). Rather than confront the content of that "disgust," however, Newman flees forward by fleeing back to other paradigms of satisfaction.

The pattern of return in Newman's desires suggests the larger pattern of repetitions around which the novel is structured. *The American* webs together repetitions that consistently reintroduce the past into the present of its characters and so unsettle both Newman's conceit of rupture in his experience and the general idea of a quotidian stability. Madame de Cintre, for example, is twice caught in controversial marriage situations that prove damaging for a male participant. Madame Bellegarde twice is involved in skullduggery concerning her daughter's marriage, over which she refuses to relinquish control. Newman twice forgoes revenge for suffered wounds, and this forbearance may itself resemble earlier incidents. Mrs. Tristram twice unsettles Newman's ease: first, by introducing him to Claire and, second, by telling him that the Bellegardes had presumed upon his good nature. M. Nioche threatens a violent and dangerous response to Noemie's sexually unrestrained behavior, just as he earlier had entertained fantasies, in response to his wife's behavior, that he was for once "a man to be afraid of" (563). Valentin announces, when he hears of his family's behavior, that "it is time . . . to withdraw" (776), just as his father had renounced life with his wife years earlier.

Even the account of Newman's earlier career had indicated a repeated rise and fall in his fortunes, and he had predicted, in terms of his erratic swerve to Europe, that he would eventually swerve back to business and back to the United States in much the same way: "I dare say that a twelvemonth hence the operation will be reversed. The pendulum will swing back again. I shall be sitting in the gondola or on a dromedary, and all of a sudden I shall want to clear out" (537). Newman's attempt to domesticate both rupture and repetition in his life in terms of a cheerful, pendulum-like inevitability, does nothing to prepare him for the devastating blow that sends him in full flight from Europe. This blow is the loss of Claire de Cintre to the Carmelite convent, but its center—the heart of Old World evil in the novel—is Mrs. Bread's vision of the murder of Claire's father, the marquis:

> What was killing him was the dreadful fits of pain in his stomach. . . .
> The doctor found something that gave him great comfort—some
> white stuff that . . . always made him easier. . . . I believe it was in
> this way. He had a fit of his great pain, and he asked her for his medicine. Instead of giving it to him she went and poured it away, before
> his eyes. Then . . . he was frightened, he was terrified. "You want to
> kill me," he said. "Yes, M. le Marquis, I want to kill you," says my
> lady, and sits down and fixes her eyes upon him. You know my lady's
> eyes, I think, sir; it was with them she killed him; it was with the
> terrible strong will she put into them. It was like a frost on flowers.
> (811, 819)

Mrs. Bread produces for Newman a vision of a primal family violence.[20] The bliss of Newman's dreaming-back derived from his uncritical belief in ste-reotypic norms of gender, his belief in the painting we initially see him view-ing with pleasure, "Murillo's beautiful moon-borne Madonna" (515). What he finds instead is a crime scene that owes its gothic power as much to the transgression of conventional roles as to its literal content of the murder of the marquis—the victim, in other words, is normative identity. The mother in this scene kills through the evil eye; she has control of a tube of milky-white medicine that suggests an erasure of the distinction between the penis and the breast; and, far from suggesting sentimental maternity, she attempts to kill Papa with her eldest son's help. The extraterrestrial mother in *Alien* pales in comparison.

At the same time, it is crucial to note that matricide, as much as patri-cide, is the hidden content of this scene. It is against Madame Bellegarde in particular that James enlists our readerly resentment for her matriarchal per-versity in relation to her family. If she were killed into the self-effacing femi-ninity of her daughter, the conventionally paternal marquis would yet live. She thus stands for a cultural possibility that must be done away with if the culturally induced suppressions of oedipal structures and the normative mas-culine identities they support are to be maintained. Newman's masculine ease, in other words, requires a backdrop of enforced sentimentality, of feminine quiescence.

Newman's vision of the marquis's murder forms a logical conclusion in *The American* to his retrogressive journey. We are prepared for such a scene not only by the persistent repetitions of the text but by the striking lack, in James's account of Newman, of a typical past. We know nothing at all about him prior to the age of fourteen; we are given no memories of anything like a family of origin. It is this puzzling lack, which unavoidably suggests a re-pressed trauma in Newman's past, that finds an answer here in a primal scene of familial disaster and maternal betrayal. What allows Newman to recall from the unconscious a trauma of this magnitude is precisely the uncanniness of its presentation to him—the uncanny finding of his own memory in the memory of another.

Rowe suggests that more and better historical and political knowledge of France might be the proper antidote to uncanniness in the text and that James plants plentiful hints through which much more complex motivations for the behavior of *The American*'s French characters can be posited.[21] His informative reading, to my mind, excessively domesticates the uncanniness of the text on Newman's behalf. If political and historical knowledge might pro-duce the French world as an everyday affair for Newman, it is also precisely the belief in a rational world that sets one up for its uncanny disruption. Rowe argues that, in the final sections of the novel, "our reading experience is now constantly at odds with Newman's impressions. While we see nothing but reflections of Newman, Newman sees nothing but unaccountable events, strange coincidences, unexpected revelations" (85). As I read it, Newman generally clings to his matter-of-fact world, while he remains largely oblivious to the uncanny repetitions and strange coincidences the reader perceives. And, while Newman demonstrably contributes to his disaster, he has not produced the gothic murder of the marquis, which is the center of uncanniness in the text and can be seen as a veritable grab bag of many Freudian signs of the uncanny: illness, paternal death, implications of castration, stories told by nurses, and the "evil eye."[22]

The phenomenon of uncanniness can be best explained at the level of authorship and narrative, largely in the terms that have guided this book. In attempting to write about a world exterior to the text, the author may well unconsciously produce reflections of his own unconscious, aided and abetted precisely by a good-faith pursuit of the real. Freud tells the story of repeatedly attempting to escape a street of "painted women" in a small town in Italy, only, each time, to find himself back where he started (143). Just so, the author may, again and again, attempt to represent exterior reality (as in the case of naturalism, for example), only uncannily to confront some moment of self-representation. Each attempt retains the charge of the inexplicable, since it is part and parcel of the experience of trying in good faith to reach some apparently commonsensical and eminently reachable object.

It is a peril and pleasure of authoring fiction that one has an enormously enlarged power to control through composition the world of one's narrative, and, if this conscious control is illusory in multiple ways, it is nonetheless true that one has appreciably less control over the actual world in which one lives, a world in which other persons with other subjectivities have other agendas to enact. Newman's response to his disaster, caused by a complex mix of his inadequate common sense and the resistant otherness of reality, is to attempt to institute a fully authorial relation to his experience. This attempt is evident in his response to receiving the marquis's note from Mrs. Bread: "I want to be the first; I want it to be my property and no one else's!" (816). When the note proves nearly illegible, "covered with pencil-marks, which at first, in the feeble light, seemed indistinct," Newman makes it make sense. It is "Newman's fierce curiosity" that "forced a meaning from the tremulous signs" (820).[23]

The possession of the note as a commodity and the experience of expending his will upon it allow Newman to wrench authority from Mrs. Bread, who, in fact, has authored most of the story Newman consumes, and who enjoys her trade like "an ancient tabby cat, protracting the enjoyment of a dish of milk" (812). As James tells us at one point, "Mrs. Bread paused again, and the most artistic of romancers could not have been more effective. Newman made a movement as if he were turning over the page of a novel" (813). She is symbolically barred, however, from contributing to the fetishized note itself. Despite years of working for a French family in Paris, Mrs. Bread, honest Englishwoman that she is, cannot read enough French to make out the marquis's brief note. She thus is framed by the text as a mute middle-woman, functioning as a transfer point in a circuit of male discourse unaffected by her mediation. Indeed, just as Poe's Dupin gallantly returns the letter to the Queen, Newman, in a fit of noblesse oblige, promises Mrs. Bread to "translate poor M. de Bellegarde's French to you," despite what must be the rather crude state of his own (820). He is willing, in other words, to extend to her what now will remain his property, the meaning he has "forced" from its "tremulous signs" (820).

The exclusion of Mrs. Bread from the symbolic has its counterpart in the scene that immediately follows, Newman's visit to the Carmelite convent where Claire is in the process of taking the veil. Behind its blank walls, from "the depths of the chapel," Newman suddenly hears "a sound which drew his attention from the altar—the sound of a strange, lugubrious chant uttered by women's voices. It began softly, but it presently grew louder, and as it increased it became more of a wail and a dirge. It was the chant of the Carmelite nuns, their only human utterance. It was their dirge over their buried affections and over the vanity of earthly desires. . . . The chant kept on, mechanical and monotonous, with dismal repetitions and despairing cadences. It was hideous, it was horrible; as it continued, Newman felt that he needed all his self-control" (832–833). This sound without sense suggests the threat of preoedipal abjection, as Newman's odyssey of regression to the maternal here reaches a limit of comprehension. Finally, the movement to rejoin with the mother uncovers a dread of obliteration that effectively short-circuits such desire. The prior scene involving Mrs. Bread suggests, however, that Newman here actively wants to abject the feminine, as opposed to merely uncovering the buried and hidden nature of maternity. Bad and tough as the Carmelite lifestyle may well be, the pain Newman hysterically perceives in their chants is his own, and this pain derives as well from economics, history, language, and death, all of which have an abjection of their own to offer. The chant he hears—as he hears it—may well suggest a threat that requires "all his self-control," but it assails that self-control from a qualitatively different outside and, thus, also serves to reinforce it (833).

Newman emerges from his visit to the Carmelites with his desire for revenge intact. The next step of that revenge, his visit to the duchess, proves far more disruptive to his masculine stability. The duchess, "monumentally stout and imperturbably serene," possesses formidable discursive powers and possesses them in the material world (723). Throughout Newman's visit she remains in complete control, not only of what can be spoken, but of who can speak: "The duchess, in her arm-chair, from which she did not move, with a great flower-pot on one side of her, a pile of pink-covered novels on the other . . . presented an expansive and imposing front. . . . She talked to him about flowers and books, . . . about the theatres, about the peculiar institutions of his native country, about the humidity of Paris. . . . All this was a brilliant monologue on the part of the duchess. . . . Newman . . . found himself in an atmosphere in which apparently no cognizance was taken of grievances" (847). As Rowe has argued, the duchess's conversation may actually contain much historical and cultural information that Newman needs to hear, and if he gives no sense of absorbing the information, his proud sense of his authorial possession of the tale of the marquis's murder is nonetheless swamped and diminished, enshrouded by complexities of which she, not he, is master.[24] This world is not under Newman's command, nor is it a world, however patriarchal in its gender asymmetries, in which reality is simply constructed and transferred, father to son, as if Newman had acquired the entire truth of the murder, rather than a confirming piece of evidence, straight from the marquis's own mouth. Cultural unmanning in the presence of a powerful woman proves a more threatening disruption of Newman's sense of self than preoedipal shadows.[25]

If Newman would do well to take instruction, his reception of her words suggests aspects of his processing of the Carmelite chant. He hears only what seems to him to be meaningless information about the "history of the love affairs of the Princess X——" (849) and does not process her interminable conversation as anything to which he needs to pay attention; indeed the *X* that signifies her name suggests Newman's eventual response to all disruptive information: he crosses it out. At length, emptied of content, it strikes him as a "wall of polite conversation in which . . . he would never find a gate" (850). Again, though this metaphor implies her exclusion of him, it also suggests his own defensive attempt to block out a feminine authority he cannot countermand, and one that shrinks his sense of his own small tale's significance. Before he leaves, she, in fact, invites him to relate it, mentioning her sense that he had "something particular to say" (850). Newman declines to submit his story to her judgment.

The power of the duchess to blunt Newman's will suggests that the novel's exposure of his ease is twofold. Private memory in general will not conform to the contents of cultural fictions of proper maternity and paternity; private memory, in fact, may contain perverse and disturbing contents that work to undo its sentimental rewriting by culture. On the other hand, historical and social relations pose complex threats to ease as well, emblematized earlier in the novel by Noemie Nioche.

In his breathless pursuit of Claire de Cintre, Newman must depend on the leverage of his wallet to make up for his lack of social status. He essentially attempts to purchase a wife from the Bellegardes and unselfconsciously poses his pursuit of a wife as a search for "the best article in the market" (549). As he picturesquely puts it, to make his wealth complete "there must be a beautiful woman perched on the pile" (548). Meanwhile, Claire de Cintre's creepy family, undeterred by the morbid disaster of her first marriage, aggressively markets her to Lord Deepmere in the hope of securing a better deal. Clearly then, much of *The American* concerns the traffic in Claire and, stripped of the trappings of class, as Carolyn Porter suggests, little essentially distinguishes her position from the novel's copyist-turned-prostitute, Noemie Nioche.[26] This equivalence is obvious in Noemie's eventual pairing with Deepmere after Claire's flight to sanctuary in the church.

Noemie, on the other hand, embraces her position as what Valentin calls "one of the celebrities of the future" (657). Noemie uses the market to gain a social foothold, albeit a tainted one in Newman's estimation: "She looked 'lady-like.' She was dressed in quiet colors, and she wore her expensively unobtrusive toilet with a grace that might have come from years of practice. Her present self-possession and *aplomb* struck Newman as really infernal" (706). Newman demonizes Noemie, thus essentially protecting himself from her effective disruption of the manifold but incoherent distinctions on which he relies, among them copy and original, art and commerce, love and money, and cherished wife and prostitute.[27]

Noemie graphically indicates her position in the novel when she draws a large red cross over the painting on which she is at work: "'I know the truth—I know the truth,' Mademoiselle Noemie repeated. And dipping a brush into a clot of red paint, she drew a great horizontal daub across her unfinished picture. 'What is that?' asked Newman. Without answering, she drew another long crimson daub, in a vertical direction. . . . 'It is the sign of truth,' she said at last" (655). An initial truth is that Noemie cannot paint, but, in crossing out her expression, she paradoxically expresses herself and, Valentin suggests, increases the value of the painting: he now offers to purchase it. Similarly, if her mark suggests the nullity of her effort, it also ennobles it by invoking the cross as the necessity of human suffering. It may not be too much to suggest that Noemie realizes the truth of her own nontranscendent position and inhabits it, as opposed to the apparent transcendence offered by a life of art. Many truths might be attached to her gesture, symbolically rich in its muteness, most of them suggesting her position at the crossing of social registers.[28] Her cross also suggests her fate in the novel at Newman's hands: he will cross her out as a person to whom attention must be paid, precisely because she herself crosses or confuses such social boundaries. Such a reading, moreover, has an echo in Newman's conversation with the complicating duchess mentioned above. In that scene, it is the "Princess X——" whose "sentimental vicissitudes" cross and complicate, but whose name is crossed out by Newman as a consequence (849).

In the wake of the text's multipronged assault on Newman's easy self-sufficiency, in the wake of the social and psychological instabilities that get uncovered as the story progresses, Newman can only attempt to reconstitute the ease of his former repression. After a period of desultory travel, Newman returns to Paris and pays a visit to the other Carmelite convent in which Claire "took the veil," as did St. Veronica, her patroness (866). As I earlier pointed out, when visiting the duchess, Newman imagines a "wall of polite conversation in which . . . he would never find a gate" (850). In visiting this new convent, located at the intersection of two streets, Newman finds a "wall" once again, but this time, not as an interpretive conclusion, but as a cold, given fact of exterior reality. The convent was

> a dull, plain edifice, with a high-shouldered blank wall all round it. . . . But these things revealed no symptoms of human life; the place looked dumb, deaf, inanimate. The pale, dead, discolored wall stretched beneath it, far down the empty side street—a vista without a human figure. . . . This seemed the goal of his journey; it was what he had come for. . . . It told him that the woman within was lost beyond recall, and that the days and years of the future would pile themselves above her like the huge immovable slab of a tomb. (867–868)

This scene of utter blankness and emptiness stands in stark contrast to the penetrating and disintegrating Carmelite chant that had unnerved Newman earlier. It suggests that Newman's project of repression has reached a nearly successful conclusion and that he will "forget" the woman he almost married. He will also, however, as the strong and emotionally charged language suggests, "remember" her in contrast to the humiliating presence of the duchess, safe forever outside of the contested space of ongoing history. Thus encapsulated, Claire can serve to ground his masculine self against a secured and idealized feminine other, the productivity of which generates the "strange satisfaction" Newman feels as a consequence of the opportunity to "gaze his fill" (867). If Newman can "close the book and put it away" (868), it is because he now contains the book.

The efficacy of Claire's internalization through Newman's process of mourning is evident in the altered and more stable ground of his reconfigured masculinity. Prior to his final visit to the monastery, Newman thinks about his loss in religious terms: "He had a fancy of carrying out his life as he would have directed it if Madame de Cintre had been left to him—of making it a religion to do nothing that she would have disliked. In this, certainly, there was no sacrifice; but there was a pale, oblique ray of inspiration. It would be lonely entertainment—a good deal like a man talking to himself in the mirror. . . . Yet the idea yielded Newman several half hours' dumb exaltation" (863).

The metaphor of the mirror here suggests the emptiness of Newman's planned project of religious adoration, as well as its identity-conferring comfort, since nothing outside of Newman's self-image has the power to disrupt the idea he labors to construct. The connection of women to religion surfaces in ironical form several pages earlier, in Deepmere's account to Newman of how the Bellegardes packaged Valentin's death, the result of a duel over Noemie Nioche, for public consumption. According to Deepmere, the fantasy has been that Valentin died defending the honor of the pope, when, in actuality, "it was about *her* morals—*she* was the Pope!" (860).

Claire de Cintre, unconsciously, becomes the pope of Newman's imagination, even as Newman ceases to think of his changes as having feminine sources. After his final visit to the Carmelite convent, though Claire is not explicitly invoked, Newman wanders into Notre Dame in meditation—but not in any conscious consideration of religious questions. He decides that he was "ashamed of having wanted to hurt them. They had hurt him, but such things were really not his game. At last he got up and came out of the darkening church; not with the elastic step of a man who has won a victory or taken a resolve, but strolling soberly, like a good-natured man who is still a little ashamed" (868–869).

Though James's narrator disingenuously pretends to have no knowledge of "what it was in the background of his soul," Newman's sense that "he didn't want to hurt them" (868) echoes the ethical unease of Claire de Cintre at the prospect of inflicting pain, even as she insists on the necessity of breaking their engagement: "I don't think I have wronged, seriously, many persons; certainly not consciously. To you, to whom I have done this hard and cruel thing, the only reparation I can make is to say, 'I know it, I feel it'" (783). As she says several pages later, "Of course I am hard. . . . Whenever we give pain we are hard. And we *must* give pain; that's the world,—the hateful, miserable world!" (789). When asked what she will do as a consequence, she announces her resignation. She will go "[w]here I shall give no more pain and suspect no more evil" (789). Newman's ethical elevation at the end of the novel, if one can call it that, consists of a similar determination to give no pain that is avoidable.

The invocation of religion in this part of the novel suggests a reshuffling of Newman's core convictions and alters his relation to business. If commerce had "cast a shadow" over his connection to Madame de Cintre, "a woman justly proud, he was willing to sponge it out of his life forever" (863). He feels "no impulse" at all "to sell all he had and give to the poor. . . . He was glad he was rich and tolerably young; if it was possible to think too much about buying and selling, it was a gain to have a good slice of life left in which not to think about them" (863). The structure of his "not thinking" about commerce is finally homologous to his "not thinking" about Claire: what he forgets still has an absolutely determining effect on his existence. In each case, "forgetting" produces a cementing of relationships in place, a double-edged process tantalizingly invoked in the oxymoronic and ironic tangle of the following: "He had a feeling that the link which bound him to a possible interest in the manufacture of cutlery was broken" (854). Newman devotes his existence in the final pages of the novel, precisely, to the cutting of links, which on a deeper level continue to exist. If commerce stands for a deindividualizing web of relations that comes to threaten Newman's idea of himself, he now establishes his identity on religious noncommercial grounds that are largely invulnerable to complex realities. These grounds are themselves guaranteed by a buried image of a woman safely located beyond the complex and challenging crossings of material life. Newman has, in effect, discovered the identity-confirming value of domesticity in the United States of the nineteenth century.[29]

The American generates a complex and ironic critique of the construction of Newman's masculinity, and one that I think has value in terms of heterosexual masculinity in general. It lacks, however, the disruptive engagement with questions of desire between men in *Roderick Hudson,* an absence that may contribute to Newman's limited, wooden character. Despite James's insistence in the preface that we are seated at the window of a consciousness that is "wide, quite sufficiently wide" (1067), Newman is not a man allowed to feel too divergently about anything, least of all other men, and undoubtedly that restraint contributes to the narrow focus of its plot. Its critique of Newman is an incisive one but lacks breadth, and it is incisive in its particular way because it lacks breadth.

Though this is so, it preserves a space for potential openness in its refusal to let Newman's masculine ease coalesce, as if James himself shares the perspective of Mrs. Tristram early in the novel: "Before I have known you six months I shall see you in a fine fury. . . . You take things too coolly. It exasperates me. And then you are too happy" (545). By perpetuating disruptions, by exposing the implication of Newman's self-protective masculinity in the complicated intersections of gender and commerce, the novel preserves spaces for kinds of desires it does not provide itself. Indeed, its final gesture is to use Mrs. Tristram to unsettle his ease once again after his final act of repression and denial. It is only when the note is "quite consumed" that she sadistically tells him that he has, in fact, only acted in accord with the Bellegardes' expectations of his "remarkable good nature" (871–872).

The American was one of James's most commercially successful novels and thus helped secure James's career at its beginning. Nevertheless, James was always dissatisfied with the novel. As late as the preface to *The Golden Bowl,* he would lament over "many of the sorry businesses of *The American*" (1337). The attempt to correct its flaws in the New York edition, however, only produced desires for even more extensive alterations. Mourns James: "If only one *could* re-write, if only one *could* do better justice to . . . the poor morsels of consciously-decent matter that catch one's eye with their rueful reproach for old stupidities of touch!" (1337). The most thorough revision, however, must be bound by the basic shape and form of the original, which in the case of *The American* was a "garment misfitted, a garment cheaply embroidered and unworthy of it" (1337). The early and flawed novels would be most searchingly reworked in the final great novels of James's career.

CHAPTER 4

Late Authorizations in The Ambassadors and The Wings of the Dove

The Ambassadors and *The Wings of the Dove* have close and crossed relations with each other. Remarkably, given the complexity and density of each, these two "major phase" texts were both composed in a space of two years and, as James parenthetically remarks in his preface to the New York edition of *The Ambassadors,* "The order of composition, in these things, I may mention, was reversed by the order of publication; the earlier written of the two books having appeared as the later."[1] *The Wings of the Dove* was published in 1902 in England and the United States, and *The Ambassadors* was serialized in the *North American Review* in 1903, although composed before its dense and difficult companion. Moreover, James had possessed the ideas for both novels for some time prior to the beginning of composition. It is to be expected, then, that two such major undertakings, performed in such a compressed span of time, should have a complementary relation and that James should come to think in terms of the similarities and differences of productions that stand as two of three capstones to his life's work.[2]

The heart of this relation replays, in reverse order, the relationship I have argued exists earlier between *Roderick Hudson* and *The American. The Ambassadors,* the first of the two composed, is another heterosexual romance set in Paris, this time marked by a carefully worked-out and consistent acknowledgment of the complicated sexualities located just beyond its borders, which is to say, just beyond the borders of Strether's heterosexualizing consciousness. *The Wings of the Dove,* in contrast, takes up the difficult task of dealing with the divergent and queer desires present in *Roderick Hudson,* this time with the resource of the late style fully at James's command. If both late novels, meanwhile, are written to embody the full weight of James's acquired experience and authority, his comments in the prefaces on the experience of composing both novels replay, at a higher level, his experience with the earlier two.[3] In writing *The Ambassadors,* James remembers in the preface to the New York edition, he had an "absolute conviction and constant clearness to deal with. . . . Even under the weight of my hero's years I could feel my postulate firm. . . . Nothing resisted, nothing betrayed" (1306). James remembers in the same preface the tendency of his subject in *The Wings of the Dove* to trouble him by a "sealing up of its face" (1306) and a breakdown of narrative. Just as Roderick's decline, set in Italy, occurs too precipitously in the early novel, in *The Wings of the Dove,* the second half, also set in Italy, is "false and deformed" and "bristles with 'dodges' . . . for disguising the reduced scale of the exhibition" (1299). The second half of my consideration of James, then, will develop the consequences of these interrelations. I begin with *The Ambassadors.*

In his study of Hawthorne, James famously comments on the list of things missing from U.S. culture—"no cathedrals, nor abbeys, nor little Norman churches," et cetera—and ends by remarking that "[t]he American knows that a good deal remains; what it is that remains—that is his secret, his joke, as one may say."[4] *The Ambassadors* is composed over James's own concealed joke, one that figuratively places the novel's critics and readers in the position of the obtuse residents of Woollett. The joke actually is quite simple and resides in the provincial assumption that the trouble into which Chad has gotten himself in Paris must involve a tie to a woman, dark and devious, rather than to a man or men, and that such a deplorable tie was *naturally* the factor preventing the homecoming of the prodigal son. Strether's own progress, then, in learning to appreciate the virtues of Marie de Vionnet, the French temptress of the Woollett imagination, is thus undercut by ironies of the deepest kind. James builds his joke about what else remains into a seamless and integrated comic romance of heterosexuality, one that borrows heavily from both *The American* and *Roderick Hudson,* but one that achieves on a higher level the narrative ease of the former. In both *The American* and *The Ambassadors,* homoerotic possibilities are discounted rather than substantively explored. In *The Ambassadors,* this process barely ruffles the surface of the novel, as its homoerotic suggestiveness helps support the heterosexual plot as well.

James describes the composition of *The Ambassadors* in terms of the same sureness and purpose, the same "ease" that marked both the writing and the narrative of *The American*. As he remarks at the beginning of the preface to *The Ambassadors*, "Nothing is more easy than to state the subject of *The Ambassadors*. . . . The whole case, in fine, is in Lambert Strether's irrepressible outbreak to little Bilham . . . in Gloriani's garden. . . . The idea of the tale resides indeed in the very fact that an hour of such unprecedented ease should have been felt by him *as* a crisis" (1304). If Newman's ease in *The American* was unconsciously replicated in the composition of a romance by an inexperienced author, the general issue of ease in terms of the composition of *The Ambassadors* has less to do with a pejorative easiness. Instead, it is related to the mature master's magisterial control of the facts of the case. In writing it, the "absolute conviction and constant clearness" that he had from the beginning—his "full and sound sense of the matter"—corresponds to the relentlessness of *The Ambassadors'* consistent excision of erotic desire between men in favor of the conventional paradigms of heterosexual male development that finally dominate its plot (1306). It corresponds to the novel's conviction of what *always* gets left out, at least as the world exists in the American heterosexual imagination of Lambert Strether.

Strether's landing in Europe begins with a discounting of his own erotic possibilities in the immediate marginalization of Waymarsh, his friend from the United States. At this introductory stage of the novel, Strether has experienced his friendship with Maria Gostrey as a betrayal of Waymarsh, whom he dreads seeing. In an attempt to cure Waymarsh's insomnia, Strether visits his friend's room late at night, much as Newman had earlier visited the lodgings of Valentin. Their conversation stages a jocular competition between Waymarsh and Mrs. Newsome for Strether's attention: "Waymarsh gloomily gazed. 'What does that mean then but that your trip is just *for* her?' . . . Strether, in impatience, violently played with his latch. 'It's simple enough. It's for both of you.' Waymarsh at last turned over with a groan. 'Well, *I* won't marry you!' 'Neither, when it comes to that—-!' But the visitor had already laughed and escaped."[5] Though Waymarsh never disappears from the text, he plays an increasingly marginalized role, while Miss Gostrey becomes a principal player as an important maternal teacher of Strether, encouraging him in his growing mastery of imaginative and cognitive complexity, regardless of James's characterization of her in the preface as a "ficelle" (1317).[6] Waymarsh, in contrast, offers precisely what his name implies, and his grumpy, irritable response to Europe represents a "marsh" for the narrative at odds with its apparent commitment to expansive experience. It realizes this commitment in heterosexual terms, however, so that Strether's turning away from his friend suggests an ironic contraction as well. Strether will simply not explore, in other words, the implications of coming "for Waymarsh."

The discounting of an attachment to Waymarsh, who after all stands in general for principles of nonpleasure, costs nothing compared to the sacrifice of the more tantalizing and palpable possibilities offered to Strether by little Bilham. Strether's initial encounter with Bilham has a voyeuristic and erotic edge: "Two or three of the windows stood open to the violet air. . . . [A] young man had come out and looked about him, had lighted a cigarette and tossed the match over, and then, resting on the rail, had given himself up to watching the life below while he smoked" (21:97). Although Strether explains his desire to himself as a longing for a surrogate home, a longing for the domesticity normally provided by the temporarily absent Maria Gostrey, thinking of Bilham in such terms brings Strether to the edge of the erotic even as he insists on the primacy of comforts women supply.

Though Strether experiences, initially, an erotic tug in little Bilham's direction, he displays an astounding obtuseness to the possible character of the latter's relation to Chad. As he relates his initial contact with Bilham to Waymarsh, Strether talks of the suggestive smell of the place: "I dawdled, I trifled; above all I looked round. I saw, in fine; and—I don't know what to call it—I sniffed. It's a detail, but it's as if there were something—something very good—*to* sniff" (21:105). This sniffing is automatically interpreted heterosexually by Waymarsh, who immediately asks, "Does he live there with a woman?" (21:106).

The discounted possibility, of course, is that Chad has lived there with little Bilham and that the latter (or even the former) produces Strether's pleasurable scent, as he subliminally perceives. Struck by the attractiveness of the apartment, Strether speaks to Waymarsh of "'a charming place; full of beautiful and valuable things. I never saw such a place . . . [f]or a little artist-man—!' He could in fact scarce express it" (21:108). Strether's problem of expression derives precisely from his Woollettian absence of a vocabulary for such relations, even as he senses that the apartment has somehow been formed *for* Bilham.

Why has Bilham been there? Miss Gostrey, a perhaps reliable guide to Europe, informs Strether that this was an elaborate first step in a plan Chad and Bilham had cooked up. Gostrey suggests that the pair had arranged "[e]very move in the game. And they've been arranging ever since" (21:133). The conventional explanation for this arranging, one that Strether obviously accepts, is that Bilham has been helping Chad prepare Strether for the descent of his mistress, Madame de Vionnet, who has been sending her partner "every day his little telegram from Cannes" (21:133). A competing possibility, however, and one that more efficiently explains Bilham's behavior, is that the two men expect that Bilham himself constitutes part of the problem. Bilham has been present by himself, not to ease Strether into acquaintance with de Vionnet, but to insert himself, as himself, into the American ambassador's favor. Strether senses the workings of a nefarious plot but remains baffled as to its purpose: "'What's he up to; what's he up to?'—something like that was at the back of his head all the while in respect to little Bilham" (21:113).

Maria Gostrey's relation to these proceedings is ambiguous at best. She accompanies Strether to little Bilham's own modest dwelling, currently occupied by one of his friends, where they meet an attractive but sexually ambiguous circle of artists and aesthetes who take turns occupying each other's rooms: "The ingenious compatriots showed a candour, he thought, surpassing even the candour of Woollett; they were red-haired and long-legged, they were quaint and queer and dear and droll; they made the place resound with the vernacular" (21:127–128). This is the same circle Chad joined when he first came to Paris in preparation, in the eyes of Woollett, for a "long dark drop of the curtain" (21:92). Though Gostrey plays a crucial role in steering the impressionable Strether in heterosexual directions—and has a stake in doing so given her own romantic interests—she produces for Strether at this gathering a patronizing sense of "how she dealt with boys" (21:128), a phrase that suggestively connects heterosexuality and maturity, homosexuality and arrested development. This last connection surfaces in the terms of her praise of little Bilham. He was "too delightful. If he'll only not spoil it! But they always *will;* they always do; they always have." This "spoiling" will be done by having "wanted so dreadfully to do something" that leaves them "never the same afterwards"; Bilham, at present, however, doesn't worry about consequences and "isn't a bit ashamed" (21:130–131). Bilham's perfection, Gostrey suggests, lies in his resistance to the teleologies of heterosexual manhood that come to claim Chad. If such manhood aims at a combination of marriage and career, one reinforcing the other, Bilham needs and should seek neither. Gostrey's description, however, also reinforces the necessity of heterosexual plotting in *The Ambassadors*. What story results from the perfection of doing nothing?

Despite their efforts to ease Strether into this complex and polysexual world, both Chad and Bilham register surprise that Strether manages to continue to understand their relations in oblivious heterosexual terms. This despite Strether's initial impression of Chad in the charged idiom of Greek art:

"It was as if . . . he just presented himself, his identity so rounded off, his palpable presence and his massive young manhood as such a link in . . . a kind of demonstration. . . . What could there be in this for Strether but the hint of some self-respect, some sense of power, oddly perverted; something latent and beyond access, ominous and perhaps enviable? . . . The intimation had the next thing, in a flash, taken on a name—a name on which our friend seized as he asked himself if he weren't perhaps really dealing with an irreducible young Pagan" (21:156–157). The ambiguities of Chad's sexuality do not distract Strether's focus on the inevitable woman, even as the former even initially displays *none* of the passionate interest in this relationship that Strether expects. Chad responds with something close to disbelief:

> *Strether:* "Do you mean . . . that there isn't any woman with you now?"
> *Chad:* "But pray what has that to do with it?"
> *Strether:* "Why it's the whole question."
> *Chad:* "Of my going home?" Chad was clearly surprised. "Oh not much!
> Do you think that when I want to go any one will have any power—"
> *Strether:* "To keep you"—Strether took him straight up—"from carry-
> ing out your wish? Well, our idea has been that somebody has hith-
> erto—or a good many persons perhaps—kept you pretty well from
> 'wanting.' . . . [B]ut if you aren't in anybody's hands so much the
> better." (21:157–158)

Chad then responds with some impatience, culminating in amazement: "One doesn't know quite what you mean by being in women's 'hands.' It's all so vague. One is when one isn't. One isn't when one is. And then one can't quite give people away. . . . I've *never* got stuck" (21:158). When Strether responds by asking, "What has kept you . . . if you *have* been able to leave," Chad expresses shock: "It made Chad, after a stare, throw himself back. 'Do you think one's kept only by women?' His surprise and his verbal emphasis rang out so clear in the still street that Strether winced till he remembered the safety of their English speech. 'Is that,' the young man demanded, 'what they think at Woollett?'" (21:159). Eventually, Strether returns to little Bilham and puts the question to him directly: "*Is* there some woman? Of whom he's really afraid of course I mean?" Bilham responds with an answer that credits Strether with some previous delicacy, saying, "It's awfully charming of you . . . not to have asked me that before" (21:177).

The ironic charm, from little Bilham's point of view, lies in Strether's forbearing to interrogate about the loss of a lover, and a lover who has gone from an immersion in a bohemian community back to the bourgeois, heterosexual world. Chad, in this narrative, is "a rare case" who has "awfully changed" (21:177). From the point of view of (pre)homophobic Woollett, if they had any sense of Parisian sexuality, the rehabilitation of Chad by Marie de Vionnet would serve as the most moral transformation on earth, one of the book's lacerating ironies. From Bilham's point of view, the transformation has not been an unmixed thing. That Chad has visibly improved, Bilham admits, is clear, but Bilham isn't "sure he was really meant by nature to be quite so good. It's like the new edition of an old book that one has been fond of. . . . I believe he really wants to go back and take up a career. . . . He won't then . . . be my pleasant well-rubbed old-fashioned volume at all. But of course I'm beastly immoral" (21:177–178). The terms of goodness and badness, improvement and decline, are heavily and ironically coded by Bilham in an effort to be as honest as possible with Strether, without dotting *i*'s and crossing *t*'s. If he will call himself "beastly immoral," Chad has shared this state. According to Bilham, he actually "wants to be free" and isn't "used . . . to being so good" (21:178). When Strether asks if he is, now, "good," Bilham remarks, again with lacerating irony, "[*D*]*o* take it from me," as if, after all, the heterosexual transformation of Chad has been one in which he, as forsaken lover, has been intimately involved (21:179).

The obdurate obliviousness of Strether to the actual situation of his quarry, to the actual complexity of the sexual intrigue of Parisian life, has its culmination in the famous speech to little Bilham in Gloriani's garden, when Strether offers his gems of regretful middle-aged wisdom: "Live all you can; it's a mistake not to" (21:217). Strether's sense that Bilham might need to hear this speech, however, has been constituted by the emptiness of the latter's life seen in heterosexual terms.[7] He has been blind, even willfully blind, to precisely the ways in which his new friend already manages to live.

It is provocative to trace the source of this irony back to the conversation James records between Jonathan Sturges and William Dean Howells. Sturges, badly crippled by polio, was one of the younger men with whom James formed a passionate friendship in the 1890s, and for whom he provided care through a series of illnesses and breakdowns. Sturges was an intimate of Wilde's London circle and a supporter of Wilde following the latter's trial.[8] Clearly, the advice to a significantly disabled person to "live, live," depending on the context, might not represent a high point in the history of conversational gambits, particularly when the self-referential focus of such advice seems to be the anxieties of the able and famous. Neither is it necessarily clear, however, that Sturges needed such patronizing advice, perhaps already, despite his physical problems, having learned to live quite well on his own. For example, James describes Sturges in the following terms to long-time friend Henrietta Reubell: "He is full of talk and intelligence, and of the absence of prejudice, and is saturated with London, and with all sorts of contrasted elements of it, to which he has given himself up. Handicapped, crippled, invalidical, he has yet made his way there in a wondrous fashion, and knows nine thousand people, of most of whom *I've* never heard."[9] Though an authoritative reading of this encounter is impossible, its ironies nonetheless seem manifold and suggestive and support the notion that Strether's relation to Bilham is finally one of avuncular obliviousness.

As a final irony in Strether's relationship to Bilham, he does *not* help his friend live, if we accept Maria Gostrey's advice that he should be left exactly as he is. The idea that Bilham should marry Mamie Pocock surfaces at Chad's dinner party, as Strether and Bilham share a "deep divan." Bilham offers himself as a support, if he's "of the least use to hold on by." Strether replies, "'You're not of the least!'—and Strether laid an appreciative hand on him to say it. 'No one's of the least.' With which, to mark how gaily he could take it, he patted his companion's knee. 'I must meet my fate alone, and I *shall*—oh you'll see!'" (22:165). Little Bilham does not exactly reciprocate Mamie's burgeoning crush, but he will do "anything in the world" for Strether, and his "happy laugh" indicates that "if pretending, or even trying, or still even hoping, to be able to care for Mamie would be of use, he was all there for the job" (22:169). It is not clear exactly what use marrying Mamie will serve in terms of Strether's designs for Chad, since it is already clear that she has practically given him up. Nonetheless, just as Marie de Vionnet has "saved" Chad, Mamie can now try to "save" Bilham, a project that may put her determination to the test. Strether, meanwhile, both acts out and suppresses his own unacknowledged homoeroticism by perversely manipulating the sexuality of his friend, a manipulation to which Bilham, with equal perversity, masochistically submits.

Strether himself betrays some reservations about the erotic content of this relation, gynophobically remarking, in the midst of an apparent appreciation of her virtues, that "Mamie would be fat, too fat, at thirty" (22:155). This comment occurs in the middle of Strether's extremely long meditation on Mamie's merits as she waits on Chad's balcony for little Bilham, the same balcony where Strether earlier spied Bilham in "the violet air" (21:97). If Strether's rich response here indicates the growth of his imagination, this growth occurs as a product of heterosexual substitution as well. In the first scene, Strether is interested but confused by Bilham's presence and by the desire this presence invokes: it leaves him with nothing to say. In the second scene, Strether has only too much to say concerning Mamie's affairs of the heart, in part because these affairs are Woollettian rather than Parisian. Finally then, the marriage of little Bilham marks the sacrifice of his negatively defined perfection to positive imperatives of narrative, imperatives served by the intelligibility of conventional heterosexual desire.

Most of the argument I have made to this point in the chapter can be given an interpretation consistent with the heterosexuality of each of the characters. Its mode of elaborate, covering double entendre allows James the magisterial consistency and control afforded by conventional heterosexual story lines. The cost of such an efficient and capacious cover story, however, is high: the novel must forgo any disruptive exploration of what the alternative desires and experiences toward which the novel gestures might actually mean for its characters. This exploration will occur in the tangled and difficult *The Wings of the Dove*. In *The Ambassadors,* however, James generally indulges the comic suppressions and limitations of Lambert Strether's own consciousness, including Strether's penchant for unconsciously allowing emulative desire and competitive resentment to govern his relations to other men.[10] These forces structure his development in the course of the novel.[11]

Two crucial relations for Strether in the novel are those with Chad and Gloriani, the artist directly imported into *The Ambassadors* from *Roderick Hudson*. The name "Chad Newsome" suggests a reincarnation of *The American*'s Christopher Newman, a connection cemented by his embodiment in the novel of the same problem of masculine "ease" that James explores in the earlier book. In the pivotal scene in Gloriani's garden, for example, Strether enviously sees Chad's behavior in the following remarkably heavy-handed terms: "Chad . . . after having easily named his companion, had still more easily turned away. . . . He was as easy, clever Chad, with the great artist as with his obscure compatriot, and as easy with every one else as with either" (21:197–198). A few pages later, Strether finds himself wishing, again in terms of Chad, that "he himself might have arrived at such ease and such humor" (21:210). Still later in the novel, when Strether has been feeling himself "rather in pieces," he compares himself to Chad's "personal magnificence": "There he was in all the pleasant morning freshness of it—strong and sleek and gay, easy and fragrant and fathomless, with happy health in his colour, and pleasant silver in his thick young hair, and the right word for everything on the lips that his clear brownness caused to show as red" (22: 27–28). The persistent envy of ease in this text suggests an envious relation to the real and imagined privileges of conventional masculinity. It consists in imagining that the position of the culturally privileged other can and does

sponds, in his final ambiguous speech of the text, "Ah, . . . you're exciting" (22:318).

Strether's competitive masculine relation to Chad actually displaces and camouflages a more important and more desiring relation between men in *The Ambassadors*. This relation is between Strether and Gloriani, the cynical older artist imported from the pages of *Roderick Hudson,* and one of the clearest markers of important intertextual relations between *The Ambassadors* and James's first major book. It is Gloriani's efforts that provide the "hour of unprecedented ease" that paradoxically oppresses Strether by reminding him of his privation, and he himself possesses a kind of ease for his envious observers, especially in his relation to women.[14] Strether imagines him as a "glossy male tiger" (21:219), and little Bilham, who as a "little artist man" also has an envious gaze (21:108), attests to his ability to more or less shepherd the flock of *femmes du monde* we find among the guests. According to Bilham, among "ambassadors, cabinet ministers, bankers, generals," there are "[a]bove all always some awfully nice women—and not too many; sometimes an actress, an artist, a great performer—but only when they're not monsters; and in particular the right *femmes du monde*. You can fancy his history on that side—I believe it's fabulous: they *never* give him up. Yet he keeps them down: no one knows how he manages" (21:199). The phallic order of the garden, with Gloriani at its center, attests to the artist's demonic genius. The nearly prostrate Strether, for example, experiences Gloriani's eyes as "all unconscious, unintending, preoccupied . . . the source of the deepest intellectual sounding to which he had ever been exposed" (21:197). Strether wonders whether this sounding has been produced by "the most special flare, unequalled, supreme, of the aesthetic torch, lighting that wondrous world for ever, or . . . the long straight shaft sunk by a personal acuteness that life had seasoned to steel. . . . The deep human expertness in Gloriani's charming smile—oh the terrible life behind it!" (21:197). Strether's adoration of Gloriani constitutes *The Ambassadors'* most powerful erotic moment, a masturbatory fantasy of his own physical violation at the hands of his imagined master, as Strether comes "quite to cherish his vision of it, to play with it in idle hours; only speaking of it to no one" (21:197). The desire in this passage, however, only functions to enable Strether's oedipal identification with the famous artist. Finally, this identification serves James's narrative of the construction of heterosexual male identity. In terms of his relations with women, key for Strether in this text, he demonstrates how, in little Bilham's terms, he "keeps them down" even though "they *never* give him up" (21:199).

At the time of his visit to Gloriani's garden and throughout the novel,

James has Strether mute the power of his own identification with the master artist. In fact, Strether executes a perceptual switch from Gloriani to a less exalted role model, Chad himself. As he watches Gloriani talking to a duchess, he admires the artist's confidence and is sure that despite the duchess's "latent insolence" she "had met her match" in Gloriani's "equal resources" (21:219). This small moment suggests another intertextual relation, since it is precisely Christopher Newman's inability to talk on equal terms with *The American*'s duchess that leads to the collapse of his revenge. As Strether watches this display of mastery, he stands on the brink of proclaiming to little Bilham that Gloriani is the person "whom I should enjoy being" (21:220). Suddenly, however, Strether spots Chad and the virginal Mademoiselle de Vionnet, appearing like a twin vision of young felicity, and sees the truth like "the click of a spring" (21:220): "'Oh Chad!'—It was that rare youth he would have enjoyed being 'like.' The virtuous attachment would be all there before him. . . . Jeanne de Vionnet . . . would be . . . the object of it. Chad brought her straight up to him, and Chad was, oh yes, at this moment—for the glory of Woollett or whatever—better still even than Gloriani" (21:220–221). James reinforces Strether's quick, sleight-of-hand substitution later in *The Ambassadors*, when Chad himself occupies the structural position of Gloriani, at a dinner he magically orchestrates and Gloriani attends. Strether here marvels that he "had perhaps seen, on Fourths of July and on dear old domestic Commencements, more people assembled, but he had never . . . known so great a promiscuity to show so markedly as picked. . . . So could things go when there was a hand to keep them consistent—a hand that pulled the wire with a skill at which the elder man more and more marvelled" (22:159–161). Though Strether seemingly abandons Gloriani, in reality the powerful identification with him formed in the garden scene works only more effectively for its apparent effacement. Gloriani represents what Emerson means by a sufficiently "other" genius: his apotheosis takes him beyond envy and resentment.[15] Strether, finally, comes to feel the difference as such an abyss that the famous sculptor seemed to signal "almost condolingly, yet oh how vacantly! as across some great flat sheet of water. . . . That idea . . . performed the office of putting Strether more at his ease" (22:262–263).

    This expanse between Gloriani and Strether functions to allow the former's values to remain veiled, transcendent, and untouched. As the masculine God of the text, Gloriani in fact functions as the trope his name suggests, "glory," which, I suggested in the introduction, plays a key role in James's account of his development in *A Small Boy and Others*. Such a trope inhabits myths, legends, histories, and works of art, but it works best at a remove from the pedestrian clay of everyday life. It is for this reason that Gloriani is nearly absent—yet powerfully present—throughout the text of *The Ambassadors.*

At the same time, seen intertextually, James's appropriation of Gloriani allows him covertly to ground glory as a material possibility in culture and works against the possibility that Strether and little Bilham cook up a completely fatuous idea of greatness. James's attitude toward Gloriani's art in *Roderick Hudson* is less than wholehearted approval; his knowing aesthetic complications and Hudson's jejune purity balance each other as insufficient positions. But his resurrection in *The Ambassadors* at a later phase of his career nonetheless pays tribute to survivalist longevity—as if Gloriani, despite all the inevitable obstacles, failures, depressions, and the like, had kept sculpting, just as James had kept indefatigably writing.[16] Persistence and durability are precisely the key qualities we would expect him to display, based on his behavior in the earlier novel.

Gloriani thus fills the paternal function for Strether in *The Ambassadors* and complements his much more obviously present "mothers," like Maria Gostrey and Marie de Vionnet, whose efforts in schooling Strether's powers of perception and his power to generate narrative have been noted by other critics.[17] This paternal function is left largely unperformed in the earlier two texts. It is a paradox of James's late novels that, as they engage homoerotic issues more systematically, they do so within a more conventional oedipal structure that also restricts the terms of engagement.

The Ambassadors borrows and reworks much of *The American*'s narrative of heterosexual male development. In the later novel, James employs this narrative positively to suggest the triumph, however equivocal, of a character to whom he refers in the preface as a man of "imagination galore" (1307), a man more like Rowland Mallet in *Roderick Hudson* than like the commercial Newman. If, in *The American,* James's authority was created inversely through critique, in *The Ambassadors* he makes its metanarrative construction through Strether an issue at the center of the text.[18]

A key moment in Strether's aestheticized, narrative creation of power occurs in his crucial and critically prominent visit to the French countryside, where he realizes that Madame de Vionnet and Chad have had an ongoing sexual relationship. James frames this scene in terms of rural pictures, especially of a "certain small Lambinet" that Strether had failed to buy at a Boston establishment years before (22:245). Though this Lambinet is a commodity and remembered by Strether as part of a capitalist aesthetic adventure, it immediately identifies Strether's day trip as a search for earlier pleasures, and these pleasures finally lie deeper than adventures in the purchase of art. It is the "background of fiction, the medium of art, the nursery of letters" that Strether seeks, "practically as distant as Greece" and as "consecrated" (22:245). The actual target of regressive desire is less classical antiquity, however, than the buried contents of Strether's unconscious, as James's description plainly demonstrates. The kind of aesthetic experience carried to life in this passage facilitates a release of the defenses of consciousness, on the grounds that the objects of such desire are intrinsically benign. What Strether enacts in this crucial passage of the text is a romance of the maternal, a "nursery" romance he learns must be renounced in order to consolidate masculine identity.

James wraps the episode in the machinery of uncanniness.[19] Strether begins his journey by abandoning any effort at control or pretense as to specific destination. He selects the station at which he departs by train "almost at random" and "observed in respect to his train almost no condition save that it should stop a few times after getting out of the *banlieue*" (22:245–246).

Strether has been nursing heterosexual hopes as a consequence of his visits to Marie de Vionnet. He has formed "[t]he brave intention of frequency" and has advanced so far as to meditate on an odd "special shyness that had still made him careful" (22:249). He immediately links this shyness to the danger of lapsing from the good faith of his original mission, but the suggestion that an attack of conscience might make one "shy" seems incongruous, as if the truth of the "shyness" has just been neatly ducked. In any case, he has to some extent abandoned restraint, and, consistent with the melting beneficence of rural France, relations between the two have advanced "smoothly, mild but not slow, and melting, liquefying into his happy illusion of idleness." The pleasing erotic suggestiveness of Strether's memory yields in the next paragraph, though some time later in the day, to "a stout white-capped deep-voiced woman at the door of the *auberge*" (22:251–252). The aesthetic machinery of what James characterizes in the space of a single page as a "picture," a "scene and a stage," a "text," and a "play" "melt[s] together" in this maternal woman's "broad sketch of what she could do for her visitor's appetite" (22:253–254). It is in the midst of this comprehensive ease at the fancied breast of the world, this release from watchfulness and restraint, that the traumatic vision of the two lovers magically drifts into Strether's painting. These lovers are "expert, familiar, frequent. . . . They knew how to do it" (22:256). They also, of course, turn out to be Madame de Vionnet and Chad, a fact "queer as fiction, as farce" (22:257). As Madame de Vionnet exclaims, "*Comme cela se trouve!*" (22:260).

This scene repeats the trajectory of Newman's heterosexuality in *The American*. Newman, too, entertains fantasies of a regression to the maternal, a regression that begins with his indolent ease in the Louvre at the beginning of the text. This ease suggests a relaxing of necessary psychic defenses—until he finds himself rocked by a revelation of the primal violence at the heart of heterosexual relations, served for him by the pacific and nurturant Mrs. Bread. The apparently aversive content of this episode and the tragedy of losing his beloved Claire to the Carmelite convent, I argue, while true enough at the level of the shocked Newman's emotions, have positive functions as well, as Newman attempts to reconfigure, albeit blindly as ever, his masculine ease. He ends, fortified against a dangerous femininity, by creating and containing a resentimentalized femininity in consciousness. This reconstituted femininity is superimposed over the chant of the Carmelite nuns, over a language of mere, meaningless sound.

Strether's primal scene arguably serves the constitution of masculine identity as well, as it signals for him the necessity of shifting his fundamental relation to experience. Strether initially experiences the lovers as an aesthetic touch that makes his scene "but the more idyllic" (22:256). This isn't an obvious scene of violence or kinky permutations of gender roles—Madame de Vionnet doesn't push Chadwick overboard or even try to gain control of the oars. What makes the scene primal are the terms in which James frames it: Strether's sexual fantasies and the easeful, unconscious drift of his day. Its disruptive jolt, however, resides somewhere beneath its heterosexually correct surface and somewhere beneath its status as, for Strether, the revelation of a serious error in judgment. Its buried content, however we imagine it, comes to us wrapped in the dreamwork of heterosexuality in *The Ambassadors*.

This trauma represents an essential step in constituting Strether's masculine independence, his ability, in the words of Maria Gostrey, to "toddle alone" (22:39). His perception of the two lovers institutes a rupture from romantic vision in favor of the real. If earlier he had been guilty of dressing up the raw truth as "a little girl might have dressed her doll" (22:266), he suddenly has discovered a new tough-minded attention for the lie previously concealed, "a lie on which one could now, detached and deliberate, perfectly put one's finger" (22:262–263).

As a consequence of the trauma of his rural idyll, Strether must pay a farewell visit to Madame de Vionnet, who by the end of the novel clearly has transferred her desperate affections to him, even as we find in *Roderick Hudson* that Christina Light has been carrying at least a dim and smoky torch for Rowland Mallet. Leland S. Person, Jr., argues that Strether's final visit represents his attempt imaginatively to manipulate his perceptions into an idealized "loaf on the shelf" of his memory (22:276), a process in which Madame de Vionnet masochistically participates.[20] Such a process suggests the kind of emergency consolidation of memory that I have argued Christopher Newman undertakes in *The American*. Person may underestimate, however, the extent to which his conversation with Madame de Vionnet breaks up his fantasizing process. When Strether meretriciously suggests that she "ought . . . to be easy" based on what she has done for them all, she perceives that Strether wishes to seal off their relationship on the best terms possible. "'And not trouble you any more, no doubt,'" she responds, "'not thrust on you even the wonder and the beauty of what I've done; only let you regard our business as over, and well over, and see you depart in a peace that matches my own? No doubt, no doubt, no doubt,' she nervously repeated. . . . 'Yes, as you say,' she continued after a moment, 'I ought to be easy and rest on my work. Well then here am I doing so. I *am* easy. You'll have it for your last impression. When is it you say you go?'" (22:283). There is little ease in this speech, however, and Strether responds as if he understands the uneasy subtext: "He took some time to reply—his last impression was more and more so mixed a one. It produced in him a vague disappointment, a drop that was deeper even than the fall of his elation the previous night" (22:284).

Person cites but discounts this passage, arguing that Strether quickly finds refuge in a standard cultural fantasy of Marie as exploited and hunted victim. If Strether seems to achieve some kind of recognition of the "mixed" position of Madame de Vionnet, this recognition serves his own sense of a new authority over experience. This authority is constituted by a shift in aesthetic modes from romance, as the feminized nursery of letters, to realism, as the ability to make accurate judgments and recognitions. This authority is not directly challenged, I would argue, by the possibility that even in their last encounter Strether fails to accurately perceive Marie de Vionnet. An anxiety that realist vision perpetually fails is endemic to realism, and mandates an intensification of the perceiver's effort to form better, more nuanced pictures of the world. This effort is consistent with the gradual expansion of consciousness Strether has tried to achieve and feels he has achieved in the novel. The larger problem with realism of Strether's variety, however, is that while it dabbles with nailing down the nuances of its fetishized objects of microscrutiny, and in part because it does fixate on these nuances, it excludes an entire range of objects and experiences from consideration. Strether's concentration on Marie de Vionnet as a problem for his augmented consciousness, particularly following the revelation that she and Chad are actual lovers, works to shore up his continuing obliviousness to anything other than the heterosexual modes of social experience realism typically serves.

If encounters with women such as Marie de Vionnet in complex domestic spaces pose challenges for Strether's cultivated mastery, he reinforces his new sense of self through his access to the public urban sphere of Paris. He has a vision of "the vibration of the vast strange life of the town, the influence of the types, the performers concocting their messages; the little prompt Paris women, arranging, pretexting goodness knew what, driving the dreadful needle-pointed public pen at the dreadful sand-strewn public table. . . . After he had put in his paper he had ranged himself, he was really amused to think, on the side of the fierce, the sinister, the acute. He was carrying on a correspondence, across the great city, quite in the key of the *Postes et Télégraphes* in general" (22:270–271). Later, as he heads for his final showdown with Marie de Vionnet, he remains newly attentive to the city itself, to the violent and brutal side of its history, and to revolution and independence: "From beyond this, and as from a great distance . . . came, as if excited and exciting, the vague voice of Paris. Strether had all along been subject to sudden gusts of fancy, . . . odd starts of the historic sense, suppositions and divinations with no warrant but their intensity. . . . They were the smell of revolution, the smell of the public temper—or perhaps simply the smell of blood" (22:274). This dawning mastery of an adopted city shows most in his outings with Miss Gostrey: "He proposed amusements to her; he felt expert now in proposing amusements; and he had thus, for several days, an odd sense of leading her about Paris, of driving her in the Bois, of showing her the penny steamboats—those from which the breeze of the Seine was to be best enjoyed. . . . He found means even to take her to shops she didn't know" (22:291). This mastery of urban space works to shield Strether's masculinity from unconscious shocks. If this kind of knowledge has had feminine sources in *The Ambassadors*—"it took women, it took women"—its appropriation has been naturalized as a maternal contribution to male independence (22:285). Whatever primal threat lurks in maternal relations, meanwhile, vanishes against the exteriority, the brute reality, of commercialized masculine space. The cultivation of such mastery constitutes the triumph of Strether's identification with Gloriani in the pivotal scene in his garden. It is not that such gardens contain only objects gendered male. Rather, the successful man "keeps them down" regardless of gender (21:199).

This space itself poses a threat to James's men of imagination. It is possible, as Christopher Newman discovered, to be too commercial, a fate into which Chad Newsome is fated to descend. Chad has embraced the new art of advertisement: "'It's an art like another, and infinite like all the arts.' . . . He went on as if for the joke of it. . . . 'In the hands, naturally, of a master. The right man must take hold'" (22:316). Against the too masculine world, which threatens with another kind of decentering nonbeing, Strether counterpoises a domestic, feminine realm, occupied by Maria Gostrey: "He had sent Maria Gostrey a word early, by hand, to ask if he might come to breakfast; in consequence of which, at noon, she awaited him in the cool shade of her little Dutch-looking dining-room. This retreat was at the back of the house, with a view of a scrap of old garden that had been saved from modern ravage; and . . . the place had never before struck him as so sacred to pleasant knowledge, to intimate charm, to antique order, to a neatness that was almost august" (22:319). Secure masculinity of an aesthetic type requires a balance: the feminine against commerce; commerce against the feminine. If Strether renounces this refuge, he nonetheless at this moment, no doubt exquisite, seems in full cognitive and emotional command of it. And even his abandonment of Maria Gostrey and his contemplated return to the United States suggest an augmentation of Rowland Mallet's power in *Roderick Hudson*. In that novel, the failed hero returns to America to continue his interminable and guilt-ridden courting of Mary Garland, who clings for her part to her memories of Hudson.

Gostrey's garden suggests a reduced but analogous version of the garden of Gloriani, the place where Strether first encounters the figure who defines the trajectory of desire for him in the text:

> Far back from the streets and unsuspected by crowds, reached by a
> long passage . . . it was as striking to the unprepared mind . . . as a
> treasure dug up; giving him too, more than anything yet, the note of
> the range of the immeasurable town. . . . It was in the garden, a spa-
> cious cherished remnant . . . on the other side of which grave *hôtels*
> stood off for privacy, spoke of survival, transmission, association, a
> strong indifferent persistent order. The day was so soft that the little
> party had practically adjourned to the open air, but the open air
> was . . . a chamber of state. Strether had presently the sense of a great
> convent, a convent of missions. . . . [H]e had the sense of names in
> the air, of ghosts at the windows, of signs and tokens, a whole range
> of expression, all about him. (21:195–196)

Strether has now moved into a position of reduced but analogous splendor. If he turns his back on what Maria Gostrey offers, he affirms that he now "keeps them down" as well.

Finally, I might here take slight issue with what I take to be Carren Kaston's framing of Strether's renunciation. Kaston argues that Strether fails to assume full authorial stature because of his secondary "ambassadorial" consciousness, which involves a refusal of a full (and necessarily self-aggrandizing) assertion of self over experience: "Although it would seem that in refusing to carry out Mrs. Newsome's mission Strether would himself become the author of his experience, his insistence on not getting anything for himself, not profiting personally, implies that he is still prototypically ambassadorial. He defines his identity negatively."[21] I have argued that Strether gets quite a lot for himself and that, given the centrality of his consciousness to the telling of the novel, he has to do so, whether he professes renunciation or not. Authorship regularly implies a disinterested failure to "get" anything from the fictions it produces, a failure that paradoxically constitutes the fiction's "rightness" or perfection. But for the author, as for the unconscious, there is no negative. The author (like Strether) always profits.

The Wings of the Dove

James would devote his next project, *The Wings of the Dove,* to the development of the complicating vectors of desire that form the barely explored frame of *The Ambassadors.* It is likely that the two late projects actually have an enabling relation to each other as expressions of divergent and contradictory pressures in James's writing. *The Ambassadors* represents a smooth and masterful performance within the tradition of the novel, and its twelve-part serialization even demonstrates James's capacity to pirouette within the confines dictated by nineteenth-century commerce. *The Wings of the Dove,* according to James in the preface, assumed its shape because of the absence of market constraints and pressures. Its complexity was produced by a "free hand" that James owed "to the fact that the work had ignominiously failed, in advance, of all power to see itself 'serialised.'" As a consequence, as a "considerable production," it was "born not otherwise than a little bewilderedly, into a world of periodicals and editors, of roaring 'successes' in fine, amid which it was . . . to lose itself" (1293).

A turn away from the impositions of commerce, voluntary or not, freed James for an exploration of queer or wayward desires located in a perverse relation to his heterosexual plots. *The Wings of the Dove* is a text about perversion in the sense historically traced in Jonathan Dollimore's *Sexual Dissidence.* Dollimore locates an anxiety about perversion at the heart of the Western humanist tradition. As Dollimore defines it, perversion "is a concept involving: (1) an erring, straying, deviation, or being diverted from (2) a path, destiny, or objective which is (3) understood as natural or right—usually right because natural (with the natural possibly having a yet higher legitimation in divine law)."[22] Though, as Dollimore shows, perversion can be, has been, and continues to be modeled in different ways, its use as a concept implies an interrelation of the deviant and the dominant in which each assumes some of its identity or character from the other, so that the perverse and straight are dynamically locked together. The degree to which the perverse can finally be said to subvert or resist culturally dominant formations remains a crucial subject of debate.[23]

The Wings of the Dove suggests, for its part, the capacity of deviance dialectically to reinforce dominant cultural formations. I have suggested that James, in both *The American* and *The Ambassadors,* constructs authority through a heterosexual plot of masculine, authorial self-making that marginalizes and suppresses homoerotic dynamics. In *The Wings of the Dove,* James opens his prose to such dynamics by deferring the plot of masculine self-making; the final result of this deferral is an increase in its affective intensity, as if James deploys it directly against the energies he also liberates.

There have been two important queer readings of the novel in the last several years, from Michael Moon and Eve Kosofsky Sedgwick, which have changed the way in which the novel must be understood. Although I am indebted to both essays here and to Sedgwick's imaginatively empowering work in general, I think that both arguments miss aspects of the complex representation of sexuality in the novel. The intertextual dynamics I have been tracing in James in the case of *The Wings of the Dove* suggest a less productively queer text than Sedgwick does, but a more integratedly queer text than Moon does.

In the case of Moon's argument, most of the novel consists of an exercise in retrograde heterosexual politics. As Moon puts it, "*The Wings of the Dove* is frequently a rebarbative text because in many of its parts it reproduces in uncritical fashion a lethal form of sexual politics which continually stultifies relations among its characters."[24] This uncritical project, in Moon's view, is rescued by a homosexual thematics that magically "irrupts" in the great Venetian climax, when the novel escapes "from the trammels which hold its energies in check for most of the rest of its course" (428). Moon unpacks these Venetian energies with great skill, but sees them as encased in a plot of stifling heterosexuality with which they have little to do.

Sedgwick writes about the novel after Moon and, in a powerful reading, exposes and traces the queer desires that course through the novel. She convincingly identifies Lionel Croy's oblique disgrace as a homosexual one, and she unpacks at length the erotic tensions between Kate and Milly. She suggests that Milly's ravaging illness should, in fact, be understood as a profound melancholia produced by her transgressive desires for Kate and her inability to enact them.[25]

Sedgwick's commitment to demonstrating directly queer productivity at work in the novel, to seeing "queer people as not only what the world makes but what makes the world" (95), directs her away from addressing the different kinds of sexualities at work in the novel. Her argument, crucially, hinges on the construction of a queer plot in the novel. This plot begins with Lionel Croy, whom Sedgwick compellingly argues is almost certainly homosexual because of exchanges like the following:

Kate: "I don't know what you're like."

Lionel: "No more do I, my dear. I've spent my life in trying in vain to discover. Like nothing—more's the pity. If there had been many of us and we could have found each other out there's no knowing what we mightn't have done." (19:20)[26]

Sedgwick argues that Croy passes on his queerness to Kate, whose "construction as a woman, her sexing and gendering, have her father's homosexual disgrace installed at their very core" (77). If this claim is correct—and I think it is—we might also supplement it by noting that, in a book that stages the opposition between hetero- and homoeroticism as a devastating and murderous dialectic, that core is also overwritten in heterosexual terms.

At the center of *The Wings of the Dove,* one finds a tale of the consolidation of masculine identity consistent with similar consolidations in *The American* and *The Ambassadors.* In famously "turn[ing] her face to the wall," Milly effectively embodies an important image from earlier novels, as she becomes a blank space that may be projectively filled in as Densher pleases.[27] As part of this project, Densher refuses Milly's actual words, preferring not to know the content of her final note, which Kate burns after he places the letter in her hands:

The part of it missed for ever was the turn she would have given her act. . . . It had made of them a revelation the loss of which was like the sight of a priceless pearl cast before his eyes . . . into the fathomless sea, or rather even it was like the sacrifice of something . . . that, for the spiritual ear, might have been audible as a faint far wail. . . . He sought and guarded the stillness, so that it might prevail there till the inevitable sounds of life, once more, comparatively coarse and harsh, should smother and deaden it—doubtless by the same process with which they would officiously heal the ache in his soul that was somehow one with it. It moreover deepened the sacred hush. (20:396)

Densher's final consolidation of an idealized feminine other is remarkably similar to Newman's. It involves an erasure of material content so that an idealized and completely controlled image can be instituted in its stead. The difference between *The Wings of the Dove* and *The American* in this regard lies in the former's formalization and foregrounding of the process. Milly is so dressed for sacrifice that she barely holds her integrity as a conventionally realist character. The pathos her death produces, always on the edge of tipping into camp, results less, in my judgment, from a direct sense of the death of a real woman at the hands of a nefarious plot than from the power of this heavily symbolic death to invoke the broad and remorseless representational violence done to women. The famous scene in which Milly confronts her supposed double in the Bronzino portrait and perceives that its subject is "dead, dead, dead" speaks directly to this aspect of the novel (19:221).

The Ambassadors, I argue, dramatizes Strether's self-development in heterosexual terms that comically marginalize homosexual possibilities. Strether imagines that one can only acquire certain things from women, an assumption that suppresses what one might (and Chad arguably does) acquire from men as well. By enacting a teleological narrative that naturalizes male appropriation of feminine goods and rupture from the maternal, Strether moves smoothly into a position of consolidated independence, enacting an identification with his imaginative father, Gloriani. Strether's "good" and the novel's "good," in adhering to this developmental paradigm, are indistinguishable. The novel thus performs the cultural hegemony of the heterosexual marriage plot, a hegemony that cannot be undone by reading the novel's marginalized homosexual markers against it.

The same narrative core exists at the heart of *The Wings of the Dove*. Since this is a novel arguably more interested in exposing Densher's imagination than in celebrating it, he does not have "imagination galore," to repeat James's phrase about Strether. Indeed, he is positioned between Strether and Newman, with perhaps closer ties to the obliviousness of the former. Densher's status as a journalist does not entitle him to a seat of honor in James's pantheon of characters, as the acidic, withering tone of the following suggests: "[H]e wrote, as for print, with deplorable ease; since there had been nothing to stop him even at the age of ten, so there was as little at twenty; it was part of his fate in the first place and the wretched public's in the second" (19:64).

The story of the generation of Densher's independence from Kate chiefly occupies the second half of the book and is told in metafictive terms. Carolyn L. Karcher has described *The Wings of the Dove* in general in terms of James's campaign against women writers (visible in his patronizing treatment of Susan Stringham) and argues that Densher wins back authorship as a male prerogative by substituting his own "idea" for Kate's entrapping plan (20:236). He thus wins his freedom from the "circle of petticoats" that, in his view, obliterates his masculinity (20:209).[28] As Julie Olin-Ammentorp has argued, this authorship occurs through Densher's oedipal identification with Sir Luke Strett, who represents in the novel a fantasy of undiluted masculine mastery analogous to that of Gloriani in *The Ambassadors,* but is more obviously installed in the practical world.[29] Strett possesses, in fact, the same expertness that Strether displays, as Sir Luke moves effortlessly from public to private space and back again. An expert traveler, he knows, for example, that when getting on a train the first task is "the right bestowal of his numerous effects, about which he was particular" (20:307). An adept at negotiating Venice, in his "prowl or two" with Densher, "Sir Luke knew just what he wanted; haunted a little the dealers in old wares; sat down at Florian's for rest and mild drinks; blessed above all the grand weather" (20:303–304).

Realism undergirds the desire for male authority in this section of the novel. In *The Ambassadors,* Strether finds that "it was the quantity of make-believe involved and so vividly exemplified that most disagreed with his spiritual stomach" (22:265). He had "dressed the possibility" of an affair between Chad and Madame de Vionnet "in vagueness, as a little girl might have dressed her doll" (22:266). In *The Wings of the Dove,* inspired by Strett's presence, Densher concludes, "He had also, with every one else, as he now felt, actively fostered suppressions which were in the direct interest of every one's good manner. . . . It was a conspiracy of silence, as the *cliché* went, to which no one had made an exception, the great smudge of mortality across the picture, the shadow of pain and horror, finding in no quarter a surface of spirit or of speech that consented to reflect it. 'The mere aesthetic instinct of mankind—!'"(20:298–299). Even though Densher repudiates "aesthetic instinct" as a cause of cultural mystification, he quickly employs those instincts in his transformation of Milly's death. Densher invokes realism as a crucial cultural ground upon which masculine authority rests, but this authority resides in no ascertainable epistemological certainty. Sir Luke's healing effect on

132 Circuits of Desire

Densher, in fact, succeeds precisely because it begs tricky questions about the reliability of ideas about the world: "The beauty was also that this wasn't on system or on any basis of intimate knowledge; it was just by being a man of the world and by knowing life, by feeling the real, that Sir Luke did him good. There had been in all the case too many women. A man's sense of it, another man's, changed the air. . . . The grand thing . . . was the way he carried off . . . the business of making odd things natural" (20:305). The "business of making odd things natural" is precisely the work performed by conventional ideas of the real.

At the same time, Sir Luke's authority is not confined to a masculine, exterior realm, although that is where he has his personal effect on Densher. On the contrary, his power makes itself more felt in his effortless penetration of the private domestic realm, a penetration especially evident in his unchallenged access to Milly at a time when Densher feels himself to be exiled and in disgrace. Just as masculinity in *The American* and *The Ambassadors* requires a final balancing of exterior mastery against domestic feminization and domestic integration against the disintegrating power of economic and commercial life, Sir Luke's power resides in his effortless fusion of social antinomies. When Strett first meets Milly, she describes him as having a face "half like a general and half like a bishop, and she was soon sure that, within some such handsome range, what it would show her would be what was good, what was best for her." If he would seem to her a "friend," he would nonetheless "somehow wear the character scientifically, ponderably, proveably— not just loosely and sociably" (19:230–231). Even his office speaks to Milly of a perfect balance of the public and the private, both in the world and apart from it, much like Gloriani's garden in *The Ambassadors:*

> The very place, at the end of a few minutes, the commodious "handsome" room, far back in the fine old house, soundless from position . . . put on for her a look of custom and use, squared itself solidly round her as with promises and certainties. She had come forth to see the world, and this then was to be the world's light, the rich dusk of a London "back," these the world's walls, those the world's curtains and carpet. She should be . . . one of the circle of eminent contemporaries, photographed, engraved, signatured, and in particular framed and glazed, who made up the rest of the decoration. (19:237)

Whatever James's bottomless ironies about doctors and dead patients, Sir Luke represents a style of masculine authority that James preferred, both in the world and committed to the private and domestic. His worried sense that the

U.S. businessman had simply abdicated domestic responsibility is evident, for example, throughout *The American Scene*. It is worth listening, against the interpretive possibilities of his fiction, to what James says outside of it: "From the moment it is adequately borne in mind that the business-man, in the United States, may . . . never hope to be anything *but* a business-man, the size of the field he so abdicates is measured. . . . It lies there waiting, pleading from all its pores, to be occupied—the lonely waste, the boundless gaping void of 'society.' . . . Here it is then that the world he lives in accepts its doom and becomes, by his default, subject and plastic to his mate."[30] For her part, James suggests in a late essay on U.S. women published in *Harpers*, that "the wisdom of the ages has everywhere quite absolved her from the formidable care of extracting a conception of the universe and a scheme of manners from her moral consciousness alone—the burden that among ourselves she has so rashly and complacently assumed [when women] . . . with their immense delusion . . . collectively launch themselves upon the world."[31] I do not believe that the interpretive possibilities of James's fiction ought to be bound by his worst public moments. By way of appreciating the deeply reactionary and conservative side of a divided book, however, it is worth remembering the extent to which James was capable of simply and directly sympathizing with the efforts of characters like Lambert Strether and Merton Densher to achieve a release from their respective "circle[s] of petticoats" (20:209).

The female character who has had to "launch" herself upon the world in the absence of proper masculine guidance is, of course, Kate Croy. The teleology of the narrative development of her character, I will argue, largely serves but also ironizes the masculinizing self-constructions of Merton Densher outlined above. For much of the novel, she clearly occupies a female tutelary position, as does Marie de Vionnet or Maria Gostrey in *The Ambassadors,* and so normalizes and naturalizes the male hero's separation as the cultivation of adult independence. Hers is the chief petticoat of the circle and, prior to the pathetic self-assertion of his seduction of her, she persistently (but lovingly) patronizes his deficiencies in addition to refusing to grace his bed. This account opens volume 2, chiefly devoted to Densher's dilemmas: "'I say, you know, Kate—you *did* stay!' had been Merton Densher's punctual remark on their adventure after they had, as it were, got out of it; an observation . . . she . . . let him see that she forgave in him only because he was a man. . . . But the amount of light men *did* need!—Kate could have been eloquent at this moment about that" (20:3). It is against this sexual/intellectual pressure that Densher (journalist, man of the mind) has his "idea" that Kate must come to his rooms: "It had simply *worked*, his idea, the idea he had made her accept; and all erect before him, really covering the ground . . . was the fact of the gained success that this represented" (20:236). The success of Densher's lone "idea" to this point in the text, however, paradoxically only adds assertive sexuality to Kate's power and sends him flying to the vitiated image of Milly Theale in full-fledged gynephobic sexual panic.

Much of the question of Kate's heterosexual relations is framed by the lens of Merton Densher's fantasy life. Early in the book, for example, it is his perception that Kate is insufficiently sexual despite the fact that she cannot get enough of his "long looks" (19:61). Their difference here reads like a parody of male avidity and female sexlessness: "She looked it well in the face, she took it intensely home, that they were lovers; she rejoiced to herself and, frankly, to him, in their wearing of the name; but . . . she took a view of this character that scarce squared with the conventional. . . . Life might prove difficult . . . but meanwhile they had each other. . . . For *him* each other was what they didn't have" (19:61–62). Densher will feel, in fact, that the absence of sexual relations with Kate produced "an impatience that, prolonged and exasperated, made a man ill" (20:7). Though the sexual disgrace of Kate's father might logically equip her with a commitment to sexual propriety, Densher's description of her behavior suggests a cold disinterest in sexual pleasure.[32] This disinterest, however, forms part of his (and possibly James's) repugnant fantasy of innocence, violation, and sexual awakening that underlies Densher's relationship with Kate.

Before she agrees to see him, Densher fantasizes that his sexual insistence pleases her. First, when he breaks out, "Good God, if you'd only *take* me!" he imagines that "she felt his rebellion more sweet than bitter" (20:198–199). Then, as she continues to resist, he suggests that "her rigour was more to him, nevertheless, than all her readiness; for her readiness was the woman herself, and this other thing a mask, a stop-gap and a 'dodge'" (20:230). Immediately after she comes to see him, Densher includes Kate in his fantasies of sexual bliss. Though Kate "had come to him," it was "only once," but in Densher's memory this was not "from any failure of their need" (20:235). These are conventionally suspicious sentiments to be sure, and no particular reason at this point to attribute passion to Kate in her relation to Densher.

Kate and Densher next meet after the return of both to London. Although Densher has been back a "fortnight" he has not informed Kate of his presence (20:213). In fact, Densher now smugly perceives that she wants him:

He might have struck her as expert for contingencies in the very degree of her having in Venice struck *him* as expert. He smiled over his plea for a renewal with stages and steps, a thing shaded, as they might say, and graduated; though—finely as she must respond—she met the smile but as she had met his entrance five minutes before. Her soft gravity at that moment—which was yet not solemnity, but the look of a consciousness charged with life to the brim and wishing not to overflow—had not qualified her welcome; what had done this being . . . the footman . . . who had been interrupted in preparing the tea-table. (20:315–316)

The point, I take it, is that this intercession forestalls a greeting that would be substantially more passionate, suggested by the effort required to prevent the "consciousness charged with life to the brim" from overflowing.

When Kate takes over the preparation of tea, she uncharacteristically lacks poise. The tea has been left to boil too long and is "hissing too hard," and Kate "rather too profusely . . . ladled tea into the pot," a sign that, we are told, "her friend noticed" (20:330). Kate's enthusiastic awkwardness passes into confusion at Densher's brutal indifference, made more striking by the disappearance of constraints that have previously bound their interactions. Aunt Maude has now been "squared." When Densher remarks that he must be "a brute" to please so many people, Kate responds as follows: "'Ah,' said Kate with a gleam of gaiety, 'you've done it to please *me*.' But she was already, with her gleam, reverting a little. 'What I don't understand is—won't you have any sugar?'" (20:331). Within the context I am establishing, the sudden shift in the flow of Kate's conversation suggests that she begins to ask one question concerning Densher's sudden unresponsiveness, cannot bring herself to ask it, and presents it instead in barely disguised form.

Of Milly and love, Kate now apparently speaks from firsthand experience. In speaking of Milly's death, Kate offers the opinion that she will have "the peace of having loved," to which she adds the following as qualification: "'Of having *been* loved,' she went on. 'That is. Of having,' she wound up, 'realised her passion. She wanted nothing more. She has had *all* she wanted.' Lucid and always grave, she gave this out with a beautiful authority that he could for the time meet with no words" (20:332). Almost immediately following this pronouncement, Densher and Kate renew the physical passion of Venice, this time at Kate's instigation. "She was once more close to him, close as she had been the day she came to him in Venice, the quickly returning memory of which intensified and enriched the fact. He could practically deny in such conditions nothing that she said, and what she said was, with it, visibly a fruit of knowledge. 'We've succeeded.' She spoke with her eyes deep in his own" (20:333). Such a reading of this scene as an erotic one is immediately reinforced by James. When the now "squared" Aunt Maude enters the room, "Kate and he, no doubt, . . . had fallen apart with a certain suddenness, . . . but the effect of this lost itself, to his mind, the next minute, in the effect of his companion's rare alertness. She instantly spoke to her aunt . . . inviting her thereby intimately to join them" (20:334).

The sum of this evidence suggests a renewal of sexual relations, chiefly at Kate's now eager instigation but with Densher's participation. Since Milly lies grotesquely dying in Venice at the time, such a reading lays permanently to rest arguments that Densher achieves any substantive nobility. He does achieve a renewed anxiety about his own authority in light of Kate's passion, however, that chases him defensively into his chaste love for the dying Milly Theale. His perception of Kate suggests, in fact, Pater's description of Leonardo da Vinci's *La Gioconda* in a familiar passage of *The Renaissance*. In this passage, women's sexual knowledge, understood as a defilement of their purity, literally embodies centuries of cultural corruption: "All the thoughts and experience of the world have etched and moulded there. . . . She is older than the rocks among which she sits; like the vampire. . . . Certainly Lady Lisa might stand as the embodiment of the old fancy, the symbol of the modern idea" (80). The sign and center of all this embodiment is her "unfathomable smile, always with a touch of something sinister in it" (79). Now the mythologized Kate's "large strange smile" (20:348) discomfits Densher, as does his imputation to her of unfathomable and unalterable wisdom. This passage again emphasizes the strangeness of her smile: "He had brought her there to be moved, and she was only immoveable—which was not moreover, either, because she didn't understand. She understood everything, and things he refused to; and she had reasons, deep down, the sense of which nearly sickened him. She had too again most of all her strange significant smile" (20:348–349).

Kate's Mona Lisa grin in these passages suggests sexual knowingness of a kind that converts her into Densher's personal Medusa. She once again has gained the upper hand in erotic terms, and has created in him a

> failure of insistence when it brought up *that* challenge, and his sense
> of her personal presence, and his horror, almost, of her lucidity. They
> made in him a mixture that might have been rage, but that was turn-

ing quickly to mere cold thought, thought which led to something else and was like a new dim dawn. It affected her then, and she had one of the impulses, in all sincerity, that had before this, between them, saved their position. When she . . . made him sink with her, as she leaned to him, into their old pair of chairs, she prevented irresistibly, she forestalled, the waste of his passion. She had an advantage with his passion now. (20:350)

Though distorted by misogynist sexual paranoia, Densher's "reading" of Kate's behavior corresponds to actual physical actions on her part consistent with a reading of them as desiring. If Kate has been cold earlier in the book, the coldness now is Densher's, despite his sense of her "personal presence." It is at this moment that the "new dim dawn" of Densher's final idea occurs, that of renouncing Kate, even as she uses her "advantage with his passion" (20:350).

Kate and Densher, then, cross roles in *The Wings of the Dove,* Densher going from a position of assertive sexuality to sexual fear, and Kate, from a position of at least posited sexual innocence to sexual desire. This particular cross heterosexually "crosses out" Kate's much more complicated and disruptively queer positioning in the first volume of the novel. It is this beginning section that constitutes the chief difference between *The Wings of the Dove* and James's other novels of masculine self-making, a difference that again highlights the importance of thinking intertextually about James's project. Unlike both *The American* and *The Ambassadors,* the entirety of the plot of *The Wings of the Dove* does not center exclusively on the male protagonist's attempt to developmentally integrate his psyche against the assaults of experience. James begins the novel by deliberately stepping back from this plot in order to see the complications that surround it, complications that are confined and generally absent from *The American* and present but radically marginalized by the workings of Strether's imagination in *The Ambassadors.* This radical decentering of the plot of masculine self-making both exposes and consolidates its authority. We see with clarity the dispersive force of the desires that surround it, but this dispersive force dialectically produces the elevated intensity of the novel's final deployment of Milly Theale's covering wings.

The Wings of the Dove opens with Kate. "Croy," as has commonly been remarked, suggests *croix,* or "cross," and marks her relation to the crosspainting Noemie Nioche of *The American.* Like Noemie, she embodies the commercial, nontranscendent reality of the social positions of women, and like Noemie she sets out to remedy the deficiencies of her personal position by any necessary means. A desire for money underlies all of her motives. Arguably, she sleeps with Densher in order to forward her scheme to appropriate Milly's millions, and Milly's millions are what she ends up with as a consequence. More complex motives can always be attributed to Kate, but the space for these motives depends on the ultimate ineffability of everything in the novel beyond Aunt Maude's furniture. We can "cling," as Kate puts it for herself, "to some saving romance in things" precisely because the romance might exist: its nonexistence, at least, cannot be proven (19:72).

It is consistent with her transgressive position in the first part of the text that nothing definitive can be said about Kate's sexuality or the sexuality of other characters in *The Wings of the Dove*. Erotic desire darts everywhere and is inextricably tied to a greedy, social acquisitiveness: if sex and money are not precisely the same thing, they behave in a similar fashion. Just as anyone and anything can be ranked and desired as a commodity in the social world of the novel, so anyone can be sized up and sexually desired. Few things could exceed the erotic, capitalist, sadomasochistic fusion of Kate's account to Milly of the workings of the social system: "Kate did explain, for her listening friend; every one who had anything to give—it was true they were the fewest—made the sharpest possible bargain for it, got at least its value in return. The strangest thing furthermore was that this might be in cases a happy understanding. The worker in one connexion was the worked in another; it was as broad as it was long—with the wheels of the system, as might be seen, wonderfully oiled" (19:179). The rhetoric of *The Wings of the Dove* works as a desire-creating machine precisely through its endless sadomasochistic specification and exaggeration of differences, so that the penetration of or by another person can offer up the requisite fantasy of pleasure. Milly, for example, has the following complexly evolving fantasy about her relation to Lord Mark and Kate:

> It was the handsome girl alone, one of his own species and his own society, who had made him feel uncertain; of his certainties about a mere little American, a cheap exotic, imported almost wholesale and whose habitat, with its conditions of climate, growth and cultivation, . . . he was perfectly satisfied. The marvel was too that Milly understood his satisfaction—feeling she expressed the truth in presently saying: "Of course; I make out that she must be difficult; just as I see that I myself must be easy." . . . She was more and more content herself to be easy; she would have been resigned, even

had it been brought straighter home to her, to passing for a cheap exotic. . . . They *had* all affected her as inevitably knowing each other, and if the handsome girl's place among them was something even their initiation couldn't deal with—why then she would indeed be a quantity. (19:166)

If power, as Marcia Ian suggests, consists in this text in not letting oneself be penetrated or known by others,[33] pleasure often involves allowing and wishing such violation to occur. Thus Milly wills herself to be, in three loaded words, "cheap," "easy," and "exotic," the better to be desired herself by a handsome girl who, she later perceives, is "the least bit brutal" (19:181).

A sadomasochistic desire to penetrate and to be penetrated informs Densher's relations to a variety of men in the Venice section of the novel, including Strett, Eugenio, Pasquale (the gondolier), and Lord Mark, as Moon has suggested. These interactions reinforce the novel's vision of a potentially terrifying fluidity of desire. Moon persuasively suggests that visiting Victorian gentlemen had sexual relationships with Italian men. As he writes, "male-homosexual tourists commonly made contact with men of Venice's large lower-class population of gondoliers and sailors, some of whom engaged in prostitution" (439). Furthermore, he writes, "James can hardly have been unaware either of the 'trade' in gondoliers going on around him during his stays in Venice or of the frequency with which men of his class and official level of cultivation sought sex and sometimes more from men of Eugenio's class" (440).

Such sexual trade paradigmatically uses barriers of nationality, ethnicity, and class to compartmentalize dangerous desires apart from the reality of bourgeois daily life and the identity that depends on it. Part of Eugenio's threatening presence in *The Wings of the Dove,* then, lies in his refusal as a character to be so contained. Densher cannot free himself from Eugenio's judging gaze, a gaze that posits an essential equality: "It had been . . . far from occult to our young man that Eugenio took a view of him not less finely formal than essentially vulgar, but which at the same time he couldn't himself raise an eyebrow to prevent" (20:257). Eugenio even haunts Densher's saving relationship with Sir Luke Strett and, hence, deconstructively challenges its essential nature. If Strett represents Densher's fantasy of a powerful and beneficent father, Densher has nonetheless felt judged by Eugenio as well. If, on the other hand, Eugenio occupies a position conventionally marked as a sexual one, he unmasks the erotics of Densher's oedipalized relation to Strett. No absolute distinction can be drawn, finally, between either kind of man or kind of experience, and all of this gazing between men occurs in public space, in Densher's exile from a relation to a stabilizing feminine domesticity. In the following passage, for example, Densher watches Strett, but finds his attention inevitably redirected to Eugenio. The scene ends with his recognition of the similarity between the two:

> What he had been doing was proof of a huge interest as well as of a huge fee; yet . . . his companion . . . studied his fine closed face as much as ever in vain. It was like a lesson, from the highest authority, on the subject of the relevant, so that its blankness affected Densher of a sudden almost as a cruelty. . . . The strain, though probably lasting, at the carriage-door, but a couple of minutes, prolonged itself so for our poor gentleman's nerves that he involuntarily directed a long look at Eugenio, who met it, however, as only Eugenio could. . . . Eugenio resembled to that extent Sir Luke—to the extent of the extraordinary things with which his facial habit was compatible. (20:306–307)

This twilight amorphousness of experience and desire threatens to drown Merton Densher. Even in James's initial description of him, his identity flickers like a loose light bulb:

> He was a longish, leanish, fairish young Englishman, not unamenable on certain sides, to classification—as for instance by being a gentleman, by being rather specifically one of the educated, one of the generally sound and generally civil; yet, though to that degree neither extraordinary nor abnormal, he would have failed to play straight into an observer's hands. He was young for the House of Commons, he was loose for the Army. He was refined, as might have been said, for the City and, quite apart from the cut of his cloth, skeptical, it might have been felt, for the Church. On the other hand he was credulous for diplomacy, or perhaps even for science, while he was perhaps at the same time too much in his mere senses for poetry and yet too little in them for art. (19:48)

The ongoing, demasculinizing threat of disintegration, implicit in nearly every amorphous aspect of this social world, produces the countervailing energy of Merton Densher's enshrining of Milly Theale as the stabilizing "other" of masculine identity.[34]

Lionel Croy, as Kate's parent, serves as the parent of the text's instabilities and as a paranoid marker of their danger.[35] Kate initially presents herself to him as a faithful daughter if only he will agree to serve as an agreeable father, and although the form of her utterance initiates the novel's cynicism about verbal pledges, we have little reason to doubt her sincerity. As she says, "I wish there were some one here who might serve—for any contingency—as a witness that I *have* put it to you that I'm ready to come" (19:20–21). He does not agree, but the power of paternity in Western culture only partly depends on the compliance of particular actors in particular roles. Even as his blankness suggests his homophobic near erasure, it simultaneously has an eerie theological character produced by his remoteness and silence. The beginning of the novel suggests a postlapsarian world of necessarily failed authority, and in such a world Kate is fated, as she puts it, to "go my way— as I see my way" (19:23). The entire scene suggests the structure of a fall that is inevitable, whether fortunate or not. No one has the phallus; all paternity fails; all children swerve.

Queerness thus has a dual character at the beginning of the text as something produced by a specific, material position of a specific character, Lionel Croy, and as a general experiential feature of the world of *The Wings of the Dove,* as something that just *is.* In this latter sense it inheres in the comprehensive queerness of style that at times threatens to dissolve the integrity of any individual character. To Leo Bersani, a single voice, that of the "single psychological perspective" of the narrative, runs through all of the text's major characters or narrative centers. To Quentin Anderson, "*The Wings of the Dove* treats 'representatives' of a *single* complex abstraction—human nature as James conceived it." To Laurence Holland, "[t]he narrative convention of *The Wings of the Dove* is founded on neither the author's voice alone nor on the center of consciousness alone but on the intimate connection between them."[36] The decentering of character by narrative voice in the novel is a clear part of the experience of reading it: one returns again and again to its remarkable style and to what James acknowledges in his preface to the New York edition as his "instinct everywhere for . . . *indirect* presentation" (1303). Such diffuse queerness prevents the compartmentalization of queer identity as the province of certain historically discrete, historically marked individuals, but it also suggests the potential of queerness to serve as the abjected ground of normative heterosexuality. *The Wings of the Dove* models queerness chiefly in the latter terms precisely because it finally subjects its differences and distinctions to the consolidation of the heterosexual identity of Merton Densher and, in a less explicit sense, consolidates the heterosexuality of Kate Croy as well.

The most immediate sacrifice to such consolidation might be Lionel

Croy himself, whose virtual absence from the text James mourns in the preface: "But where do we find him, at this time of day, save in a beggarly scene or two which scarce arrives at the dignity of functional reference? He but 'looks in,' poor beautiful dazzling, damning apparition that he was to have been; he sees his place so taken, his company so little missed, that, cocking again that fine form of hat . . . he turns away with a whistle of indifference" (1295). As opposed to Croy, the most markedly homosexual figure in the text, who has barely an explicit foothold in it, James must concern himself, *for* his text, apparently regardless of what else he does or does not want to do, with Merton Densher, the male whose character undergoes consolidation: "It wasn't, after this fashion, by making good one's dream of Lionel Croy that my structure was to stand on its feet—any more than it was by letting him go that I was to be left irretrievably lamenting. The who and the what, the how and the why, the whence and the whither of Merton Densher, these, no less, were quantities and attributes that should have danced about him with the antique grace of nymphs and fauns circling round a bland Hermes and crowning him with flowers" (1296). What I think is striking about this passage is the degree to which James continues to mourn for Lionel Croy even as he shifts to a description of the massive, hegemonic power of the heterosexual Densher to command our attention.

This tension between homosexual and heterosexual narratives in *The Wings of the Dove,* and in James's career as a whole, seems alluded to in another difficult passage preceding his comment on Lionel Croy, again made in the key of mourning:

> Yet one's plan, alas, is one thing, and one's result another. . . . I mourn for them all as I remount the stream, the absent values, the palpable voids, the missing links, the mocking shadows. . . . Such cases are of course far from abnormal—so far from it that some acute mind ought surely to have worked out by this time the "law" of the degree in which the artist's energy fairly depends on his fallibility. How much and how often, and in what connexions and with what almost infinite variety must he be a dupe, that of his prime object, to be at all measurably a master, that of his actual substitute for it—or in other words at all appreciably to exist? (1294–1295)

James has just articulated his own version of the intentional fallacy, but the stakes are higher, I think, than simply the question of the divergence of actual practice from original intention. The passage suggests the possibility of massive displacements in the compositional process, and in these displacements it is far from clear what occupies the position of unconscious "substitute." Conventionally, one might assume that James's homosexuality would find means of circumventing cultural prohibitions against it, so that the homosexual would come to substitute for an intentional heterosexuality. It is just as true to argue, however, that heterosexuality always functions as a cultural default value and thus unconsciously expresses its dominance unless consciously counteracted. In the passages just cited, it is Lionel Croy who best answers to the description of a "prime object" missed, while the "mastery" equated with the "actual substitute for it" might well suggest the resurgence, once again, of a dominant heterosexual plot. However one chooses to read the relation between an artist's "prime object" and "substitute for it," James suggests that the ability of the artist "to exist" is at stake. Without this mysterious two-tiered writing process in operation, the writer might be, just as Lionel Croy, "like nothing" (19:20).

Sedgwick points out that the rhetoric of the unspeakable that circulates around Lionel Croy circulates around Milly Theale as well. As she says, "One of the most astounding effects in *The Wings of the Dove* is the way Milly's relation to her illness winds up, rhetorically, as an echo precisely of Lionel Croy's homosexual disgrace. The strangeness of this is of course that Milly's illness is supposed to be the most sacralizing element of the novel, as Lionel's disgrace is the most sordid. Yet the same compulsive, reifying gestures of disavowal surround both secrets" (88). Even more than Milly's illness ties her to Lionel Croy's queerly marginal position in the novel. Like Lionel, Milly has a curious almost transparent quality, as if her only real corporeal presence is her money—the rest is indescribable. According to Susan Stringham's assessment, Milly has "arts and idiosyncrasies of which no great account could have been given, but which were a daily grace if you lived with them; such as the art of being almost tragically impatient and yet making it as light as air; of being inexplicably sad and yet making it as clear as noon; of being unmistakably gay and yet making it as soft as dusk" (19:115). She is like Lionel as well in that the narrative essentially asks her to efface herself in the interests of another character. If the narrative effaces Milly as a self-sacrifice to Densher's need for the integration of sublime heterosexual transcendence, Lionel Croy offers to fade from existence for his daughter Kate: "You must do me the justice to see that I don't do things, that I've never done them, by halves—that if I offer you to efface myself it's for the final fatal sponge I ask, well saturated and well applied" (19:20). If Lionel Croy has not had a describable life, the advice offered to Milly by Sir Luke Strett is simply and fully to resist such a fate. She must make up her mind to live. As he says, "My dear young lady, . . . isn't to 'live' exactly what I'm trying to persuade you to take the trouble to do?" (19:246).

The question of what it means to live—or more precisely, how it is possible to live without living—represents an obsession of James's late fiction. It is far from easy to say what the essence of living consists of, other than to suggest that it might well consist of something other than falling in love with Merton Densher. This, unfortunately, is what Milly chooses to do, even advertising a willingness to visit his carefully selected rooms.

The question of living commonly surfaces in James in terms of a choice of homosexual or heterosexual being. If we see Milly as most powerfully defined by her desires for Kate, the scene between Strett and Milly repeats the scene between Strether and Bilham, especially if we remember the source of this scene in a conversation between W. D. Howells and Jonathan Sturges. Sturges, like Milly, is also physically afflicted and, like Milly, receives ambiguous advice "to live" from a voice of middle-aged, autumnal authority, an authority whose own sexuality is at least open to interrogation.[37] This question of what it means, exactly, "to live" in a sexual context receives another and perhaps more searching interrogation in "The Beast in the Jungle." The most positive answer I can see that James supplies to this question is a knowing version of Strether's advice: "[I]t doesn't so much matter what you do in particular, so long as you have your life. If you haven't had that what *have* you had?" (21:217). Marcher, in short, should do *something* passionately, preferably with another person but even by himself, and the kind of act or person he chooses is not at the heart of the matter. Of course it *is* at the heart of the matter socially and politically, and the problem with James's late fiction is that the alternatives to choosing heterosexual life are never fully or convincingly developed, even if one admits the daunting difficulty of the task.[38] The anxiety, I have tried to suggest, is not just the question of what it means to exist as a person, but what it means to exist as an author, and James's fiction, I have suggested, sacrifices homosexual possibility for the authority granted by heterosexual narratives.

It is the value of *The Wings of the Dove* that it makes, of all of James's fiction, the world of marginalized and transgressive desire most visibly "there," most palpably felt, in the wayward circumlocutions of every sentence. It nonetheless fuses these desires into a heterosexual apotheosis and frames the excision of homosexual possibility as a preordained sacrifice of transcendent beauty. For Milly Theale and for the narrative, finally, "to live" means to choose, once again, narratable heterosexual experience.

Milly's sacrifice has important resonances with the death of Roderick

Hudson in James's first major novel. Like Roderick, Milly lives fast—"too fast"—a sure sign of foreordained doom. Says James of Milly, "[H]er doom was to live too fast. It was queerly a question of the short run and the consciousness proportionately crowded" (19:159). Similarly, Rowland Mallet "at moments felt vaguely uneasy for the future; the boy was living too fast, he would have said, and giving alarming pledges to ennui in his later years" (225). In both cases, the narrative itself seems interested in crowding experience into its characters' lives before their narrative executions. James, at any rate, knows what is coming.

The silence concerning what precisely causes Milly Theale's decline and death resembles, as well, what I argued earlier was a suppressive silence in *Roderick Hudson* concerning Roderick's remarkably fast drop to disaster. As I indicated, James suggests in the preface that the chief flaw of the novel was its foreshortened failure to account authentically for the decline of its hero: "Everything occurs, none the less, too punctually and moves too fast: Roderick's disintegration, a gradual process . . . swallows two years in a mouthful. . . . One feels indeed . . . on how much too scantly projected and suggested a field poor Roderick and his large capacity for ruin are made to turn round" (1047). The same flaw uncannily comes to haunt *The Wings of the Dove:* "The latter half, that is the false and deformed half, of 'The Wings' would verily, I think, form a signal object-lesson for a literary critic bent on improving his occasion to the profit of the budding artist. This whole corner of the picture bristles with "dodges" . . . for disguising the reduced scale of the exhibition, for foreshortening at any cost, for imparting to patches the value of presences, for dressing objects in an *air* as of the dimensions they can't possibly have" (1299–1300). Both foreshortenings, in turn, correspond to a heterosexualization of the narrative that, I would suggest, not only reduces the scale of the exhibition, but actively represses it. The veiled questions of the dynamics between Rowland and Roderick, and of the Paterian relation between homosexuality and Roderick's sculpture, and the further question of how such dynamics might be textually represented are suddenly obscured by the spread of Christina Light's own obscuring wings. The "false and deformed" latter part of *The Wings of the Dove,* also set in Italy, hurriedly forecloses erupting desires between men through Densher's abrupt return to London and the death of Milly.

Also uniting the two novels are similarities between scenes of Milly's temptation and Roderick's death, connections it will take some time to develop. Early in the novel, Susan Stringham and Milly form a "couple" based on mutual accommodation (19:111). Milly replaces the "love-interest" at the heart of Stringham's domestic fiction and Stringham offers herself as the personification of "culture" to the starved Milly (19:109). If this friendship lacks the sadomasochistic romance of Milly's relationship to the smart, beautiful, and secretive Kate, it nonetheless contributes to the novel's relentless blurring of conventional forms.

Susan takes her charge to Switzerland, as a consequence of her memories of her own earlier experiences of "cool upper air and of everything else that hung like an indestructible scent to the torn garment of youth—the taste of honey and the luxury of milk, the sound of cattle-bells and the rush of streams, the fragrance of trodden balms and the dizziness of deep gorges" (19:120). Milly is willing to be provided for as, after all, a princess, assenting to their "staying over," but ignoring all practical questions, such as rooms, carriages, horses, and other cares (19:120). While there, Susan realizes Milly's alarming absence: "When at the end of an hour she hadn't returned to the house Mrs. Stringham . . . took, with precautions, the same direction." The path leads her high up the hillside, past chalets and one "bewildered old woman" who is "fearful . . . to behold" (19:121–122). As she continues the search with increasing anxiety, she finds Milly seated, at a great height, on a rock, and is terrified by a perception of a potential to "slip, to slide, to leap, to be precipitated by a single false movement . . . into whatever was beneath." If an accident was a possibility, so too was suicide as a product of "some betrayed accordance of Milly's caprice with a horrible hidden obsession." This perception immediately yields to the perception that Milly wasn't meditating a jump but "sat . . . in a state of uplifted and unlimited possession that had nothing to gain from violence" (19:123–124). Between these opposing perceptions, Stringham's next perceptions more or less split the difference between a perception of Milly's power and her self-destructive vulnerability: "It wouldn't be for her a question of a flying leap and thereby of a quick escape. It would be a question of taking full in the face the whole assault of life, to the general muster of which indeed her face might have been directly presented as she sat there on her rock" (19:125). Milly's position here resembles nothing else in James's novels so much as Roderick's accidental or suicidal fall at the end of *Roderick Hudson*. Rowland, like Stringham, has powerful memories of Switzerland, associated with "cool air stirring about his temples, the wafted odors of the pines in his nostrils, the tinkle of the cattle-bells in his ears" (468). Like Stringham, Rowland must handle all practical questions, since Hudson "concerned himself not a particle about the itinerary, or about any of the wayside arrangements; he took no trouble . . . and led for a week a perfectly contemplative life" (469). Like Stringham, Rowland must set off in search of his alarmingly missing charge, a path that leads to encounters with grotesque alpine persons and finally Hudson's dead but beautiful body.

Earlier, I suggested Hudson presented a narrative problem in *Roderick Hudson* and embodied, both in his own aesthetic practice and in his fall, the difficulty of how to make same-sex desire between men the central focus of one's tale. His apocalyptic death—at best a sort of an ending—suggests the failure of the young James to solve this problem adequately. Roderick, finally, must be gotten rid of, but his death leads to nothing despite its disguising patina of redemptive beauty:

> He had fallen from a great height, but he was singularly little disfigured. The rain had spent its torrents upon him, and his clothes and hair were as wet as if the billows of the ocean had flung him upon the strand. An attempt to move him would show some hideous fracture, some horrible physical dishonor; but what Rowland saw on first looking was only a strangely serene expression of life. The eyes were dead, but in a short time, when Rowland had closed them, the whole face seemed to awake. The rain had washed away all blood; it was as if Violence, having done her work, had stolen away in shame. (509–510)

In *The Wings of the Dove,* James suggests the possibility of a similar violent end to Milly—and then defers it in the name of "taking full in the face the whole assault of life" (19:125). The lingering narrative of Milly's death, if we see her as an embodiment of queer desire, is as grotesque as Roderick's suicide, since she is slowly fashioned by the text into a sacrifice to heterosexual purity, a sacrifice redeemed by its ability to be cast in terms of transcendental beauty. In a final irony, Milly and Roderick die for the same cause. Roderick kills himself because he realizes he is too mixed and distorted to produce the pure and transcendental art he values; the purified but obliterated Milly dies as the art Roderick is unable to produce.

Postscript

Though I argue for the value of an intertextual reading of James, the practice of reading two pairs of texts, each pair consisting of roughly contemporaneous productions, works to make the drawing of conclusions difficult. I will, however, risk three:

Conclusion One

I have argued that the texts of the major phase function as a reenact-ment of oppositions and conflicts already present in rougher form at the be-ginning of James's career. What both *The Ambassadors* and *The Wings of the Dove* finally suggest, when read against *Roderick Hudson* and *The Ameri-can,* is a mastery of James's basic conflicts as aesthetic problems without mastering the conflicts themselves. The authority-disrupting conflicts of the early texts, in other words, are centered as the subject matter of the late ones, and centered precisely as questions that can be recognized as such, but that must be ultimately and even violently suppressed for the production of beauty, itself linked to the consolidation of masculine power. The positive beauty of such texts, if one can find positive beauty in such morally ambiguous condi-tions, lies in the precision with which they balance the value of what art pro-duces and what it costs, psychologically, socially, and politically. If one is unable to affirm the transcendences of characters such as Densher and Strether, these costs begin to look monstrously high. The foregrounding of such conflicts, meanwhile, consolidates authority for James even as he puts it at risk. Strether and Densher blindly and unconsciously enact a process of authority creation; James, as author, demonstrates that he is at least not blind.

Conclusion Two

I have made much of questions of "crosses" and "crossing," particu-larly in my discussion of *The American* and *The Wings of the Dove.* These tropes or marks—"the sign of truth" to Noemie Nioche—are at the heart of James's fiction and suggest why simple conclusions are hard to draw from an intertextual reading of his novels (655). Jamesian "crosses" and the re-lated figure x produce information and excise it with near simultaneity, sug-gesting a balance between James's desire to articulate culturally suppressed and unsayable truths and to control the socially and aesthetically disruptive consequences of his own excavations (see conclusion 1). The crossed rela-tion elicits such material without positive or essential content, the point be-ing that culturally dissonant registers have come into collision. With a forty-five-degree tilt, the cross becomes an x, a sign that stands for the re-pressive obliteration already implicit in the cross to begin with. Thus, Newman's aggressive effacement of Noemie Nioche yields to a blanket re-pression of the complexities of his experience as he fails to register the duchess's tale of "Princess X——."

In *Wings of the Dove,* the figure of x quietly creeps into the proceed-ings through the empty yet complicating presence of Lord Mark, whom James first refers to in his notebooks as "Lord X."[39] Mark's place in the book consists of nothing but a crossroads that enables certain kinds of relations to occur between characters, as, at the same time, he suggests the threatening nullity of such completely decentered identity. Through attributed value, he suggests to Kate the possibility of what "the really clever had in common with the really void," although on the whole "she was blank about Lord Mark" (19:177–178). In fact, he serves as the supposedly intellectual Densher's threatening double: his description by Milly occurs in precisely the same "longish, leanish, fairish" language that defines Merton Densher (19:48): "It was difficult to guess his age—whether he were a young man who looked old or an old man who looked young; it seemed to prove nothing, as against other things, that he was bald and, as might have been said, slightly stale, or more delicately perhaps, dry. . . . Very neat, very light, and so fair that there was little other indication of his moustache than his constantly feeling it—which was again boyish—he would have affected her as the most intellectual person present if he had not affected her as the most frivolous" (19:151). Mark suggests the threat of a permanent absence of substance, a threat Densher's quasi-theological absorption of Milly acts against.

Even Milly, as the "dove," suggests an aestheticized figure for an x or cross. The cross and the dove are metonymically linked in any case by their copresence as elements in Christian liturgy, and James repeatedly emphasizes Milly as a dove with wings extended for flight, so that the line of the wings and the line of the body intersect. Her crossed desires for Kate and Densher early in the novel suggest that her situation is as complex as Kate's own, yet at the end she stands for a beautiful obliteration of those complexities. As Kate puts it, "I used to call her, in my stupidity—for want of anything better—a dove. Well she stretched out her wings, and it was to *that* they reached. They cover us" (20:404).

The cross or x figures in a fascinating if ambiguous fashion in James's notebooks as well, where I first began to think about its significance. The published versions of the notebooks fail to convey the striking nature of James's practice of marking pages of notebooks with long rows of crosses, since they record the presence but not the number of such marks. Between passages or within them, James at times strings as many as thirty xs across a page, sometimes bending a line of xs to continue $x$ing down a margin. In the midst of so much intelligence at work, such mute and unintelligible signs, often present for no apparent reason, register the unknowable physiology of writing—the inscriptive equivalent of a twitching leg or chattering teeth, and a related excess of somatic/cognitive energy.

At other times, such marks seem positively to signify in James the interrelations of intertextual complexity, repression, and transcendence. I will give one substantial example. In a meditation in his notebooks on his childhood, dated "Cambridge, December 26th" (1881), James writes the following:

> It was a time of suffering so keen that that face might serve to give its dark colour to the whole period; but this is not what I think of today. When the burden of pain has been lifted, as many memories and emotions start into being as the little insects that scramble about when, in the country, one displaces a flat stone. Ill-health, physical suffering, in one's younger years, is a grievous trial; but I am not sure that we do not bear it most easily then. In spite of it we feel the joy of youth; and that is what I think of today among the things that remind me of the past. The freshness of impression and desire, the hope, the curiosity, the vivacity, the sense of the richness and mystery of the world that lies before us—there is an enchantment in all that which it takes a heavy dose of pain to quench and which in later hours, even if *success* have come to us, touches us less nearly. Some of my doses of pain were very heavy; very weary were some of my months and years. But all that is sacred; it is idle to write of it today. (224–225)

Suddenly, with no line break, James lists ten *x*s across the page and continues:

> What comes back to me freely, delightfully, is the vision of those untried years. Never did a poor fellow have more; never was an ingenuous youth more passionately and yet more patiently eager for what life might bring. Now that life has brought something, brought a measurable part of what I dreamed of then, it is touching enough to look back. . . . What strikes me is the definiteness, the unerringness of those longings. I wanted to do very much what I have done, and success, if I may say so, now stretches back a tender hand to its younger brother, desire. . . . I remember more than I can say here today. (225)

James follows with seventeen *x*s across an entire page and resumes on a different note: "Again, in New York the other day, I had to break off: I was trying to finish the little history of the past year. There is not much more to be said about it" (225). The first set of *x*s are necessitated by no change of theme, but they do signal a distinct change of mood by their presence. Without the

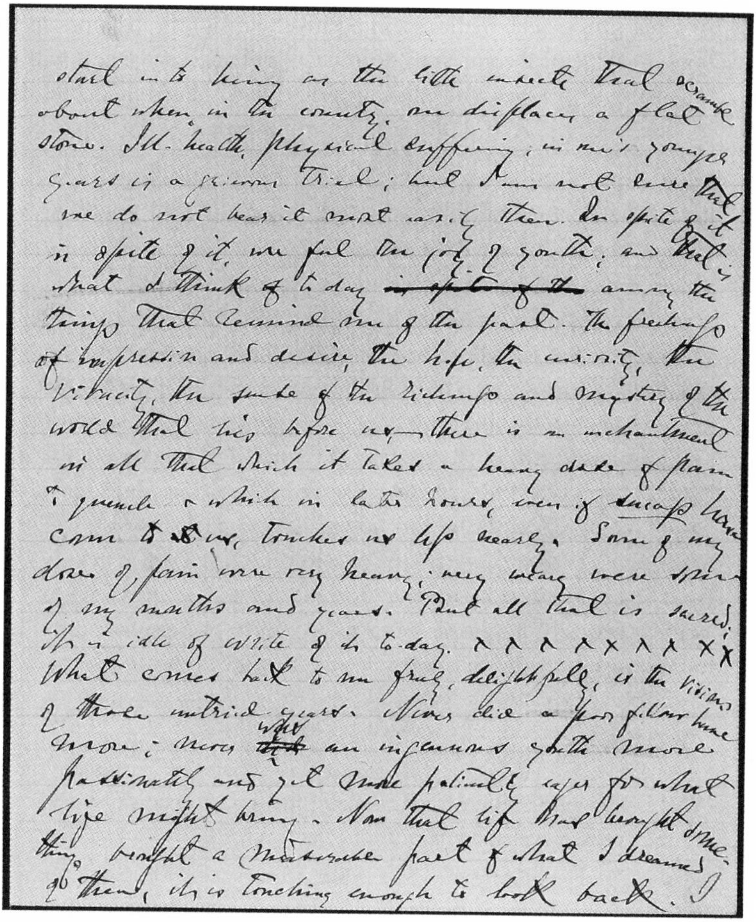

FIGURE 1. *American Journal 1,* Cambridge, December 26, 1881 (bMS Am 1094). *Reprinted by permission of the Houghton Library, Harvard University and the James family.*

*x*s, in other words, I doubt that we would feel so acutely that James has broken off a string of negative and disordering memories, which he feels scrambling (crossing?) like insects under a large, flat stone. (See fig. 1.)

After his row of *x*s, James so clearly converts the energy of those negative emotions into affirmations of his creative power that one can feel the shifting of emotional gears. Again, without the *x*s demarcating the boundary between them, the sense of shift would not be so firm, the sense of damaging disorder fenced off and sublimated not nearly so acute. At the same time,

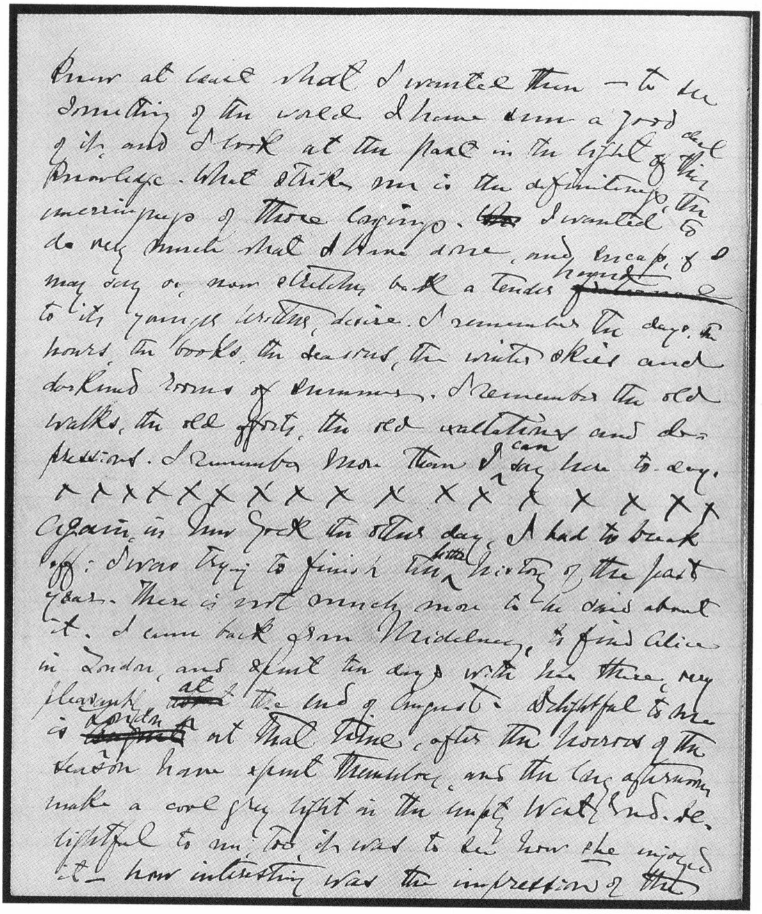
know at least what I wanted then — to see
something of the world. I have seen a good deal
of it, and I look at the past in the light of this
knowledge. What strikes me is the definiteness, the
unerringness of those longings. I wanted to
do very much what I have done, and, because I
may say so, now stretching back a tender hand
to its younger, restless desire. I remember the days, the
hours, the books, the seasons, the winter skies and
darkened rooms of summer. I remember the old
walks, the old efforts, the old exaltations and depressions. I remember more than I can say here to-day.
x x x x x x x x x x x x x x x x x x
Again in New York the other day I had to break
off: I was trying to finish the little history of the past
year. There is not much more to be said about
it. I came back from Middlemore to find Alice
in London, and spent ten days with her there, very
pleasantly, at the end of August. Delightful to me
is London at that time, after the horrors of the
season have spent themselves, and the long afternoons
make a cool grey light in the empty West End. Delightful to me too it was to see how she enjoyed
it — how interesting was the impression of the

FIGURE 2. *American Journal 1,* Cambridge, December 26, 1881 (bMS Am 1094). *Reprinted by permission of the Houghton Library, Harvard University and the James family.*

these *xs* also serve deconstructively to cross and complicate the passages by virtue of excessively insisting on their separation. What actual interrelation, we ask, does the latter passage have to the former?

The second set of *xs* that divides the quoted passages, so far as I can see, signifies nothing definitive at all. There is not a consistent domesticating meaning that can be given to this inveterate writing habit in James's notebooks. Rather, they persistently signify the outside boundary of writing, a nonwriting of scrambling insects that produces the energy of James's prose, and a linked threat of nonbeing that causes him to transform and suppress it. (See fig. 2.)

The enigmatic quality of these *x*s only intensifies as James ages. In the pocket diaries of 1910 from September to December, James has pages and pages of nothing but black and red *x*s, virtually uninterrupted by any connecting prose. These entries occur in a period of physical and mental anguish for James, following the commercial failure of the New York edition and during the final serious illness of his brother William. As the editors of his notebooks put it, "Their considerable number suggests that the symbols were a totality of nervous release either of comfort or despair, and a substitute for words."[40] Their mute eloquence suggests the level of despair contained in the report of his nephew Harry: "There was nothing for me to do but sit by his side and hold his hand while he panted and sobbed for two hours. . . . He talked about Aunt Alice and his own end and I knew him to be facing not only the frustration of all his hopes and ambitions, but the vision looming close . . . of a lingering illness such as hers. In sight of that, he wanted to die."[41] In filling his notebooks with *x*s, it seems possible to suggest, Henry James was acknowledging by way of crossing out the wretchedness of his own condition. If so, this ongoing practice is itself crossed by the dream of July 21, 1910, often taken as the date of the famous dream in the Galerie d'Apollon, noted in his *Autobiography* as the "most appalling yet most admirable" of his life.[42] In this dream, James is disturbed at his rest by a threatening "agent, creature or presence," who, "whatever he was," pushes with "hard pressure" on the "lock and bar" of a door James defends from the other side. Suddenly, James has the "great thought" that he, in his appalled state, was "still more appalling than the awful agent, creature or presence, whatever he was." So, "surpassing him for straight aggression and dire intention," James forces the door open himself and puts his opponent to flight through halls James suddenly recognizes as the Galerie (348). James and his oppressor, in other words, cross positions. In his notebooks, James notes the dream (if this is the time of its occurrence) only by remarking, "Woke up in great relief," and putting down twenty-three red *x*s (318). (See fig. 3.) On the fifteenth of September, James refers back to the date of his dream in curious fashion: "I am better and can really make my [and here he lists seven red *x*s] again as on July 21st last—date never to be forgotten" (321).[43]

The presence of *x*s in James's notebooks suggests by way of replication the centrality of crossings and crossings-out in his fiction, but everything is still in search of a conclusion.

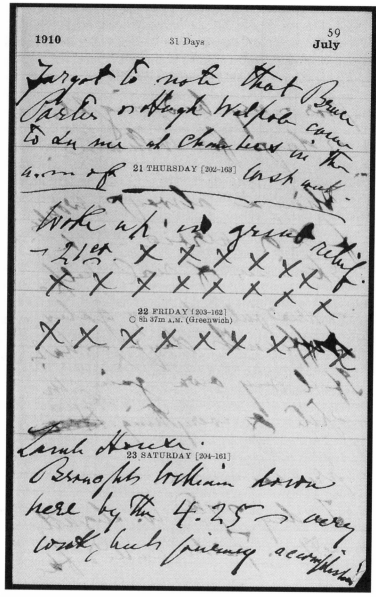

FIGURE 3. *The Pocket Diaries,* Thursday, July 21, 1910 through Saturday, July 23, 1910 (bMS Am 1094). *Reprinted by permission of the Houghton Library, Harvard University and the James family.*

Conclusion Three

James's fiction is powerfully and palpably inhabited by processes of denial and avoidance, a crossing-out that produces complex narrative crossings and displacements. These crossings themselves constitute transgressions of cultural boundaries and borders and represent a destabilizing mobility of desire that must be crossed out through the construction of a stabilizing myth of self. Such a myth is erected against and undercut by the ironies of its own constitution in specific narratives, and it is destabilized intertextually by the alteration of James's desires for, on one hand, the cultural power and aesthetic ease produced by the telling of heterosexual tales, and, on the other, for the unsettling energy and aesthetic difficulties of a destabilizing homoeroticism. The interrelations of the four texts I have read here are chiastic.[44] *The American* gains its authority through a heterosexual erasure of the conflicts that disrupt and disfigure *Roderick Hudson,* but nonetheless ruthlessly critiques the heterosexual masculinity of its protagonist. *The Wings of the Dove,* on the other hand, composed after *The Ambassadors,* undoes the suppressive heterosexual ease of the earlier text, but as a consequence generates the countervailing force of Milly Theale's heterosexualizing, aestheticized, and repressive obliteration. If all of James's writing bears the mark of the oppressive power of heterosexual presumption, such reversals nonetheless reveal the deeply unsatisfying nature to James of the choices he was forced to make, early and late in his career, between conflicting alternatives that could not be resolved or avoided.

PART 3

꙳Ꙩ꙳

Ruptured Bodies, Ruptured Tales

MASCULINE INJURY AND TRANSCENDENCE IN TURN-OF-THE-CENTURY U.S. LITERATURE

*I*t is in this period that culture gener-
ates such mechanisms of masculinization as the Boy Scouts, muscular Chris-
tianity, bodybuilding, institutionalized sports such as football and baseball,
and the public modeling of martial aggressiveness by figures such as Theodore
Roosevelt.[1] Such mechanisms of male acculturation point to a growing unease toward signs of feminine presences in the masculine psyche, presences
it had been the project of "true womanhood" systematically to cultivate
throughout the previous century. The insistence on specifically masculine virtues, in other words, reflects the success of domestic ideology in producing
the feminine as an ongoing and ineradicable challenge to male authority, both
intrapsychically and in the material world of social relations. The twin halves
of this cultural crisis coincide with the much noted crystallization of homo-
sexuality/homophobia in the late nineteenth and early twentieth centuries. The
intense desire for the redeeming stuff of masculinity is shadowed by a growing panic that, experientially, masculine affiliations, enthusiastically cultivated,
cannot be separable in kind from erotic desires for other men. Such a threat
is in part contained by the casting of the homosexual as a recognizable figure antithetical to normative masculinity, but this defense against homoeroticism paradoxically also intensifies the threat of impermissible, feminizing
desires alien to the specular, manifest masculinity of the touchdown run, the
heroic charge, or the Western duel.

The broad turn-of-the century crisis of masculinity is coterminous with the emergence of naturalist literature. Naturalism's raison d'être is the possibility of a masculine authority grounded in a tough-minded and accurate appraisal of the world, shored against and hence containing the threat of an unleashed and dangerous feminine nature. The naturalist writer had to contend, as Christine Van Boheeman concisely puts it, with "a suddenly powerful and prolific Mother Nature dethroning the ancient figure of God the Father."[2] As part of its cultural authority, naturalist literature insists on the importance of a right to depict physical realities such as birth, poverty, injustice, violent death, and sexuality graphically, in pursuit of the general truth of human experience.

It is also the case, however, that naturalism carries internally the seeds of its own dissolution. As I will argue in terms of Upton Sinclair's *The Jungle*, its very pursuit of the truth of social and cultural relations, often in spheres and situations outside the reality of middle-class life and across lines of ethnicity, class, and personal experience, makes its fantasies powerfully projective and produces a continuing vulnerability to uncanny and psychoanalytically resonant disruptions. The encounter with femininity as an external threat, in other words, uncannily mirrors the threat of an internalized femininity produced by middle-class domestic ideology, a threat linked to potentially feminizing and/or unreadable erotic desires.

Such disjunctions thus intensify a crisis in the conditions of knowing and paradoxically challenge the epistemological basis of the styles of masculine authority they labor to create, as both world and self decompose. The solution often is a deus ex machina installation of intellectual order after a failure of naturalist narrative to construct a bulwark of authority against the entropic death spiral of its own logic. Naturalism thus enacts, in its characteristic settings and in terms of its characteristic themes, an exacerbated version of the dynamics of masculine authority and dissolution I have been tracing throughout this book. These dynamics, then, however foregrounded by naturalism, are not specific to it.

Such dynamics inform as well Stephen Crane's *The Red Badge of Courage*, the text that first catapulted him to substantial acclaim and success.[3] I will argue that the text displaces powerful homoerotic investments visible in much of Crane's work through Crane's famous encounters with the wounded and the dead. These encounters, mixing desire and aversion, push experiences of male desire beyond the limit of intelligibility and beyond narratability as well. As a consequence, in order to complete the novel Crane must return to a conventional plot of heroism and homosocial bonding, now both energized and ironized by its status for Crane as a necessary repression.

CHAPTER 5

What a Beating
Feels Like

AUTHORSHIP, DISSOLUTION, AND MASCULINITY
IN UPTON SINCLAIR'S *THE JUNGLE*

*I*n *The Jungle,* Upton Sinclair strives to produce a socialist critique of the horrific living and working conditions for turn-of-the-century immigrant laborers in the Chicago stockyards. This account of the brutal poverty that afflicts Jurgis Rudkus and his family, however, blends indistinguishably into an account of Jurgis's subjective terrors of imprisoning familial relationships, terrors expressed in the novel as a gynephobic fear of the maternal body. The vertiginous transport in Jurgis's story between macropolitical critique and irrational dread results, I will argue, from Sinclair's own abject dread of the feminine sources of his writing and the conflicted struggle for authority this dread produces.

In *The Jungle,* "nature" seems characterized by the threatening fecundity one finds in Darwin's vision. Certainly, nature as we find it in Packingtown is characterized by an anxiety-inducing profusion of life, especially of children. In the first paragraph of the novel, for example, as Marija argues with a carriage driver in two languages, she is pursued by a "swarm of urchins" (3).[1] At the wedding of Jurgis and Ona, Sinclair tells us that the number of babies in attendance was "equal to ... all the guests invited." In a "collection of cribs and carriages ... babies slept, three or four together" (5). Later, Sinclair indicates that even the city dump, a place with "an odor for which there are no polite words," is "sprinkled over with children" (29). Odors form a part of this profusion, as do animals. One can smell Packingtown from miles away, with its "elemental odor, raw and crude; it was rich, almost rancid, sensual, and strong. There were some who drank it in as if it were an intoxicant; there were others who put their handkerchiefs to their faces" (25). The ubiquity of odor, which penetrates the body and signals the permeability of its boundaries, is mirrored by the vast number of cattle, described in a way that suggests the vastness and heterogeneity of humanity itself: "[A]s far as the eye can reach there stretches a sea of pens . . . —so many cattle no one had ever dreamed existed in the world. Red cattle, black, white, and yellow cattle. . . . The sound of them here was as of all the barnyards of the universe" (33). This numerical profusion of animals, in turn, yields to a chaos of animal sounds: "The uproar was appalling, . . . one feared there was too much sound for the room to hold. . . . There were high squeals and low squeals, grunts, and wails of agony" (35).[2]

The narrative's fear of an entrapping world swarming with disreputable life blends into a fear of family life and, within the confines of the family, misogynistic fears of maternal women and their reproductive powers.[3] Such a link is most evident at the single most wrenching scene in the novel, the death of Ona in childbirth. As the midwife, Madame Haupt, descends from the garret where Ona is dying, we are told that "[s]he had her jacket off, like one of the workers on the killing-beds. Her hands and arms were smeared with blood, and blood was splashed upon her clothing and her face" (184). Though this death is horrific, it also uncovers for Jurgis a previously veiled portion of reality, the hidden, horrible nature of nature. Sinclair tells us that "[i]t was all new to him, raw and horrible—it had fallen upon him like a lightning stroke. When little Antanas was born he had been at work, and had known nothing about it until it was over; and now he was not to be controlled" (175).

As it proceeds, *The Jungle*'s hatred of the capitalist burdens of social injustice, poverty, and suffering is increasingly indistinguishable from a gynephobic aversion to the body and all of its fluids, smells, and processes. At the height of her desirability, for example, the frail Ona barely has a corporeal presence in the novel. Even at her death, *The Jungle* displaces its distaste for its vision of female biology onto the massive figure of Madame Haupt. When Jurgis seeks the midwife, he finds her engaged in the affairs of the flesh, "frying pork and onions": she seems to be the only immigrant in Packingtown who has enough to eat (177). Sinclair tells us that "she was a Dutch woman, enormously fat," and that "[s]he wore a filthy blue wrapper, and her teeth were black" (177). After rubbing her hands with a saucer of "goose-grease" in her kitchen—good luck, Sinclair explains—Madame Haupt goes to minister to Ona (180). When she emerges, the blood displayed on her person, signifying the horror of childbirth and of the natural, allows Ona to be rescued from the body once more, for one last sentimental scene: when Jurgis finally sees his wife, "she was so shrunken he would scarcely have known her—she was all but a skeleton, and as white as a piece of chalk" (184).

A passage in the original version of *The Jungle,* published in *The Appeal to Reason* but edited out of the Doubleday edition, expresses the metonymic link between women's bodies and the stockyards themselves.[4] "Cannot anyone in his right senses," Sinclair's narrator cries, "see that such troubles as Ona's must continue to be the rule so long as women, whom 'God in his infinite wisdom' has condemned to be manufacturing machines, will insist upon having children just as if they were ordinary human creatures?" (DeGruson, 96). The phrase "manufacturing machines," hovering suggestively between women's oppressed positions in industry and women's oppressed positions in biological reproduction, and its juxtaposition to the abstract emptiness of "ordinary" humanity highlight *The Jungle*'s tendency to whirl uncertainly in the vortex of its own horror.

The wavering of the novel, between a macropolitical account of Jurgis's problems under capitalism and a micromasculine account of Jurgis's woman trouble, corresponds to the complex relation between Sinclair's muckraking goals for his novel and the projective mix of literary ambitions, gender anxieties, and family troubles that work in and through his narrative.[5] Sinclair had an enormous desire for literary success early in his career and faced enormous difficulties in its pursuit. The roots of his desire to write, according to Sinclair's *Autobiography,* were located in a vision of the essential salubrity of genius he had in the midst of his adolescence. In this vision, he imagined a kind of teetotaling boys' camp of literature, in which he could join a mix of great characters and great authors gathered around the fire: "There was a campfire by a mountain road, to which came travelers who hailed one another and made high revelry there without alcohol. Yes, even Falstaff and Prince Hal were purified. . . . There came the melancholy Prince of Denmark, and Don Quixote. . . . Also Shelley. . . . I was laughing, singing, with the delight of their company."[6] Unfortunately for Sinclair, at the time of *The Jungle*'s composition, this vision of the felicity of literary success had not been realized in the realm of experience, despite several efforts to produce literature of a monumental kind. One of these texts, *The Journal of Arthur Stirling,*[7] in fact, took for its subject the fate of the man of "genius" trapped in a culture that fails to recognize and reward—and hence actively thwarts—his ambitions and abilities.[8]

If Sinclair's ambition would make *The Jungle* a desperate project in any case, this desperation was augmented by the poverty in which he found himself at the time of his novel's composition and by the disintegration of his marriage. Sinclair wrote much of *The Jungle* in a small cabin he built himself in Princeton, New Jersey, as a space in which he could isolate himself from the problems of family life. His son, David, had been diagnosed with malnutrition and rickets in 1903, and his marriage to his first wife, Meta, had fallen into disrepair. Apparently acting out of a fear of fathering any more children who might complicate his life, Sinclair had adopted a regimen of sexual abstinence, arguing the common position of numerous health authorities that sexual activity ought to occur only for purposes of reproduction. One night, according to Leon Harris, Sinclair found his wife, Meta, in bed with a pistol, weeping because she was unable to pull the trigger.[9] Sinclair himself readily admitted the connection of such unmitigated suffering to his novel. As he says,

> [E]xternally, the story had to do with a family of stockyard workers, but internally it was the story of my own family. Did I wish to know how the poor suffered in wintertime in Chicago? I had only to recall the previous winter in the cabin when we had had only cotton blankets, and had put rugs on top of us and cowered shivering in our separate beds. It was the same with hunger, with illness, with fear. Ona was Corydon, speaking Lithuanian but otherwise unchanged. Our little boy was down with pneumonia that winter, and nearly died, and the grief of that went into the book. (*Autobiography*, 112)

Sinclair responded to such difficulties by increasing his commitment to writing, in pursuit of the kind of authorial success that promised rescue.

The overdetermination of trouble in Sinclair's narrative creates a jungle of disjunctions and contradictions, aptly represented by the novel's repeated images of bodily disintegration—of the loss of fingers, the loss of feet, the loss of ears broken off in the cold, and even the loss of little Stanislovas (who, shut in a dark cellar, is cornered and eaten by rats). Bodily anxieties are coterminous in the novel with a metaphorics of entrapment, as if a failure to rise from the body equals a life of imprisonment in an enveloping maternal womb that fundamentally undoes the illusion of autonomous masculine selfhood. As the novel progresses, it is increasingly dominated by images of enclosure in small dark spaces: in cellars and stairwells, prison cells and basement workrooms, pits and abysses. These fears, in turn, produce or are produced by a claustrophobic masculine inability to tolerate the emotions of women. After the rape of Ona by Connor, her anguish is so intense that Jurgis can "bear it no longer," and he "sprang at her . . . shouting into her ear: 'Stop it, I say! Stop it!'" (144). Jurgis has a similar reaction to her tears during her pregnancy: "She had never been like this before. . . . [I]t was monstrous and unthinkable. . . . [T]he world . . . ought to kill them at once. . . . They ought not to marry, to have children . . . —if he, Jurgis, had known what a woman was like, he would have had his eyes torn out first" (136).

The swirl of emotions Jurgis cannot tolerate as signs of the "monstrous and unthinkable" suggests the difficulty the narrative has in generating a convincing and exhaustive account of his ills, the symptoms of which rapidly threaten to swamp the diagnosis. This rupture of conscious control, however, this abandonment of systematic analysis, generates a compensatory unconscious capacity in Jurgis magically to shape reality into the form of his urges. This capacity, explicable only at the level of authorship, is incompatible with the naturalist reality of *The Jungle* and fails to lead to any supportable analysis of Jurgis's difficulties. Rather, it further submerges him in a world of blind, mechanical repetitions.

For example, Jurgis's horror at family life destroys his family, with no direct agency on his part in evidence, and gains for him the masculine freedom of rural life. After Jurgis's imprisonment for his attack on Connor, he simply concludes that death would serve his wife best: "The shame of it all would kill her . . . and it was best that she should die" (151). Jurgis's wish for her death serves as a death sentence. Ona will soon perish, but not before Jurgis makes a mistake of astounding proportions. Immediately after Jurgis is released from prison, even as he declares his willingness to "do battle" for his family against the world, he heads in the wrong direction on the strength of some bad navigational advice he receives from a child (168). After miles of journeying westward, a farmer informs him of his mistake. Jurgis quickly alters his course, but his legs have betrayed the direction in which he wants the developing narrative to carry him.

Ona's death and his devotion to young Antanas, his Nietzschean superbaby son, retain him in Chicago, but the narrative places Jurgis in an International Harvester factory, which once again sounds a proleptic note of rural life. And, when the Harvester factory closes, he gains employment in a steel mill and uncannily encounters still another foreshadowing of his approaching flight. In one of the novel's most remarkable passages, Jurgis sees the protean molten steel as a kind of life essence, which assumes first a masculine shape and then a determined and determining objective form. As he watches, the molten steel is a "pillar of white flame, dazzling as the sun . . . with a whiteness not of earth, scorching the eyeballs" (200). In another place, where the "crashing" and "groaning" of machines seem like "the centre of earth, where the machinery of time was revolving," this cosmic plasma of molten steel becomes a phallic "great red snake escaped from purgatory," which "writhed and squirmed . . . until it was cold and black—and then it needed only to be cut and straightened to be ready for a railroad" (201). At this point in the novel, what was formerly protean about Jurgis is similarly "cut and straightened" and unalterable. Several pages later, he will hop a passing freight train and ride these iron rails into the novel's curious rural idyll.[10]

First, however, young Antanas, the last obstacle to the desire of the text, must perish in a death that itself serves as an uncanny foreshadowing of his father's flight. While Jurgis labors in the steel mill, Antanas bursts from a restricting house, plunges into a mud puddle, and drowns. As a sobbing Marija informs Jurgis, "We couldn't make him stay in" (205). As a consequence, Jurgis makes his own break for freedom from a familial womb and is soon "peering out with hungry eyes, getting glimpses of meadows and woods and rivers" (207). Once in the country, Jurgis repeats Antanas's watery plunge, not in a puddle, but in a "deep pool, sheltered and silent," where he "splashed about like a very boy in his glee" (208).

Again, the uncanniness of this progress in the context of the rest of the novel is hardly liberating. On the contrary, it contributes to the novel's decentering of consciousness because the force that moves Jurgis, if it is his at all, is not subject to his control and has nothing to do with a logical mastery of events. Whatever progress Jurgis seems occasionally to make, as politician, worker, or criminal, sinks beneath his susceptibility to the uncanny repetitions that come to entrap him even in his moments of sleazy prosperity. The most startling of these is his second attack on Connor for raping Ona, which reenacts the first: "[P]recisely as before, Jurgis came away with a piece of his enemy's flesh between his teeth; and, as before, he went on fighting with those who had interfered with him" (268). It is difficult to generate a sufficient account for this capstone of the novel's many repetitions in terms of either capitalist or naturalist worldviews. Something is happening here, but neither the reader, nor Jurgis, nor, one suspects, Sinclair himself can say with precision what it is.

Fortunately, Sinclair pulls onto the stage someone who can explain, in general and abstract terms that conveniently ignore the messy particulars listed above. This figure is Schliemann, a German intellectual whose authoritative

socialist monologues offer explanations of the ills of the novel and propose
regulatory solutions:

> Nicholas Schliemann was familiar with all the universe, and with
> man as a small part of it. He understood human institutions, and blew
> them about like soap-bubbles. It was surprising that so much destruc-
> tiveness could be contained in one human mind. Was it government?
> The purpose of government was the guarding of property-rights, the
> perpetuation of ancient force and modern fraud. Or was it marriage?
> Marriage and prostitution were two sides of one shield, the preda-
> tory man's exploitation of the sex-pleasure. The difference between
> them was a difference of class. If a woman had money she might
> dictate her own terms. (322)

Schliemann stands for a voice of absolute male intellectual authority, one that
controls the body and its desires. According to Sinclair, Schliemann "studied the compositions of food-stuffs, and knew exactly how many proteins and
carbohydrates his body needed. . . . That was the nearest approach to independence a man could make 'under capitalism,' he explained; he would never
marry, for no sane man would allow himself to fall in love until after the
revolution" (321). At the same time, Schliemann has an erotic power over
women, produced, evidently, by his intellectual greatness. As Jurgis listens
to this disavowal of marriage, he notices a "beautiful young girl" listening to
Schliemann "with something of the same look that he himself had worn, the
time when he had first discovered Socialism" (332). This "young college
student . . . only spoke once or twice while Jurgis was there—the rest of the
time she sat by the table in the centre of the room, resting her chin in her
hands and drinking in the conversation" (321). The style of masculine authority Schliemann embodies, I would suggest, represents a solution to the
problems of the novel that Sinclair can only ambivalently embrace. If he stands
for the encapsulation of messy masculine emotions, if he dehystericizes *The
Jungle*'s plot, he nevertheless threatens the source of Sinclair's writing in, precisely, such feminizing forces. Sinclair can finally only ambivalently embrace
the intellectual authority his narrative creates.

   The practice of authorship itself had feminine roots and components
for Sinclair. For example, *The Jungle*'s most important literary predecessor
was arguably Stowe's *Uncle Tom's Cabin*, which Sinclair refers to in *Manassas*
as "the most unquestionable piece of inspiration in American fiction." According to Sinclair, nowhere in the world "is there a book more packed and
charged with the agony and heartbreak of *woman*" (Sinclair's italics).[11] Jack

London, of course, famously called *The Jungle* "the *Uncle Tom's Cabin* of wage slavery,"[12] and Sinclair betrays a competitive relation to Harriet Beecher Stowe in the text of the recently recovered first edition: "She had many things in her favor which cannot be counted on by him who would paint the life of the modern slave. . . . Who can make a romance out of the story of a man whose one life adventure is the scratching of a finger by an infected butcher knife?" (DeGruson, 65).

If Stowe was a literary foremother, biographically Sinclair's mother also had a substantial influence on the formation of his character. He remembered, for example, his mother reading to him from early childhood, and he was abysmally ignorant in his early schooling in the (masculine) business of mathematics. As he says in his autobiography, "I knew everything but arithmetic. This branch of learning, so essential to a commercial civilization, had shared the fate of alcohol and tobacco, tea and coffee; my mother did not use it, so neither did I" (*Autobiography,* 21). At the same time, his interest in reading alienated him from his alcoholic, navy-obsessed father: "'The social position of a naval officer is the highest in the world,' pronounced my father. 'He can go anywhere, absolutely anywhere.' . . . And meantime the little son was reaching out into a strange world of books; reading things of which the father had never heard. 'What are you reading?' he would ask, and the son would reply, none too generously, 'A book.' . . . The chasm between the two was widening, never to be closed in this world" (20).

Though Sinclair's mother was a key figure in his childhood and adolescence and helped form both his commitment to reform and his interest in literature, the author broke with her completely in later life, apparently over issues of his own authority. According to Leon Harris, Sinclair told his son, David, at the time of her death, "She was the best of mothers up to about the age (my age) of 16. Then I grew beyond her, & she wouldn't follow, or couldn't. If she'd let me alone, it could have been all right; but she still thought I was a child & stubbornly fought to direct my life & *mind*. So for 35 years I could not meet her without a controversy starting" (99).

As Sinclair's autobiographical writings underline, a paradox of naturalism, in and out of *The Jungle,* is that it revels in images of female power, which then serve as problems for male identity. For example, Sinclair's Marija Berczynskas, located outside any and all conventions of feminine gentility, is clearly the most remarkable and powerfully conceived character in *The Jungle.* In his account of the wedding that opens the text, Sinclair tells us that "[i]t was all Marija Berczynskas. Marija was one of those hungry souls who cling with desperation to the skirts of the retreating muse. . . . Whether it was by beer, or by shouting, or by music, or by motion, she meant that it should not go" (14). In addition, Sinclair thought of himself as a kind of feminist man, and *The Jungle* clearly contains an explicit critique of marriage as a form of prostitution. Quite early in the novel Jurgis tries to buy Ona from her parents for his father's two horses. As the narrator's summary of Schliemann's thought suggests at novel's end, "Marriage and prostitution were two sides of one shield, the predatory man's exploitation of the sex-pleasure" (322). Indeed, Sinclair dedicates his autobiographical account of his troubled first marriage, *Love's Pilgrimage,* which he refers to as "this woman's book," to "those who throughout the world are fighting for the emancipation of woman."[13]

In general, then, *The Jungle* massively and misogynistically defends against a feminine power that it creates itself. It also works to expose the inadequacy of Jurgis's conventional masculinity, ridiculing the conceit of his pride in his own self-sufficiency and strength. This assurance apparently has masculine origins, given that the text credits Jurgis's upbringing to his father and never mentions his mother at all.[14] The adult Jurgis "could not even imagine how it would feel to be beaten. 'That is well enough for men like you,' he would say, '*silpnas,* puny fellows—but my back is broad'" (21). *The Jungle* will teach Jurgis, distinctly not a writer himself, what a beating feels like, as Sinclair gropes toward new forms of male identity.

The unmaking of Jurgis's masculinity, the exposure of its weaknesses and contradictions, creates space for an exploration of an alternative, "feminine" subjectivity. The forces of unleashed femininity, however, surface in the novel chiefly as a terrifying negation, necessitating the construction of a new form of masculine authority lest the novel share in Jurgis's abjection. The problem of this authority is, at the same time, the problem of how to find an ending for the narrative after the dissolution of its middle, an ending necessary if Sinclair's own act of authorship is to have a successful conclusion. At stake in this ending, finally, is the novel's capacity to imagine something like a fundamental transformation of late-nineteenth-century conventions of gender, a transformation that can still supply an aesthetically necessary sense of narrative closure. Can, in other words, an attempt to step outside of a stultifying social reality for men produce anything but anomie and abjection? I have argued that the cold and clinical Schliemann represents one kind of male authority at the end of Sinclair's narrative. In fact, *The Jungle* has multiple and contradictory endings that work to qualify Schliemann's authority and create space for Sinclair's ambivalence about it. Schliemann's appearance in the text is preceded by another figure of intellectual authority, a wildly passionate speaker who first wins Jurgis to socialism. This man, like Schliemann, has the power to transfix not only Jurgis but a young and beautiful woman. Jurgis initially finds her presence at the public lecture disturbing:

> He turned a little, carefully, so that he could see her better; then he began to watch her, fascinated. She had apparently forgotten all about him, and was looking toward the platform. A man was speaking there. . . . A feeling of alarm stole over him as he stared at her. It made his flesh creep. What was the matter with her, what could be going on, to affect any one like that? . . . There was a faint quivering of her nostrils; and now and then she would moisten her lips with feverish haste. Her bosom rose and fell as she breathed, and her excitement seemed to mount higher and higher . . . like a boat tossing upon ocean surges. (290)

The woman's response, we find, mirrors the emotional state of the speaker, whose power on the stage seems produced by his own borderline disintegration:

> It was like coming suddenly upon some wild sight of nature,— a . . . ship tossed about upon a stormy sea. Jurgis had an unpleasant sensation, a sense of confusion, of disorder, of wild and meaningless uproar. The man was tall and gaunt, as haggard as his auditor himself; a thin black beard covered half of his face, and one could see only two black hollows where the eyes were. He was speaking rapidly, in great excitement; he used many gestures—as he spoke he moved here and there upon the stage. (290)

As Jurgis listens, he feels a surfacing of unmasterable forces that represents a transformation of his earlier abjection into bliss: "There was an unfolding of vistas before him, a breaking of the ground beneath him, an upheaving, a stirring, a trembling; he felt himself suddenly a mere man no longer—there were powers within him undreamed of, there were demon forces contending, age-long wonders struggling to be born" (296–297).

The body-shattering danger of these first relations requires the introduction of Schliemann, who, as opposed to the figure on the platform, quietly sits "without emotions; with the manner of a teacher setting forth to a group of scholars an axiom in geometry" (321). It is Schliemann, finally, who represents the power of male intellectual authority in naturalism to hold the disruptions of the body, sexuality, and gender in check, precisely by the generation of an abstract account of them. At the same time, the voice of

Schliemann has little in common with the impassioned prose Sinclair produces or with the prose of the woman Sinclair invokes as his literary predecessor, Harriet Beecher Stowe. Devoid of emotion, Schliemann also seems devoid of literature, and so represents a style of masculine authority that suppresses the masculine writer.

The two speakers, then, suggest a masculinity divided between its masculine and feminine selves and also divided between eroticized and noneroticized male relations. The differences in the two editions of the novel have similar implications. In the earliest edition of the novel, Sinclair makes even more explicit the feminine aspects of the first speaker: "He was a man of electric presence, . . . with a face worn thin by struggle and suffering. The fury of outraged manhood gleamed in it—and the tears of suffering little children pleaded in his voice. He was represented in the papers as a man of violence, but he had the tenderness of a woman" (DeGruson, 309). The prominence of the feminine in this figure of authority coexists with his vulnerability to the disruptive presence of actual women. The novel ends with the interrogation of the "Pitchfork Senator" by a woman in the audience who will not be put in her place. The senator tries mockery, saying, "I can face any man, but, my God, I'm not used to arguing with women." According to Sinclair, "The laughter over this would have cleared the atmosphere in any meeting less determined; but when it ceased, the woman was still there. She kept shaking her finger at the speaker—she would have answers" (DeGruson, 313–314). One page later, Sinclair refers to this woman as the senator's "Nemesis," as she leaps to her feet and interrogates him again. The speaker's vulnerability to the woman and her wagging finger, in turn, signals a continuing vulnerability for Jurgis Rudkus. As opposed to the standard edition's solutions to Jurgis's problems, the first edition returns him once again to prison and so refuses to rescue him from the irrational repetitions of its plot. It thus also answers ambiguously the question of whether for men an underlying femininity is tolerable.

Taken together, the endings of *The Jungle* suggest naturalism's discontent with the masculine authority that, because of the imperatives of culture and the dynamics of literature, it also strives to compose. Its investment in depictions of a powerful and omnipresent femininity, finally, contains a wish that its own repressive structures be shattered as well as a fear that such a wish might be granted. It powerfully depicts male disintegration, and it uses the energy of disintegration to generate new forms of confining masculine power. It veers wildly from the iron rails of probability, and it clings desperately to the structure of normative masculine plots. It wrestles manfully with the appalling inconsistencies and contradictions of late nineteenth-century gender roles, but it finally cannot transcend them.

The Jungle's anxieties, I have suggested, chiefly concern an entrapping, maternal femininity that threatens the construction of masculine authority and yet, as in the case of *The Scarlet Letter,* is crucial to it. Its representation of a disruptive homoeroticism, however, as opposed to a disruptive femininity, is muted. It nonetheless contains enough signs of same-sex desire to suggest the possibility of an additional disruption of masculine authority in the text. If Marija Berczynskas ends in *The Jungle* in the hopeless position of prostitute, the text implies that Jurgis might be tempted by workingman's prostitution as well and reinforces this point by having Jurgis receive a gift of one hundred dollars—for services not rendered. Down on his luck, as he mostly is, Jurgis is accosted by a rich, physically familiar, drunk, and "lonesome" youth named Freddie (226): "Then he lurched toward Jurgis, and the hand upon his shoulder became an arm about his neck. 'Up against it myself, ole sport,' he said. 'She's a hard ole world'" (225). Freddie invites Jurgis to his apartment, under the close scrutiny of the butler, who is clearly afraid of what might occur and peers through the keyhole. Lest we miss the implications of what might occur, Sinclair inserts a reference to Antinous, youthful consort of Hadrian: "He was clad in spotless evening dress, was Freddie, and looked very handsome—he was a beautiful boy, with light golden hair and the head of an Antinous" (234). There is no sign that this encounter has much to do with desire, as opposed to providing Sinclair with an opportunity to indict the decadence of upper-class life.

As desiring relations to masculine authority intensify at novel's end, however, so do increasing suggestions of a surfacing of erotic desire. These are evident in the powerful physical and emotional response of Jurgis to the androgynous inspirational speaker that alters his life—he felt "a breaking of the ground beneath him, an upheaving, a stirring, a trembling" (296)—and his subsequent employment by a benevolent socialist aptly named "Tommy Hinds." Sinclair speaks of this relation in terms that combine desire, restraint, and fragmentation: "[H]e would have cut off one hand for Tommy Hinds; and to keep Hinds's hotel a thing of beauty was his joy in life" (312).

CHAPTER 6

Behind the Lines

HOMOEROTIC ANXIETY AND THE HEROIC IN
STEPHEN CRANE'S *THE RED BADGE OF COURAGE*

$\mathcal{M}$ark Seltzer, in *Bodies and Machines,* suggests that *The Red Badge of Courage* contains two stories being worked simultaneously, "a love story and a war story." Continues Seltzer, "On the one side, there is an 'inside' story of the 'quiver of war desire,' of male hysteria and the renegotiation of bodily and sexual boundaries and identities. . . . On the other the side, there is an 'outside' story of social discipline and mechanization, of territory taken and lost. . . . These primal scenes of battle are, finally, struggles to make interior states visible: to gain knowledge of and mastery over bodies and interiors by tearing them open to view."[1] Though Seltzer posits an "inside" love story that apparently is different from the "outside" story of social discipline and mechanization, he does not attempt to give the "love story" in the novel a separate account. Instead, to the extent that he acknowledges the "inside" tale, he folds it indistinguishably back into the "outer" story that serves as a focus of his book.

One would not want to deny the complex relation of bodily anxieties related to sexuality to other kinds of anxieties about corporeality in mechanized, industrial society. Indeed, it seems clear throughout the nineteenth century that the codes of masculinity are propped against threats from without and within: from without, by an industrializing, multiple culture that menaces masculine authority based either on cognitive control or achieved social power; and from within, by desires, memories, capacities, and internalized contradictions that are in incongruous tension with the social poses of a rigidified masculinity. Despite the range of interpretive possibilities produced by the common overdetermination of any feature of social life, however, it remains important to focus specific attention on the unsettled question of the historical role of expressed and displaced homoerotic desire in U.S. cultural history. This will remain an important question so long as sexuality serves as a crucial marker of contemporary identity and community, and so long as deviant sexualities remain targets of persecution.

In this chapter, then, I want to suggest the extent to which homoerotic anxiety about nonnarratable, nonpermissible bodily relations between men disrupts the narrative creation of authority for Henry Fleming and his author. I will focus on *The Red Badge of Courage,* but I will also refer to a number of Crane's other works in order to establish a context for untangling the displacements of Crane's prose, the nature of which, in isolation, easily escapes recognition.

The claim that *The Red Badge of Courage* must be understood in terms of its homoerotic investments is difficult to make on one level and obvious on another. The difficulty of the claim has nothing to do with the biographical fact of Crane's sexual relations with women. That Crane had an active heterosexual life seems amply documented, but such a life does not make questions concerning the nature of Crane's relations to either women or men a simple matter. Apparent heterosexual avidity proves little in and of itself and does not preclude homosexual interests or anxieties; in fact, the reverse might be as easily maintained.

In general, Crane's notorious elusiveness as a biographical subject makes it difficult to make reliable or definitive claims about his sexuality. There has been no successful narrativization of his life, and he has left a paper trail that seems sparse even for such a mercurially brief career, so that one ends up relying on collected anecdotes about an individual notorious in his own time.[2] Such reticence in itself is suggestive in terms of Eve Kosofsky Sedgwick's claim that, since the late nineteenth century, homosexuality has centered itself as *the* unspeakable secret in male lives, the power of which depends on its epistemological elusiveness—its complex interimplication in systems of knowledge and power.[3] Nonetheless, beyond remarking on the fact of Crane's remarkable, beckoning reticence, one can draw no reliable conclusion. Even for his contemporaries, Crane's enigmatic life was a dangerous invitation to transference.

In one account by a journalist and admirer, Robert H. Davis, for example, Crane's oddly flamboyant attempt to rescue a prostitute causes his entire person to flower.[4] Having at last succeeded in meeting Crane, Davis was unsuccessful in getting the "cold" (xiii) author to "unchain [his] tongue" and talk about himself (xvi). With nothing else to do, Davis studied his physical characteristics and "was struck by the weakness of his chin and the paleness of his lips. The nose, while quite thin, was delicately molded. . . . The eyes, about which I had heard much, did not seem to be in any way remarkable" (xvi). Suddenly, however, at the appearance of a prostitute, Crane sprang forward with an elaborate bow and Davis reports that he saw "an almost indescribable luminous beauty in the eyes of this modern Villon. They were large, the iris seemingly out of proportion to the pupil, blue in general tone, brilliant, flashing. . . . The girl stood there . . . lured by the beauty of his eyes and forehead or startled by the weakness of his chin and the poverty of his garb" (xviii). Davis may be making up or embellishing this tale, which he recalls years afterward—we have no way of knowing. What the anecdote may relate most reliably is the strength of Davis's own attraction to those suddenly luminous blue eyes, as Crane's fascination with a prostitute threatens to short-circuit their own conversation. And, if we credit the story, for whom was Crane performing and for what reason? Certainly, the power of the wastrel author's mixture of manliness and delicate vulnerability to fascinate other men is a marked characteristic of what biographical information we have concerning him. Part of the interest in Crane's brief career consists in his chain of famous acquaintances, including James Huneker, Richard Harding Davis, William Dean Howells, Hamlin Garland, Henry James, H. G. Wells, Joseph Conrad, Ford Madox Ford, and Harold Frederic.[5]

The fascinated attraction other men feel for the elusive Crane, however, still leaves us short of understanding the character of Crane's feelings for other men. James Huneker, in a famous but, so far as I can tell, unreliable account, remembers Crane as remarkably innocent about even the possibility of sexual desire between men, a contention that places Huneker in the position of a benign but potentially molesting uncle. According to Huneker, Crane, who was "damned innocent about everything but women," was approached by a young boy who "was painted. He was very handsome—looked like a Rossetti angel—big violet eyes—probably full of belladonna—Crane was disgusted. Thought he'd vomit. Then he got interested. He took the kid in and fed him supper. Got him to talk. The kid had syphilis, of course—most of that type do—and wanted money to have himself treated."[6] As a consequence of this encounter, Crane supposedly began a novel of New York street life entitled "Flowers of Asphalt," no trace of which has ever been found. Here, again, the anecdote seems as enlightening about the fascination of others with Crane as it is about the author's own enigmatic person. The boy's large and beautiful eyes, poverty, disease, and use of drugs all mime characteristics that have been imputed to Crane, so that Huneker's anecdote suggests a fantasy of Crane meeting a less "damned innocent" Crane, a fantasy that would be realized if "Flowers of Asphalt" were written.

But, as Berryman asks, how innocent can we imagine Crane in any case? Is it credible that the Crane who even in his Syracuse years interviewed prostitutes at police court had no sense of other men as erotic possibilities? Is it possible that the military boarding school Crane attended should have been entirely free of homoerotic experience, even though nineteenth-century health writers issued dire warnings about the shared masturbatory experiences (with clear homosexual implications) of improperly supervised young men in groups? Is it possible, given photographic evidence of Crane cozily sharing a bed with other men at the Students' Art League, that, at midnight after a little too much beer, or in the half doze of dawn, a stray limb had never cozened up a little enlightening heat in the pleasure centers of the body?[7]

Is it possible that Crane had no sense of homoerotic possibility despite his fascination with the underworld of New York life? According to George Chauncey's important recent history, *Gay New York*, the Bowery was home to a significant and visible homosexual subculture in the latter part of the nineteenth century.[8] According to Chauncey, "going slumming in the resorts of the Bowery and the Tenderloin was a popular activity among middle-class men (and even some women)" (36). He quotes one Mary Casal, who recalled, despite the popularity of slumming, her shock at "'the ugliness of the displays we saw as we hurried from one horrid but famous resort to another in and about the Bowery,' many of them full of male 'inverts'" (36). Chauncey adds,

> A number of resorts made "male degenerates" pivotal figures in their portrayal of working-class "depravity." Billy McGlory had realized as early as the late 1870s that he could further the infamy of Armory Hall . . . by hiring fairies—powdered, rouged, and sometimes even dressed in women's clothes—as entertainers. Circulating through the crowd, they sang, danced, and sometimes joined the best-paying customers in their curtained booths to thrill or disgust them with the sort of private sexual exhibitions (or "circuses") normally offered only by female prostitutes. By 1890, several more halls had added fairies as attractions, and the Slide . . . had taken Armory Hall's place as New York's "worst dive." . . . The fairies' presence made such clubs a mandatory stop for New Yorkers out slumming. . . . As a *New York Herald* reporter observed in 1892: "It is a fact that the Slide and the unspeakable nature of the orgies practised there are a matter of common talk among men who are bent on taking in the town." (37–38)

Chauncey's resurrection of lost history suggests that Crane's representations of lower-class New York life are selective in their urban grittiness. If
editorial practices of the time censored his brave realism, an ongoing critical
concern in terms of both *Maggie: A Girl of the Streets* and *The Red Badge of
Courage,* the evidence suggests that in some respects, at least, Crane censored himself. He may also, however, have textually marked such moments
of self-censorship. In *Maggie,* for example, Maggie and Pete visit a Bowery
saloon whose entertainment is marked by relentless counterfeiting and fal-
sity. An opening singer wears "some half dozen skirts" when "[i]t was patent
that any one of them would have proved adequate."[9] The singer is followed
by a ventriloquist whose fakery fools Maggie; by two girls posing as sisters
suggestively dancing to a song heard occasionally at church concerts; by a
woman "of debatable age" posing as a "plantation darkey;" and by a "small
fat man" who "looked like a pictured devil on a Japanese kite" in his "shock
of red wig" (32–33). All of these acts foreground the question of authenticity in Bowery entertainment, yet what must have been the preeminent challenge to authenticity in Bowery life, that of a cross-dressing man, is not
explicitly present. It may be implicitly present, however, precisely in Crane's
focus on masquerade and artificiality as the unifying thread of saloon entertainment in the Bowery.

The questions of the homoerotic that play suggestively about Crane's
life, often in terms of the relations of others to him, would not be worth specifying were it not for the central and manifest concern of his best fiction with
the dynamics of interactions between men, either as individuals or in groups.
Like Whitman, Melville, or London, Crane realizes that relations between
men are physical, bodily, desiring relationships.

A corollary of such a claim is the common observation that Crane does
not write well about women. To the generally admiring Beer, "only a frantic
admirer" would call Crane "a profound student of the female mind." Adds
Edwin H. Cady, "in dealing with women . . . , Crane's irony deserted him.
He did not have a clear single view of them, much less a double or triple
vision."[10] Such limits led Crane, according to Carol Hurd Green, "as artist
and as man, to the battlefield and the decks of ships, to places where women
could not follow."[11] Even in *Maggie: A Girl of the Streets,* which represents
the strongest counterargument, Maggie is an idealized construct or hypothesis who organizes the narrative through her absence of substance, and who
mediates homosocial relations between Jimmy and Pete. When Crane returns
to his analysis of the Bowery in the weaker *George's Mother,* he empties the
world of women aside from George's one-dimensional, Christian, and long-

suffering mother and a cameo appearance by Maggie herself. The energy in this book shifts wholly to George's relation to his male peer group.

In *The Red Badge of Courage,* Henry Fleming is a man with a secret, but, as stated, the secret seems inadequate to its textual representation. Henry's problem consists of his fear that he might run in his first major engagement, and this fear separates him from his comrades. He is completely unable to wrench similar anxieties out of his fellow soldiers, although he seems willing enough to talk about himself to any sympathetic audience. The world of male interactions the novel depicts stands categorically against any confession of weakness between men. The only person who will confess any doubt to Fleming is Jim Conklin, the tall soldier who admits that "it might get too hot for Jim Conklin in some of them scrimmages, and if a whole lot of boys started and run, why, I s'pose I'd start and run. And if I once started to run, I'd run like the devil, and no mistake. But if everybody was a-standing and a-fighting, why, I'd stand and fight. By jiminey, I would. I'll bet on it" (90).[12] Henry "was in a measure reassured" by this admission, but it does nothing in the long term to reassure him (90). The tall soldier still displays "serene unconcern," and Henry, meanwhile, must conclude that "he could not sit still and with a mental slate and pencil derive an answer" (91). He continues to "occasionally . . . fathom a comrade with seductive sentences. He looked about to find men in the proper mood. All attempts failed to bring forth any statement which looked in any way like a confession to those doubts which he privately acknowledged in himself" (91–92). It is not clear that it is impossible to find men willing to converse honestly about fear of death before a major battle, nor is it clear that the mere entertaining of such doubts about oneself institutes such extreme psychic distance, such shame, between the doubter and his fellow soldiers. It is clear that doubts about one's masculinity lodged in phobic anxieties about impermissible sexual desires would cause such separation, and that such anxieties would be felt to constitute "shameful crimes against the gods of traditions" (92).

The language of this last phrase might remind one of Dimmesdale's secret shame in *The Scarlet Letter.* I argued that this shame was connected, not just to adulterous guilt toward Hester Prynne, but to impermissible desires in his relation to Chillingworth that expressed themselves as breakdown or dissolution for both Dimmesdale and the narrative. An analogous dissolution threatens Densher in *The Wings of the Dove,* particularly in the swirling glances exchanged among men in the Venice portion of the novel—the sense, as Moon indicates, of being penetrated by and penetrating others.[13]

In *The Red Badge of Courage,* the revelation of Henry's wound, of his difference, also occurs in the midst of moments of breakdown in the order of narrative, as the conventional and predictable narrative of battle—Henry runs or fights, is or is not heroic, wins or loses the battle, does or does not achieve manhood—yields to the disorder of his rambles in the chaos behind the lines. This chaos produces Henry's uncanny and seemingly random encounters with corpses and wounded soldiers. These encounters have a structure, I will suggest, albeit not one so easy to apprehend or narratively to sustain.[14]

The first of several encounters with corpses occurs as Henry and his cohorts march toward the coming engagement. The following moment is one of the most famous in the text:

> Once the line encountered the body of a dead soldier.
>
> He lay upon his back staring at the sky. He was dressed in an awkward suit of yellowish brown. The youth could see that the soles of his shoes had been worn to the thinness of writing paper, and from a great rent in one the dead foot projected piteously. And it was as if fate had betrayed the soldier. In death it exposed to his enemies that poverty which in life he had perhaps concealed from his friends. (102)[15]

The protruding foot suggests a fear of a shameful exposure projected by the narrative upon the corpse, one for which literal "poverty" seems insufficient as an explanation, given the generally impoverished state of the Confederate Army. It suggests that Henry's shame has a sexual component, indicated by the narrative's interest in improper unveilings of body parts and by the foot as a conventional site of fetishism, a connection that quickly shifts shame from the viewed body to the viewer, as one whose "poverty" consists of an absence of resistance to the forbidden pleasures of unconventional displays. That the encounter contains perverse pleasures is supported by Henry's imagined tactile relations with the corpse in the next paragraph: "The youth looked keenly at the ashen face. The wind raised the tawny beard. It moved as if a hand were stroking it. He vaguely desired to walk around and around the body and stare" (102). The dead soldier seems to accept and even invite such scrutiny, as "he lay upon his back staring at the sky," in a conventionally nonthreatening, defenseless position.

As Michael Fried suggests, the passage indicates a metaphorics of writing as well, but the argument that Crane's prose obsessively represents writing as an alien, material, mechanized process profits from a focus on the intersection of writing and homoerotics in Crane's prose.[16] It may be that the productions of the imagination always suggest a mechanization, since fantasy is at best only a partially willed category of thought—our imaginings often come to us unbidden. In any case, the representation of fiction writing as mechanized dramatizes the author's lack of responsibility for what his or her prose produces, as opposed to the myriad signs of conscious, nonmechanized artistry good prose also commonly contains. Metaphors of mechanization, then, suggest the decentering mystery of desiring and imagining, yet they also suggest a defense against the assumption of responsibility for the contents of writing that hovers uncertainly on the borders of conscious intention.

Typically, writing marches Henry into scenes of grave perceptual and psychic danger. After his flight from battle, for example, he confronts another corpse, this one more horrifically and phobically (yet compellingly) described:

> He was being looked at by a dead man who was seated with his back
> against a columnlike tree. . . . The eyes, staring at the youth, had
> changed to the dull hue to be seen on the side of a dead fish. The
> mouth was open. Its red had changed to an appalling yellow. Over
> the gray skin of the face ran little ants. . . . The youth gave a shriek
> as he confronted the thing. He was for moments turned to stone be-
> fore it. He remained staring into the liquid-looking eyes. The dead
> man and the living man exchanged a long look. (126)

In this second scene, positive desire seems to be phobically rendered as a monstrous impossibility, as opposed to the intellectualized abstraction of the previous scene, yet the insects, in addition to serving as an appropriate naturalist detail, suggest a desiring restlessness (allied to the energy of the ants Henry James imagines scurrying under an uplifted rock in his notebooks). In the first scene, the confrontation with the corpse occurs as a consequence of narrative but threatens to derail its continuation, as Henry wants to "walk around and around" the corpse. His absorption in the line of march, in the ongoing narrative line of battle, means that he must continue regardless of personal desires and plans: he cannot stop. The second and more threatening encounter occurs because Henry has fallen out of the line of narrative. It occurs as a consequence of Henry's searching in the wilderness for "dark and intricate places" (125) and interrupts a sudden idyllic perception of "Nature" as "a woman with a deep aversion to tragedy" (125), a fantasy of blissful regression that suggests Lambert Strether's dangerous, oedipally charged abandonment to pleasure in his country excursion in *The Ambassadors.*

Crane's second scene effectively punishes Henry for his previous desires to "walk around and around" the earlier corpse. In this scene, he has
the freedom to contemplate the revealed body until the cows come home,
but at the price of abandoning the defenses of realist order, an order indicated in the first scene by the continuing line of march, and perhaps even by
the invocation of the conventional realist category of poverty as the source
of the scene's shame.

The second corpse presents to Henry the possibility of immediate and
threatening participation in the scene before him—as "the dead man and the
living man exchanged a long look," in fact, the metaphor of cruising irresistibly presents itself (126).[17] Henry loses the luxury of detached voyeurism, Crane's own preferred aestheticized vantage point outside—or barely
inside—the scenes he depicts. The gain of forgoing detachment is access to
something like primal energy, embodied in random "ants swarming greedily
upon the gray face" (127). If the wind stroking the first body's beard "like a
hand" indirectly suggests Henry's desire to do so as well in the first scene,
the desire receives a direct expression in the second, as "with it all he received a subtle suggestion to touch the corpse" (127). The phobic trappings
of the encounter, the direct linkage between desire and disintegration, over-
whelm its content of positive desire and send Henry fleeing, ultimately back
to the ordered comprehensibility of his unit. His final vision is of the ants
swarming "horribly near to the eyes" of the corpse, an indication that commitment to homoerotic desire threatens to blind and, if we read oedipally,
threatens symbolically to castrate as well. In capitalist culture, typically, seeing produces desire, and desiring produces a desire to see. In Crane's fiction, seeing often happens in the absence of desire, or produces an aversion
to desiring as its consequence.[18]

In the midst of Henry's wanderings, as his "mind flew in all directions"
(128), he stumbles into three connected encounters that extend the consequences of the phobic desire to the realm of relations between the living. First,
he meets a tattered, wounded soldier; second, he witnesses the agonizing death
of his friend Jim Conklin; and third, he deserts his tattered acquaintance.

Crane explicitly feminizes the wounded soldier, indicating that "[h]is
voice was gentle as a girl's voice and his eyes were pleading." In addition, a
bearded sergeant refers to him in explicitly feminine terms when he catches
the soldier gaping at his tall tales: "Be keerful, honey, you'll be a-ketchin'
flies." Despite such explicit feminization, the tattered soldier has the psychic
comfort of his wounds, one in the head, "bound with a blood-soaked rag,"
and the "other in the arm, making that member dangle like a broken bough"
(131).

The wounded soldier poses a threat to Henry, who lacks a famously justifying "red badge of courage" of his own (133). It isn't the case that Henry has escaped all wounding. His defensive yet revealing gesture of "picking nervously at one of his buttons" indicates that he might actually feel that he possesses a wound as well (132). This wound would be a feminization akin to that the wounded soldier displays, except Henry has no masculinizing exterior wound to cover the inward hurt of a perceived masculine deficiency.[19] It is this inward vulnerability that Henry unconsciously begins to unveil under the pressure of the wounded soldier's interrogation, an interrogation made, finally, as a consequence of this soldier's feminized avidity for information. Lacking manly restraint, he forces himself upon Henry, freed for such behavior by his covering masculine wounds. Even here, however, Henry's companion slides toward excess: he has two wounds, when one would plainly do (as one will do for Henry), the second, the "broken bough" of his arm, arguably reinscribing his feminized condition.

The probing of this excessively emotional man has erotic implications: if Henry's fascination with his uniform buttons suggests the presence of an nonvisible wound, it suggests a symbolic undressing as well. These implications, however, are largely displaced onto the next scene of the novel, the famous death of Henry's friend Jim Conklin. Jim's death has a commonly noted orgasmic quality that might remind one, once again, of the end of *Billy Budd:*

> There was another silence while he waited. Suddenly, his form stiffened and straightened. Then it was shaken by a prolonged ague. He stared into space. To the two watchers there was a curious and profound dignity in the firm lines of his awful face. He was invaded by a creeping strangeness that slowly enveloped him. For a moment the tremor of his legs caused him to dance a sort of hideous hornpipe. His arms beat wildly about his head in expression of implike enthusiasm. His tall figure stretched itself to its full height. There was a slight rending sound. Then it began to swing forward, slow and straight, in the manner of a falling tree. A swift muscular contortion made the left shoulder strike the ground first. (137)

Henry finds it possible to respond emotionally to his friend's death. We are told at one point that his pain was such that "[h]is heart seemed to wrench itself almost free from his body" (135) and, at another, that "[h]is face . . . twisted into an expression of every agony he had imagined for his friend" (137). This affection, however, seems paradoxically enabled by defenses against its physical expression. Though Jim's writhings lend an orgasmic quality to death, he repeatedly tells Henry to "[l]eave me be—don't tech me—leave me be" (137). What Crane refers to as the "passion of his wounds," then, finally belongs to Jim alone (133). In fact, when Henry shapes his expressions into his imagined version of his friend's experience, a process that lends an oddly separated mutuality to the scene, he nevertheless finds he is quite wrong. Jim died with his "mouth . . . open and the teeth showed in a laugh" (137).

After Jim's death, Henry fails once again to lend aid to the tattered soldier, even though his aid in this case would be helpful and possibly efficacious. If the strength of Henry's feeling for Jim was enabled by the impossibility of physically expressing his affection, in this third instance its expression is prevented once again by an absence of insulating distance. Henry makes his companion into a sign of "a society that probes pitilessly at secrets until all is apparent. His late companion's chance persistency made him feel that he could not keep his crime concealed in his bosom. It was sure to be brought plain by one of those arrows . . . pricking, discovering, proclaiming those things which are willed to be forever hidden" (141). This broad description of scrutiny is an apt expression of panic arising from the fear that one's secret lack of compliance with heterosexual masculine norms might be discovered. It reminds us that Henry's anxieties about discovery are not local to the dynamics of his particular present situation; indeed, Henry has had a general fear of a discovery of his secrets from the novel's opening scene.

If Henry's anxieties in the novel are necessarily broader than the circumstances produced by his flight, it is also necessary to emphasize the specificity of the threat posed to Henry by the guileless affection of the tattered, feminized soldier. Early in the novel, the toughness and distance of male homosocial relations prevent covert inquisitions from being successful: Henry fathoms no other secrets, and the other soldiers wrest no illicit secrets from him. Nor are the other wounded soldiers Henry encounters particularly inquisitive about his possession or lack of wounds. It is only this wounded soldier who actively threatens to unveil the secrets Henry wishes to keep concealed.

In addition to the danger of being "found out" by his companion, the empathy Henry displays in his encounter with Jim suggests another source of danger. His identification with Jim, as already indicated, is powerful but finally impossible, so that it has no consequences in the text. If transferred to the third scene of this sequence, however, identification would produce a dangerous miming of the feminine proclivities of a protohomosexual man, a miming that would dangerously equal the state of being homosexual oneself. It is this identification that Henry brutally finds himself withholding as he dehumanizes his affectionate companion. This withholding of empathy produces a retrospective dehumanization of Jim as well: "The youth looking at him, could see that he, too, like that other one, was beginning to act dumb and animal-like" (140).

At another point, the tattered soldier suggests that he was "commencin' t'feel pretty bad" (139). Henry responds with a marked absence of feeling: "The youth groaned. 'O Lord!' He wondered if he was to be the tortured witness of another grim encounter" (139). His suffering companion responds with a suggestive joke, reassuring Henry that he does not intend to die, making a joke about "th' swad a' chil'ren I've got, an' all like that" (139). On the one hand, this statement may act subliminally to calm Henry's anxieties by suggesting his own heterosexuality. On the other hand, Henry's sense that the wounded man was making "some kind of fun" reinforces the sense of the latter's otherness to norms of conventional masculinity as well, since it implies either an absence of conventional ties or an absence of conventional feeling toward them, and in any case a joke that cannot be completely fathomed by its intended audience (139). If Henry withholds his own sympathies from his feminine friend, this friend tortures him through his own emotionally unencumbered responses. These continually reassert, moreover, a secret inner sympathy between the two that only exacerbates Henry's anxieties: "They went on slowly in silence. 'Yeh look pretty peek-ed yerself,' said the tattered man at last. 'I bet yeh've got a worser one than yeh think. Ye'd better take ker of yer hurt. . . . It might be inside mostly, an' them plays thunder. . . . So, yeh wanta watch out. Yeh might have some queer kind'a hurt yerself. Yeh can't never tell'" (139–140). It is Henry's anxiety that he has a "queer kind'a hurt" that has separated him from his fellows from the beginning of the novel, and the wounded soldier is only too successful in giving this hurt, broader than simple cowardice, a visible representation.

It is Crane's own fascination with a "queer kind'a hurt" that persistently produces some of the most wrenching dislocations of his prose. Typically, these dislocations produce passages of stunning writing, often involving erotically charged relations to the male body that exist in a relation of surplus to the manifest subject of his narrative. Often, the subject such passages begin to broach must be simply abandoned, as Crane cannot or will not proceed any further. Though I will return to *The Red Badge of Courage* in order to discuss Crane's extrication of Henry from his dilemmas, I want now to look at charged moments involving the male body in other examples of Crane's fiction, as a way of establishing an expanded context for the arguments I am making.

*I*n much of Crane's fiction the mark of homoerotic investment is narrative disjunction and rupture involving some vertiginous plunge into what Crane treats as the ineffable attractions, repulsions, and dangers of physical life. The consequence of the fall into such negative epiphanies, unless, as in "The Upturned Face," the fall is the sum of the (brief) tale, must be another rupture on the far side of the experience that returns us to conventional perception, now both exposed and phobically reinforced.

One such suggestive moment occurs in *George's Mother,* mentioned earlier as a novel chiefly concerned with same-sex relationships. In this text, the guilt produced by Kelcey's Christian mother consistently competes with his desire to mix with other men over drink, mixed and otherwise. At a party of men that the drunken Kelcey thinks of as a "festival of a religion," he finds himself twice forced to the floor: "Jones seized him and dragged him toward a chair. He heard him laugh. . . . He threw out his hand violently, but Jones grappled him close and he was no more than a dried leaf. . . . As he lay, he reflected in great astonishment upon Jones's muscle. It was singular that he had never before discovered it" (247). When George wakes up and tries to rejoin the party, the assault begins anew: "He felt them hurl him to a corner of the room and pile chairs and tables upon him until he was buried beneath a stupendous mountain. Far above, as up a mine's shaft, there were voices, lights, and vague figures. He was not hurt physically, but his feelings were unutterably injured. He, the brilliant, the good, the sympathetic, had been thrust fiendishly from the party" (247–248).

The sense of this scene as a symbolic rape gains support from the compressed anal erotics of the phrase "up a mine's shaft," but it receives support as well from its context. Prior to his violent suppression, George has been attempting drunkenly to articulate his romantic passion for Maggie Johnson to "[t]he adorable Jones, the supremely wise Jones," who was "erect and tranquil" following his abortive attempt to dance with George to a tune with a "rippling waltz movement" (246). George's romantic reference to Maggie, the scene suggests, has improperly interrupted ritualized male bonding between George and his newfound friends. Though in Crane's fiction heterosexual romance is more a category of cultural transcendence than a category of sexual desire for women, George's transgression triggers a metaphorical rape as a result.

George wakes up the next morning, as "mellow streams of sunshine poured in, undraping the shadows to disclose the putrefaction," and immediately has a phobic reaction to old Bleecker, the host of the party, whom he now sees as "a tottering old beast," both "disgusting" and "weak as sin" (249–250). George perceives Bleecker, in short, as a degenerate in the cold, logical light of day.

Crane's use of narrative rupture to explore and contain desire between men is especially apparent in the famous sketch "An Experiment in Misery," his undercover exploration of the world of homeless men in the Bowery, which also involves the problem of degeneracy. If this sketch conventionally aligns lower-class experience and the body, it nonetheless represents a remarkable plunge into the body's polymorphous possibilities as a perceptual object, and it finally suggests that these possibilities cannot be restricted to a particular class but represent the omnipresent repressed underside of nineteenth-century bourgeois culture, localized and allowed to surface in the Bowery. Crane's own experiment, then, mimes the nineteenth-century voyeurism uncovered by Chauncey.

Crane's experience of poverty is one of unstinting and omnipresent fetid sensuality. Crane describes the doors of a "voracious" saloon "snapping to and fro like ravenous lips" as the saloon "gorged itself with plump men." After receiving soup and taking pleasure in the "warmth of the mixture," Crane and his companion find a place to sleep (539). In this place Crane finds himself assaulted by "strange and unspeakable odors that assailed . . . like malignant diseases with wings . . . from human bodies closely packed in dens." These are the fumes "from a hundred pairs of reeking lips . . . a thousand bygone debauches" (541). The body's vulnerability to perception, its permeable boundaries, comes to threaten its very integrity as a separate, integrated object. As Crane rests on a leather cot "like a slab," he views his companion, whose "wet hair and beard dimly glistened" and whose "inflamed nose shone with subdued luster" (542). Within arm's reach is a man with exposed "yellow breast and shoulders," with one arm that "hung over the side of the cot and the fingers lay full length upon the wet cement floor of the room" (542). The tactile power of the description of this hand, for which Crane has prepared us by the account of his chilled cot, produces a characteristic phobic withdrawal from Crane: "Beneath the inky brows could be seen the eyes of the man exposed by the partly opened lids. To the youth it seemed that he and this corpse-like being were exchanging a prolonged stare and that the other threatened with his eyes. He drew back. . . . The man . . . lay . . . like a body stretched out, expectant of the surgeon's knife" (542–543). Now the "tawny hues of naked flesh" and the assorted limbs filling the room seem "statuesque, carven, dead" (543).

The association of the male body with death suggests the threat such bodies pose in the amorphousness of night to the perception and stability of the onlooker. I take it that death in general, and especially death in Crane, threatens chiefly as a null set, about which no verifiable claim can be made or ever will be made. The nothingness with which it threatens us when invoked is beyond thought, and though its invocation seems to trump and erase all merely quotidian anxieties, the imagination of death can only be a nothing inflected by various lived, quotidian fears—and this is the case even for imaginations haunted, as Crane's must have been, by a foreboding sense of an early, horrific demise. We cannot treat, then, the fear of death as something with its own essential properties; we must ask what other fears act as source and context for what is usually considered the most primal and universal of terrors, what other fears might extend into or out of the fear of death.

In Crane's best work, repeatedly, a threatening richness or fecundity of perception finds its ultimate expression in, yet is canceled by, the gaze at death's relentless blankness. Though such issues can be framed abstractly as philosophical problems, as I have been arguing, such anxieties commonly cluster around eroticized relations to other male bodies in Crane's fiction.[20] In the case of "An Experiment in Misery," perception is in fact threatened by the overwhelming sensuality of Crane's underclass experience—by a plunge into poverty imagined as a plunge into bodily experience unmasked and heightened by deprivation. If the potential contents of this file are expunged by the invocation of death as a state of perception with no discursive object, this dead end for analysis and narrative is avoided by another of the sudden displacements that repeatedly mark Crane's prose. Just as George's drunken nighttime revel in *George's Mother* yields to a comforting world of daylight stability and objective vision, so daylight makes "the room comparatively commonplace and uninteresting," even though the bodies of his companions are now fully exposed to scrutiny. "The men, whose faces seemed stolid, serene or absent, were engaged in dressing, while a great crackle of bantering conversation arose" (544). If the conventions of daylight work with the story's patina of conventional social commentary to confine the threatening mobility of nighttime perception and experience, they also paradoxically expand the story's range of reference. If, in other words, we suddenly see that these male bodies can be like all other male bodies regardless of class, then the sensuality of the story has no necessary class location either, aside from the capacity of poverty to produce a propinquity of sleeping males outside bourgeois norms of social space and privacy. The potential universality of the human body, represented by the "men of brawn, whose skins shone clear and ruddy," reattains its class specificity only by redonning garments: "[T]hey then showed bumps and deficiencies of all kinds" (544).

The manipulation of narrative rupture characterizes as well Crane's Sullivan County stories, which he composed at the beginning of his career, prior to *The Red Badge of Courage,* the novel that first earned him acclaim as an author. In "A Ghoul's Accountant," a man sleeping with his companions is forcibly and ominously abducted from his campsite by a sadistic intruder carrying a pickerel spear, who, as he "gazed at the four passive bundles, . . . smiled a smile that curled his lips and showed yellow, disordered teeth." Taken to a remote and decrepit house, the man discovers he must only resolve an accounting dispute between his captor and his equally mad companion, a "wild, gray man" (498–499). He must answer a query about the price of "thirty-three bushels of pertaters at sixty-four an' a half a bushel" (500).

It is impossible to specify the kidnappers in this tale as sexually degenerate.[21] The story requires, however, that we imagine a kind of dire depredation practiced against its central character, from which the story's ending swerves away. The same pattern applies to Crane's story "Four Men in a Cave." In this tale, a group exploring the "black mouth" (489) of a cave find themselves trapped by an old hermit "with a long, thin knife" (492). Crane tells us that he wears "a brown checked shirt of the ploughs and cows" and that "[t]he rest of his apparel was boots"—Crane makes us imagine, in other words, a stretch of nakedness in between (491). The group finds, however, that, despite the obvious threat of sexual assault, their captor only demands that one of their party play poker until he is "dead broke" (492). The chastened adventurers find themselves ejected from the cave without suffering physical harm, although the condition of being "dead broke" might continue the story's ominous subtext by implying a metaphorical sexual exhaustion. They later find that their attacker has been ruined and driven mad by gambling away the family farm.

In both cases, the stories work by conjuring up dangers for the readers that Crane then deflates. In both cases, the dangers would seem to involve either some form of sexual violation—witness the absence of pants—or sadistic killing, or some combination of the two. Not even the greatest mathphobe among us fears that nighttime abduction will lead to forced arithmetic. Nor can "Four Men in a Cave" work only in terms of gambling, even if Crane means the story to parody the moral hysteria of his own religious background. A fear of gambling cannot be the fear invoked as the men are held at knife point.

In a structurally similar third tale, "The Octopush," Crane again injects sexual overtones into a tale of captivity. In "The Octopush," a group of pickerel fishermen employs a local to guide them through a stump-covered lake. Having conveyed each of the four fishermen to his own stump, the local occupies a stump of his own and refuses to return the sportsmen to shore until well into the night, thus effectively holding them prisoner. As each man grapples with his fear of the dark and "feels that he was compelled to sit on something that was damply alive," the now drunken local suddenly hallucinates that his stump is an "octopush" and that he is "a-settin' on his mouth" (497). The stumps themselves suggest some kind of phallic anal violation, an implication rendered obvious by the fantasy of the octopus. The changing of "pus" to "push" mutes the sexual implications of the former, but "push" also anthropomorphizes the creature and may add to the mathematical resonance between the eight-armed creature and the four men, who have between them, precisely, eight arms. In the daytime, the separate stumps suggest a rigid, homophobically enforced separation of male bodies, but this separation is undone by the unconscious, erotic fluidity of night.

In The Red Badge of Courage, Crane employs several ruptures to emphasize and formalize the commonly observed discontinuity between the first half of the novel and the second half, which emphasizes Henry's heroic ascension. The first is the disorienting effect of the wound itself, as Henry focuses his attention on the question of his health: "It had come to pass that his wound pained him but little. He was afraid to move rapidly, however, for a dread of disturbing it. . . . His thoughts, as he walked, fixed intently upon his hurt. There was a cool, liquid feeling about it and he imagined blood moving slowly down under his hair. His head seemed swollen to a size that made him think his neck to be inadequate" (151). The second rupture is represented by the mysterious guide who finds Henry and helps him to his unit, a man described by the text as having a mysterious agency: "In the search which followed, the man of the cheery voice seemed to the youth to possess a wand of a magic kind. He threaded the mazes of the tangled forest with a strange fortune. In encounters with guards and patrols he displayed the keenness of a detective and the valor of a gamin. Obstacles fell before him and became of assistance. . . . As he who had so befriended him was thus passing out of his life, it suddenly occurred to the youth that he had not once seen his face" (75). This faceless character, Amy Kaplan suggests, must be seen as a figure for the author, who shepherds Henry back to his unit so that the narrative of the construction of courage can begin.[22] He suggests the author's own intrusive stake in the narratability of his materials, a stake that would be heightened by the difficult professional and financial conditions facing Crane at the time of his novel's composition.

Just as gender in *The Jungle* must be understood in terms of Sinclair's narrative construction of cultural authority, sexuality in *The Red Badge of Courage* must be understood in a similar context. Like Sinclair, Crane was a writer of great ambition who had apparently failed texts behind him. *Maggie: A Girl of the Streets* was printed at his own expense and read by virtually no one, although the young Crane had hoped to create a sensation. Also, like Sinclair, Crane wrote the text that solidified his reputation in conditions of extreme poverty. As Hershel Parker somewhat romantically puts it, "The reality is that during much of the time he wrote *The Red Badge of Courage,* Stephen Crane was, in winter, cold—cold as street people are. . . . To be malnourished and poorly clad was bad enough, but, we need to remind ourselves, Crane was also sick. Those racking spasms of coughing . . . were probably . . . early symptoms of the tuberculosis that killed him."[23]

Crane, I think, was continually ambivalent about the pressure of the need for success to force aesthetic compliance upon his text, as the following exchange with Howells indicates. In 1896, Howells sends a congratulatory note: "I have been enjoying for your sake your English triumphs. I am glad you are getting your glory young. For once, the English who habitually know nothing of art, seem to know something."[24] To which Crane responds, "I had just become well habituated to abuse when this bit of a flurry about the red badge came upon me. I am slightly rattled and think it best to cling to Hartwood where if I choose to shout triumphant shouts none can hear me. However I have not yet elected to shout any shouts. I am, mostly, afraid. Afraid that some small degree of talk will turn me ever so slightly from what I believe to be the pursuit of truth" (192). Crane also apparently suggested a deep ambivalence about such pressure to Louis Senger, one of his close friends. According to Senger's comment to Hamlin Garland, Crane said the following: "I deliberately started in to do a pot-boiler, . . . something that would take the boarding-school element—you know the kind. Well, I got interested in the thing in spite of myself, and I couldn't, I couldn't. I *had* to do it my own way."[25] He also, however, had to do it the world's way if the novel would assume a marketable form and produce for him more than a reputation as an interesting eccentric, a function admirably filled by *The Black Riders and Other Lines,* which appeared shortly before the publication of his novel.[26]

A third rupture employed in *The Red Badge of Courage* is the division common in Crane between nighttime and daytime experience. When the stranger returns Henry to his unit, darkness makes faces so "pallid and ghostly" that "[t]his bit of forest might have appeared to an ethereal wanderer as a scene of the result of some frightful debauch" (156). Shrouded in the fluidity of nighttime experience, justified by his covering wound, Henry now gratefully receives caring, physical attention from his male companions. Henry's wounds are ministered to by the voluble Wilson, whom, like the tattered soldier, Crane earlier characterized in feminized terms, referring at one point to the "trembling" of "his girlish lip" (106). Now, Wilson's attentions are justified and welcomed, precisely because Henry has a wound (albeit problematically received). Wilson has "the bustling ways of an amateur nurse." He makes Henry drink from a canteen of coffee that goes "caressingly down his throat," and administers a damp cloth that feels like "a tender woman's hand" to his head. In response to these attentions, Henry begins "to fumble with the buttons of his jacket" (80), a gesture that again resonates with his earlier encounter with the tattered soldier, and he beds down next to Wilson for the night on the latter's blanket.

After a night in which Henry "snuggled down into his blanket, and in a moment was like his comrades," he awakes once more to his corporeal separateness, resisting any further ministrations or aid. Wilson notices that his bandage has slipped and begins to "tinker at the wound in a rather clumsy way." Henry has had enough: "'Gosh-dern it!' he said in sharp irritation; 'you're the hangdest man I ever saw! You wear muffs on your hands. Why in good thunderation can't you be more easy?'" (82). Henry's brusqueness restores distance after the soothing indeterminacy of night and signals his willingness to hurl himself into combat.

The description of much of the fighting itself will be phantasmatic and erotically loaded, as Henry has sensations that "he and his fellows, at bay, were pushing back, always pushing fierce onslaughts of creatures who were slippery. Their beams of crimson seemed to get no purchase upon the bodies of their foes" (95). The decentering power of this language, however, remains solidly encased and justified in the cultural comprehensibility of battle narratives. The cultural acceptability of all language and all depiction in *The Red Badge of Courage* related to everyday mass violence remains one of the novel's staggering messages. Eroticism between men, fashioned even as an everyday exchange of affection and concern, must furtively inhabit the secret interstices of the text. Eroticism phobically sublimated into genocidal violence, into the phantasmatic tearing and rending of male bodies, needs never to hide its face.

In *The Red Badge of Courage,* narrative authority, however ambivalently and ironically, is generated through Henry's journey to adult masculinity from the mother-centered world of his childhood, through the testing of battle, to his achieved sense of self at the text's end: "He had been to touch the great death, and found that, after all, it was but the great death. He was a man" (212). Kaplan has provided a valuable analysis of the social creation of Henry's sense of selfhood. She argues that Henry only succeeds in stabilizing his own self-image performatively: "For Henry to become a man or to have a self, he needs to imagine an audience watching him, and can only represent his actions in the eyes of others. . . . Thus Crane's representation of war as a spectacle both adopts and subverts the interpretation of the battlefield as a crucible for virility, as well as the concept of manhood as an internal primal quality."[27] Kaplan's sense that Crane's novel simultaneously adopts and subverts its paradigms of manhood leads directly to the longstanding critical question of the nature of irony in *The Red Badge of Courage*. The evidence that Crane's irony is considerable is strengthened by the restoration of sections deleted from the first published version, most of which work to satirize Henry's self-importance and capacity for self-delusion, especially this passage from chapter 12, which Crane later deleted in its entirety: "It was always clear to the youth that he was entirely different from other men; that his mind had been cast in a unique mold. Hence laws that might be just to the ordinary man, were, when applied to him, peculiar and galling outrages. . . . He regarded his sufferings as unprecedented. No man had ever achieved such misery."[28]

Crane's evident irony, nonetheless, may not indicate simple disapproval so much as a recognition of the culturally enforced distortions and denials at the base of masculine identity, particularly given the less egregiously self-inflated Henry of the Appleton version. Nearly identical questions of irony occur in terms of Hawthorne's relation to Dimmesdale's ambiguous triumph at the end of *The Scarlet Letter*, or of James's relation to that of either Lambert Strether or Merton Densher. In each case, the desire to celebrate any kind of securing transcendence on the part of the male hero requires that we forget the full complexity of the relations the texts themselves have apparently made a point of revealing. To approve of the construction of heterosexual masculine identity, all three endings suggest, it is also necessary to grant it power to construct itself through denial and repression: Its paradigms never are and never can be adequate to either social or psychological experience. The necessity of what amounts to masculine and narrative bad faith, however, is reinforced rather than exposed through the phobic depiction of its alternative as masochistic disintegration—one of the reasons why the political productivity of paradigms of male masochism must always be suspect.

Beyond Influence, Beyond Homoeroticism, and Beyond the Pleasure Principle in J. Scott Fitzgerald's The Great Gatsby

*F*reudian psychoanalysis in the first part of the twentieth century assumes a central role in the genesis of understandings of gender and sexuality, as it formalizes and institutionalizes as knowledge the anxious accomodations I have been tracing in nineteenth- and turn-of-the-century literature. Freud, though hardly a product of U.S. culture, provides a conflict-ridden narrative of how the male subject passes from an early maternal identification, through the hazards of female identification and homosexuality, to a separated, male-identified, and heterosexual adulthood. A string of male U.S. authors, I have argued, have produced their own literary versions of this story throughout nineteenth-century literature, as a consequence of the need to produce a distinctly masculine literary authority out of the received materials of culture and through the structures of narrative. These versions explore the conflicts of masculinity, but ultimately take refuge in an aestheticized transcendence of its conflicts. Their endings may be ironically undercut, but narratively necessary and culturally powerful nonetheless. Indeed, the nineteenth-century authors I have examined at times seem to construct masculine authority through a difficult-to-resist transcendence of their own ironical self-consciousness, as if intimations of immorality finally provide no help.

If Freudian psychoanalysis represents a culturally powerful force in the institutionalization of narratives of male development, twentieth-century literature participates in this process as well through the complex interface that emerges between psychoanalysis and literature, evident in the not-very-latent developmental Freudianism of something like Hemingway's *In Our Time*. I want to conclude, then, by examining a text that perhaps most expertly engineers the construction of authorship through a masterful managing of the inherited literary anxieties of female influence and homosexuality: F. Scott Fitzgerald's *The Great Gatsby*.[1]

F. Scott Fitzgerald had considerable anxiety about issues of literary influence, produced by his yearning investment in ideas of a Western tradition of largely male greatness. In a July 18, 1940, letter to his daughter, Scottie, he tries to shape her summer reading by recommending texts such as *The Brothers Karamazov, Ten Days That Shook the World,* Renan's *Life of Christ, Père Goriot, Crime and Punishment, The Doll's House,* St. Matthew, and *Sons and Lovers*. These are good summer reads, to be sure, but Fitzgerald has more than July or August pleasure in mind. The list is meant to contribute to the future good of Scottie's style: "A good style simply doesn't *form*, unless you absorb half a dozen top-flight authors every year. . . . [I]nstead of being a subconscious amalgam . . . it is simply a reflection of the last writer you have read."[2] If Fitzgerald felt aspiring authors ought seriously to read conventional great literature, he was also capable of criticizing other writers for a lack of originality in relation to the wealth of the Western tradition. In a November letter of the same year, he complains to her that Thomas Wolfe, for example, essentially has nothing to add to his particular "amalgam": "[H]is awful secret transpires in at every crevice—he did not have anything particular to say! . . . [W]hat Walt Whitman said and Dostoyevsky said and Nietzsche said and Milton said, but he himself . . . has nothing really new to add." [3]

Fitzgerald's own debatable intellectual limits, his respect for intellectuality, and his desire to be recognized as a great writer produced an anxiety about the literary company he kept that renders suspicious all of his somewhat coy hints about his own sources scattered throughout his correspondence. On the one hand, they constitute arguments for *Gatsby*'s pedigree; on the other, such sources seem so removed in time and place from his novel that they pose no threat to its pristine originality. For example, Fitzgerald proposes in a letter to Maxwell Perkins that the book be called "Trimalchio in West Egg," an allusion to Petronius's *Satyricon* that suggests his high-culture aspirations for his book.[4] In two instances he mentions *The Brothers Karamazov,* a book with a somewhat indirect relation to *The Great Gatsby,* so far as I can tell. To Edmund "Bunny" Wilson, Fitzgerald remarks, regarding Mencken's charge that his novel was based on "an anecdote," that "if my novel is an anecdote so is *The Brothers Karamazov*." In responding to Mencken, at about the same time, Fitzgerald insists that "the influence on it has been the masculine one of *The Brothers Karamazov,* a thing of incomparable form, rather than the feminine one of *The Portrait of a Lady*."[5] At a later date, Fitzgerald invokes Thackeray as his model, suggesting that "*Gatsby* was shooting at something like *Henry Esmond*."[6]

Fitzgerald's affinity for far-flung sources suggests an adult literary version of a Freudian "family romance," a search for the "right" parents he pursued as a child,[7] and one of the sins of the child in "Absolution," the short story Fitzgerald indicated was originally written as the opening section of *Gatsby*.[8] In this tale, a young boy creates an alter ego named "Blatchford Sarnemington," and confesses to, among other things, the sin of not believing he was his parents' offspring. This lie is connected to the transcendental bent of his imagination, to his search for "something ineffably gorgeous somewhere that had nothing to do with God."[9] In his attempt, then, to create an ineffably gorgeous cultural object symbolized in the novel by the disreputable and flawed beauty of Gatsby himself, Fitzgerald, I will suggest, distorted the question of his novel's literary antecedents. If *Gatsby* clearly does deserve to claim cultural space of its own, it nonetheless is too much to claim, as Fitzgerald argued to Maxwell Perkins, that *Gatsby* was "like nothing I've ever read before."[10]

If Fitzgerald's target of aspiration in writing a serious novel—"something *new*—something extraordinary and beautiful and simple + intricately patterned"[11]—was the roster of great masculine art, criticism has long been aware of the extent to which his art drew on feminine sources. One of crucial sources for Fitzgerald's fiction was Zelda's experience and writing. She half playfully accuses him of plagiarism, in fact, in her review of *The Beautiful and the Damned,* the novel that precedes *The Great Gatsby*: "It also seems to me that on one page I recognized a portion of an old diary of mine which mysteriously disappeared shortly after my marriage, and also scraps of letters, which, though considerably edited, sound to me vaguely familiar. In fact, Mr. Fitzgerald—I believe that is how he spells his name—seems to believe that plagiarism begins at home."[12] If Fitzgerald drew generally upon his wife's emotional life and at times specifically upon her own writing, he also felt himself to write *for* women in important respects, an audience *Gatsby* abandons. In a December, 1924, letter to Maxwell Perkins, he worried that "it may hurt the book's popularity that it's *a man's* book."[13] This anxiety precedes its publication by several months and suggests Fitzgerald knew as he wrote the book that his relation to women readers was an aggressive one. In an April letter of the following year, Fitzgerald returned to the subject, arguing to Perkins that "the book contains no important woman character, and women control the fiction market at present."[14] In a letter written in October, 1925, to Marya Mannes, Fitzgerald explicitly thanked her for an appreciation of his novel, apparently unusual among its women readers: "Thank you for writing me about *Gatsby*—I especially appreciate your letter because women, and even intelligent women, haven't generally cared much for it. They do not like women to be presented as *emotionally* passive—as a matter of fact I think most women are, that their minds are taken up with a sort of second rate and inessential bookkeeping which their apologists call 'practicality.'"[15] In fact, Fitzgerald viewed most of his work for his female audience as second rate, and in the wake of his disappointment over Gatsby's sales would speak quite openly to Perkins about getting "ahead again on trash" in order to begin a new novel.[16]

Though Fitzgerald could express aggression against a readership he believed was dominated by women, he understood his own writing as an occupation distanced from conventional masculine concerns.[17] In a letter to Van Wyck Brooks concerning Brooks's book on Henry James, he first asks Brooks why he didn't treat James's supposed impotence at great length. He concludes by identifying himself with James: "Novelists like he (him) + in a sense (to descend a good bit) me, have to have love as a main concern since our interest lies outside the economic struggle or the life of violence, as conditioned to some extent by our lives from 16–21."[18]

Fitzgerald's affinity for listing far-flung sources, and his anxiety about much nearer feminine ones, may be evident in two consecutive paragraphs of a letter he sent to Thomas Boyd during the composition of *Gatsby*. In the first, Fitzgerald indicates that "[w]e missed Edith Wharton by one day—she left yesterday for Paris + won't return until next season. Not that I care, except that I met her in New York + she's a very distinguished grande dame who fought the good fight with bronze age weapons when there were very few people in the line at all" (141).

In the second, Fitzgerald apparently changes the subject to engage in what strikes one as intellectual muscle flexing: "I'm going to read nothing but Homer + Homeric literature—and history 540–1200 A.D. until I finish my novel. . . . My novel grows more + more extraordinary; I feel absolutely self-sufficient + I have a perfect hollow craving for loneliness . . . + I'm going to satisfy it at last" (*Letters*, 141). It is extremely difficult for me to see precisely what Homer has to do with *The Great Gatsby*, though perhaps a case could be made that makes this more than Fitzgeraldian pretension. One possible interpretation of Fitzgerald's letter is that he means there to be no connection: though he means his reader to believe that he indeed was reading Greek literature, he is reading it as a kind of stage-clearing act, as the suppression of all influence, rather than as a real source, in order to keep his imagination somehow pristine.

If so, Wharton may be a particular influence he is escaping by fleeing to the safety of ancient Greece, a reading supported by more than the logic of association. Indeed, the entire letter consists of defensive intimations of differences between Fitzgerald and Wharton that collapse under closer inspection. First, Fitzgerald's declaration that he "doesn't care" has a defensive ring, since the letter contains no excessive feeling for Wharton that needs to be explained. Second, this suppression is followed by a suggestion that Wharton is "bronze age," a condescending phrase that serves to exaggerate the distance between two authors whose careers overlapped. Among other things, one might remember that if the Bronze Age died with Wharton, Fitzgerald outlived it by only three years himself. Third, the military metaphors seem to introduce a note of gender difference into the context of their relations, especially if one views, in Hemingwayesque terms, the war as a source of crucial metaphysical revelations. In literal terms, Wharton was never "in the line" at all. Neither, of course, was Fitzgerald, yet here he manages graciously to extend the privilege of participation to one whose general service in World War I was more meritorious than his own.[19] Fourth, it is exceedingly odd that he characterizes his loneliness as "hollow." It implies that what Fitzgerald hopes for is not so much an escape from external contacts as an escape from what he contains, in order to be "absolutely self-sufficient." What he may have contained, I would suggest, is a considerable quantity of Edith Wharton's prose.[20] If so, it is against this prose that Fitzgerald would "satisfy" his "hollow craving for loneliness."

A connection between Wharton and Fitzgerald has long been noted in Fitzgerald criticism. Fitzgerald, after all, sent to Wharton an inscribed copy of *The Great Gatsby,* visited Wharton in Paris, wrote the titles for a silent movie version of a Wharton novel, *The Glimpses of the Moon,*[21] and included Wharton at the top of a list of Scribner's authors he felt should be republished in 1921.[22] Moreover, in Fitzgerald criticism, both *Ethan Frome* and *The Custom of the Country* have been listed among the numerous texts and authors suggested as Fitzgerald's sources.[23] Generally overlooked in Fitzgerald criticism, however, has been the Wharton text that, I think, has close and important connections to *The Great Gatsby:* Edith Wharton's *The House of Mirth.*[24]

It is with some reluctance, I freely confess, that I enter at a late date into a perhaps unwinnable argument concerning source texts for *The Great Gatsby*. How, after all, can one ever prove the importance of a particular source when all of culture is alive with reverberating echoes of its own past? If it finally is the case that, like most works of literature, *The Great Gatsby* has complex and multiple relations to the general culture that has produced it, nonetheless a reasonable case for the particular importance of *The House of Mirth* can be made—if influences are complex, they are not necessarily equal or equally diffuse. An appreciation of this particular connection, moreover, helps us to see what kind of cultural labor *The Great Gatsby* undertakes. Fitzgerald's text, I will argue, is constructed against the possibility of feminine literary influence.

Wharton's novel occupies much of the same cultural ground as *The Great Gatsby*. It is this direct threat to the originality of *Gatsby*'s subject matter, as opposed to questions of technique or narration, that makes it a source of anxiety for Fitzgerald. If Joseph Conrad's work, for example, had some influence upon Fitzgerald, his subject was not upper-class New York society; Wharton wrote about it obsessively.[25] Like *Gatsby*, Wharton's novel treats the corrupt and empty world of New York wealth, and it records the power of that world to destroy not a yearning boy from the Midwest, but a character of limited means, Lily Bart, who clings to romantic aspirations that short-circuit the ruthless pragmatism she needs to survive. Though Wharton's naturalism might seem far removed from Fitzgerald's interest in the cultural possibilities of belated and corrupt romanticism, the question of the possibilities of transcendence animates both novels. Lily Bart and Lawrence Seldon are drawn together by the possibility that love might carry them beyond the operations of the culture that divides them; in fact the grey seal on Lily's stationery consists of *"Beyond!"* printed "beneath a flying ship" (249). They might reach something like Seldon's "republic of the spirit," defined in solely negative terms. His idea of success is freedom "[f]rom everything—from money, from poverty, from ease and anxiety, from all the material accidents" (108). *The House of Mirth* suggests such hopes are illusory, but in the meantime, the question of transcendence generates some remarkably purple prose from Wharton. After the *tableaux vivants* scene of the novel, for example, Seldon and Lily kiss in a scene similar to the scene of the first kiss between Gatsby and Daisy. This kiss occurs

> in the fragrant hush of a garden. Gravel grated beneath their feet, and about them was the transparent dimness of a midsummer night.

Hanging lights made emerald caverns in the depths of foliage, and whitened the spray of a fountain falling among lilies. The magic place was deserted: there was no sound but the plash of the water on the lily-pads, and a distant drift of music that might have been blown across a sleeping lake. Seldon and Lily stood still, accepting the un-reality of the scene as a part of their own dream-like sensations. It would not have surprised them to feel a summer breeze on their faces, or to see the lights among the boughs reduplicated in the arch of a starry sky. (221)

Lily turns to Seldon "with the soft motion of a flower" as "their lips touched." When Lily leaves, we are told that Seldon "knew too much the transiency of exquisite moments to attempt to follow her" (222).

This, of course, is precisely what Gatsby does not know. The vision of the first kiss of Gatsby and Daisy seems triggered by Gatsby's insistence to Nick that "of course" you can "repeat the past" (116). Rather than "lights among the boughs reduplicated in the arch of a starry sky," Gatsby imagines that "the blocks of the sidewalk really formed a ladder and mounted to a se-cret place above the trees." Instead of "turning her face to him like a flower," we are told that "at his lips' touch she blossomed for him like a flower and the incarnation was complete" (117). Fitzgerald's passage, with its insistence that Gatsby's mind "would never romp again like the mind of God" and its reference to "the tuning fork that had been struck upon a star" (117), finally seems more interesting and justly famous among prose of the purple variety— it isn't a question, finally, of whether *Gatsby* must surrender all of its claims to distinctive value to *The House of Mirth*. The two passages have suggestive similarities, nonetheless, and occupy parallel moments in their respective texts. Both are emotional high tide for the love affairs of their central characters, love affairs that are thwarted by the nontranscendental realities of wealth, class, and power.

The congruences of these two scenes would not be worth remarking on were it not for other elements of *The House of Mirth* that appear to serve as precursors for aspects of *The Great Gatsby*. Fitzgerald's famous distinc-tion between East Egg and West Egg and his account of the wild parties of the latter are anticipated by Wharton in 1905. The equivalent in Wharton's novel of the West Egg world, in which Lily must take refuge after losing her foothold among more established New York society, circulates around the Sam Gormers. According to Carrie Fisher, who engineers the connection, the Gormers have "struck out on a line of their own: what they want is to have a good time, and to have it in their own way. . . . [T]hey've started a sort of continuous performance of their own, a kind of social Coney Island, where everybody is welcome who can make noise enough and doesn't put on airs. *I* think it's awfully good fun myself—some of the artistic set, you know, any pretty actress that's going, and so on" (374). This "easy promiscuity" (377) occurs on Long Island at Roslyn, where we find that the Gormers are in the process of building a large country house.[26] Their guests disperse themselves "over the grounds in quest of the various distractions the place afforded: distractions ranging from tennis courts to shooting galleries, from bridge and whiskey within doors to motors and steam-launches without. Lily had the odd sense of having been caught up into the crowd as carelessly as a passenger is gathered in by an express train" (375). This world strikes Lily as a "flamboyant copy" of her former world in a higher key: "more noise, more colour, more champagne, more familiarity—but also greater good-nature, less rivalry, and a fresher capacity for enjoyment" (376). After the weekend, on Monday, "the party disbanded with uproarious adieux" (378). Prophetically for *The Great Gatsby,* Lily can never lose her elite society reserve and unbend. Like Daisy, she instinctively dislikes the world of the West Egg party as a corruption of ingrained distinctions.

The famous scene in which Gatsby throws his apparently endless supply of beautiful shirts across the bed also has a predecessor in Wharton's novel. According to Nick, Gatsby

> was running down like an overwound clock. Recovering himself in a minute he opened for us two hulking patent cabinets which held his massed suits and dressing gowns and ties, and his shirts piled like bricks in stacks a dozen high. . . . He took out a pile of shirts and began throwing them one by one before us, shirts of sheer linen and thick silk and fine flannel which lost their folds as they fell and covered the table in many-colored disarray. (97)

Shortly before her death, Lily

> was seized with a sudden fever of activity. . . . [N]ow she began to examine systematically the contents of her drawers and cupboard. . . . The remaining dresses, though they had lost their freshness, still kept the long unerring lines, the sweep and amplitude of the great artist's stroke. . . . An association lurked in every fold: each fall of lace and gleam of embroidery was like a letter in the record of her past. . . . She put back the dresses one by one, laying away with each some

gleam of light, some note of laughter, some stray waft from the rosy shores of pleasure." (512)

The thwarted love of Lily's life is Lawrence Seldon, the literary, priggish, self-important, slightly shabby voyeur who clings to the fringes of Lily's wealthy world. His own affair with Bertha Dorset troubles him not at all in ambivalent and often harsh judgments of Lily. Likewise, the priggish, self-important Nick Carraway has apparently just broken an engagement with a midwestern woman before becoming involved with Jordan Baker, but he minimizes his own errors, judges others unsparingly, and has difficulty overcoming his ambivalence toward both Gatsby and Jordan Baker. Just as Seldon must regretfully put Lily's affairs in order after her lonely death, Nick is left to bury the abandoned Gatsby.

Nick finally and ironically takes moral instruction from Meyer Wolfsheim, who says, "Let us learn to show our friendship for a man when he is alive and not after he is dead" (180). Such advice might also apply to Seldon, who discovers Lily's real value only after her death. Though Sim Rosedale, the Jewish financier in *The House of Mirth,* says nothing so morally pithy, he emerges as a more sympathetic figure, one who understands the corrupt and shadowy world that underlies the social world's glitter, and one who produces its wealth. Just as Wolfsheim uses Gatsby as a man who at least appears to be "a man of fine breeding" (76), Rosedale would like to use Lily to serve his own desires for upward mobility. One senses that both characters are intended to suggest the degradation of a culture that can be corrected by the moral sense of its Jewish members. When she read *The Great Gatsby,* Wharton apparently recognized an anti-Semitic tie to Fitzgerald. In the note she sent him, she pointedly refers to "your *perfect* jew."[27]

My purpose, let me repeat, is not to extinguish all differences between *The Great Gatsby* and *The House of Mirth,* but to establish a kinship between the novels that would produce anxiety for Fitzgerald about Wharton as a precursor. Rather than absolutely replicating Wharton's novel, Fitzgerald's novel is written against it, emptying out its women characters in order to deny feminine influence, and substituting for such influence a principle of masculine inspiration Gatsby embodies. In the process of containing the feminine, Fitzgerald simultaneously constructs a containing heterosexual narrative for the exploration and even celebration of a homoeroticism that need not speak its name. The often celebrated formal perfection of *Gatsby*, I would argue, results from the compatability of these two projects of the novel, neither of which should be reduced to the other.

In some ways, the character Lily Bart most resembles in *The Great Gatsby* is Gatsby himself. Even if she has inherited her tragically divided temperament, as the naturalist machinery of *The House of Mirth* implies, her intelligence and her struggle to find a suitable object for her aspirations make our concern for the plight of her character equal to our concern for any other character in the novel. She serves as the chief victim of the novel's metaphysical machinery and patriarchal social structure. Like Gatsby, Lily possesses an extraordinary personal beauty, and, like Gatsby, her tragedy in part results from her attachment to shallow values and unworthy objects of desire—even though Wharton's depiction of Seldon is several shades more sympathetic than Fitzgerald's depiction of Daisy.

Though I would not simply argue that Lily Bart serves as a direct model for Jay Gatsby, the connections between the two characters suggest Fitzgerald's comparative diminishment of the feminine. He accomplishes this through splitting Lily's character in two. I earlier suggested, in terms of the splitting of Hester's letter in *The Scarlet Letter,* that splitting represented an important technique through which the feminine could be absorbed and masculinized. The important, positive aspects of Lily's character are embedded in heightened form by the construct of Gatsby (I use the term *construct* because clearly he can barely exist as a character within any realist frame for the novel). Daisy, then, is refuse—the eviscerated shell of Lily Bart.[28] As Judith Fetterley argues, she embodies the empty, material world that finally traps and destroys Gatsby, the "perishable breath" to which he weds his "unutterable visions" (117).[29] If Gatsby must be doomed by the structure of experience as surely as Wharton's naturalism dooms Lily, it is difficult not to feel that Daisy's radical absence of value is somehow at fault. *The Great Gatsby* has little interest in exploring her victimization despite the ease with which one could concoct arguments for it. Nor is the novel particularly interested in any of its other women characters. The novel reserves its energies for the relation between Nick and Gatsby, a relation with which nothing else in the novel is allowed to compete.

The reduction of Lily Bart serves Fitzgerald's larger purpose of denying feminine influence in general, and, I have argued, Edith Wharton's influence in particular. In writing the book that he hoped would represent the full use of his talent and earn him permanent fame, Fitzgerald composed a book about the writing of a book. We learn quite early that Nick Carraway was "rather literary in college," and that he now intended to "bring all such things into my life" (8) from his position of somewhat resentful marginality. If he has literary aspirations, the story he tells allows him to realize them; as first-person narrator, the living of his story and the writing of his book are indistinguishable. Within the frame of the fiction, our only undoubtable narrative fact is that Nick Carraway forms and tells the narrative we receive, and that the narrative we read must therefore have some self-reflexive correspondence to the shape of his desires.

Nick writes his book out of his desire for Gatsby, who thus functions as a male muse. It is always scrutiny of Gatsby that triggers Nick's "literary" lyrical flights and so generates the purple prose on which the reputation of the book itself partly rests. Gatsby stands, moreover, for the self-contained nature of male literary imagination, since he "sprang from his Platonic conception of himself" and is a son not of a woman, nor even of a man, but a "son of God" (104). Gatsby *nearly* stands for the obverse of feminine influence, since the novel presents Daisy as an unworthy object of his desiring imagination. The most effective obverse of feminine influence is Nick's desire for Gatsby.

As an embodiment of Nick's desire, Gatsby exists in a dialectical relation to the degrading and degraded world that surrounds him. It is immediately after returning from his first visit with Tom and Daisy, a visit marked by the revelations of their complete indifference as parents (however specifically this lack is aimed at Daisy), by the revelation of Tom's sordid affair, and by Nick's meditation on his own broken engagement, that Nick watches Gatsby and finds his full, lyrical voice: "The wind had blown off, leaving a loud bright night with wings beating in the trees and a persistent organ sound as the full bellows of the earth blew the frogs full of life. . . . I saw that I was not alone. . . . [I]t was Mr. Gatsby himself, come out to determine what share was his of our local heaven" (25). Fitzgerald's "masculine" book, then, has been constructed by shifting his usual romantic focus on the figure of a desirable woman to a focus on a male object of desire instead, a homoerotic psychic transaction that allows him to generate lyricism while systematically degrading women. At the same time, the surplus intensity of this lyricism arguably suggests that same-sex desire is primary to *The Great Gatsby*, and not only a secondary product of Fitzgerald's anxious relation to the problem of feminine influence, however structuring this relation may be for its expression.

The sexual ambiguity of the world of *The Great Gatsby* has received critical attention of late.[30] Nick involves himself with the androgynous Jordan Baker, whom he describes as having "shoulders like a young cadet" (15). He describes Tom Buchanan in the language of sadomasochistic desire, remarking that he "seemed to fill those glistening boots until he strained the top lacing," and that he had "a great pack of muscle shifting . . . under his thin coat" (11). Nick may have as well a one-night stand with a photographer named McKee, an incident that at a minimum is in danger of turning into a sexual encounter. After Tom brutally breaks Myrtle Wilson's nose, Nick follows McKee out the door. As they "groaned down" in the elevator, the elevator boy snaps "keep your hands off the lever," to which McKee replies, "I didn't know I was touching it." As the intelligibility of the narrative breaks down, consistent with the metaphors of disintegration the homoerotic has generated in other novels I have discussed, Nick tells us only that

> . . . I was standing beside his bed and he was sitting
> between the sheets, clad in his underwear, with a great
> portfolio in his hands.
>   "Beauty and the Beast . . . Loneliness . . . Old Grocery
> Horse . . . Brook'n Bridge. . . . "
>   Then I was lying half asleep in the cold lower level of the
> Pennsylvania station, staring at the morning "Tribune" and
> waiting for the four o'clock train. (42)

This homosexual encounter, however, does not serve as a revelation of the sexual nature of Nick's obsession with Gatsby, but as a defense against its erotic implications. True to the dialectic structure of the book, Nick's degrading night (as Fitzgerald would have us see it) produces one of Nick's most lyrical rhetorical flights. Immediately following Nick's account of his night with McKee, we are told that "[t]here was music from my neighbor's house through the summer nights. In his blue gardens men and girls came and went like moths among the whisperings and the champagne and the stars" (43). The implication is clear that Nick's passionate identification with Gatsby lifts Nick from the messy world and should not be understood as a product of the sex/gender corruption that world contains.[31]

Nick's male muse falters, of course, and reveals himself to be a sordid part of the world Nick's rhetoric seeks to transcend. Frances Kerr suggests that Gatsby himself is humiliated, and hence feminized, by Tom Buchanan, so that in trying to preserve Gatsby's value, Nick attempts to lift and dignify the world of ambiguous sex/gender relationships.[32] In effect, however, the novel plunges all of masculinity into this ambiguous and corrupt world and detaches its own authority from it. Even Tom himself, the novel's icon of abusive masculinity, joins the world of sentimental degradation, pointedly humiliated by Nick's narrative. When we last see him, he confesses that he, too, has suffered over Myrtle's death: "[W]hen I went to give up that flat and saw that damn box of dog biscuits sitting there on the sideboard I sat down and cried like a baby. By God it was awful—" (187).

In effect, the novel sheds Gatsby like (to repeat a phrase I used to characterize Sinclair's treatment of Jurgis Rudkus) a spent puppet. The death and exposure of Gatsby marks a kind of oedipal triumph of Nick's lyrical voice, which now, in the words of *The Ambassadors,* can toddle alone. Gatsby may join the world of feminizing mass culture and corruption, or may have always belonged to it, but Nick's rhetoric maintains its transcendent posture. Its transcendence and triumph can only be insured, in fact, by its final disembodiment. It is detached from a man revealed to be the Bill Cody of literary inspirations—a kind of carnival huckster.

The detachment of this voice from the corpse of Gatsby marks the novel's final defense against the homoeroticism of its own model of masculine literary creation and against homoeroticism in general. A disembodied masculinity exists as a target of identification only, not erotic desire. Meanwhile, erotic desire aims again at its conventional heterosexual target. The feminine is displaced safely into the past, removed from any role or place in culture and associated with a maternity lyrically naturalized. Nick's Gatsby-inspired voice celebrates "a fresh green breast of the new world. Its vanished trees, the trees that had made way for Gatsby's house, had once pandered in whispers to the last and greatest of all human dreams; for a transitory enchanted moment man must have held his breath in the presence of this continent, compelled into an aesthetic contemplation he neither understood nor desired, face to face for the last time in history with something commensurate to his capacity for wonder. . . . Gatsby believed in the green light, the orgiastic future that year by year recedes before us. . . . So we beat on, boats against the current, borne back ceaselessly into the past" (189). In the words the novel uses to describe Gatsby's death, "the holocaust was complete" (170).

Ironically enough, Fitzgerald's final lyrical passage also suggests the possibility of a source text in Wharton. In *The Glimpses of the Moon,* as I indicated earlier a late Wharton novel made into a silent movie for which Fitzgerald wrote the titles, we are told that her hero, also named Nick, had arrived at his current station in life because of his "large resolve not to miss anything. There stood the evergreen Tree of Life, the Four Rivers flowing from its foot; and on every one of the four currents he meant to launch his little skiff. On two of them he had not gone very far, on the third he had nearly stuck in the mud; but the fourth had carried him to the very heart of wonder. It was the stream of his lively imagination, of his inexhaustible interest in every form of beauty and strangeness and folly."[33]

It is possible to see *The Great Gatsby,* for Nick, as a response to the dislocations of the war. Nick indicates that he "participated in that delayed Teutonic migration known as the Great War." He suggests that he "enjoyed the counter-raid so thoroughly" that he "came back restless" so that "the middle-west now seemed like the ragged edge of the universe"(7). If one sees the war as a precipitating event, it is striking that, also in the first pages, Nick expresses a fondness for standards of military conduct as his reaction to the events his narrative will record. As he says, "I felt I wanted the world to be in uniform and at a sort of moral attention forever" (6). The invocation of a military masculinity as regulative emphasizes *The Great Gatsby*'s investment (ironically, given the homoeroticism of military life and the capacity of war to unsettle gender roles) in the control and finally denial of transgressive desires. This apparent refuge in regulation dovetails with the chief portion of Gatsby's character Fitzgerald saves from his general exposure. If nearly everything about Gatsby is finally a fraud, the quality of his military service retains some authenticity.[34] According to Nick's narrative of Gatsby's actual life, he "did extraordinarily well in the war. He was a captain before he went to the front and following the Argonne battles he got his majority and the command of the divisional machine guns" (158). Nick thus preserves a military side to Gatsby's character against his humiliation by Tom, a side that quietly responds to Nick's own stated desires, both for Gatsby and for emotional order.

Nick's splitting of a military-based, regulative, nonpassionate masculinity, with which the male subject identifies, and a naturalized maternity represented as a lost breast, might be suggestively compared to the structure of sexuality and gender implied by Freud's *Beyond the Pleasure Principle,* published several years earlier.[35] Freud's book begins with a consideration of the problem of war neuroses, the subject of a book by his followers to which Freud wrote the introduction.[36] It is again exceedingly interesting that while considering the problem of war-torn men, Freud establishes war as his masculine norm. I refer to his positioning of masculinity in the famous "fort/da" episode, which has been fetishized in this text undoubtedly because it stands as a clear and illustrative human example in a text given over to ruminating (even if fascinating) consideration of the metaphysics of the sex lives of protozoa and "germ cells."

Freud argues that the game of throwing away and retrieving a small toy enables the child to cope with absence, and simply presumes absence pertains exclusively to the mother, despite the remarkable fact that the boy's father is away "at the front" fighting a war. Freud presumes that the child regards his father as a rival, and never considers that the child might desire his father as well, and that desire might be complicated by anger and frustration at his father's real absence. Just as Nick invokes military masculinity as a regulating norm at the beginning of *Gatsby,* Freud unthinkingly takes the father's war-necessitated military remoteness as illustrative of the father's conventional position, one that is completely compatible with conventional oedipal relations.

Freud's anecdote suggests his interest in this essay in institutionalizing the father's nonerotic position and in stabilizing the threatening potential fluidity of desire. If Freud generally argues for a distinction between desire and identification in masculine oedipal adjustment, he also commonly advertises that other (less desirable) configurations of desire and identification are possible.[37] In *Beyond the Pleasure Principle,* Freud produces potentially his most radical splitting of desire and identification by locating this distinction in a division of the drives themselves, or at least in a division of the directions in which the desire for death might be achieved: "The backward path that leads to complete satisfaction is as a rule obstructed by the resistances which maintain the repressions. So there is no alternative but to advance in the direction in which growth is still free—though with no prospect of bringing the process to a conclusion or of being able to reach the goal" (51). One might paraphrase Freud's claim with Fitzgerald's famous "so we beat on, boats against the current, borne back ceaselessly into the past."

The tableau of the fort/da episode (and much subsequent psychoanalytic theory) presents the mother as the desired object in the past representing the subject's desired (and feared) disintegration. The father, standing for culture, thus occupies the path of the forced trajectory through life, toward which we are propelled despite ourselves. This tableau is complicated, in this endlessly self-deconstructing essay, by Freud's discussion of sexuality as a life instinct, as that which binds together. "Is it really the case that, *apart from the sexual instincts,* there are no instincts that do not seek to restore an earlier state of things?" Freud asks at one point (49). Though this sense of sexuality is potentially quite expansive, *Beyond the Pleasure Principle* in fact contains Freud's most reactionary account of human sexuality. Freud's great contribution to the history of thinking about sex is to place it in the realm of culture and in the history of human development. Here, sex finds its evolutionary origins in the tendency of "animalculae" to "'conjugate'" and hence to be "saved from growing old" and to be "rejuvenated" (57). Comments Freud, "conjugation is no doubt the fore-runner of the sexual reproduction of higher creatures; it is as yet unconnected with propagation and is limited to the mixing of the substances of two individuals" (42). Sexuality, in short, becomes reproductive, and hence intrinsically heterosexual. Freud further cements heterosexuality in its position of teleological privilege by his reference to Plato's *Symposium*.[38] He cites the myth, credited within the dialogue to Aristophanes, that "'the sexes were originally three in number, not two as they are now; there was man, woman, and the union of the two . . .'. Everything about these primaeval men was double: they had four hands and four feet, two faces, two privy parts, and so on. Eventually Zeus decided to cut these men in two. . . . After the division had been made, 'the two parts of man, each desiring his other half, came together, and threw their arms about one another eager to grow into one'" (69–70).

Potentially, such an allusion might have liberatory potential, since the *Symposium* acknowledges different kinds of splittings, different kinds of coming together, and refuses simply to privilege reproductive heterosexuality. Freud, however, adds a supplemental footnote that makes its explicitly conservative and heterosexual import clear. In this footnote, he suggests that Plato's source may be a passage in the Upanishads, in which the split self gives rise to "husband and wife. . . . Therefore the void which was there, is filled by the wife" (70 n. 20).[39]

Why does Freud produce this conservative, heterosexualizing account of human sexuality at such a late stage in his career? The suspicion, perhaps reinforced by Fitzgerald's use of related schematic divisions in *Gatsby,* is his active interest in controlling and suppressing his own homosexuality, with which, contemporary scholarship has made clear, he persistently struggled. This homosexuality is most evident and acknowledged in his early friendship with Wilhelm Fliess, but as Peter Gay indicates, the ghost of Fliess haunted Freud's subsequent professional friendships with men.[40] Gay quotes Freud's remarks to Ferenczi that "Adler is a little Fliess redivivus, just as paranoid. Stekel, as appendix to him, is at least named Wilhelm." Adler, Freud once wrote to Jung, "awakens in me the memory of Fliess, an octave lower (274)." In terms of Jung, at the time when the tone of Jung's letters changed from "tenderness to overbearing insolence," Freud had fainting spells. Writing to Ernest Jones, Freud remarked that the first time he had seen Munich, the site of these spells, "was when I visited Fliess." As a consequence, "this town seems to have acquired a strong connection with my relation to this man. There is some piece of unruly homosexual feeling at the root of the matter." In an exchange with Ernest Jones, Freud in fact admits that "I had transferred to Jung homosex[ual] feelings from another part" (275–276). The theory of dual drives directly attacks the apostasies of Jung: "Our views have from the very first been *dualistic,* and to-day they are even more definitely dualist than before—now that we describe the opposition as being, not between ego-instincts and sexual instincts but between life instincts and death instincts. Jung's libido theory is on the contrary *monistic;* the fact that he has called his one instinctual force 'libido' is bound to cause confusion, but need not affect us otherwise" (64). Sexuality might be the force that binds together, but it evidently would not bind Freud to Jung.

If *Beyond the Pleasure Principle* struggles with Freud's unruly homo-sexuality and subdues it by separating masculinity from same-sex desire, it must also struggle with questions of feminine influence. I refer to the contri-butions of Sabina Spielrein to its genesis, as a patient of Jung, and his lover, and a practitioner of psychoanalysis herself. Spielrein was entangled in the relations between Freud and Jung at the time of their famous split and re-ceived support from Freud in overcoming her feelings for Jung, even as Freud struggled with his own. Freud writes to her at one point that he is "sorry to hear that you are consumed with longing for J[ung], and this at a time when I am on such bad terms with him, having almost reached the conclusion that he is unworthy of all the interested concern I have bestowed on him."[41]

Freud cites Spielrein as a source for *Beyond the Pleasure Principle* in a footnote to the text. According to Freud, "A considerable portion of these speculations have been anticipated by Sabina Spielrein (1912) in an instruc-tive and interesting paper which, however, is unfortunately not entirely clear to me. She there describes the sadistic components of the sexual instinct as 'destructive'" (66 n. 16). Freud's acknowledgment of Spielrein is most odd because of its remarkable and seemily disingenuous claim that Freud finds her work "not entirely clear." Its claim of noncomprehension (certainly not a common reading experience for Freud) suggests a defense against influence partly disabled by its own transparency. It suggests the possibility that Spielrein's influence has been partly an unconscious one, since it occurs un-derneath or apart from a conscious grasp of her work, yet this suggestion uncannily places Spielrein in the unconscious, pre-Symbolic position that de-fines the general place of femininity in *Beyond the Pleasure Principle.* Thus, Freud's late essay uncannily repeats the process Wayne Kostenbaum finds in his discussion of the complicated earlier interrelations of Freud, Anna O. (a pseudonym for Bertha Pappenheim, a feminist activist), Josef Breuer, and Wilhelm Fliess: it seeks to "appropriate the power of female reproduction" and to resolve as well "homoeroticism's unsettling presence," a presence in his own life Freud consciously struggled to overcome.[42]

Madelon Sprengnether suggests that Freud employs Spielrein's work to conceal a more threatening debt to Bachofen's *Das Mutterrecht*, but if this is this case the masculine influence for which the acknowledgment of Spielrein substitutes stakes an even greater claim for the cultural authority of women,[43] a claim also at stake in Freud's relations with Jung, who was himself influenced by Bachofen.[44] Spielrein, then, is related to a great many things about which we are "not entirely clear" in *Beyond the Pleasure Principle*, including her complex positioning between Freud and Jung.[45]

It is not surprising that as one delves into Freud's text one uncovers a subtext of sex/gender instabilities.[46] Indeed, as Freud's apparent reduction of the richness of *The Symposium* to a heterosexualizing tableau of complementarity might suggest, *Beyond the Pleasure Principle* exists in a dialectical relation to an underlying complexity and indeterminancy that it resists and attempts to structure.

Like that of *The Great Gatsby*, its desire for order seems situated in the perception of chaos spawned by the war, a chaos bound up, for modernist writers such as Fitzgerald, Hemingway, and Eliot, with their experience of indeterminancies of sex and gender. Like Fitzgerald in *The Great Gatsby*, Freud's solution is to author a fiction of dual drives that seems to put gender and sexuality—more or less—back in their proper bifurcated places: women are targets of reproductive desires and impossible regressive longings, but are not imagined as agents of cultural production; men are targets of identification but are not objects of desire, their relations to each other characterized by taken-for-granted norms of distance and violence that ought to be seen as the real symptoms of war.[47] Taken together both texts suggest the collaboration of literature and psychoanalysis simultaneously to defend masculine authority from the fragmenting energies of same-sex eroticism, and to effect and obscure its appropriative relation to the ongoing cultural production of women.

It has been a temptation to read *Beyond the Pleasure Principle* as Freud's reaction to the death of his beloved daughter Sophie, whose death occurs close to the date of composition of the text. Freud's own insistence that most of the text was composed prior to this death seems uncontroverted by any substantial evidence to the contrary.[48] I am not sure that a reading of the text as inflected by personal mourning, however, is at odds with my sense of it. It is often the case that deeply felt and powerfully conveyed feelings are at the same time powerfully conventional, just as doubt and ambivalence accompany experiences substantially outside the path of the ordinary. The installation of conventional patterns of sexuality and gender upon experience, then, may well be accompanied by powerful expressions of emotion. In terms of *The Great Gatsby,* for example, I have argued that Fitzgerald's lyricism is linked to anti-feminist and homophobic strategies that allow Fitzgerald to shake free from the fetters of his ambivalence, and passionately embrace the ordinary as the transcendent. Indeed, it has seemed to be the case, in the texts I have discussed in this book, that containment is emotional work.

NOTES

INTRODUCTION *Authoring the Self*

1. There is a danger of reinscribing the male canon through the act of critiquing it, as Nina Baym suggests in the cautionary and still relevant "Melodramas of Beset Manhood." If I cannot entirely avoid such a danger, I nonetheless hope that articulating the sex/gender dynamics at work in this tradition justifies dwelling on such a traditional body of masculine texts. See "Melodramas of Beset Manhood: How Theories of American Fiction Exclude Women Authors," *American Quarterly* 33, no. 2 (summer 1981): 123–139.

2. This transformation has been well documented. See, for example, William Charvat's *Literary Publishing in America, 1790–1850* (Philadelphia: University of Pennsylvania Press, 1959); Nina Baym, "The Triumph of the Novel," in *Novels, Readers, and Reviewers: Responses to Fiction in Antebellum America* (Ithaca: Cornell University Press, 1984), 26–43; Michael T. Gilmore, introduction to *American Romanticism and the Marketplace* (Chicago: University of Chicago Press, 1985), 1–17; and John F. Kasson, "Etiquette Books and the Spread of Gentility," in *Rudeness and Civility: Manners in Nineteenth-Century Urban America* (New York: Hill and Wang, 1990), 34–69, and especially 37–44.

3. For a useful review of this debate, see Stuart M. Blumin, "The Hypothesis of Middle-Class Formation in Nineteenth-Century America: A Critique and Some Proposals," *American Historical Review* 90, no. 2 (April 1985): 299–338.

4. John Greenleaf Whittier, "The Nervous Man," in *Whittier on Writers and Writing,* ed. Edwin Harrison Cady and Harry Hayden Clark (Syracuse: Syracuse University Press, 1950), 99.

5. Letter quoted by Perry Miller in "John Greenleaf Whittier: The Conscience in Poetry," in *Critical Essays on John Greenleaf Whittier,* ed. Jayne K. Kribbs (Boston: G. K. Hall, 1980), 216.

6. Whittier, "American Literature," in *Whittier on Writers and Writing,* 25–26.

7. For the first quoted passage, see Nathaniel Hawthorne, "To Elizabeth C. Hathorne, Raymond," Tuesday, March 7, 1820, in *The Letters, 1813–1843, vol. 15,* ed. Thomas Woodson, L. Neal Smith, and Norman Holmes Pearson, The

Centenary Edition of The Works of Nathaniel Hawthorne (Columbus: Ohio State University Press, 1984), 117. For the second, see Hawthorne, "To Elizabeth C. Hathorne," March 13, 1821, in *The Letters,* 139. T. Walter Herbert uses these passages in *Dearest Beloved: The Hawthornes and the Making of the Middle-Class Family* (Berkeley and Los Angeles: University of California Press, 1993), 71.

8. Julian Hawthorne, *Nathaniel Hawthorne and His Wife,* 2 vols. (Boston: James R. Osgood, 1885), 1:96.

9. Quoted by Lewis Simpson, *The Man of Letters in New England and the South: Essays on the History of the Literary Vocation in America* (Baton Rouge: Louisiana State University Press, 1973), 95.

10. Henry James, *Notes of a Son and Brother* (London: MacMillan, 1914).

11. William bore the brunt of this parental disapproval and arguably suffered the greatest damage as a consequence, as Howard M. Feinstein makes clear in *Becoming William James* (Ithaca: Cornell University Press, 1984), 117–145

12. Mary Ryan indicates that, in a census taken in Utica in 1855, less than 4 percent of the boys under the age of fifteen listed an occupation, and that less than 1 percent of those employed listed their occupation as "apprentice." Finding an occupation, then, would be a central task of males' late adolescence and early adulthood. See Ryan, *Cradle of the Middle Class: The Family in Oneida County, New York, 1790–1865* (New York: Cambridge University Press, 1981),

13. According to Ryan, in *Cradle of the Middle Class,* 167, by 1855 in Utica, 16 percent of young men filled white-collar positions, as opposed to 6 percent of middle-aged men, while the percentage of young men in artisan occupations was 15 percent lower than in older generations. The nature and definition of the "middle class" in nineteenth-century America continues to be the subject of scholarly debate, even as it seems to remain an indispensable category of analysis. See also Blumin, "The Hypothesis of Middle-Class Formation"; Burton J. Bledstein, *The Culture of Professionalism: The Middle Class and the Development of Higher Education in America* (New York: W. W. Norton, 1976); Alexis de Tocqueville, *Democracy in America,* The Henry Reeve Text, revised by Francis Bowen, ed. Phillips Bradley, 2 vols. (New York: Alfred A. Knopf, 1945); and David Leverenz, "Three Ideologies of Manhood," in *Manhood and the American Renaissance* (Ithaca: Cornell University Press, 1989), 75.

14. G. Stanley Hall, *Adolescence: Its Psychology and Its Relations to Physiology, Anthropology, Sociology, Sex, Crime, Religion, and Education,* 2 vols. (New York and London: D. Appleton, 1904). Texts such as *Adolescence* undoubtedly help produce and change the phenomena they purport to study, but they also, I would argue, should be taken seriously as efforts to describe cultural phenomena that predate the texts' publication and the terminology they generate. In general, we take our own efforts as contemporary cultural critics seriously on precisely these grounds.

15. Alfred J. Beveridge, *The Young Man and the World* (New York and London: D. Appleton, 1905), 75–76.

16. Carroll Smith-Rosenberg cites Blumin's findings that between the 1820s and the 1850s—in Philadelphia, at least—downward mobility far exceeded upward move-

ment. It did likewise in Buffalo in the 1850s and 1860s. Within this unknown and evolving world, few could be certain where they would find either places of power or zones of safety. See Smith-Rosenberg, "Bourgeois Discourse in the Age of Jackson: An Introduction," in *Disorderly Conduct: Visions of Gender in Victorian America* (New York: Alfred A. Knopf, 1985), 79–89

17. Nina Baym, *Woman's Fiction: A Guide to Novels by and about Women in America, 1820–1870* (Ithaca: Cornell University Press, 1978), 30–31

18. These lectures are discussed in Milton Rugoff's *The Beechers: An American Family in the Nineteenth Century* (New York: Harper & Row, 1881), 268–272. The quotations that follow are taken from Henry Ward Beecher, *Addresses to Young Men* (Philadelphia: Henry Altemus, 1895).

19. Gillian Brown, *Domestic Individualism: Imaging Self in Nineteenth-Century America* (Berkeley and Los Angeles: University of California Press, 1990), 3.

20. See Mary Ryan, "The Empire of the Mother: American Writing about Domesticity, 1830–1860," *Women and History* 2/3 (summer/fall 1982): 47–70.

21. See E. Anthony Rotundo's discussion of shifts in parental responsibilities in *American Manhood: Transformations in Masculinity from the Revolution to the Modern Era* (New York: Basic Books, 1993), 25–30.

22. Ryan, *Cradle of the Middle Class,* 173–174.

23. Robert Wiebe reports this change. See Robert Wiebe, *The Opening of American Society: From the Adoption of the Constitution to the Eve of Disunion* (New York: Alfred A. Knopf, 1984), 270.

24. Rotundo, *American Manhood,* 33.

25. Christopher Newfield has recently argued that family relations for persons such as Emerson ideally should be understood as equal and nonhierarchical, and that the dominance of men was a product of "well-placed passivity" (131). Nonetheless, in Newfield's argument, the liberal family still preserves masculine dominance, albeit as a form of submission to social structures outside the family's domain, and Emerson's desires and demands in practical reality conflict with his theoretical desire to avoid the direct exercise of authority. Newfield's family, then, is finally one in which liberal men ultimately support (and are supported by) patriarchal structures in the face of conflicted and competing desires for other kinds of relationships to women. This view is compatible with my own, that patriarchal privilege must be repeatedly wrung from angst-ridden conflict and turmoil, but that it typically emerges victorious at narrative's end. See Newfield, "Loving Bondage: The Authority of Domestic Remoteness," in *The Emerson Effect: Individualism and Submission in America* (Chicago: University of Chicago Press, 1996), 129–150.

26. The first part of a transition to adult masculinity might be occupied by what E. Anthony Rotundo calls "boylife." According to Rotundo, after the age of six boys would continue to live formally in the home; they also became inhabitants of a rough world of streets, fields, forests, vacant lots, and playgrounds, in general rebellion against parental control of all kinds, but in specific rebellion against the domestic world of their mothers. The "energy, self-assertion, noise, and frequent recourse to violence" of this world ended generally in the boy's midteens, when attention turned to the world of adult sexuality and work had to be con-

fronted. See Rotundo, "Boy Culture," in *Meanings for Manhood: Constructions of Masculinity in Victorian America,* ed. Mark C. Carnes and Clyde Griffin (Chicago: University of Chicago Press, 1990), 17–19.

27. Ryan, *Cradle of the Middle Class,* 168 and 179. The number of foreign-born youths living with their parents was much lower, according to Ryan. Their different experiences help to ground the existence of a distinctively middle-class experience in Ryan's argument.

28. Quoted in Joe Dubbert, *A Man's Place: Masculinity in Transition* (Englewood Cliffs, N. J.: Prentice-Hall, 1979), 39.

29. Nancy Cott makes this case at length in *The Bonds of Womanhood: "Woman's Sphere" in New England, 1780–1835* (New Haven: Yale University Press, 1977).

30. Joel Pfister in general sees the sentimental devices of the family as a protection against the material labor of women in external culture. Such sentimentalization, I would argue, also protects the male subject against the material reality of women's labor within the middle-class family. The family itself and the contested psychological space it produces are also threatening, and, in turn, force the male subject back into the world, a step the family-centered oedipalized narratives of male selfhood make necessary. Male representations of the feminine are persistently unstable and ambivalent in nineteenth-century life because there is no stable ground of male subjectivity, particularly for male authors, whose relation to the domestic is particularly fraught. I finally see men and male authors such as Hawthorne, then, less in the position of producing the psychological with close to conscious intentionality than as (always already) inscribed agonistically within it. Concomitantly, though particular figurations of the psychological are historically contingent, the cultural origins of such figurations are not easy to specifiy or locate. See Joel Pfister, *The Production of Personal Life: Class, Gender, and the Psychological in Hawthorne's Fiction* (Stanford: Stanford University Press, 1991), 37, 120–121, 157.

31. Sandra M. Gilbert and Susan Gubar discuss the broader importance of the maternal in Western culture, as opposed to psychoanalytic and literary arguments that align the father with language and the mother with "lack." I am broadly sympathetic to their argument but hesitant about the terms in which they make it. Their discussion may still be too circumscribed because of their focus on questions of language, and because of their tendency to use a language of feminist countermyth, talking of the broad suppression of a "*materna lingua*" in favor of a "*patrius sermo*" (253). The question of women's contributions to history is much broader than questions of the origins of language, and reducing such contributions to the mythic is a persistent mode of circumscribing the feminine while seeming to celebrate it. See Sandra M. Gilbert and Susan Gubar, *The War of the Words,* vol. 1, *No Man's Land: The Place of the Woman Writer in the Twentieth Century* (New Haven: Yale University Press, 1988).

32. Leslie Fiedler notes the importance of women's presence as cultural producers. See "The Bourgeois Sentimental Novel and the Female Audience," in *Love and Death in the American Novel,* revised ed. (New York: Stein and Day, 1982), 74–104. See also Ann Douglas's epic treatment of this theme in *The Feminization of American Culture* (New York: Avon Books, 1977).

33. Octavius Brooks Frothingham, *George Ripley* (Boston: Houghton Mifflin, 1882), 1–2; Peter Revell, *James Whitcomb Riley* (Boston: Twayne, 1970), 28; Glenn O. Carey, *Edward Poupon Roe* (Boston: Twayne, 1985), 9; Rollo Ogden, *William Hickling Prescott* (Boston: Houghton Mifflin, 1904), 13.

34. Henry James, *The American Journals*, "February 9th, 1882," in *The Complete Notebooks of Henry James,* ed. Leon Edel and Lyall H. Powers (New York: Oxford University Press, 1987), 229.

35. Alfred Habegger makes an interesting case that James does sympathize in "The Return of the Father in *The Bostonians,*" in *Henry James and the Woman Business* (New York: Cambridge University Press, 1989), 182–229.

36. James quotes Eliot as to the importance of women in the world and notes that "in *Romeo and Juliet* Juliet has to be important, just as, in *Adam Bede* and *The Mill on the Floss* and *Middlemarch* and *Daniel Deronda*, Hetty Sorrel and Maggie Tulliver and Rosamond Vincy and Gwendolen Harleth have to be." It is interesting that Dorothea Brooke is not on this list, given that she is an obvious literary predecessor for Isabel Archer. Henry James, "Preface to *The Portrait of a Lady,*" in *Henry James, Literary Criticism: French Writers; Other European Writers; The Prefaces to the New York Edition*, ed. Leon Edel with the assistance of Mark Wilson (New York: Library of America, 1984), 1077.

    James also profited from a host of less celebrated women writers. William Veeder has traced James's appropriations and transformations of many of the standard plots and characters of women's fiction in *Henry James, The Lessons of the Master: Popular Fiction and Personal Style in the Nineteenth Century* (Chicago: University of Chicago Press, 1975).

37. See, especially, Alfred Habegger's "Who Made James the Modern American Master, and Why?" in *Gender, Fantasy, and Realism in American Literature* (New York: Columbia University Press, 1982), 289–302. See also Gilbert and Gubar, "Tradition and the Female Talent: Modernism and Masculinism," in *The War of the Words,* 125–162.

38. See Richard Poirier, *A World Elsewhere: The Place of Style in American Fiction* (New York: Oxford University Press, 1966).

39. Samuel G. Goodrich, *Recollections of a Lifetime, or Men and Things I Have Seen: In a Series of Familiar Letters to a Friend, Historical, Biographical, Anecdotical, and Descriptive,* 2 vols. (New York and Auburn: Miller, Orton, and Mulligan, 1856).

40. Cathy N. Davidson, *Revolution and the Word: The Rise of the Novel in America* (New York: Oxford University Press, 1986), 29–31.

41. On the possibility of female genius, see Baym, *Novels, Readers, and Reviewers,* 259.

42. This crisis of authority has in recent years been a prominent topic in nineteenth-century U.S. cultural criticism. See, for example, Thomas L. Haskell, *The Emergence of Professional Social Science: The American Social Science Association and the Nineteenth-Century Crisis of Authority* (Urbana: University of Illinois Press, 1977), 65; Mark Patterson, *Authority, Autonomy, and Representation in American Literature, 1776–1865* (Princeton: Princeton University Press, 1988); and Kasson, *Rudeness and Civility.*

43. Nathaniel Hawthorne, "To J. T. Fields, Boston," December 11, 1852, in *The*

Letters, 1843–1853, ed. Thomas Woodson, L. Neal Smith, and Norman Holmes Pearson, vol. 16, The Centenary Edition of The Works of Nathaniel Hawthorne, (Columbus: Ohio State University Press, 1985), 624.

44. Nevertheless, Hawthorne's creativity, as I will suggest in chapter 3, relies on access to the cultural "feminine" in important ways. As James D. Wallace has suggested, even the metaphor of "scribbling" is one he often applied to himself. See "Hawthorne and the Scribbling Women Reconsidered," *American Literature* 62 (June 1990): 201–222.

45. Quoted by Kasson, *Rudeness and Civility,* 39–40.

46. Goodrich, *Recollections of a Lifetime,* 86.

47. Quoted by Lewis Simpson, *The Man of Letters in New England and the South: Essays on the History of the Literary Vocation in America* (Baton Rouge: Louisiana State University Press, 1973), 145.

48. Lora Romero, "Vanishing Americans: Gender, Empire, and New Historicism," in *Subjects and Citizens: Nation, Race, and Gender from "Oroonoko" to Anita Hill,* ed. Michael Moon and Cathy N. Davidson (Durham: Duke University Press, 1995), 87–105. See especially 96–97. Romero makes her argument in terms of the antebellum literary culture. For an account of naturalism's later capacity to conflate the feminine generativity of nature and the industrial generativity of capitalism, see Mark Seltzer, "The Naturalist Machine," in *Bodies and Machines* (New York: Routledge, 1992), 25–44.

49. Walt Whitman, *Democratic Vistas,* vol. 2, *The Complete Poetry and Prose of Walt Whitman as Prepared by Him for the Deathbed Edition,* ed. Malcolm Cowley (New York: Pellegrini & Cudahy, 1948), 244–245.

50. It is not a new claim that literature in some way self-reflexively signifies itself, or "writing," or stages a drama of the autonomy of the self. In U.S. literature, such issues commonly surface in work on "authority," a problem recently addressed in texts such as Patterson's *Authority, Autonomy, and Representation*; Kenneth Dauber's *The Idea of Authorship in America: Democratic Poetics from Franklin to Melville* (Madison: University of Wisconsin Press, 1990); and Gregory Jay's *America the Scrivener: Deconstruction and the Subject of Literary History* (Ithaca: Cornell University Press, 1990). Also important are texts that stress writing as a material practice, especially Michael Fried's *Writing, Realism, and Disfiguration: On Thomas Eakins and Stephen Crane* (Chicago: University of Chicago Press, 1987); and Seltzer's *Bodies and Machines.* My attempt here is to give a particular version of such self-reflexivity, one that is interpretively useful in addressing a particular set of cultural and historical dynamics.

51. "Authorship" has exhibited, in recent years, a remarkable ability to withstand even postmodern critique. We still have, for example, a roster of names of cultural "authorities." Even a determined critique of cultural authority produces the authority of having the vision and ability to make it and inevitably produces power and authority for the person who does so. Such authority, finally, cannot be easily given away. The position of the author will not be equivalent to the position of the reader, for example, so long as the productions of authors are circulated to mass audiences, while individual readings and interpretations barely circulate at all. I am more comfortable with authority, then, or perhaps less hopeful that

its workings can be altered than, for example, Dauber is in *The Idea of Authorship in America.*

52. Jonathan Auerbach suggests that particular novels ought to be thought of as a process through which the concerns of the author are worked out. The author "invents, discovers, makes something of himself in everything he or she composes. The objective text is not so much a reflection of the self as its very embodiment." Auerbach's sense of the mechanisms of this working out vary from mine. See Auerbach, *The Romance of Failure: First-Person Fictions of Poe, Hawthorne, and James* (New York: Oxford University Press, 1989), 3–19.

53. Henry James, "Preface to *Roderick Hudson,*" in *Literary Criticism,* 1041–1042.

54. The possibility of writing to "deface" or otherwise undo the centered subject has been a persistent theme of poststructuralism. See, for example, Paul de Man's "Autobiography as Defacement," in *The Rhetoric of Romanticism* (New York: Columbia University Press, 1984), 67–81; Allan Stoekl's *Politics, Writing, Mutilation: The Cases of Bataille, Blanchot, Roussel, Leiris, and Ponge* (Minneapolis: University of Minnesota Press, 1985); Michel Foucault's discussion in "What Is an Author?" in *Language, Counter-Memory, Practice: Selected Essays and Interviews by Michel Foucault,* ed. Donald F. Bouchard, trans. Donald F. Bouchard and Sherry Simon (Ithaca: Cornell University Press, 1977), 113–138; and Roland Barthes's "The Death of the Author," in *The Rustle of Language,* trans. Richard Howard (Berkeley and Los Angeles: University of California Press, 1989). As Barthes usefully puts it, the writer "is only that *someone* who holds collected into one and the same field all of the traces from which writing is constituted" (54). All of these figures also testify to the persistent power of authoring to produce the author in the position of "one who knows" or, in recent years, the "one who knows the conditions of not-knowing."

55. Henry James, "Preface to *The Spoils of Poynton,*" in *Literary Criticism,* 1138–1139.

56. Roland Barthes, *The Pleasure of the Text,* trans. Richard Miller (New York: Hill and Wang, 1975), 14.

57. Leo Bersani and Ulysse Dutoit argue for linear narrative as inherently repressive in *The Forms of Violence: Narrative in Assyrian Art and Modern Culture* (New York: Schocken, 1985). See, for example, the section entitled "Narrativity and Violence," 40–56.

58. Gillian Brown discusses the longstanding interrelation of the problem of interiority and the feminine in a long note to *Domestic Individualism,* 205. She valuably provides a series of sources for this idea as well, which I repeat here, including Ian Watt, *The Rise of the Novel* (London: Chatto and Windus, 1957); Myra Jehlen, "Archimedes and the Paradox of Feminist Criticism," *Signs* 6, no. 4 (summer 1981): 575–601; Frances Ferguson, "Rape and the Rise of the Novel," *Representations* 20 (fall 1987): 88–112; and Nancy Armstrong, *Desire and Domestic Fiction* (New York: Oxford University Press, 1987).

Myra Jehlen puts the matter usefully for my argument in terms of the relation of male writers to the feminine:

I want to propose the thesis that this interior life, *whether lived by man or woman, is female,* so that women characters define themselves and have power only in this realm. Androgyny, in the novel, is a male trait enabling men to act from their male side and feel from their female side. . . . It is precisely the drama of the suppressed self, the self who assumes the universal duty of self-realization but finds its individual model in absolute conflict with society. . . . If there is a tragic dimension to the novel, it is here in the doomed encounter between the female self and the middle-class world. (596–597)

59. My sense of the problem of homosexuality in nineteenth-century texts and its relation to questions of narrative structure corresponds to what D. A. Miller has labeled the "nonnarratable" in the text. To Miller, "what defines a nonnarratable element is its incapacity to generate a story. Properly, or instrinsically, it has no narrative future—unless, of course, its nonnarratable status is undermined" (5). This should be sharply distinguished from the "unspeakable," though obviously the boundaries between these two categories are shifting and ambiguous. The nonnarratable and the desires it represents exist in tension with the imperative of closure. See Miller, *Narrative and Its Discontents: Problems of Closure in the Traditional Novel* (Princeton: Princeton University Press, 1981). The case that narrative is both heterosexual and heterosexualizing has been made recently by Paul Morrison. See Morrison, "End Pleasure," *GLQ* 1 (1994): 53–78.

60. I believe this claim will remain generally reliable, despite ongoing efforts to uncover more and more of a lost nineteenth-century homosexual culture. Steps in this direction have been taken recently by George Chauncey, who, in the first part of his book "Male (Homo)sexual Practices and Identities in the Early Twentieth Century," has a frame of reference that extends, tantalizingly for the nineteenth-century critic, back to the New York of 1870. Nonetheless, unless one was actually a member of this subculture, it would not seem to suggest access to a narratable sense of homosexuality for most of U.S. culture, or for writers in particular. See Chauncey, *Gay New York: Gender, Urban Culture, and the Making of the Gay Male World, 1890–1940* (New York: Basic Books, 1994), 32–127.

61. The order and intelligibility of linear narrative may exist in tension with something fundamentally unintelligible and unrepresentable in sexuality, a position that finally implies a tension even in heterosexuality between sexual experience and the heterosexual plot. According to Leo Bersani's reading of Freud, "The investigation of human sexuality leads to a massive detachment of the sexual from both object-specificity and organ-specificity. We desire what nearly shatters us, and the shattering experience is, it would seem, *without any specific content*—which may be our only way of saying that the experience . . . belongs to the nonlinguistic biology of human life." See Bersani, *The Freudian Body: Psychoanalysis and Art* (New York: Columbia University Press, 1986), 39–40.

   One must be cautious, of course, in assuming that all of sexual experience—or that "real" sexual experience—is necessarily apocalyptic. Though I believe Bersani's formulation is valuable, it is difficult finally to say what sexuality is or is not. This mobility, of course, finally contributes to the difficulty of rationalizing sexuality, which returns one to its potential disruptiveness.

62. Fiedler, *Love and Death*. See, for example, 282–283, 360–390. Fiedler's book, unfortunately, is clouded by the familiar homophobic narrative of homosexuality as developmental failure, as he refers in his introduction to "[t]he failure of

the American fictionist to deal with adult heterosexual love and his consequent obsession with death, incest and innocent homosexuality" (12).

Joseph Boone updates Fiedler's work by suggesting that wilderness in U.S. literature often serves as a "wild zone," which allows an exploration of desires difficult to articulate within the setting of conventional culture. See Boone, "Male Independence and the American Quest Romance as Counter-Traditional Genre: Hidden Sexual Politics in the Male World of *Moby Dick, Huckleberry Finn, Billy Budd*, and *The Sea Wolf*," *Tradition Counter Tradition: Love and the Form of Fiction* (Chicago: University of Chicago Press, 1987), 226–227.

63. See Jonathan Dollimore, *Sexual Dissidence: Augustine to Wilde, Freud to Foucault* (Oxford: Clarendon Press, 1991), 305. See also Eve Kosofsky Sedgwick's discussion of "homosexual panic" in *Between Men: English Literature and Male Homosocial Desire* (New York: Columbia University Press, 1985), 83–91, and her own discussion of the homosocial, 1–5.

64. See Herbert's account of Hawthorne's marital relations in *Dearest Beloved*.

65. Michael Warner usefully examines Freud's problematic separation of desire and identification in "Homo-Narcissism; or Heterosexuality," in *Engendering Men*, ed. Joseph A. Boone and Michael Cadden (New York: Routledge: 1990), 190–206. Warner suggests that the narratives of psychoanalysis are by no means theoretically sound or necessary, but that they replicate cultural mechanisms through which the sex/gender system is perpetuated, leading, for example, to an ease of confirmation of the link between homosexuality and narcissism (203).

Other critics have noted that nineteenth-century U.S. cultural structures seem to anticipate Freud's formulation of them. See Pfister's argument that Hawthorne's fiction "makes Freud's invention of psychoanalysis . . . historically *predictable*" (50), in "Hawthorne Explains Freud (Historically)," *The Production of Personal Life*, 49–58. Newfield also talks in terms of the nineteenth century's generation of the material for Freudian paradigms in *The Emerson Effect*, 109–117.

66. Henry James, *A Small Boy and Others* (New York: Charles Scribner's Sons, 1913). I discuss this scene at greater length in "A Small Boy and the Ease of Others: The Structure of Masculinity and the Autobiography of Henry James," *Arizona Quarterly* 45 (winter, 1989): 25–56.

CHAPTER 1   *Gender and the Scene of Writing*

1. Nathaniel Hawthorne, *The Scarlet Letter*, vol. 1, *The Works of Nathaniel Hawthorne*, The Centenary Edition of The Works of Nathaniel Hawthorne, ed. William Charvat, Roy Harvey Pearce, and Claude M. Simpson (Columbus: Ohio State University Press, 1962).

This chapter is a version of an essay I published in *Novel: A Forum on Fiction* 28, no. 3 (spring 1995): 308–326, entitled "'A Curious Subject of Observation and Inquiry': Homoeroticism, the Body, and Authorship in Hawthorne's *The Scarlet Letter*."

2. *The Scarlet Letter*'s concern with intertwined anxieties related to gender and authorship has been noted in a variety of ways by other critics. See, for example, John T. Irwin, *American Hieroglyphics: The Symbol of the Egyptian Hieroglyphics*

in the American Renaissance (New Haven: Yale University Press, 1980), 271–284; Robert K. Martin, "Hester Prynne, *C'est Moi*: Nathaniel Hawthorne and the Anxieties of Gender," in *Engendering Men: The Question of Male Feminist Criticism*, ed. Joseph A. Boone and Michael Cadden (New York: Routledge, 1990), 122–139; and Leland S. Person, Jr., *Aesthetic Headaches: Women and a Masculine Poetics in Poe, Melville, and Hawthorne* (Athens: University of Georgia Press, 1988), 94–145.

3. Nathaniel Hawthorne, "To H. W. Longfellow, Cambridge," June 4, 1837, in *The Letters: 1813–1843*, ed. Thomas Woodson, L. Neal Smith, and Norman Holmes Pearson, vol. 15, The Centenary Edition of The Works of Nathaniel Hawthorne (Columbus: Ohio State University Press, 1984), 251–253. See especially 252.

4. John Irwin notes the relentlessness of Hawthorne's campaign against normative masculinity in "The Custom-House," noting that "[t]he reversal of masculine and feminine traits (whereby the supposedly passive artist is shown to be more truly active than the men of customary business) underlies most of the other reversals in the autobiographical preface." See Irwin, *American Hieroglyphics*, 274.

5. Lauren Berlant suggests that "A Rill from the Town-Pump" resembles "The Custom-House" itself by serving as an imagined site of nationalist collectivity. It thus serves as a site of both real and imagined power for both Hawthorne and his text. See Berlant, *The Anatomy of National Fantasy: Hawthorne, Utopia, and Everyday Life* (Chicago: University of Chicago Press, 1991), 186–189.

6. Mark Seltzer argues that, in Norris's *The Octopus*, "The colossal mother is thus rewritten as a machine of force that brings men into the world. . . . And crucially, if the mother is merely a 'carrier' of force, the mother herself is merely a medium—mid-wife and middleman—of the force of generation." See Seltzer, "The Naturalist Machine," *Bodies and Machines* (New York: Routledge, 1992), 29.

7. The feminine sensitivity of General Miller to beauty has been noted by Irwin in the "Hawthorne and Melville" section of *American Hieroglyphics*, 275.

8. Hawthorne's often-noted comments in his notebooks at the time of his mother's death indicate how important and difficult this relation was for him:

> I love my mother; but there has been, ever since my boyhood, a sort of coldness of intercourse between us, such as is apt to come between persons of strong feelings, if they are not managed rightly. I did not expect to be much moved at the time—that is to say, not to feel any overpowering emotion struggling, just then. . . . but I was moved to kneel down close by my mother, and take her hand. . . . [A]nd then I found the tears slowly gathering in my eyes. I tried to keep them down; but it would not be—I kept filling up, till, for a few moments, I shook with sobs. For a long time, I knelt there, holding her hand; and surely it is the darkest hour I ever lived.

Nathaniel Hawthorne, "Sunday, July 29th, 1849, $1/2$ past 9 o'clock A.M.," in *The American Notebooks*, ed. Claude Simpson, vol. 8, The Centenary Edition of The Works of Nathaniel Hawthorne (Columbus: Ohio State University Press, 1972), 429.

9. T. Walter Herbert suggests the depths of domestic conflicts in Hawthorne's personal life, specifically in terms of gender, in "Nathaniel Hawthorne, Una Hawthorne, and *The Scarlet Letter*: Interactive Selfhoods and the Cultural Con-

struction of Gender," *PMLA* 103, no. 3 (May 1988): 285–297. Una in particular suffered in the Hawthorne family from her Pearl-like inability to conform to such relentlessly idealizing pressure.

10. Nathaniel Hawthorne, "To Sophia Hawthorne, West Newton," in *The Letters: 1843–1853*, ed. Thomas Woodson, L. Neal Smith, and Norman Holmes Pearson, vol. 16, The Centenary Edition of the Works of Nathaniel Hawthorne (Columbus: Ohio State University Press, 1985), 226–227.

11. Joel Pfister suggests that Hawthorne uses the "psychological" as a defense against women's wider roles, particularly in literature. While I think this is in some senses true, it also understates the psychological as a realm of conflict and breakdown that produces a need for a return to public space as well. Idealized domesticity in Hawthorne is a defense against both the psychological and the public. See Pfister, *The Production of Personal Life: Class, Gender, and the Psychological in Hawthorne's Fiction* (Stanford: Stanford University Press, 1991), 138.

12. Nathaniel Hawthorne, "Mrs. Hutchinson," in *Hawthorne: Tales and Sketches* (New York: Library of America, 1982), 18–19. This sketch figures in a number of considerations of Hawthorne's novel. See, for example, Amy Schrager Lang, *Prophetic Woman: Anne Hutchinson and the Problem of Dissent in the Literature of New England* (Berkeley and Los Angeles: University of California Press, 1987), 1–4; and Pfister, *Production of Personal Life* 71–72. For a useful consideration of Hawthorne and women writers, see James Wallace, "Hawthorne and the Scribbling Women Reconsidered," *American Literature* 62, no. 2 (June 1990): 201–222.

13. Nathaniel Hawthorne, "To William D. Ticknor, Boston," February 2, 1855, in *The Letters: 1853–1856*, ed. Thomas Woodson, James A. Rubino, L. Neal Smith, and Norman Holmes Pearson, vol. 17, The Centenary Edition of The Works of Nathaniel Hawthorne (Columbus: Ohio State University Press, 1987), 307–308.

14. Hawthorne, "Mrs. Hutchinson," 24.

15. Hawthorne's investment in this ideal and its middle-classness are examined at length by T. Walter Herbert, Jr., in *Dearest Beloved: The Hawthornes and the Making of the Middle-Class Family* (Berkeley and Los Angeles: University of California Press, 1993).

16. This remark is recorded by Edwin Haviland Miller in *Salem Is My Dwelling Place* (Iowa City: University of Iowa Press, 1991), 381. Miller reports Hawthorne's own comment: "Though the story is true, yet it took a romancer to do it."

17. Eve Kosofsky Sedgwick, *Between Men: English Literature and Male Homosocial Desire* (New York: Columbia University Press, 1985).

18. Michael Warner, "Thoreau's Bottom," *Raritan* 11 (winter 1992): 53–79. See especially 54–55. See also James Creech's discussion of this problem in *Closet Writing/Gay Reading: The Case of Melville's "Pierre"* (Chicago: University of Chicago Press, 1993). Cautions Creech, "Even as we wisely caution against naive projection by a contemporary critic, we find it impossible to avoid the conclusion that there were, in nineteenth-century America, what we today can only call homosexuals" (68).

19. Chuck Jackson, a gifted graduate student at Rice University, first pointed out to

me the difficulties of seeing Chillingworth's violation of Dimmesdale as metaphorical rape.

20. James R. Mellow makes this argument in a speculative footnote in his biogra-
phy, *Nathaniel Hawthorne in His Times* (Boston: Houghton Mifflin, 1980), 610–
611. His position is cautiously seconded as a suggestive one by David Leverenz.
To Leverenz, "[t]he threat of homosexual rape seems much more central to
Hawthorne's narrative tensions than does homosexual desire" (245). Gloria
Ehrlich, on the other hand, feels the suggestion of actual violation is excessive
given Robert Manning's reputation for "probity and self-discipline" (118). To
Ehrlich, in an argument that may understate the conflict generated in many vic-
tims of rape, if Hawthorne had been assaulted, his rebellion against his uncle
would have been "more retributive" and "less conflicted." See Gloria C. Ehrlich,
Family Themes and Hawthorne's Fiction: The Tenacious Web (New Brunswick:
Rutgers University Press, 1984), 118; and see David Leverenz, *Manhood and
the American Renaissance* (Ithaca: Cornell University Press, 1989).

21. James Fenimore Cooper, *The Pathfinder* (New York: Oxford University Press,
1992), 271–272.

22. See Elaine Scarry's argument in *The Body in Pain* (New York: Oxford University Press, 1985), 3–11.

23. John D'Emilio and Estelle B. Freedman indicate that "[d]espite extremists . . .
most health reformers and medical writers who supported male continence did
not reject sexual pleasure completely. Rather, they attempted to train men to ex-
ert self-control and channel their desires toward procreative, marital relations"
(69). Even middle-ground understandings of sexuality involved the rational regulation of pleasure. See D'Emilio and Freedman, *Intimate Matters: A History of
Sexuality in America* (New York: Harper & Row, 1988), 69–72.

24. Sylvester Graham, *A Lecture to Young Men* (1834; reprint, New York: Arno Press,
1974).

25. Herbert has recently argued that Hawthorne's sexual relations with Sophia were
marked by nineteenth-century theories about sexuality's potentially debilitating
effects. These theories suggested that Hawthorne's notoriously feminine person-
ality and his love of solitude might have had origins in sexual deviance. See
Herbert, *Dearest Beloved* , 140–142. Stephen Nissenbaum notes as well that in-
triguing parallels exist between Graham's work and some of Hawthorne's characters, including Dimmesdale, in *Sex, Diet, and Debility in Jacksonian America:
Sylvester Graham and Health Reform*, Contributions in Medical History, no. 4,
(Westport, Conn.: Greenwood Press, 1980), 154 n. 3. Pfister notes as well the
similarity between Dimmesdale and "a lubricious lad liberated from the pages
of antimasturbation tracts of the 1830's and 1840's" penned by Graham, among
others (*Production,* 139). Though Nissenbaum offers no proof that Hawthorne
was directly influenced by Graham, he does indicate how Graham's cultural presence was quite familiar, as when Emerson referred to him as "the prophet of
bran bread and pumpkins" (Nissenbaum 3), and he notes also that Graham was
"mobbed" twice in Boston during the winter of 1837, and that a boarding house
there, which Graham helped to found, was devoted to Graham's principles (14–
15). Throughout his life, Hawthorne had an interest in Utopian communities and

reform, as his personal sojourn at Brook Farm and *The Blithedale Romance* clearly indicate.

26. Carroll Smith-Rosenberg, "Sex as Symbol in Victorian Purity: An Ethnohistorical Analysis of Jacksonian America," *American Journal of Sociology*, 84 supplement (1978): 226.

27. Let me be clear that I am not, however, arguing that homosexuality has a privileged relation to narcissism; rather, I am arguing that homosexuality disrupts the narcissism of male homosocial mirroring.

28. For a discussion of the connections between gender and the "heterosexual matrix," see Judith Butler, *Gender Trouble: Feminism and the Subversion of Identity* (New York: Routledge, 1990), 151 n. 6. For a discussion of heterosexuality and narrative, see Paul Morrison, "End Pleasure," *GLQ* 1 (1994): 53–78. See especially 68.

29. In fact, Chillingworth, as a (pre)homosexual in the text, suggestively embodies the signifying disarray that Thomas Yingling argues becomes characteristic of modern homosexuality. To Yingling, homosexuality always has an evocative relation to modernism and postmodernism precisely because the homosexual finds himself vertiginously suspended outside conventional codes of gender and sexuality. See Thomas Yingling, *Hart Crane and the Homosexual Text: New Thresholds, New Anatomies* (Chicago: University of Chicago Press, 1990), 72.

30. Sedgwick, in her extended reading of *Billy Budd* in *Epistemology of the Closet*, simply names Claggart as the "homosexual in this text." Her apparently arbitrary insistence marks an inevitable problem of a gay critical practice, given the secrecy that often has necessarily attended gay writing. Claggart must be taken as gay; his homosexuality cannot be proven regardless of the suggestiveness of the text. At the same time, a critical assumption of a character's heterosexuality may finally be equally ungrounded—just less self-conscious. See Eve Kosofsky Sedgwick, *Epistemology of the Closet* (Berkeley and Los Angeles: University of California Press, 1990), 92.

31. Christopher Newfield offers a significant reading of this scene in terms of masochism in "The Politics of Male Suffering: Masochism and Hegemony in the American Renaissance," *Differences* 1, no. 3 (fall 1989): 55–87. Newfield's suspicion of any attempt to find a political productivity in male feminization seems correct to me; indeed, I will be arguing consistently that the operations of narrative and writing serve the consolidation of masculine authority in the texts I analyze. I have reservations, however, about the productivity of addressing the text in terms of "male masochism." Sadism and masochism at the level of fantasy are easily deconstructible categories, as slippery as any theoretical distinction between pain and pleasure, and the political content of any particular masochistic scenario depends heavily on who frames and controls it. The effort to fix inherently slippery terms produces a stabilization of the psychoanalytic framework that gives them their meaning (and an involuted concentration upon this framework), and hence often has a conservative instead of a liberatory effect. By the end of his discussion, Newfield himself seems partly to discard male masochism as insufficient, suggesting that another less individualist mode of discourse is necessary.

224 Notes to Pages 55–62

32. This scene in Dimmesdale's study, however, is the most psychologically resonant scene in *The Scarlet Letter*, and it suggests why the "psychological" in
Hawthorne cannot be understood only as a cultivated defense against cultural
anxieties in the novel, as Pfister argues. Dimmesdale, in fact, can only stabilize
his identity by escaping the psychological and returning to public space—the
project of the rest of the novel. Michael T. Gilmore has recently pointed out the
oddity of confirming the supposedly private family on a public scaffold in the
marketplace, in "Hawthorne and the Making of the Middle Class," in *Rethink-
ing Class: Literary Studies and Social Formations*, ed. Wai Chee Dimock and
Michael T. Gilmore (New York: Columbia University Press, 1994), 232.

33. Nina Baym, "Nathaniel Hawthorne and His Mother: A Biographical Speculation," *American Literature* 54, no.1 (March 1982): 1–27. See especially 7. Though
this is a useful argument, I'm not sure it is necessary to rescue Elizabeth Hathorne
from her son's own comments. Given the structural importance of the maternal
position in the nineteenth century, even a reclusive mother might well be crucial
to the structure of her son's creativity.

34. Nathaniel Hawthorne, "Letter to William D. Ticknor, Boston," May 17, 1862, in
The Letters: 1857–1864, ed. Thomas Woodson, James A. Rubino, L. Neal Smith,
and Norman Holmes Pearson, vol. 18, The Centenary Edition of The Works of
Nathaniel Hawthorne (Columbus: Ohio State University Press, 1987), 456–457.
I suggest the possibility of rhetorical inflation because Hawthorne obviously
hopes in the letter that Ticknor might help Ebe find employment in some position connected to literature. Nevertheless, Hawthorne's praise of his sister does
not seem feigned nor false.

35. Nathaniel Hawthorne, "To Sophia Peabody, Salem," April 17, 1839, in *The Letters: 1813–1843* , 299.

36. Herbert, *Dearest Beloved*, 100.

37. Nathaniel Hawthorne, "To Sophia Hawthorne, Boston," July 13, 1847, in *The
Letters: 1843–1853*, 174.

38. Lang notes that the novel continually recalls Hester "from masculine thought"
to "feminine feeling." See Lang, *Prophetic Woman*, 173.

39. Luce Irigaray, *This Sex Which Is Not One*, trans. Catherine Porter with Carolyn
Burke (Ithaca: Cornell University Press, 1985), 179–180.

40. If, as Lang argues, the text has systematically established everything Hester maintains as error, this status helps reinforce her separation from thought. The content of her speech, even as Verena Tarrant's in *The Bostonians*, is simply
disposable, though also a necessary vehicle for the production of passion. See
Lang, *Prophetic Woman*, 183–184.

41. Person notes Hester's alienation from the scene of Dimmesdale's final triumph
and notes as well the irony of this alienation given her role as the source of the
"energy" for Dimmesdale's sermon. See Person, *Aesthetic Headaches*, 136–138.

42. See Lauren Berlant's argument that successful masculinity in *The Scarlet Letter*
is such that men must be indistinguishable from the law. Berlant argues that adultery in the novel forces men to face "that *within themselves* which is 'outside'
or in excess of the law that founds their authority and self-identity" (117), and
that "Dimmesdale's self-combustion can be traced to his need *to not know* that
he has a body" (121). This is because "for the fully lawful man there is neither a

split nor a fantasy of a split between his official and his private self. His relation to the law is his subjectivity" (121). See Lauren Berlant, *The Anatomy of National Fantasy* (Chicago: University of Chicago Press, 1991).

43. Christine van Boheemen suggests that novels often work to substitute fantasies of patrilineal generation for the threatening generativity of women and nature. See *The Novel as Family Romance: Language, Gender, and Authority from Fielding to Joyce* (Ithaca: Cornell University Press, 1987).

44. Berlant notes this "eruption and validation of homosocial desire" and sees the eroticism it suppresses: "[T]he narrator's dream of a utopian world of men invests the male gender (but *not* the male body) with another, purer kind of power." See Berlant, *Anatomy of National Fantasy*, 120.

CHAPTER 2   *Poe and the Purloined Mother*

1. See, for example, Daniel Hoffman, *Poe Poe Poe Poe Poe Poe Poe* (Garden City, N.Y.: Anchor Books, 1973), 19–33. John Irwin provides the following general summary of Poe's relation to women: "From what we know of Poe's life, he was a man whose relationships with women characteristically involved the need to be mothered. But to judge from his fiction, he was highly ambivalent about this need, at once wanting maternal care and affection from women, and yet resenting it as childish dependency." See John Irwin, *The Mystery to a Solution: Poe, Borges, and the Analytic Detective Story* (Baltimore: Johns Hopkins University Press, 1994), 231.

2. See Kenneth Silverman, *Edgar A. Poe: Mournful and Never-Ending Remembrance* (New York: HarperCollins, 1991), 136.

3. See Silverman, *Edgar A. Poe*, 280–290, 355–390, 398–399. Silverman suggests that Poe's support of Sarah Anna Lewis's poetry marks "a deterioration of [his] literary morals" and was done for pragmatic reasons (398–399). Particularly in the case of Sarah Helen Whitman, however, it seems difficult to believe that Poe would passionately court a woman whose writing he despised, especially since this courtship involved the exchange of poems (354, 358–359). What Poe's precise feelings were toward such poetry, or whether he had precise feelings, must remain ambiguous.

An early treatment of Poe's relations to nineteenth-century women writers may be found in Richard Cary's "Poe and the Literary Ladies," *Texas Studies in Literature and Language: A Journal of the Humanities* 9 (1967): 91–101.

4. For an account of Poe's relations with John Allan, see Silverman, *Edgar A. Poe*, 29–99. See as well Hoffman, *Poe, Poe, Poe*, 33–35. For an account of Poe's early ambitions, see Silverman, 24, 40, 122.

5. Silverman indicates Poe's continuing desire for respect (232–233) and cites as well at least one instance of his insistence that he was "*not* ambitious" (487 n). Silverman concludes by quoting Poe to the effect that "genius of the highest order lives in a state of perpetual vacillation between ambition and *the scorn of it*." Scorn for conventional ambition, of course, can often imply an equally intense ambition of higher and more exclusive form. See Silverman, *Edgar A. Poe*, 232–233.

6. Recent critics have tended to find in Poe a complex exposure of the nature of cultural authority. See Stephen Rachman, "'Es lässt sich nicht schreiben': Plagiarism and 'The Man of the Crowd,'" in *The American Face of Edgar Allan Poe*, ed. Shawn Rosenheim and Stephen Rachman (Baltimore: Johns Hopkins University Press, 1995), 49–87; Joseph Riddel, "The Crypt of Edgar Poe" and "Poe's Fable of Criticism," in *Purloined Letters: Originality and Repetition in American Literature*, ed. Mark Bauerlein (Baton Rouge: Louisiana State University Press, 1995), 121–176; and Jonathan Elmer, *Reading at the Social Limit: Affect, Mass Culture, and Edgar Allan Poe* (Stanford: Stanford University Press, 1995), especially "The Cultural Logic of the Hoax," 174–223.

7. All citations in this volume to Poe's detective stories refer to *The Short Fiction of Edgar Allan Poe*, ed. Stuart Levine and Susan Levine (Urbana: University of Illinois Press, 1990). See "The Murders in the Rue Morgue," 175–197; "The Mystery of Marie Roget," 197–225; and "The Purloined Letter," 225–244.

8. There a few exceptions. The most notable is a valuable recent reading by Laura Saltz of "The Mystery of Marie Roget." See Laura Saltz, "'(Horrible to Relate!)': Recovering the Body of Marie Roget," in *American Face*, 237–267. Saltz correctly argues that the story makes Mary Rogers, the actual victim on whom Poe's tale is based, a sacrifice to Poe's efforts to stabilize masculine (authorial) identity (253). David Leverenz offers as well a reading of "The Purloined Letter" in terms of gender, but focuses not on the story's purloining of the feminine, but on the story as a homosocial competition, in which Dupin "remasculinize[s]" the marginalized role of southern "gentleman of leisure" (229). See Leverenz, "Poe and Gentry Virginia," in *American Face*, 210–236. Cynthia Jordan sees Poe's stories sympathetically, arguing that "Dupin becomes virtually a feminist critic" (251), but she notes the violence against women and the silencing of women the stories contain. See Jordan, "Poe's Re-Vision: The Recovery of the Second Story," in *On Poe: The Best from "American Literature,"* ed. Louis J. Budd and Edwin H. Cady (Durham: Duke University Press, 1993), 247–265. See especially 248–249.

   This trio of stories, particularly "The Purloined Letter," has received some of the most intricate treatments in the history of literary criticism. The three most famous in this regard are those of Jacques Lacan, in "Seminar on the 'Purloined Letter'"; Jacques Derrida, in "The Purveyor of Truth"; and Barbara Johnson, in "The Frame of Reference: Poe, Lacan, and Derrida." These are all collected, along with other useful essays, in *The Purloined Poe: Lacan, Derrida, and Psychoanalytic Reading*, ed. John P. Muller and William J. Richardson (Baltimore: Johns Hopkins University Press, 1988). To these three one must add Irwin's *Mystery to a Solution* and recent treatments such as Jonathan Elmer's "The Cultural Logic of the Hoax," in *Reading at the Social Limit*, 192–201; and Shawn Rosenheim's "Detective Fiction, Psychoanalysis, and the Analytic Sublime," in *American Face*, 153–176. These are valuable and often brilliant readings that I want to acknowledge without reading through them in producing my own readings, and thus yielding to their own prior constructions of Poe's tales. My sense, however, is that, in overlooking the aggressive gender politics of these stories in regard to women, even intricate readings have missed what is in plain sight.

9. Cynthia Jordan argues for a relatively feminist Poe and, relevant for this study, finds in Dupin a hero who does "justice to women." As she says, "Dupin, more forcefully than Roderick, provides readers with a model of the cultural detective work that needs to be done to bring such criminal acts of forgetfulness to light" (145). I would be cautious about such a generous assessment of the dynamics at work in Poe's fiction. As Jordan admits at the end of her chapter, in Poe's life one finds "precious little biographical evidence of any behavior that we could consider even remotely feminist today" (150). Leland S. Person, Jr., also finds a relatively feminist Poe who critiques "a male tendency to disembody women [and repress] those very aspects of human being which the male would rather not face in himself" (46).

   I see little evidence in Poe's tales of any sensitivity to the historical and material suffering of women. I sympathize with Jordan's and Person's evident desire to be as generous as possible in their readings, but such generosity is a problem if it masks patterns of appropriation in which authors themselves are implicated. It is difficult for male authors to step outside of fundamental structures of masculinity. I would be reluctant to embrace, on the other hand, the totalizing argument of Judith Butler that within language and culture all definable positions are masculine ones—that masculinity inhabits, not a particular position within a structure, but the structure itself. Such a position negates the cultural work of women, and thus arguably completes the work of nineteenth-century masculinity. See Cynthia S. Jordan, *Second Stories: The Politics of Language, Form, and Gender in Early American Fictions* (Chapel Hill: University of North Carolina Press, 1989), 133–151; Leland S. Person, Jr., *Aesthetic Headaches: Women and a Masculine Poetics in Poe, Melville, and Hawthorne* (Athens: University of Georgia Press, 1988), 19–47; and Judith Butler, *Bodies that Matter: On the Discursive Limits of Sex* (New York: Routledge, 1993), 27–56.

10. See Saltz's cogent suggestion in terms of "Marie Roget" that Poe needs to "contain and obscure questions about the public visibility of women and their participation in a market economy. . . . He subordinates Marie and her body's productions to his own literary production, attempting to secure his place in the market that so provokes him." See Saltz, "'(Horrible to Relate!),'" 240.

11. Naomi Schor discusses the importance of this "female body" in criticism of "The Purloined Letter" in "Female Paranoia: The Case for Psychoanalytic Feminist Criticism," *Yale French Studies* 62 (1981): 204–219. She notes that the intricate detail of this description becomes a sign of the "clitoral," in which "those details of the female anatomy which have been generally ignored by male critics" are put into critical play (216).

12. Marie Bonaparte, "Selections from *The Life and Works of Edgar Allen Poe*," in *The Purloined Poe*, 130.

13. In Lacan's psychoanalytic reading, the blankness of the letter makes it a sign of its status as pure signifier, which has its effects, like the unconscious itself, regardless of its contents.

   Derrida works to undo theoretically the blankness of the letter, suggesting its divisibility in order to prevent the letter's "elevation toward the ideality of a meaning" (195). He resists what he sees as Lacan's interest in an equation of woman and lack, attributes to the Queen a desire to reappropriate power ceded to the King (184), and interestingly cites Lacan's failure to acknowledge Marie Bonaparte's prior treatment of the story, a move that suggests the importance of women as actual cultural producers. He remains in general less interested in the operations the story undertakes than in critiquing Lacan's particular use of it and, using the story as a base for a reading supportive of deconstruction, fails to articulate the extent to which the story itself represents the construction of masculine power in the historical context of nineteenth-century U.S. literature. See Lacan, "Seminar on 'The Purloined Letter,'" trans. Jeffrey Mehlman, in *The Purloined Poe,* 51. See Derrida, "The Purveyor of Truth," trans. Alan Bass, in *The Purloined Poe,* 184–188.

14. Jordan notes that this epigraph is suggestive in terms of the problem of gender in Poe. See Jordan, "Poe's Re-Vision: The Recovery of the Second Story," 259.

15. Achilles is cross-dressing in hiding himself among women. Marjorie Garber suggests that cross-dressing often serves to ground an essentialist view of gender, performing, rather than discounting, the importance of the penis/phallus. As she says, "Rather than regarding the penis (or the phallus) as incidental equipment contributory toward a general sense of 'male subjectivity' that transcends the merely anatomical, both male transvestites and transsexuals radically and dramatically *essentialize* their genitalia." See Marjorie Garber, "Spare Parts: The Surgical Construction of Gender," in *Vested Interests: Cross-Dressing and Cultural Anxiety* (New York: Routledge, 1992), 98.

16. Joanne Feit Diehl argues that we should think of Hawthorne's letter as a fetish, though her understanding of this term conforms more to the classic terms of its operation. See Joanne Feit Diehl, "Re-Reading *The Letter*: Hawthorne, the Fetish, and the (Family) Romance," *New Literary History* 19, no. 3 (spring 1988): 655–673.

17. Sigmund Freud, "Fetishism," in *Sexuality and the Psychology of Love*, ed. Phillip Rieff (New York: Macmillan, 1963), 216.

18. Kaja Silverman has a useful model of the maternal voice that brings the mother's presence into the symbolic as a problem for male identity. Speaking about the maternal voice, Silverman suggests seeing Freud's "equation of woman with lack as a *secondary construction,* one which covers over *earlier sacrifices* " (14). Silverman speaks of a "constantly renewed Oedipal structuration, which resituates the loss of the object at the level of the female anatomy, thereby restoring to the little boy an imaginary wholeness" (23). See Kaja Silverman, *The Acoustic Mirror: The Female Voice in Psychoanalysis and Cinema* (Bloomington: Indiana University Press, 1988).

See as well Eve Cherniavsky's discussion of fetishism in *That Pale Mother Rising: Sentimental Discourses and the Imitation of Motherhood in Nineteenth-Century America* (Bloomington: Indiana University Press, 1995), 61–74. Cherniavsky continues the discourse of the "maternal phallus," a metaphor I find troublesome because it continuously suggests women's cultural contributions are phantasmal. She differentiates male and feminist fetishism, and suggests the maternal phallus for the latter represents "the possibility of investing subjects with authority in excess of and in opposition to the distribution of authority within the economy of patriarchal gender" (73). I agree if one also specifies that such an excess of authority continuously exists and is contained at the level of the social real. Feminist fetishism, in other words, is the culturally repressed content of male fetishism.

Of course the attribution to women of cultural power and influence could itself be labeled fetishistic. To my mind there needs to be some preserved difference, however, between the effort to appreciate women's contributions to culture and the tendency to counterproductive "idealization" that Marcia Ian finds represented by the "phallic mother." To Ian, the phallic mother is the "very 'type' of idealization itself, and therefore more pernicious and persistent than we thought." See Marcia Ian, *Remembering the Phallic Mother: Psychoanalysis, Modernism, and the Fetish* (Ithaca: Cornell University Press, 1993), 7.

19. Madelon Sprengnether refers to these effects as "spectral" and attributes them in her extended reading of Freud to his refusal to theorize adequately the maternal position and the repression of the maternal in his own life. She thus reads Freud as a figure whose theories represent and help produce a cultural castration of women. See Madelon Sprengnether, *The Spectral Mother: Freud, Feminism, and Psychoanalysis* (Ithaca: Cornell University Press, 1990).

20. This sense of the fetish is related to what D. W. Winnicott calls a "transitional object," which he suggests can in later life develop into a fetish object. Winnicott says that "the transitional object stands for the breast, or the object of the first relationship." It thus is constructed from the maternal against loss, rather than given to the mother to defend against the spectacle of "lack." See Winnicott, *Playing and Reality* (New York: Routledge, 1990), 9.

Behind Winnicott's formulation is the work of Melanie Klein. Klein's work suggests that the child's first object relations involve the internalization of gendered objects such as the breast, and that such internalizations involve crucial subsidiary processes such as splitting, projection, reparation, and mania. I attempt to explore some of these possibilities for the former in "A Small Boy and the Ease of Others: The Structure of Masculinity and the Autobiography of Henry James," *Arizona Quarterly* 45 (winter 1989): 25–56. Though I may not use Klein's work in explicit ways in this book, I am nonetheless, in general, in her intellectual debt.

21. Luce Irigaray valuably analyzes the commodification of women in a Marxist/feminist framework in *This Sex Which Is Not One,* trans. Catherine Porter with Carolyn Burke (Ithaca: Cornell University Press, 1985), 185.

22. Eve Cherniavsky treats this story in terms of disruptive memories of the preoedipal mother, memories that disrupt the male subject's claim to identity and must be contained. Her reading is valuable, but the invocation of the pre-oedipal tends to have the conservative effect of reinforcing male identity by explaining its anxieties as presymbolic and inevitable symptoms of a structure that cannot be changed. See Eve Cherniavsky, "Revivification and Utopian Time: Poe versus Stowe," in *American Face,* 121–138.

23. Cynthia Jordan notes the striking similarity between Ligeia and Dupin in "Poe's Re-Vision," 259.

24. David Van Leer notes the problem of "homosexualization" and "sexual oddity"

in "The Purloined Letter," although it does not serve as the main focus of his general reading. See "The World of the Dupin Tales," in *New Essays on Poe's Major Tales,* ed. Kenneth Silverman (New York: Cambridge University Press, 1993), 65–91.

25. Eve Kosofsky Sedgwick makes this comment in *Between Men: English Literature and Male Homosocial Desire* (New York: Columbia University Press, 1985), 25.

PART 2   *Circuits of Desire*

1. Richard Brodhead, *The School of Hawthorne* (New York: Oxford University Press, 1986), 123.
2. John Carlos Rowe, *The Theoretical Dimensions of Henry James* (Madison: University of Wisconsin Press, 1984). See especially "Feminist Issues: Women, Power, and Rebellion," 85–118.

CHAPTER 3   *Early Authorizations in James*

1. Henry James, "Preface to *Roderick Hudson,*" in *Henry James, Literary Criticism: French Writers; Other European Writers; The Prefaces to the New York Edition,* ed. Leon Edel with the assistance of Mark Wilson (New York: Library of America, 1984), 1039–1052. See especially 1040.
2. Henry James, "Preface to *The Golden Bowl,*"in *Literary Criticism,* 1336.
3. Henry James, *Roderick Hudson,* in *Henry James, Novels 1871–1880: "Watch and Ward"; "Roderick Hudson"; "The American"; "The Europeans"; "Confidence,"* ed. William T. Stafford (New York: Library of America, 1983), 163–511; see 171.
4. Craig Milliman discusses Gloriani in a recent essay and argues that he emerges as a much more respected character in *The Ambassadors.* This increase in respect also marks James's revisions of the earlier novel for the New York edition. See "The Fiction of Art: Roderick Hudson's Pursuit of the Ideal," *Henry James Review* 15 (1994): 234–235.
5. Eric Savoy, "*Hypocrite Lecteur*: Walter Pater, Henry James and Homotextual Politics," *Dalhousie Review* 72 (spring 1992): 25. Savoy notes as well the Paterian nature of Roderick's theories about art (29). The relation of *Roderick Hudson* to Pater's *The Renaissance* has also been discussed by Richard Ellmann in "Henry James among the Aesthetes," the Sarah Tryphena Phillips Lecture on American Literature and History, *Proceedings of the British Academy* 69 (1983): 209–228; and by Jonathan Freedman, "James, Pater, and the Discovery of Aestheticism," in *Professions of Taste: Henry James, British Aestheticism, and Commodity Culture* (Stanford: Stanford University Press, 1990), 133–166.
6. Walter Pater, "Winckelmann," in *The Renaissance,* ed. Adam Phillips (New York: Oxford University Press, 1986), 138–139.
7. Robert Aldrich, "Winckelmann and Platen," in *The Seduction of the Mediterranean: Writing, Art, and Homosexual Fantasy* (New York: Routledge, 1993), 41–68.
8. Michael Moon, "Sexuality and Visual Terrorism in *Wings of the Dove,*" *Criticism* 28, no. 4 (fall, 1986): 427–443. See also Daniel J. Murtaugh's recent essay,

"An Emotional Reflection: Sexual Realization in Henry James's Revisions to *Roderick Hudson*," *The Henry James Review* 17 (1996): 182–203.

9. Robert K. Martin has argued that the central concern of *Roderick Hudson* is the homoerotic love of Rowland for Roderick. See Martin, "The 'High Felicity' of Comradeship: A New Reading of *Roderick Hudson*," *American Literary Realism* 2 (1978): 100–108.

10. Priscilla L. Walton argues that a disruptive heterosexuality in *Roderick Hudson* nevertheless is less disruptive than an amorphous and difficult to articulate homosexuality, and observes as well that Roderick's death is "convenient" because the problem of homosexuality dies with him. See Walton, *The Disruption of the Feminine in Henry James* (Toronto: University of Toronto Press, 1992), 34–48. See especially 43–46.

11. The circumstances surrounding the novel's composition, including financial pressures, have been usefully described by Martha Banta. See her introduction to *New Essays on "The American,"* ed. Martha Banta (New York, Cambridge University Press, 1987), 1–42.

12. According to Leon Edel, James received $1,350 for the serialization of *The American* in twelve issues of the *Atlantic*. As a consequence, his "livelihood was assured until the following year." See Edel, *The Conquest of London: 1870–1881* (New York: Avon, 1962), 261.

13. See Cheryl Tornsey, "Henry James, Charles Sanders Peirce, and the Fat Capon: Homoerotic Desire in *The American*," *Henry James Review* 14 (1993): 166–178.

14. William Veeder, "The Portrait of a Lack," *New Essays on "The Portrait of a Lady,"* ed. Joel Porte (New York: Cambridge University Press, 1990), 113.

15. Henry James, *The American*, in *Novels 1871–1880*, 513–872. See 586.

16. Banta, in *New Essays*, argues that James writes *The American* as an exploration of a national identity he essentially shares, even though this sharing is to some extent formed negatively, through James's sharp sense of his differences from his countrymen (see Banta, introduction, 16–18). Even if Newman's rebuff parallels James's own difficulty in gaining admission to Parisian society, it strains credulity to believe that one would rebuff Henry James *as* a Christopher Newman. On the contrary, the antithesis between author and character is clear and sharp. James arguably sees some strengths in Newman's character and patriotically sees much of which to disapprove in France. Nevertheless, Newman's shortcomings in terms of aesthetic consciousness, leading to shortcomings of actual perception, are ones upon which James would insist through his entire career as a basis for the authority of his art. Reverse Newman's strengths and shortcomings and you will have a better facsimile of Henry James.

Despite these significant shortcomings, we may still "like" Newman as the novel's generally well-intentioned chief character and wish that he were less oblivious to his surroundings. I do not believe, however, that Newman's flaws should be seen only as "localized ones, scattered here and there," as Richard Poirier puts it, "transmuted into delightfully natural characteristics." See Poirier, "*The American* and *Washington Square*: The Comic Sense," in *Henry James*, ed. Harold Bloom (New York: Chelsea House, 1987), 51.

17. Eric Haralson has a useful account of the cultural sources of Newman's style of masculinity. See "James's *The American*: A (New)man Is Being Beaten," *American Literature* 64, no. 3 (September 1992): 475–495. Haralson argues that Newman's masculinity is defined primarily by his body and suffers from a corresponding limitation in conscious perception (478–479).

18. I unpack the implications of the word "ease" at length in "A Small Boy and the Ease of Others: The Structure of Masculinity and the Autobiography of Henry James," *Arizona Quarterly* 45, no. 4 (winter 1989): 25–56.

19. For an informing account of the political and cultural information Newman lacks, see John Carlos Rowe's "The Politics of Innocence in Henry James's *The American*," in *New Essays on "The American*," 69–97.

20. Ultimately the author produces all fantasies in a text, so that this scene at least suggests a primal scene for James as well. See Kaja Silverman's discussion, "Too Early/Too Late: Subjectivity and the Primal Scene in Henry James," *Novel* (winter/spring 1988): 147–173.

21. John Carlos Rowe talks about *The American* as a text of the uncanny in "The Politics of the Uncanny: Newman's Fate in *The American*," *Henry James Review* 8, no. 2 (winter 1987): 79–90.

22. Sigmund Freud, "The Uncanny," in *On Creativity and the Unconscious* (New York: Harper & Row, 1958), 122–161.

23. Mark Seltzer discusses this moment in *The American* in terms of a thematics of writing. See "Physical Capital: *The American* and the Realist Body," *New Essays on "The American*," 131–167. Note especially 148–150.

24. For an account of these complexities, see Rowe's "The Politics of Innocence," especially 88–90.

25. My argument intersects here with that of Carolyn Porter, who has an extensive discussion of Newman's feminization in the novel. She argues that Newman's masculinity is threatened by his paradoxical relations to commerce and sees Claire de Cintre's importance as a marker for both James and Newman as a "pure, transcendent value" (102). See Porter, "Gender and Value in *The American*," in *New Essays on "The American*," 99–129.

26. Porter, "Gender and Value," 108–110.

27. See Porter's discussion, "Gender and Value," 107–110.

28. Seltzer discusses the implications of the cross Noemie draws in both "*The American* and the Realist Body" (esp. 139 and 149) and an expanded version of this argument in the section entitled "Physical Capital: The Romance of the Market in Machine Culture," in his *Bodies and Machines* (New York: Routledge, 1992), 67–68. His interests in seeing the interrelatedness of bodies, stories, and commercial exchanges are congruent with mine here.

29. Gillian Brown makes the argument, in *Domestic Individualism*, that domesticity plays a crucial role in anchoring individualism against the deindividualizing forces of commerce. See her introduction, 1–10.

CHAPTER 4   **Late Authorizations in James**

1. Henry James, "Preface to *The Ambassadors*," in *Henry James, Literary Criticism: French Writers; Other European Writers; The Prefaces to the New York Edition*, ed. Leon Edel (New York: Library of America, 1984), 1304–1321. See 1306.

2. David McWhirter notes the remarkable differences between *The Wings of the Dove* and *The Ambassadors*, and he sees the style and difficulty of the former as a reaction against the suppressions of the latter. See McWhirter, "The Contracted Cage," in *Desire and Love in Henry James: A Study of the Late Novels* (Cambridge: Cambridge University Press, 1989), 83–113.

3. My argument is less interested in a theorizing of James's entire career than are other recent intertextual accounts, such as Carren Kaston's *Imagination and Desire in the Novels of Henry James* (New Brunswick: Rutgers University Press, 1984), and William Veeder's more recent essay, "The Feminine Orphan and the Emergent Master: Self-Realization in Henry James," *Henry James Review* 12 (1991): 20–53. These are valuable and interesting efforts, but the price they pay for their narrative reach is a constriction of the possibilities for reading individual texts in terms of their particular teleologies. I have tried to restrict the number of texts I consider, thereby enlarging their points of possible relation, and to leave open the question of the relation of this particular set of interrelations to numerous other possible juxtapositions.

4. Henry James, *Hawthorne* (1879), in *Henry James, Literary Criticism: Essays on Literature—American Writers, English Writers*, ed. Leon Edel (New York: Library of America, 1984), 315–457. See 352.

5. Henry James, *The Ambassadors,* 2 vols., *The Novels and Tales of Henry James,* vols. 21 and 22, New York Edition (1909; reprint, New York: Charles Scribner's Sons, 1937). See 21:33–34.

6. Judith Wilt, "A Right Issue from the Tight Place: Henry James and Maria Gostrey," *Journal of Narrative Technique* 6, no. 2 (spring 1976): 86–87.

7. Kaston notes that Strether simplifies sexuality in the novel but sees him simplifying heterosexual questions. My argument, then, is designed to show the full extent of Strether's simplifications. See Kaston, *Imagination and Desire,* 83–84.

8. This relation is detailed in Fred Kaplan's recent biography, *Henry James: The Imagination of Genius* (New York: William Morrow, 1992), 401–406.

9. Quoted by Leon Edel, *Henry James: A Life* (New York: Harper & Row, 1985), 475.

10. For a useful recent discussion of the problem of the relation of the homosocial to the homosexual, see Jonathan Dollimore, *Sexual Dissidence: Augustine to Wilde, Freud to Foucault* (Oxford: Clarendon Press, 1991), 242–245. See also Eve Kosofsky Sedgwick's important discussion in *Between Men: English Literature and Male Homosocial Desire* (New York: Columbia University Press, 1985), especially 1–20.

11. A term like "sublimation" suggests itself here, since Strether's supposed achievement in *The Ambassadors* has such close ties to conventional aesthetic achievement. I will avoid it, however, in order to avoid its flattening effects on analysis:

its excessive and finally suppressive conceptual neatness. It implies too quickly an opposition between identification with other men and desire for them, when, if repressive conversion from one to the other often occurs, this conversion is not a necessary condition of either desire or identification, or achievement, and occurs when it occurs in different ways to different extents. For a useful recent discussion of such problems, see Dollimore, *Sexual Dissidence,* 244–248.

12. Dollimore, *Sexual Dissidence,* 305.

13. Gordon S. Haight makes the point that others in the novel seem always to recognize Chad's bent for business—especially Madame de Vionnet. From the reactions of others, he believes, we have no doubt that Chad will return to America and manufacturing. See Haight, "Strether's Chad Newsome: A Reading of James's *The Ambassadors,*" in *From Smollet to James: Studies in the Novel and Other Essays Presented to Edgar Johnson,* ed. Samuel I. Mintz, Alice Chandler, and Christopher Mulvey (Charlottesville: University of Virginia Press, 1981), 275–276.

14. Henry James, "Preface to *The Ambassadors,*" 1304.

15. Ralph Waldo Emerson indicates that "[e]ach man seeks those of different quality from his own, and such as are good of their kind; that is, he seeks other men, and the *otherest*" (616). Nevertheless, we also discover that "[t]here is . . . a speedy limit to the use of heroes. Every genius is defended from approach by quantities of unavailableness. . . . The more we are drawn, the more we are repelled. . . . The best discovery the discoverer makes for himself" (628). Greatness that is too available, in other words, must also be resisted as directly threatening. See Emerson, "The Uses of Great Men," in *Emerson: Essays and Lectures* (New York: Library of America, 1983).

16. Craig A. Milliman discusses the increase in Gloriani's stature in *The Ambassadors.* See Milliman, "The Fiction of Art: Roderick Hudson's Pursuit of the Ideal," *Henry James Review* 15, no. 3 (fall 1994): 231–241.

17. See Wilt, "Right Issue," 77–91.

18. The idea that Jamesian characters execute authorial functions as they attempt to "compose" experience has been a theme of much James criticism. See, for example, Kaston, *Imagination and Desire,* 3, and, concerning Strether in *The Ambassadors,* 82–83; Leo Bersani, "The Jamesian Lie," *Partisan Review* 36 (winter 1969): 57–58; Poirier's discussion of *The Ambassadors* in *A World Elsewhere,* 124–143; or Rowe, *Theoretical Dimensions,* 91–95.

19. John Carlos Rowe mentions the uncanniness of this scene in passing. See "James's Rhetoric of the Eye: Re-Marking the Impression," *Criticism* 24, no. 3 (summer 1982): 240.

20. Leland S. Person, Jr., "Strether's 'Penal Form': The Pleasure of Imaginative Surrender," *Papers on Language and Literature* 23 (winter 1987): 27–40. See as well Kaston's argument that Madame de Vionnet has been "Stretherized, sold on his ideas of renunciation, converted to his wish 'not . . . to have got anything for myself'" (*Imagination and Desire,* 102).

21. See Kaston, *Imagination and Desire,* 99.

22. Dollimore, *Sexual Dissidence,* 104. Also relevant to my argument are 103–275.

23. Judith Butler directly addresses such problems in the influential *Gender Trouble.* Her quest is to work out a productive politics when (and given that) perverse

subject positions are inevitably circumscribed within heterosexual dominance. See Butler, *Gender Trouble* (New York: Routledge, 1990).

24. Michael Moon, "Sexuality and Visual Terrorism in *The Wings of the Dove*," *Criticism* 28, no. 4 (fall 1986): 428.

25. Eve Kosofsky Sedgwick, "Is the Rectum Straight?: Identification and Identity in *The Wings of the Dove*," in *Tendencies* (Durham: Duke University Press, 1993), 73–103. Sedgwick draws on Butler's argument about melancholia in *Gender Trouble*, 57–72.

26. This passage is cited by Sedgwick, "Rectum," 79.

27. Henry James, *The Wings of the Dove*, 2 vols., in *The Novels and Tales of Henry James*, vols. 19 and 20, the New York Edition (1909; reprint, New York: Charles Scribner's Sons, 1937). See 20: 274. See also *The American*, 867, and my discussion of this image in chapter 3.

28. Carolyn L. Karcher, "Male Vision and Female Revision in James's *The Wings of the Dove* and Wharton's *The House of Mirth*," *Women's Studies* 10 (1984): 227–244.

29. Julie Olin-Ammentorp, "A Circle of Petticoats: The Feminization of Merton Densher," *Henry James Review* 15 (1994): 38–54.

30. Henry James, *The American Scene* (Bloomington: Indiana University Press, 1968), 345.

31. Henry James, "The Speech of American Women," *French Writers and American Women: Essays*, ed. Peter Buitenhuis (Branford, Conn.: Compass, 1960), 78–79.

    Alfred Habegger notes that James's essays on the speech and manners of women in the United States, which appeared in *Harper's* in 1906–1907, make "queerly explicit" his desire to maintain masculine authority (235). He wants women to serve the transmission of masculine culture, despite the "shabby deceptions" of those who represent culture for them. While I think Habegger's work valuably points out the conservative side of James's politics, I am never sure of a necessary and absolute continuity between his stated politics and his fiction. At a minimum, James embeds his politics in a framework that complicates and clouds his views. See Habegger, *Henry James and the "Woman Business"* (New York: Cambridge University Press, 1989), 230–238.

32. Sedgwick twice suggests that Kate is "frigid," a position I do not think the text finally supports, however in tune it may be with the logic of her life and early actions. See Sedgwick, "Rectum," 82, 94.

33. Marcia Ian has written of the importance of penetrating the subjectivities of others in *The Wings of the Dove*, and has argued that power depends on one's ability to resist such penetration. See Ian, "The Elaboration of Privacy in *The Wings of the Dove*," *ELH* 51, no. 1 (1984): 107–136.

34. Habegger's discussion of the extent to which James simply appropriates memories of Minnie Temple, long regarded as a source for Milly Theale, is illuminating in this context, especially given the unconventionality Habegger finds in the biographical Minnie and the importance he believes it has to James. See Habegger, "Minnie Temple's Death and the Birth of Henry James's Imagination," in *"Woman Business,"* 126–149.

35. I see Croy as a clearly homosexual figure in the novel, as Sedgwick argues, but

I also see his productivity in the novel as tied to his not completely jettisoned familial role. Since he only appears in the novel as a father in relation to his daughter, the salience of the family seems difficult to deny. So does, however, the salience of his queerness, and I suspect that Sedgwick minimizes the former in her argument as much as possible in order to prevent it from effacing (as it so often does) the latter.

36. Leo Bersani, "The Narrator as Center in *The Wings of the Dove*," *Modern Fiction Studies* 6, no. 2 (summer 1960): 131–144. The quotation is on 135. Quentin Anderson, *The American Henry James* (New Brunswick: Rutgers University Press, 1957), 239. Laurence Bedwell Holland, *The Expense of Vision: Essays on the Craft of Henry James* (Princeton: Princeton University Press, 1964), 286.

37. Sedgwick notes that Strett is a Victorian bachelor figure of a kind linked historically to the emergence of gay identities. For her discussion of Strett, see "Queer Tutelage," in *Tendencies,* 90, and, for her larger discussion of metropolitan bachelors, see *Epistemology of the Closet* (Berkeley: University of California Press, 1990), 189–195.

38. See Sedgwick's argument about "The Beast in the Jungle" in *Epistemology of the Closet,* 195–212. These pages contain an impassioned interrogation of the politics of reading James straight or gay and opt, correctly, for the latter. Sedgwick suggests, for example, that the absence of a positive homosexual presence in "The Beast in the Jungle" creates a potentially perfect symmetry between the "nothing" that defines Marcher's life and the "something" suggested by his love for May Bartram. To allow this false symmetry to stand uninterrogated, however, is simply to capitulate to the effects of homophobic terrorism, a terrorism that deeply marked James's life and fiction.

39. Henry James, "November 7, 1894," in *The Complete Notebooks of Henry James*, ed. Leon Edel and Lyall H. Powers (New York: Oxford University Press, 1987), 106.

40. Edel and Powers, *The Complete Notebooks,* 319–320.

41. Quoted by Edel, *Henry James: A Life,* 666.

42. See James, *A Small Boy and Others,* 347 in *Henry James, Autobiography,* ed. Frederick W. Dupee (Princeton: Princeton University Press, 1983), 196.

43. Edel suggests this date for the "admirable nightmare." See the final volume of his biography, *The Master, 1901–1916* (New York: Avon Books, 1972), 445. John Paul Eakin has a suggestive reading of the dream as potentially reflective of the psyche of both the small boy and the mature author. See Eakin, *Fictions in Autobiography* (Princeton: Princeton University Press, 1985), 79. I also discuss the dream in "A Small Boy and the Ease of Others: The Structure of Masculinity and the Autobiography of Henry James," *Arizona Quarterly* 45, no.4 (winter 1989): 47–52.

44. The centrality of chiasmus in James's fiction has been commented on by Ralf Norrman, in *The Insecure World of Henry James's Fiction: Intensity and Ambiguity* (New York: St. Martin's Press, 1982), 137–184.

PART 3   ***Ruptured Bodies, Ruptured Tales***

1. Joe Dubbert offers a broad and useful account of these cultural anxieties and alterations. See Dubbert's *A Man's Place: Masculinity in Transition* (Englewood Cliffs, N.J.: Prentice- Hall, 1979). See also Mark Seltzer, *Bodies and Machines* (New York: Routledge, 1992), 149–155.

2. Christine Van Boheeman, *Novel as Family Romance: Language, Gender, and Authority from Fielding to Joyce* (Ithaca: Cornell University Press, 1987), 114.

3. James Nagel has made an important argument that Crane's impressionism marks his distinction from other more conventional naturalists, such as Sinclair. My own sense of naturalism is that it represents a capacious but vexed and contradictory genre, a sense that informs in differing ways recent considerations of naturalism by Walter Benn Michaels, Mark Seltzer, Lee Clark Mitchell, and Jonathan Auerbach. On the one hand, much of Crane's work inarguably (if inconsistently) has characteristics compatible with naturalism, such as its commitment to graphic honesty, its fascination with violence, its interest in the interrelations of environment and behavior, its interest in lower-class experience, and its ruthless decentering of subjectivity. If naturalism in general often seems more interested in embodying abstract truths of experience than Crane's fictions do, it is nonetheless true that naturalism's paradoxical insistence on the limits of humanist consciousness produces internally important countercurrents of scepticism. Many of naturalism's most powerful moments of social description also have a local, impressionist quality, such as Dreiser's famous account of Carrie's factory work. Consequently, I see no reason to insist on a strict categorical difference between Crane and more conventional naturalists. Because generic categories are notoriously difficult to define (as Mitchell makes clear in *Determined Fictions*), however, it is important to see the differences of individual authors and fictions.

   See Nagel, *Stephen Crane and Literary Impressionism* (University Park: Pennsylvania State University Press, 1980); Seltzer, *Bodies and Machines;* Michaels, *The Gold Standard and the Logic of Naturalism* (Berkeley: University of California Press, 1987); Mitchell, *Determined Fictions: American Literary Naturalism* (New York: Columbia University Press, 1989), especially "Naturalism and the Excluded Self," 1–33; Auerbach, *Male Call: Becoming Jack London* (Durham: Duke University Press, 1996), especially his cogent summary of different contemporary versions of naturalism in his introduction, 1–20.

CHAPTER 5   ***What a Beating Feels Like***

1. Upton Sinclair, *The Jungle* (Urbana: University of Illinois Press, 1988). All references will be to this edition unless otherwise stated.

   This chapter is a version of an essay I published in *Studies in American Fiction* 23, no. 1 (spring 1995): 85–100, entitled "What a Beating Feels Like: Authorship, Dissolution, and Masculinity in Sinclair's *The Jungle.*"

2. Sinclair's account of all this "uproar" at times seems uncomfortably close to his accounts of the uproar caused by the numerous foreign languages of Packingtown.

It seems clear, at points in *The Jungle*, that ethnicity itself is an aspect of the profusion, the entrapping productivity, of nature.

3. Mark Seltzer argues that such fears are in fact characteristic of a broad range of U.S. naturalist texts, which work to substitute a safely masculine narrative of the creation of life. See Seltzer, "The Naturalist Machine," in *Bodies and Machines* (New York: Routledge, 1992), 23–44.

4. Upton Sinclair, *The Lost First Edition of Upton Sinclair's "The Jungle,"* ed. Gene DeGruson (Atlanta: St. Luke's Press, 1988). This edition was compiled from a manuscript discovered in a barn in Kansas and contains some significant differences from the Doubleday version that earned Sinclair fame. Page numbers for citations from this edition will be given parenthetically, but I will include the editor's name, DeGruson, to distinguish them from the standard edition.

5. See Christopher P. Wilson's account of the influence of Sinclair's position as a writer on *The Jungle* in *The Labor of Words: Literary Professionalism in the Progressive Era* (Athens: University of Georgia Press, 1985), 113–140. Wilson provides a valuable account of Sinclair's early career and the extent to which he projected himself and his literary troubles onto his work. To Wilson, this projection chiefly accounts for the inconsistencies and failures of *The Jungle*, as incommensurate registers of experience are somewhat randomly registered in the novel. I argue for a more thoroughgoing and consistent determination of the plot by Sinclair's authorial anxieties about feminine influence, a determination that makes the novel a tortured example of U.S. literature's tales of authorial self-construction, and confers a largely unconscious unity upon the book.

6. Upton Sinclair, *The Autobiography of Upton Sinclair* (New York: Harcourt, Brace & World, 1962), 54.

7. Upton Sinclair, *The Journal of Arthur Stirling: "The Valley of the Shadow"* (New York: Doubleday, Page, 1906).

8. This subject is a common one in naturalist literature in the United States. Characters who might be described as thwarted geniuses include Basil Ransom in *The Bostonians*; Martin Eden in the text that bears his name; Wolf Larsen in *The Sea-Wolf*; and Eugene Witla in *The Genius*.

9. Leon Harris, *Upton Sinclair: American Rebel* (New York: Thomas Y. Crowell, 1975), 62.

10. Such metaphors, of course, suggest the problem in naturalism of the articulation of the body and subjectivity in industrial metaphors. Such metaphors imply an alienation of the subject from his or her own desires. While industrialism provides the possibility of such metaphors, and hence of such understandings of the self, it is not clear what the relation of such metaphors are to a body that resists perpetual refiguration, to a body-as-inertia. Seltzer seems to leave a place in discourse for such a body, which contradicts the "interpretive standard in recent cultural criticism" of "the unnaturalness of nature." To Seltzer, the suspect conventional wisdom is that "when confronted by the nature-culture opposition, choose the culture side." The issue is an important one, in that opening up a space for a subject who is different from discourse reconstitutes a space for a historical psychoanalysis as an attempt to map the intersection of the subject and culture. We cannot give such an account by yielding to the metaphors of a particular

historical moment as the exhaustive "truth" of subjectivity. See Seltzer, *Bodies and Machines*, 155.

11. Sinclair's assessment of the novel includes both an aggressive reference to those critics who still "speak of it as having historical rather than literary interest" and a judicious critical acknowledgment that "its literary faults are evident enough." Nevertheless, anyone who can read it with "dry eyes" is "not an enviable person." See Upton Sinclair, *Manassas: A Novel of the War* (New York: Macmillan, 1904), 57–58.

12. Reported by Leon Harris, *Upton Sinclair,* 64.

13. Upton Sinclair, "Dedication," *Love's Pilgrimage* (London: William Heinemann, 1912).

14. Sinclair relates Jurgis's past in mythic terms that suggest the possibility of a masculinity not complicated by the presence of women. The onset of Jurgis's love for Ona represents a fall from this masculine fairy-tale world into a "foolish trap": "His father, and his father's father before him, and as many ancestors back as legend could go, had lived in that part of Lithuania known as *Brelovicz*, the Imperial Forest. This is a great tract of a hundred thousand acres, which from time immemorial has been a hunting preserve of the nobility. There are a very few peasants settled in it, holding title from ancient times; and one of these was Antanas Rudkus, who had been reared himself, and had reared his children in turn, upon half a dozen acres of cleared land in the midst of a wilderness" (22).

CHAPTER 6   *Behind the Lines*

1. Mark Seltzer, *Bodies and Machines* (New York: Routledge, 1992), 162–163. See also 111–112.

2. Thomas Beer's fictionalized but famous biography of Crane has produced much distress as the corrupting "fall" of Crane studies from reliability, but Crane would doubtless be a difficult subject even if Beer had not produced a compelling but distorted version of his life. Despite the helpful and recent *The Crane Log*, it is still remarkably difficult to tell what constitutes a reliable fact about Crane. See Beer, *Stephen Crane: A Study in American Letters* (New York: Alfred A. Knopf, 1923). See also Stanley Wertheim and Paul Sorrentino, *The Crane Log: A Documentary Life of Stephen Crane, 1871–1900* (New York: G. K. Hall, 1994).

3. See Eve Kosofsky Sedgwick, *The Epistemology of the Closet* (Berkeley: University of California Press, 1990). Relevant pages include but are not limited to 6–12 and 91–97. Of particular interest might be this statement concerning "The Beast in the Jungle"; "In 'The Beast in the Jungle,' written at the threshold of the new century, the possibility of an embodied male-homosexual thematics has, I would like to argue, a precisely liminal presence. It is present as a—as a very particular, historicized—thematics of absence, and specifically of the absence of speech. The first (in some ways the only) thing we learn about John Marcher is that he has a 'secret'" (201).

4. Robert H. Davis, "Introduction: Tales of Two Wars," *The Work of Stephen Crane*, vol. 2, ed. Wilson Follett (New York: Russell and Russell, 1963), ix–xxiv.

5. For contemporary readers, this chain might be extended to include his biogra-

phers, according to John Clendenning's recent account of the tangled and powerful investments of Thomas Beer, John Berryman, Melvin Harold Schoberlin,
and R. W. Stallman in their subject. See Clendenning, "Stephen Crane and His
Biographers: Beer, Berryman, Schoberlin, and Stallman," *American Literary Realism, 1870–1910* 28, no. 1 (fall 1995): 23–57. Crane's capacity to generate
transferential fascination also crosses gender lines, as indicated by "The Red
Room: Stephen Crane and Me," a personal essay by a recent biographer, Linda
H. Davis, in *The American Scholar* 64, no. 2 (spring 1995): 207–220.

6. A recent account of this problematic incident can be found in Wertheim and
Sorrentino, *The Crane Log*, 105. They cite as their source the Beer Papers. The
first published account seems to be given by John Berryman, though he also lists
Beer as his source. Berryman mentions that Beer chose not to use the information himself, a fact that says little about its reliability since Beer was apparently
willing to use absolute fiction. See John Berryman, *Stephen Crane* (n.p.: William Sloane Associates, 1950), 86–88.

One wonders about the dynamics of Beer's apparent fictionalization of
Crane. If, as Clendenning suggests, Beer "remained a closeted gay man writing
tributes to the heterosexual order," his heterosexual idealization of Crane represented his own self-idealization. By the same token, Crane's veiled exploration
of homoerotic dynamics between men must have appealed to Beer, even as the
latter aided in its suppression as a manifest subject in Crane criticism. See
Clendenning, "Stephen Crane and His Biographers," 26.

7. Christopher Benfey, *The Double Life of Stephen Crane* (New York: Alfred A.
Knopf, 1992), 105.

8. George Chauncey, *Gay New York: Gender, Urban Culture, and the Making of
the Gay Male World, 1890–1940* (New York: Basic Books, 1994), 1–99. Beer
also refers to the Bowery's reputation for "incredible debauchery" in *Stephen
Crane*, 78. He doesn't specify same-sex activity.

9. Stephen Crane, *Maggie: A Girl of the Streets*, in *Stephen Crane: Prose and Poetry*, ed. J. C. Levenson (New York: Library of America, 1984), 5–78. See 31.

The question of how much Crane actually uses observation in *Maggie* is,
of course, a difficult one to answer given the text's veiled compositional history.
Christopher Benfey, who actually is interested in arguing that Crane inverts the
usual relationship between observation and composition, reasonably concludes that
"it's hard not to believe that some version of *Maggie* was written before Crane arrived in New York, though he probably rewrote and revised it, drawing on his New
York experience, before its publication in 1893." See Benfey, *The Double Life*, 63.

10. Beer, *Stephen Crane*, 206. Edwin H. Cady, *Stephen Crane*, revised ed. (Boston:
Twayne, 1980), 148. See also Lilian B. Gilkes's criticism of Crane's treatment
of women in *"The Third Violet, Active Service*, and *The O'Ruddy*: Stephen Crane's
Potboilers," in *Stephen Crane in Transition: Centenary Essays*, ed. Joseph Katz
(De Kalb: Northern Illinois University Press, 1972), 106–126, especially 114;
and Carol Hurd Green, "Stephen Crane and the Fallen Woman," *American Nov-
elists Revisited: Essays in Feminist Criticism*, ed. Fritz Fleischmann (Boston: G.
K. Hall, 1982), 225–240.

11. See Green, "Fallen Women," 240.

12. Stephen Crane, *The Red Badge of Courage,* in *Stephen Crane: Prose and Poetry,* ed. J. C. Levenson (New York: Library of America, 1984), 79–212. All references will be to this edition unless otherwise noted.

13. Michael Moon, "Sexuality and Visual Terrorism in *The Wings of the Dove, Criticism* 28, no. 4 (fall 1986): 427–443.

14. It is worth repeating that the "nonnarratable" is a relative, descriptively useful category rather than an absolute one. It reflects the degree of resistance certain kinds of material pose to the author's need to fashion his material into a coherent shape. The reader participates as well in the construction of narrative through interpretation and, through his or her efforts, thus produces narrative from difficult and seemingly detached moments of a text.

15. According to Seltzer, this "projection of the body through a 'sole' worn to the thinness of writing paper, the very surfacing of the pun and the effect of the pun as a materialization both of writing and of personhood, are evident enough. It is, again, the correlation of the writing of writing and the body-machine complex." I am less concerned with signs of writing as a material practice than with writing as a cognitive event, structured by the requirements of narrative. See Seltzer, *Bodies and Machines,* 112.

16. Michael Fried suggests that the text contains an "irruption in the text of an alien—more accurately, an unacknowledgeable—agency, which I take to be that of writing as such" (125). It is Crane's fixation on faces, he further suggests, that allows his "unconscious fixation on the scene of writing" to come "closest to *surfacing . . .* but also, precisely . . . (to be) most emphatically *repressed*" (121). See Fried, *Realism, Writing, and Disfiguration: Thomas Eakins and Stephen Crane* (Chicago: University of Chicago Press, 1987), 93–161.

17. For a useful parallel discussion of an implied relation between homoerotic desire, vision, and death, see Eve Kosofsky Sedgwick's treatment of the looks exchanged between Marcher and an unidentified male fellow mourner, in "The Beast in the Closet: James and the Writing of Homosexual Panic," *Sex, Politics, and Science in the Nineteenth-Century Novel*, ed. Ruth Bernard Yeazell (Baltimore: Johns Hopkins University Press, 1986), 148–186. See especially 180–181.

18. For a valuable recent account of this detachment, see Mary Esteve, "A 'Gorgeous Neutrality': Stephen Crane's Documentary Anaesthetics," *ELH* 62 (1995): 663–689. Esteve presents an intellectual and aesthetic framework for Crane's detachment but threatens to accede too uncritically, I think, to what also must be read as defenses against threats of participation.

   Crane's entwined anxieties about vision and desire would seem to have a relation to the reform-minded religion of his upbringing. This upbringing would suggest that one can see (indeed, may have a duty to do so) if one doesn't desire. The converse is that if one does desire, one's vision must be sacrificed, a fear Crane may literalize. For a reading of Crane that consistently emphasizes his interest in religion, see R. W. Stallman, *Stephen Crane: A Biography* (New York: George Braziller, 1968).

19. Stallman suggests that Henry has a "guilt-wound" that has no physical sign. See "The Red Badge of Courage," *Stephen Crane*, 174.

20. David Halliburton has produced a broad, philosophically informed framing of

much of Crane's work. Though Halliburton valuably produces Crane as a serious and complex writer, a sense of the uncanny compulsive side of Crane's writing seems not to be accounted for in his book because of the breadth of its treatment. The compulsive side of Crane's writing surfaces with more force in studies that focus themselves on a particular complex in Crane, such as Fried's *Realism, Writing, and Disfiguration* or Seltzer's recent *Bodies and Machines.* The danger, of course, is that the compulsions thus unveiled are the writer's own, rather than Crane's. See David Halliburton, *The Color of the Sky: A Study of Stephen Crane* (New York: Cambridge University Press, 1989).

21. The significance of degeneracy in naturalist fiction has been valuably discussed by Sherwood Williams, who reminds us that premature degeneracy is commonly posited throughout the nineteenth century as a symptom of sexual excess. The prime example of such excess was masturbation, but the imagined scene of the transmission of masturbatory practice, as I have previously indicated, had homosexual implications as well. Williams places such degeneration in relation to the decadence of late nineteenth-century aestheticism embodied in a Wildean text such as *The Picture of Dorian Gray.* The connections Williams traces are less causal than associative, as a distinctive notion of "homosexual identity" becomes fused from the materials of late nineteenth-century culture. See Sherwood Williams, "The Rise of a New Degeneration: Decadence and Atavism in Vandover and the Brute," *ELH* 57 (1990): 709–736.

22. Amy Kaplan, "The Spectacle of War in Crane's Revision of History," in *New Essays on the Red Badge of Courage*, ed. Lee Clark Mitchell (New York: Cambridge University Press, 1986), 77–108. See p. 94.

23. Hershel Parker, "Getting Used To the 'Original Form' of *The Red Badge of Courage*," *New Essays on the Red Badge of Courage*, 25–47. See especially 27.

24. Stephen Crane, *The Correspondence of Stephen Crane*, vol. 1, ed. Stanley Wertheim and Paul Sorrentino (New York: Columbia University Press, 1988), 188.

25. Quoted by Wertheim and Sorrentino, *The Crane Log*, 91–92.

26. See Benfey's important discussion of these poems, *Double Life,* 123–139.

27. See Kaplan, "Spectacle of War," 100. Kaplan further argues that the novel demonstrates the limits of storytelling and of speech, and that as a substitute it "frames a new sense of the real as a highly mediated spectacle" (95).

28. See Stephen Crane, *The Red Badge of Courage: An Episode of the Civil War*, ed. and restored by Henry Binder (New York: Avon Books, 1987), 60. The Binder version of the novel was significantly altered by Crane for publication. It never was published in unaltered form, unlike the recently reconstructed first version of Sinclair's *The Jungle*, and there is little direct evidence that Crane's changes were a consequence of editorial censorship, which can only be inferred from the changes themselves. I prefer the Appleton version, as my argument here indicates. Inclusion of omitted material seems to weaken rather than strengthen the text by shifting the novel's focus from general structures and problems of masculine culture to the problem of Henry's individual and exaggerated vaingloriousness.

For arguments for the restored edition, see Binder's essay, "The *Red Badge of Courage Nobody Knows*" in the same volume, 123–175. In terms of its clear irony toward Henry, see 124–134. See also Parker, "Getting Used to the 'Original Form' of *The Red Badge of Courage*," in *New Essays on the Red Badge of Courage*, 25–47. For a pro-Appleton summary of arguments concerning different editions, see Michael Guemple's "A Case for the Appleton *Red Badge of Courage*," *Resources for American Literary Study* 21, no. 1 (1995): 43–57. See as well Donald Pizer's essay, "Self-Censorship and Textual Editing," *Textual Criticism and Literary Interpretation*, ed. Jerome J. McGann (Chicago: University of Chicago Press, 1985), 144–161.

Conclusion **Beyond Influence**

1. F. Scott Fitzgerald, *The Great Gatsby* (New York: Collier Books, 1991).
2. F. Scott Fitzgerald, "Dearest Scottie, July 18, 1940," in *The Letters of F. Scott Fitzgerald,* ed. Andrew Turnball (New York: Charles Scribner's Sons, 1963), 85–86.
3. Scott Fitzgerald, "Dearest Scottina, November 2, 1940," in *The Letters of F. Scott Fitzgerald, 97.*
4. F. Scott Fitzgerald, "Dear Max, ca. November 7, 1924," in *Dear Scott/Dear Max: The Fitzgerald-Perkins Correspondence,* ed. John Kuehl and Jackson R. Bryer (New York: Charles Scribner's Sons, 1971), 81–82. Matthew J. Bruccoli discusses the question of Trimalchio and the title in *Some Sort of Epic Grandeur: The Life of F. Scott Fitzgerald ,* rev. ed. (1991; reprint, New York: Carroll & Graf, 1991), 245.
5. F. Scott Fitzgerald, "To: Edmund Wilson, May 1925," in *F. Scott Fitzgerald: A Life in Letters*, ed. Matthew J. Bruccoli with the assistance of Judith S. Baughman (New York: Charles Scribner's Sons, 1994), 109. See also "To: H. L. Mencken, May 4, 1925," 111.
6. F. Scott Fitzgerald, "Dear John, April 7, 1934," in *The Letters of F. Scott Fitzgerald,* 363.
7. Bruccoli indicates that at the age of nine Fitzgerald suspected he was "a foundling of royal lineage." See Bruccoli, *Epic Grandeur,* 21.
8. Fitzgerald indicates this in a letter to Maxwell Perkins. See "Dear Max, June 18, 1924," in *Dear Scott/Dear Max, 72–73.*
9. See F. Scott Fitzgerald, "Absolution," in *All the Sad Young Men* (New York: Charles Scribner's Sons, 1926), 131.
10. F. Scott Fitzgerald, "To: Maxwell Perkins, September 10, 1924," in *The Correspondence of F. Scott Fitzgerald*, ed. Matthew J. Bruccoli and Margaret M. Duggan with the assistance of Susan Walker (New York: Random House, 1980), 146.
11. F. Scott Fitzgerald, "To: Maxwell Perkins, Mid-July 1922," in *Correspondence,* 112.
12. See Nancy Milford, *Zelda: A Biography* (New York: Harper & Row, 1970), 89. Milford details at some length the question of the use Fitzgerald's writing makes of his wife.
    The exact nature of this complicated relationship cannot be fathomed with

precision. That Fitzgerald appropriated the materials of his wife's life for his fiction is well known, and evidence suggests that he appropriated at least some of Zelda's writing from her now lost diary and letters as well. Neither can Zelda's own hunger for outlets for her creativity be doubted in the emotional chaos of their marriage, which casts this appropriation in an even less favorable light. It is difficult to judge, on the other hand, the extent to which Zelda, especially in the early years of their marriage, willingly participated in F. Scott's use of her writing or experience, or to judge the extent of her contributions of editorial advice to him as opposed to his contributions to her work. Bruccoli finds few signs of her writing on F. Scott's manuscripts, while he finds plentiful notations made by F. Scott on hers. There are different ways in which one can contribute to another's work, however, and even if, as Bruccoli concludes, "Zelda was not his collaborator," she still seems important in a variety of ways to his work. Given the underlying power dynamics of patriarchal culture, a suspicion that F. Scott's creative use of his wife was exploitative cannot be erased. Nor is the question of justice for Zelda finally a matter of who was the more gifted writer, the terms in which Jeffrey Meyers recently defends F. Scott. Even the rights of superior talent have limits. See Bruccoli, *Epic Grandeur,* 192–193. See Meyers, *Scott Fitzgerald: A Biography* (New York: HarperCollins, 1994), 222–223.

13. See F. Scott Fitzgerald, "Dear Max, ca. December 20, 1924," in *Dear Scott/Dear Max,* 88–90.

14. See F. Scott Fitzgerald, "Dear Max: ca. April 24, 1925," in *Dear Scott/Dear Max,* 101–102.

15. F. Scott Fitzgerald, "To: Marya Mannes, Postmarked October 21, 1925," in *Life in Letters,* 129–130.

16. F. Scott Fitzgerald, "Dear Max: Paris, May 1 [1925]," in *Dear Scott/Dear Max,* 103.

17. Frances Kerr gives a valuable account of Fitzgerald's anxieties about gender in the context of the broad gender anxieties of modernism. Working off of Mencken's comments that Gatsby is a "fat clown-woman" (408), she sees Gatsby himself as a feminine man, and argues that the novel expresses, in somewhat muddled form, Fitzgerald's sympathy with men who appear feminine to other men (424–425). I have a different perspective on Gatsby's function in the novel and its gender politics. See Kerr, "Feeling 'Half Feminine': Modernism and the Politics of Emotion in *The Great Gatsby,*" *American Literature* 68, no. 2 (June 1996): 405–431.

18. F. Scott Fitzgerald, "To: Van Wyck Brooks, Postmarked 13 June 1925," in *Correspondence,* 170.

19. For an account of Wharton's extensive charitable efforts during the war, see Shari Benstock, *No Gifts from Chance: A Biography of Edith Wharton* (New York: Charles Scribner's Sons, 1994) 301–349.

20. I am using Wharton here partly as a metonym for other feminine contributions to Fitzgerald's art, contributions that might include other women authors such as Willa Cather. In a letter to Cather, Fitzgerald expressed great admiration for *My Antonia, A Lost Lady, Paul's Case,* and *Scandal.* I do not believe Cather's influence on Fitzgerald was as direct or as threatening as Wharton's. For a posi-

tive argument for her influence, see Tom Quirk, "Fitzgerald and Cather: *The Great Gatsby*," *American Literature* 54, no. 4 (December 1982): 576–591.

Recently, Walter Benn Michaels has also argued for Cather's importance as an influence. See Michaels, *Our America: Nativism, Modernism, and Pluralism* (Durham: Duke University Press, 1995). See 46–47 and 156 n. 83. See also Fitzgerald, "To: Willa Cather, Late March/Early April 1925," in *Correspondence*, 155–156.

21. See Bruccoli, *Epic Grandeur*, 209.

22. F. Scott Fitzgerald, "To: Charles Scribner II, April 19, 1922," in *A Life in Letters*, 56–58.

23. See Robert Roulston for a general account of suggested sources over the years for *The Great Gatsby*. He concludes as a consequence of this survey that the novel is, in fact, "*sui generis.*" Roulston, "Something Borrowed, Something New: A Discussion of Literary Influences on *The Great Gatsby*," in *Critical Essays on F. Scott Fitzgerald's "The Great Gatsby*," ed. Scott Donaldson (Boston: G. K. Hall, 1984), 54–65.

24. Edith Wharton, *The House of Mirth* (New York: Charles Scribner's Sons, 1905).

25. For an account of Joseph Conrad's possible influence on *The Great Gatsby*, see James E. Miller, Jr., *The Fictional Technique of F. Scott Fitzgerald* (The Hague: Martinus Nijhoff, 1957), 79–81. Miller also argues for the importance of James Joyce and Willa Cather, 72–79.

26. While at the Gormers', Lily has several encounters with the whiny, pathetic George Dorsett, who feels victimized by his wife's affairs and whose marital difficulties help doom Lily. I am tempted to see Dorsett as a model for George Wilson, who adopts a similar pose of pathetic victim in *The Great Gatsby*, and whose marital difficulties doom Gatsby.

27. See Edith Wharton, "Three Letters About *The Great Gatsby*," in F. Scott Fitzgerald, *The Crack-Up*, ed. Edmund Wilson (New York: New Directions, 1945), 309.

28. Myrtle Wilson has the most vitality of any female character in the novel, but Fitzgerald makes her correspondingly crude and unsympathetic and generally uses class barriers to insulate her from questions of male creativity.

29. See Judith Fetterley, "*The Great Gatsby*: Fitzgerald's *Droit de Seigneur*," in *The Resisting Reader: A Feminist Approach to American Fiction* (Bloomington: Indiana University Press, 1978), 72–100. See especially 72–79.

30. See, for example, Keith Fraser's essay "Another Reading of *The Great Gatsby*," in *Modern Critical Interpretations of "The Great Gatsby*," ed. Harold Bloom (New York: Chelsea House, 1986). Fraser's valuable examination of homoeroticism in the novel was first published in 1979. See Kerr, "Feeling 'Half Feminine,'" 414–421. See also Bryan R. Washington, "The Daisy Chain: *The Great Gatsby* and *Daisy Miller* or the Politics of Privacy," in *The Politics of Exile: Ideology in Henry James, F. Scott Fitzgerald, and James Baldwin* (Boston: Northeastern University Press, 1995), 35–54.

31. Michaels has recently argued that a broad anxiety concerning miscegenation in U.S. culture structures *The Great Gatsby*: Daisy cannot marry Gatsby not simply because he was poor, but because of the ethnicity implied by his name, James

Gatz. Michaels goes on to argue in terms of other texts that the anxiety generated by the potential misalliances of women in American literature generates homosexuality and incest as an antidote. To Michaels, "[t]he homosexual family and the incestuous family thus emerge as parallel technologies in the effort to prevent half-breeds" (49). Michaels's argument often seems curiously inattentive to the ease with which heterosexual marriage and reproduction cement and serve class and race stability in the United States and solve, as a consequence, the transgressive possibilities it generates. It may be the case that some same-sex relationships are free from the anxieties concerning miscegenation that apply to heterosexuality, but I am not convinced that the former should be attributed to the displacement of the latter given the depth and virulence of twentieth-century homophobia. I would not, then, use Michaels's paradigm to account for the homoerotic energies of *The Great Gatsby*. To be fair, *The Great Gatsby* is only one of a handful of texts Michaels uses to construct his argument, and he does not address, so far as I can see, its homoerotic energies. I am thus addressing an extension of his argument that he does not explicitly make, but one I presume his readers will. See Michaels, *Our America*, 23–52.

32. See Kerr, "Feeling 'Half Feminine,'" 421–422.

33. Edith Wharton, *The Glimpses of the Moon* (New York: D. Appleton, 1922).

34. Gatsby's Oxford claims also have some justification, but fail to confer redeeming value upon him. He ends up at Oxford because of a mistake, despite trying "frantically to get home" (158).

35. Sigmund Freud, *Beyond the Pleasure Principle*, ed. and trans. James Strachey (New York: W. W. Norton, 1961). The first German edition appears in 1920; the first English translation in 1922 (xvii). *Gatsby* is published in 1925.

36. Sandor Ferenczi, Karl Abraham, Ernst Simmel, and Ernest Jones, *Psychoanalysis and the War Neuroses,* International Psychoanalytic Library, no. 2 (Vienna: The International Psychoanalytical Press, 1921).

37. For a sympathetic account of Freud's openness to different configurations of desire, see Henry Abelove's essay "Freud, Male Homosexuality, and the Americans," in *The Lesbian and Gay Studies Reader*, ed. Henry Abelove, Michèle Aina Barale, and David M. Halperin (New York: Routledge, 1993), 381–393. To Abelove, the psychoanalytic tendency to pathologize homosexuality is an American contrivance, one that cuts across the grain of Freud's own thinking.

38. See Plato, *Plato's Erotic Dialogues*, trans. William S. Cobb (Albany: State University of New York Press, 1993), 15–59. For the passage alluded to by Freud, see 29–30.

39. Freud's simplifying use of this fable is repeated in *Three Essays on Sexuality*, where he suggests that "the popular view of the sexual instinct is beautifully reflected in the poetic fable which tells how the original human beings were cut up into two halves—man and woman—and how these are always striving to unite again in love." This beautiful fable serves as an introduction, of course, to Freud's complex discussion of "inversion," which renders impossible any such simplified vision of human sexuality. Even here, however, a dialectical relation in Freud between a desire to acknowledge the multiple possibilities of experience and a

desire for formal order are evident. In *Three Essays* arguably the former pre-
vails; in *Beyond the Pleasure Principle*, the latter. See Sigmund Freud, *Three
Essays on the Theory of Sexuality*, trans. and rev. by James Strachey (New York:
Basic Books, 1975), 2.

40. I rely for my account of these relations on Peter Gay's biography, *Freud: A Life
for Our Time* (New York: Anchor Books, 1988). See especially 267–292.

41. See Aldo Carotenuto, "Letters from Sigmund Freud to Sabina Spielrein," in *A
Secret Symmetry: Sabina Spielrein Between Jung and Freud*, trans. Arno
Pomerans, John Shepley, and Krishna Winston (New York: Pantheon Books,
1982), 119. Carotenuto gives a detailed interpretation of the relations between
Freud, Jung, and Spielrein, and provides transcripts of the letters between them.

42. See Wayne Kostenbaum, "Privileging the Anus: Anna O. and the Collaborative
Origin of Psychoanalysis," in *Double Talk: The Erotics of Male Literary Collaboration* (New York: Routledge, 1989), 17–42. See especially 18.

43. See Madelon Sprengnether, *The Spectral Mother: Freud, Feminism, and Psychoanalysis* (Ithaca: Cornell University Press, 1990), 126–127. Sprengnether also
discusses the interrelations of the thought of Bachofen, Freud, and Jung, 86–105.

44. Sprengnether, *The Spectral Mother*, 96–101.

45. As Sprengnether suggests, her "between men" positioning suggests she mediates the homoerotic relations of Freud and Jung in the manner suggested by Eve
Kosofsky Sedgwick in *Between Men*. See Sprengnether, *The Spectral Mother*,
125–126 n. 3.

For a detailed and valuable account of the interrelations of Freud, Jung, and
Speilrein, see John Kerr, "Beyond the Pleasure Principle and Back Again: Freud,
Jung, and Sabina Spielrein," in *Freud: Appraisals and Reappraisals*, ed. Paul E.
Stepansky (New York: Analytic Press, 1988), 3–79. Kerr believes that Speilrein
in general "played a crucial role in the evolution of the Freud-Jung relationship"
(4), and suggests that specifically in terms of *Beyond the Pleasure Principle*,
Speilrein mediated relations between Freud and Jung through their complex mu-
tual absorption and misreading of her work.

46. Jacques Derrida provides an instructive account of the multiple interpretive possibilities of the fort/da episode, possibilities that call into question the authority
of Freud's own preferred reading of his nephew's game. See Derrida, "Coming
into One's Own," trans. James Hulbert, in *Psychoanalysis and the Question of
the Text: Selected Papers from the English Institute, 1976–1977*, new series no.
2, ed. Geoffrey H. Harman (Baltimore: Johns Hopkins University Press, 1978),
114–148.

47. Peter Brooks suggests that Freud takes pleasure in his status as "poet and phi-
losopher" in *Beyond the Pleasure Principle*, or by implication as the author of
what Brooks sees as his "human masterplot." He also usefully cites Freud's comment in *New Introductory Lectures* that "the theory of the instincts is so to say
our mythology. Instincts are mythical entities, magnificent in their indefinite-
ness." Freud, in other words, self-consciously imagines rather than discovers the
structural principles he describes, and imagines them, I would argue, as a form
of authorial transcendence of the complex reality of sex/gender relations in which

he was involved at the time. See Peter Brooks, "Freud's Masterplot: A Model for Narrative," in *Reading for the Plot: Design and Intention in Narrative* (New York: Vintage Books, 1985), 90–112. See especially 106.

48. See, for example, Elisabeth Bronfen, "The Lady Vanishes: The Death of Sophie Freud-Halberstadt (1920) and Chapter Two of *Beyond the Pleasure Principle* (Freud)," in *Over Her Dead Body: Death, Femininity, and the Aesthetic* (New York: Routledge, 1992), 15–38. See as well Gay, *Freud: A Life for Our Time,* 394–395.

INDEX

Abelove, Henry, 246n37
Abraham, Karl, 246n36
absence, in Freud, 204–205
advice books, in the 19th century, 49
aestheticism and degeneration, 242n21
Aldrich, Robert, 89
Allan, John, 66, 225n4
ambiguity, sex/gender, in Fitzgerald, 201–202
ambition, and Poe, 66, 225n5
Anderson, Quentin, 141
androgyny, 67, 73, 217–218n58
"Anna O." [pseud.], 207
anxiety: authorial, in James, 144; cultural, 3, 237n1; over homoerotic desire, in James, 90; over miscegenation, 245–246n31; about perversion, 127–128
appropriation of the feminine, 67, 75; in Fitzgerald, 200; in Freud, 207; in Hawthorne, 58; in Poe, 73
Armstrong, Nancy, 217n58
art: and femininity, 26; in James, 30–31; vs. mass culture, 22
Auerbach, Jonathan, 217n52, 237n3
authenticity: in Crane, 175; in Fitzgerald, 204
author, 216–217n51; self-making, 1–4; and writer, 31
authorial identity, in Poe, 226n8
authoring, ideal, in Hawthorne, 63
authority: and authorship, 29, 83–84, 216–217n51; consolidation of, 148; creation of, in James, 148; crisis of,

215n42; failed, 141; in heterosexual narratives, 144; intellectual, in Sinclair, 165; for James, 87, 148; in James, The Ambassadors, 121, 124, 234n18; in James, The American, 94, 121, 234n18; in James, Roderick Hudson, 87, 94; literary, in James, 5, 94; paternal, 141; in Poe, 67; for Sinclair, 166; in U.S. literature, 216n50. See also cultural authority; feminine authority; masculine authority; narrative authority
authors. See men writers; women writers; writers and publishers
authorship, 1–2; construction of, 192; desire for, 22–23; in Hawthorne, 37–40; in James, 127, 130; and masculinity, 130; for Sinclair, 165. See also writing

Bachofen, Johann Jakob, Das Mutterrecht, 208
Banta, Martha, 231nn11, 16
Barthes, Roland, 25, 217n54
Baym, Nina, 18, 57, 211nn1, 2
beauty, and masculine power, 148
Beecher, Henry Ward, Addresses to Young Men, 10–11
Beer, Thomas 175, 239n2, 240nn5, 6, 8
Benfey, Christopher, 240n9, 242n26
Benstock, Shari, 244n19
Berlant, Lauren, 220n5, 224–225n42, 225n44

Berryman, John, 174, 240nn5, 6
Bersani, Leo, 141, 217n57, 218n61, 234n18
Beveridge, Alfred J., *The Young Man and the World,* 9, 10, 13
Binder, Henry, 242–243n28
biography, of authors, 4
Bledstein, Burton J., 212n13
Blumin, Stuart M., 6n3, 212n13, 212–213n16
bodily anxieties: in Crane, 171; in the 19th century, 49; in Sinclair, 160–162
body: commodification of, 59; erotic, 48; and identity, 49; as an interpretive problem, in Hawthorne, 47–50; and mind, in Graham and Hawthorne, 49–51, 54; in naturalism, 238–239n10; and perception, in Crane, 184; and perception, in James, 232n17. *See also* female body; male body
Bonaparte, Marie, 72, 227–228n13
Boone, Joseph, 219n62
Boyd, Thomas, 194
"boylife" (Rotundo), 213–214n26
Breuer, Josef, 207
Brodhead, Richard, 83
Bronfen, Elisabeth, 248n48
Brooks, Peter, 247–248n47
Brown, Gillian, 12, 217n58, 232n29
Bruccoli, Matthew J., 243nn4, 7, 243–244n12
business, in James, *The Ambassadors,* 234n13. *See also* commerce
Butler, Judith, 223n28, 227n9, 234n23, 235n25

Cady, Edwin H., 175
capitalism, industrial, 12
capitalist culture, 11, 179
Carotenuto, Aldo, 247n41
Cary, Richard, 225n3
Cather, Willa, 244–245n20, 245n25
chaos, reactions to, 208; in Crane, 177; in Sinclair, 160
"character." *See* masculine "character"
character, decentering of, in James, 141
Charvat, William, 211n2
Chauncey, George, *Gay New York,* 174, 218n60

Cherniavsky, Eve, 228–229n18, 229n22
chiasmus, in James, 236n44
child rearing, in the 19th century, 12, 14
class and sensuality, in Crane, 185
Clendenning, John, 240nn5, 6
commerce: devaluation of, 37; and the feminine, 20–21, 126; in Hawthorne, 37–38; and individualism, 232n29; in James, 117; and religion, 106
commodification: of the body, 59; of the feminine, in Poe, 69; in Hawthorne, 36; and "splitting," 59; of women, 75, 229n21
competition: and eroticism, in Poe, 79; and masculinity, in James, 117
composition: narratives of, 23; and observation, in Crane, 240n9
compulsions, in Crane, 241–242n20
Conrad, Joseph, 196, 245n25
containment of homoeroticism, in Freud, 206–208
Cooper, James Fenimore, *The Pathfinder,* 48
Cott, Nancy, 214n29
Crane, Stephen, 158, 237n3, 239n2; as author, 187–188; *The Black Riders and Other Lines,* 188; "An Experiment in Misery," 184, 185; "Four Men in a Cave," 186; *George's Mother,* 175–176, 183–184; "A Ghoul's Accountant," 186; *Maggie: A Girl of the Streets,* 175, 240n9; "The Octopush," 187; and poverty, 188; *The Red Badge of Courage,* 4, 171–172, 176–182, 187–190, 242–243n28; and religion, 241n18; and sexuality, 172–174; and writing, 241–242n20
Creech, James, 221n18
crisis: of authority, 87, 157; of authorship, in Hawthorne, 38; of homosexual and heterosexual, in Hawthorne, 53; of masculinity, 38, 158; of midcomposition, 23–25, 86
criticism, 226n8
cross-dressing, 228n15
"crosses" and "crossing" in James, 148–155

cultural anxiety, 3, 237n1
cultural authority, 216–217n51, 226n6;
of naturalism, 158; of women, 208;
of the writer, 1, 22–23, 216–217n51
cultural castration of women, 229n19
cultural "feminine," 216n44
cultural narratives, 2
culture, U.S., at turn of the century, 1
Cummins, Maria, *The Lamplighter,* 14

Dauber, Kenneth, 216n50, 216–217n51
Davidson, Cathy, 18
Davis, Linda H., 240n5
Davis, Richard Harding, 14–15
Davis, Robert H., 172
death, in Crane, 185
decay and disintegration, in Hawthorne,
37–38
decentering: of character, in James,
141; of consciousness, in Sinclair,
164; of identity, in James, 149
degeneracy, in Crane, 184
degeneration and aestheticism, 242n21
DeGruson, Gene, 238n4
de Man, Paul, 217n54
D'Emilio, John, 222n23
denial and avoidance, in James, 155
Derrick, Scott, 219n66, 219n1, 229n20,
232n18, 236n43, 237n1
Derrida, Jacques, 226n8, 227n13,
247n46
desire: and competition, in James, 117;
and disintegration, in Crane, 179; in
Fitzgerald, 200–201, 203; and homophobia, 44–53; homosexual sources
of, 28; and identification, 28, 36,
205, 219n65, 233–234n11, 246n37;
in James, 84, 96–97, 138–140, 155;
in Sinclair, 170; transgressive, 144;
and vision, 179, 241nn17, 18
detachment, 203, 241n18
deviance, 127–128
Diehl, Joanne Feit, 228n16
difference, 120; and pleasure, 138
disintegration: and desire, in Crane,
179; and emotion, in Hawthorne,
52, 223n29; and the homoerotic,
202; in Hawthorne, 37–38; in
James, 140; of masculinity, 37, 140,
169; in Sinclair, 169

displacements: in Crane, 182–185; in
James, 143
disruption: and the homoerotic, 55; of
masculine authority, in Sinclair, 170
"dodges," in James, *The Wings of the
Dove,* 145
Dollimore, Jonathan, *Sexual Dissidence,* 28, 127, 233n10, 233–
234n11
domestic, in Hawthorne, 40–42, 220–
221n9, 221n11
domestic ideology, effects of, 157
"domestic individualism" (Brown), 12
domesticity, in the 19th century, 12,
106, 232n29
Dostoyevsky, Fyodor, *The Brothers
Karamazov,* 192–193
doubling, 79–80. *See also* identification; "splitting"
Douglas, Ann, 214n32
Dubbert, Joe, 214n28, 237n1
Dutoit, Ulysse, 217n57

Eakin, John Paul, 30, 236n43
"ease": in James, *The Ambassadors,*
109–110, 116, 119, 123; in James,
The American, 91, 94–95, 103, 107,
123; threats to, 103. *See also*
masculine ease
Edel, Leon, 153, 233n9, 236n43
Ehrlich, Gloria, 57, 222n20
Eliot, George, 16, 215n36
Ellmann, Richard, 230n5
Elmer, Jonathan, 226nn6, 8
Emerson, Ralph Waldo, 120, 213n25,
234n15; feminine influences on, 14;
on Graham, 222–223n25
emotion: and containment, 208; in
Sinclair, 162–164, 170
emulative and erotic desires, 28–29
endings for narrative, 167; in James,
24–25; in Sinclair, 167
energy, feminine, in Hawthorne, 39
entrapment, in Sinclair, 162–164
envious gaze, 117, 119
erotic, disruptive power of, 48; in
James, 111
erotic desire: and emulative desire, 28–
29; in Fitzgerald, 203; in Sinclair,
170

eroticism: in Hawthorne, 36; and
  masculinity, 28, 51; in Poe, 79; vs.
  rationality, 51
erotic triangle, in Hawthorne, *The
  Scarlet Letter,* 44
erotophobia in the 19th century, 48, 51
Esteve, Mary, 241n18
ethnicity and nature, 237–238n2

family: for Emerson, 213n25; fear of,
  in Sinclair, 160; in Hawthorne,
  214n30; influences, 11–12; in
  James, 235–236n35
"family romance," for Fitzgerald, 193
fear: in Crane, 176, 185; in Sinclair,
  160, 162–163
feeling and thought, 56, 58, 71. *See
  also* body: and mind
Feinstein, Howard M., 212n11
female body: in Poe, 72; in Sinclair,
  160–161
female power and male identity, 166–
  167
feminine: and commerce, 126;
  commodification of, 69; cultural,
  216n44; in Fitzgerald, 199–201; in
  Hawthorne, 41; and interiority, 217–
  218n58; and male authority, 71,
  157–158, 217–218n58; in Poe, 68–
  69. *See also* appropriation of the
  feminine
feminine authority, in James, 102
feminine identifications, 26, 167
feminine influence, 2, 4; in childhood,
  13; on Fitzgerald, 193, 194, 200–
  201, 244–245n20; on Freud, 207–
  209; on Sinclair, 166
feminine other, in James, 105, 130
femininity, 2; and art, 26; in Freud, 207;
  in James, 123; in male culture, 27,
  68–70; within masculine authority,
  in Sinclair, 169–170; and passion, in
  Hawthorne, 56; in Poe, 68–70, 72;
  as threat, 158
feminism, and Poe, 227n9
feminist fetishism, 228–229n18
feminization: and authorship, 7, 26, 39;
  covering, 71; in Crane, 179–180; in
  Hawthorne, 39; in James, 232n25;
  in Poe, 74; productive, 223n31; in

Sinclair, 165
Ferenczi, Sandor, 206, 246n36
Ferguson, Frances, 217n58
Fern, Fanny, 42
fetishism, 74–75, 228–229n18
Fetterley, Judith, 200
fiction, for James, 133
Fiedler, Leslie, *Love and Death in the
  American Novel,* 28, 214n32, 218–
  219n62
Fitzgerald, F. Scott: "Absolution," 193;
  and audience, 193–194; *The
  Beautiful and the Damned,* 193; and
  feminine sources, 193, 194, 244–
  245n20; *The Great Gatsby,* 4, 192–
  209; influences on, 192–200, 203,
  244–245n20, 245n23, 245–246n31;
  letters, 192–194, 244–245n20
Fitzgerald, Zelda, 193, 243–244n12
Fliess, Wilhelm, 206, 207
Forster, E. M., *Aspects of the Novel,*
  117
"fort/da" episode, in Freud, 204–205,
  247n46
Foucault, Michel, 217n54
Fowler, O. S., 13
Fraser, Keith, 245n30
Freedman, Estelle B., 222n23
Freedman, Jonathan, 230n5
Fried, Michael, 177, 216n50, 241n16,
  241–242n20
Freud, Sigmund, 204–208, 219n65;
  Beyond the Pleasure Principle,
  204–205, 207–209, 247–248n47; on
  body, 49; on desire, 29, 246n37; and
  feminine influence, 207–209; on
  fetishism, 75; fort/da episode,
  247n46; and homosexuality, 206–
  207; and Jung, 247n41; letters, 206,
  207, 247n41; on the maternal,
  229n19; narrative of male self-
  construction, 191; *New Introductory
  Lectures,* 247–448n47; *On Creativity . . . ,* 232n22; *Three Essays
  on . . . Sexuality,* 246–247n39; on
  uncanniness, 100
Freudianism in literature, 192
Frothingham, Octavius Brooks, 15

Garber, Marjorie, 228n15

Garland, Hamlin, 188
Gay, Peter, 206, 248n48
gender: and commodification, 75; discourse of, in the 19th century, 28, 67; and literature, in Hawthorne, 57; in Poe, 74, 228n14; and sexuality, 1–4, 83–84, 191, 223n28
gender anxieties, and modernism, 244n17
gender politics, in Poe, 67, 226n8
generativity, feminine, 20
genius, 18
genre and gender, 5
Gilbert, Sandra M., 214n31, 215n37
Gilkes, Lilian B., 240n10
Gilmore, Michael T., 211n2, 224n32
Goodrich, Samuel, 17–18, 19–20
Graham, Sylvester, *A Lecture to Young Men*, 49–52, 222–223n25
Green, Carol Hurd, 240n10
Gubar, Susan, 214n31, 215n37
Guemple, Michael, 242–243n28
guilt, in Crane, 183
gynophobia, in Sinclair, 160–161

Habegger, Alfred, 16–17, 215n35, 235nn31, 34
Haight, Gordon S., 234n13
Hall, G. Stanley, *Adolescence*, 9, 212n14
Halliburton, David, 241–242n20
Haralson, Eric, 232n17
Harris, Leon, 162
Haskell, Thomas L., 215n42
Hawthorne, Ebe, 57, 224n34
Hawthorne, Elizabeth, 57, 224n33
Hawthorne, Julian, 57
Hawthorne, Nathaniel, 7, 13, 19, 36–37, 190, 216n44; domestic life of, 219n64, 220–221n9; feminine influences on, 14, 41, 220n8; fiction, 219n65; "Mrs. Hutchinson," 42–43, 221n12; and politics, 43, 227n9; "A Rill for the Town Pump," 38, 220n5; *The Scarlet Letter*, 3, 27, 35–65, 71, 176, 219n1, 219–220n2; sexual life of, 222–223n25; and women, 42, 56–58, 221n12; youth of, 46, 57
Hawthorne, Sophia, 57–58

Hawthorne, Una, 41, 220n8, 220–221n9
health writers, in the 19th century, 50
Herbert, T. Walter, 51, 219n64, 220–221n9, 221n15, 222–223n25
heterosexuality: in Freud, 206; and gender, 223n28; and homosexuality, in James, 141–144; and narrative, 51, 145, 223n28; power of, in James, 123, 155
heterosexual male identity, in James, 117, 119
heterosexual paradigm, in James, *The American*, 94
heterosexual plot: in Fitzgerald, 199; in Hawthorne, 53, 55; in James, 91, 109–116, 128–132, 143–144; in Sinclair, 169–170
Hoffman, Daniel, 225nn1, 4
Holland, Laurence, 141
Homer, 194
homoerotic: in Crane, 175; and disintegration, 55, 201–202; in James, 109–110, 121; in the 19th-century novel, 53; in Poe, 79
homoerotic desire, 27–30, 172; in Fitzgerald, 201; in James, 89–90, 128, 231n9; vision, and death, 241n17
homoeroticism: and aesthetics, 88–89; in Crane, 177, 189; in fiction and biography, 4; in Fitzgerald, 199–203, 245n30; and Freud, 207; within heterosexual narrative, 199–203; and identity, in Hawthorne, 36; in James, 92, 110–119; and masculinity, 203; and writing, 177
homophobia: and desire, 44–53; and homosexuality, at turn of the century, 157; in the 19th century, 51; in the 20th century, 245–246n31
homosexual: and heterosexual narratives, in James, 141–143; and the homosocial, 233n10; identities, 236n37; vs. normative masculinity, 157; subculture, in New York, 174
homosexuality: in Crane, 183; and criticism, 223n30; as developmental failure, 112, 218–219n62, 246n37; and disruption, 52, 223n29; and

homosexuality (*continued*)
  heterosexuality, in James, 141–144;
  and homophobia, in the U.S., 44,
  157, 246n37; in James, 112, 231n10;
  marginalization of, 223n29; and
  masculinity, in Freud, 207; and
  masturbation, 50; and narcissism,
  219n65, 223n27; in 19th-century
  texts, 27, 53, 218n59; unspeakable,
  172
"homosexuality" of the sociocultural
  order (Irigaray), 79
"homosexual panic" (Sedgwick),
  219n63
Howells, W. D., 7, 144, 188
Huneker, James, 173

Ian, Marcia, 139, 228–229n18, 235n33
identification: and desire, 36, 205,
  219n65, 233–234n11; and femininity, in Crane, 181; in James, 119–
  120; as "masculine" trait, 70; in
  Poe, 79
identity: and body, 49; decentered, 149;
  and homoeroticism, in Hawthorne,
  36; in James, 140, 149; of writer,
  24. *See also* masculine identity
impressionism, in Crane, 237n3
individualism, and domesticity, 232n29
industrial capitalism, 12
influence. *See* feminine influence
interiority, and the feminine, 217–
  218n58
intuition, in Poe, 71
Irigaray, Luce, *This Sex Which Is Not
  One*, 59, 79, 229n21
irony, in Crane, 190
Irwin, John T., 219–220n2, 220nn4, 7,
  225n1, 226n8

Jackson, Chuck, 221–222n19
James, Henry, 3, 23–25, 30, 83–155,
  190, 231nn12, 16, 236n38; *The
  Ambassadors*, 84, 108–127, 130,
  131, 148, 178, 233n2; *The American*, 84, 91–107, 116, 121, 123,
  130, 137, 148, 232n23; *The
  American Scene*, 133; *Autobiography*, 153; "The Beast in the Jungle,"
  144, 236n38; *The Bostonians*, 16;

  essays, 133, 235n31; *Hawthorne*,
  109; and homosexuality, 143;
  influences on, 15–16, 30; notebooks, 149–154, Figs. 1, 2, 3; *Notes
  of a Son and Brother*, 8; and politics,
  235n31, 236n38; *Roderick Hudson*,
  23–24, 84, 85–91, 116, 117, 119,
  121, 126, 145–147, 148, 234n16; *A
  Small Boy and Others*, 29–31, 120,
  219n66; *The Spoils of Poynton*, 24–
  25; *The Wings of the Dove*, 84, 108–
  109, 127, 149, 155, 176, 233n2;
  writings, 127–149, 155, 231n16,
  233n3, 235n31, 236n38
James, Mary, 15
James, William, 212n11
Jay, Gregory, 216n50
Jehlen, Myra, 217–218n58
Johnson, Barbara, 226n8
Jones, Ernest, 206, 246n36
Jordan, Cynthia, 226n8, 227n9,
  228n14, 229n23
Jung, Carl, 206–207, 247n41

Kaplan, Amy, 187, 190, 242n27
Kaplan, Fred, 233n8
Karcher, Carolyn, 131
Kasson, John F., 211n2, 215n42
Kaston, Carren, 127, 233nn3, 7,
  234nn18, 20
Kerr, Frances, 202, 244n17, 245n30
Klein, Melanie, 229n20
Kostenbaum, Wayne, 207

Lacan, Jacques, 226n8, 227–228n13
lack, woman as, 75
Lang, Amy Schrager, 63, 221n12,
  224nn38, 40
language vs. "lack," 214n31
law and masculinity, 62
leisure and childhood, 96
Leverenz, David, 212n13, 222n20,
  226n8
Lewis, Anna Robinson, 66, 225n3
literary criticism, 226n8
literary thinking, in masculine culture,
  70
literature: and gender, 2, 57; as a
  vocation, 11
London, Jack, 165–166

Lowell, James Russell, 20

McWhirter, David, 233n2
male authoring, 3
male authority. *See* masculine authority
male body, in Crane, 184–186
male culture, 3, 10, 28, 157, 213–
214n26; in James, 93; in Poe, 68–70
male identity, 119; and female power,
166–167, 228–229n18; in Sinclair,
166–167, 239n14
male intellectual authority, in Sinclair,
165, 168–169
male masochism, 190, 223n31
male rationality, 51
manhood, paradigms of, in Crane, 190
Mann, Horace, 43
Mannes, Marya, 194
Manning, Robert, 46
marks (in writing), in James, 149–154
Martin, Robert K., 219–220n2, 231n9
masculine authority: and the feminine,
157–158, 169–170; in James, 131–
132; and narrative, 29, 223n31; in
Poe, 67, 78; psychoanalytical
defense, 208; in Sinclair, 165–169;
threats to, 171; through transcendence, 191; and women, 235n31
masculine "character," 12
masculine creativity, in Poe, 72
masculine development, cultural
narrative of, 1–2
masculine ease, defenses of, in James,
122–123
masculine identity, 2; and adolescence,
9; construction of, 33; in Crane,
190; and femininity, 27; in
Hawthorne, 40, 63; in James, 122,
123, 140; in Poe, 226n8; and
women, 60
masculine narrative, 237n3
masculine power: consolidation of,
148; construction of, 227–228n13
masculine self-construction, 1–4, 33,
133, 137
masculine writing, 3
masculinity: alienation from, in
Hawthorne, 39–40, 43; of androgyny, 73; and art, 11, 126; as
authority, in Hawthorne, 62–63; and

authorship, in James, 131; and body,
in James, 232n17; and commerce,
126; crisis of, 158; construction of,
in the 19th century, 11, 13–14, 33,
227n9; development of, 213–
214n26; and eroticism, 51, 203; in
Fitzgerald, 203; and Freud, 204–
205; in Hawthorne, 35, 39–40, 43,
62–63, 220n4; in James, 94, 105–
107, 116, 125; and law, 62, 224–
225n42; of literature, 2; and military
life, 204; self-constructed, 171; in
Sinclair, 167, 239n14; threats to, 2,
157; and violence, 60–61
masculinization, in U.S. culture, 133,
157
masochism, 190, 223n31
mass culture: and art, 22; feminine, 16–
18
masturbation, and homosexuality, 50
maternal: denied, in Hawthorne, 55;
romance of, in James, 122
maternal influence, 74, 125
"maternal phallus" (Cherniavsky), 228–
229n18
maternal power, in Poe, 70
maternal voice, 228–229n18
maternal women, in Sinclair, 160
maternity, idealized, 15
mechanization, in Crane, 178
medical writers, in the 19th century, 49,
222n23
Mellow, James R., 46, 222n20
Melville, Herman, *Pierre,* 16
memory, consolidation of, in James,
124
Mencken, H. L., 192, 244n17
men writers, and the feminine, 2,
214n30, 217–218n58
Meyers, Jeffrey, 243–244n12
Michaels, Walter Benn, 237n3, 244–
245n20, 245–246n31
midcompositional space for expression,
27, 36
middle-class culture, 8–9, 43, 212n13,
214n27
midnarrative crisis, 23–25, 27, 86
Milford, Nancy, 243–244n12
Miller, D. A., 218n59
Miller, Edwin Haviland, 221n16

Miller, James E., Jr., 245n25
Miller, Perry, 7
Milliman, Craig A., 230n4, 234n16
mind and body, in Graham and
Hawthorne, 49–51, 54
miscegenation, anxieties about, 245–
246n31
misogynist violence, in Poe, 67
Mitchell, Lee Clark, 237n3
mobility of desire, in James, 155
modernism, 244n17
Moon, Michael, 89, 128, 139, 176
Morrison, Paul, 218n59, 223n28
mother, role of, 11–12, 14, 75, 228–
229n18
Murtaugh, Daniel J., 230–231n8

Nagel, James, 237n3
narcissism, and homosexuality, 223n27
narrative: of composition, 23; in
Fitzgerald, 200–201; and heterosexuality, 51, 141–143, 223n28; in
James, 141–143; linear, 217n57,
218n61; of male self-construction,
191; and masculine authority,
223n31; needs of, 53, 55, 86, 187–
188; reader-constructed, 241n14;
and sexuality, 218n61
narrative authority, in Crane, 189
narrative ease, in James, 109–110
narrative foreshortening, 87
narrative rupture, in Crane, 183–184,
186, 187, 188
narrative voice, in James, 141
naturalism, 39, 158, 216n48, 220n6,
237n3, 238nn3, 8, 238–239n10; in
Wharton, *The House of Mirth,* 196,
200
nature, in Sinclair, *The Jungle,* 159–
161, 237–238n2
nature-culture opposition, 238–239n10
Newfield, Christopher, 213n25,
219n65, 223n31
Nissenbaum, Stephen, 222–223n25
"nonnarratable" (Miller), 218n59,
241n14. *See also* unspeakable
normative masculinity, 99, 157; in
James, 141–143; in Sinclair, 169
Norris, Frank, *The Octopus,* 220n6
Norrman, Ralf, 236–237n44

observation and composition, in Crane,
240n9
odor, in Sinclair, *The Jungle,* 160
oedipal structures, in James, 99, 121
Olin-Ammentorp, Julie, 131
order, in Fitzgerald and Freud, 208
Osgood, Frances Sargent, 66
"other" for masculine identity, in
James, 105, 140

Pappenheim, Bertha, 207
Parker, Hershel, 188, 242–243n28
passion and femininity, in Hawthorne,
52, 56
Pater, Walter, *The Renaissance,* 88–89,
136, 230n5
paternity, in James, 121, 141
patrilineal generation, fantasy of, 63,
225n43
Patterson, Mark, 215n42, 216n50
Peabody, Sophia, 57–58; "Cuba
Journal," 57
perception, in Crane, 184–185
Perkins, Maxwell, 192, 193, 194
Person, Leland S., Jr., 123–124, 219–
220n2, 224n41, 227n9
perversion, anxiety about, 127–128
Pfister, Joel, 214n30, 219n65, 221nn11,
12, 222–223n25, 224n32
"phallic mother" (Ian), 228–229n18
Phelps, Elizabeth Stuart, *The Story of
Avis,* 6
Pizer, Donald, 242–243n28
Plato, *The Symposium,* 206
plot: of death and disaster, 90; of
masculine self-making, 137. *See
also* heterosexual plot
Poe, Edgar Allan: detective stories, 67,
77–78; "Ligeia," 75–78; "The
Murders in the Rue Morgue," 67,
69, 77, 78; "The Mystery of Marie
Roget," 69–70, 226n8, 227n10;
"The Purloined Letter," 3, 66, 67,
70–81, 226n8, 227n11; and women,
66, 225n1, 227n9
Poirier, Richard, 17, 231n16, 234n18
popular literature, 18–19
Porter, Carolyn, 103, 232n25
poststructuralism, 217n54
poverty and sensuality, in Crane, 184–

185, 188
power: and beauty, 148; creation of, in James, 121; female, 166–167; of paternity, in James, 141; and pleasure, 139, 235n33
Prescott, W. H., feminine influences, 15
primal scene: in James, *The Ambassadors,* 123; in James, *The American,* 99, 232n20
productivity, in James, 235–236n35
projection, in Hawthorne, 54
psychoanalysis and literature, 191–192
"psychological," in Hawthorne, 224n32
public space, in Hawthorne, 224n32
publishers, in the 19th century, 5–6

queer desires. *See* homoerotic desire
queerness. *See* homosexuality
Quirk, Tom, 224–245n20

Rachman, Stephen, 226n6
rape: in Hawthorne, 46, 222n20; metaphorical, in Crane, 183
rationality vs. eroticism, 49–52. *See also* thought and feeling
readership: for Crane, 188; for Fitzgerald, 193–194
real as spectacle, in Crane, 242n27
realism, 124–125, 131
religion, in James, 105–106
repetitions: in James, 97–98; in Sinclair, 164
repression, in James, 155
rhetoric of the unspeakable, in James, 143
Riddel, Joseph, 226n6
Riley, James Whitcombe, 15
Ripley, George, 15
Roe, E. P., 15
romance of the maternal, in James, 122
romanticism, in Fitzgerald, 196
Romero, Lora, 20, 216n48
Rosenheim, Shawn, 226n8
Rotundo, E. Anthony, 213n21, 213–214n26
Roulston, Robert, 245n23
Rowe, John Carlos, *The Theoretical Dimensions of Henry James,* 83, 99–100, 102, 232n19, 234nn18, 19
Rugoff, Milton, 213n18

Ryan, Mary, 12, 212nn12, 13, 214n27

Saltz, Laura, 226n8, 227n10
same-sex desire. *See* homoerotic desire
same-sex relationships. *See* homosexuality
Savoy, Eric, 88, 230n5
Scarry, Elaine, 48
Schoberlin, Harold, 240n5
Schor, Naomi, 227n11
Sedgwick, Eve Kosofsky, 128–129, 143, 172, 223n30, 235n32, 235–236n35, 236nn37, 38, 239n3, 241n17; *Between Men,* 44, 79, 219n63, 230n25, 233n10
seeing and desiring, 179, 241nn17, 18
self: as author, 53; and body, 49; myth of, in James, 155
self-censorship, in Crane, 175
self-construction: authorial, 1–4, 53; in James, 133, 137. *See also* masculine self-construction
self-image, in Crane, 190
self-reflexivity, 216n50
self-representation, involuntary, 100
Seltzer, Mark, 232n23; *Bodies and Machines,* 39, 216nn48, 50, 220n6, 232n28, 237n3, 238n3, 238–239n10, 241n15, 241–242n20
Senger, Louis, 188
sensuality and poverty, in Crane, 184–185
serialization of James novels, 231n12
sex/gender instabilities, in Freud, 208
sexual ambiguity, in Fitzgerald, 201–202
sexuality: in Crane, 188; crises of, 1–4; and cultural identity, 172; dangerous, 49; and envy, in James, 117; and eroticism, 51; in Freud, 191, 205–206, 246–247n39; and gender, in Freud, 191; and gender, in James, 83–84; indefinability of, 218n61; in James, *The Ambassadors,* 110–119, 233n7; in James, *The Wings of the Dove,* 128–129, 138; and linear narrative, 218n61; in 19th-century theories, 49–51, 222n23
signs of writing, 241n15
silence, suppressive, in James, 145
Silverman, Kaja, 228–229n18, 232n20

Silverman, Kenneth, 66, 225nn3, 4, 5
Simmel, Ernst, 246n36
Simpson, Lewis, 212n9, 216n47
Sinclair, Upton, 161, 162, 166, 238n5;
    Autobiography, 161, 162, 166; *The*
    Journal of Arthur Stirling, 161; *The*
    Jungle, 159–170, 237–238n2,
    238n5; *Love's Pilgrimage,* 167;
    Manassas, 165
Smith-Rosenberg, Carroll, 10, 50, 212–
    213n16
Sorrentino, Paul, 239n2, 240n6
Southworth, E.D.E.N., *The Hidden*
    Hand, 14
spectacle, in Crane, 242n27
Spielrein, Sabina, 207–208, 247n41
"splitting": and commodification, 59;
    in Fitzgerald, 200, 204; in Freud,
    205; of masculinity, 204
Sprengnether, Madelon, 207, 229n19,
    247n43
stabilizing of desire and self, in James,
    155
Stallman, R. W., 240n5, 241nn18, 19
Stoekl, Allan, 217n54
Stowe, Harriet Beecher, *Uncle Tom's*
    Cabin, 14, 165–166, 239n11
Sturges, Jonathan, 114–115, 144
style: formation of, 17–18; queerness
    of, 141
subject and culture, in naturalism, 238–
    239n10
subjectivity, 23; "feminine," in Sinclair,
    167; and naturalism, 238–239n10
"sublimation," 233–234n11

Temple, Minnie, 235n34
Thackeray, William M., 193
thought and feeling, 56, 58, 71
thwarted genius, 238n8
Tocqueville, Alexis de, 212n13
Tornsey, Cheryl, 92
transcendence: in Fitzgerald, 203; in
    Freud, 247–248n47; in James, 29–
    31, 148; and literature, 22; and
    masculinity, 30–31, 191; in
    Wharton, *The House of Mirth,* 196
transgressive desire, 144
"transitional object" (Winnicott),
    229n20

uncanniness: in James, 99–100, 122; in
    Sinclair, 164
unspeakable, 172; in James, 143

Van Boheeman, Christine, 158, 225n43
Van Leer, David, 229–230n24
Veeder, William, 92, 215n36, 233n3
violence: and masculinity, 60–61, 80; in
    narrative, 29; against women, in
    Poe, 67
vision and desire, 241nn17, 18
vocational: crisis, 6–8; identity, 11, 24
voyeurism, in 19th-century New York,
    184

Wallace, James D., 216n44, 221n12
Walton, Priscilla L., 231n10
war, and masculinity, 204
Warner, Michael, 44, 219n65
Warner, Susan, *The Wide, Wide World,* 14
Washington, Bryan R., 245n30
Watt, Ian, 217–218n58
Wertheim, Stanley, 239n2, 240n6
Wharton, Edith, 194–200, 244n19; *The*
    Custom of the Country, 195; *Ethan*
    Frome, 195; *The Glimpses of the*
    Moon, 195, 203; *The House of*
    Mirth, 196–200, 245n26
"white-collar" jobs, 8
Whitman, Sarah Helen, 66, 225n3
Whitman, Walt, *Democratic Vistas,* 21–
    22
Whittier, John Greenleaf, "The
    Nervous Man," 6–7
Wiebe, Robert, 213n23
Wilde, Oscar, 114
Williams, Sherwood, 242n21
Wilson, Christopher P., 238n5
Wilson, Edmund, 192
Wilt, Judith, 233n6, 234n17
Winckelmann, Johann Joachim, 88–89
Winnicott, D. W., 229n20
women: in American literature, 2, 245–
    246n31; "bodies" of, 59–60; in
    Crane, 175, 240n10; commodi-
    fication of, 229n21; cultural
    authority of, 208; cultural castration
    of, 229n19; cultural contributions
    of, 2, 13–17, 26, 75, 227n9, 227–
    228n13, 228–229n18; and Haw-

thorne, 56–58; and James, 83–84, 133, 235n31; labor of, 214n30; and lack, 75; and literature, 14; and masculine authority, 60, 235n31; and Poe, 67, 227n9; and religion, in James, 105; roles of, 2, 11, 13, 42, 59–60, 68, 83–84, 138; suppression of, in Poe, 67; and writing, 6
women characters: in Fitzgerald, 200, 245n28; in James, 133
women poets, in the 19th century, 66
women's culture, in the 19th century, 56–57, 66
women writers, 19, 215n36, 244–245n20; and Hawthorne, 42, 221n12; and James, 131; and Poe, 66, 225n3

work, and masculine identity, 11
writers and publishers, 6. *See also* men writers; women writers
writing, 33, 177–178, 216n50, 241nn15, 16; anxieties of, 38; in Crane, 177; as a crisis of self-definition, 22; in Hawthorne, 38, 53, 62; and homoerotics, in Crane, 177; for James, 151–153; and masculinity, 27, 36, 223n31; as a profession, 5–8; of writing, 241n15. *See also* authorship

x, in James, 148–154

Yingling, Thomas, 223n29

ABOUT THE AUTHOR

Scott Derrick is currently an associate professor of English at Rice University, specializing in nineteenth-century American literature. He was born in Harrisburg, Pennsylvania, in 1953, received his Ph.D. in English from the University of Pennsylvania in 1987, and has also taught at George Mason University and Brandeis.